The Illustrated Directory of

SUBMARINES
OF THE WORLD

The Illustrated Directory of

SUBMARINES
OF THE WORLD

David Miller

SALAMANDER

A Salamander Book

Published by Salamander Books Ltd.,
8 Blenheim Court,
Brewery Road,
London N7 9NT,
United Kingdom

© Salamander Books Ltd., 2002

A member of **Chrysalis** Books plc

ISBN 1 84065 375 2

Credits

Project Manager: Ray Bonds
Designed by: Interprep Ltd.
Colour reproduction by: Anorax Imaging Ltd.
Printed in: Slovenia

The Author

David Miller is a former officer in the British armed forces, who spent his service in England, the Falkland Islands, Germany, Malaysia, the Netherlands, Scotland, and Singapore. He subsequently worked as a freelance author and for three years as a journalist for Jane's Information Group. He was Editor of the two-volume *Jane's Major Warships*, and has written more than forty other works, many of them related to sea warfare and naval weapons.

Acknowledgements

The publishers are grateful for the help given by many institutions and private individuals who have provided photographs for this book, in particular Anchor Consultancy Photo Library for the photographs on pages 47 (bottom), 159 (bottom), 185, 187, 197, 204-5, 207, 209 (top), 263 (bottom), 322-3, and 479 (bottom).

Contents

Introduction

The early history of the submarine was similar to that of the aeroplane. From the 15th century onwards a few individuals dreamt of diving and travelling in the depths of the ocean. Who conducted the first successful dive is open to argument, but a Dutchman, van Drebbel, is credited with conducting the first public demonstration, which took place in the River Thames, London, in 1620; it is even suggested that King James I was aboard for one dive. The first person to foresee the potential of the submarine as a weapon of war was an American, David Bushnell, who produced two submersibles to attack the British, the first in 1776 and the second in 1812. He was followed by a Bavarian, Bauer, in 1851, a spate of inventors during the American Civil War, and the Peruvian, Blume. By the 1890s the basic problem of submerging and returning to the surface had been solved, but the question of propulsion was not solved until J. P. Holland established that the solution was the use of electric storage cells, with internal combustion engines being employed on the surface for both propulsion and the recharging of the batteries. Practical use of the various options – petrol, kerosene and diesel – eventually established the latter as the most satisfactory and least dangerous, and for fifty years diesel-electric was the only practicable means of propulsion, with steam an unpopular and dangerous alternative.

In 1914 there were many submarines in service with European, United States and Japanese navies, and it was supposed that their primary use would be against enemy warships. As events unfolded, however, it was their role against merchant shipping that predominated, and the statistics for the twelve months from February 1917 to January 1918 summarise the story. During that period an average of 46 German U-boats were at sea in any one month, sinking a total of 2,684 British merchant ships (6,069,724 tons), a loss which brought the British Empire to the brink of defeat and established the strategic maturity of the submarine for all to see.

The inter-war period saw a few years of consolidation, mixed with a few experiments as navies tested ideas for specialised submarines, such as monitors, aircraft carriers, minelayers and boats that could keep pace with the main surface battlefleet. Many concepts were short-lived and the main focus of attention remained the patrol submarine, which increased steadily in size, and improved in efficiency and capability. However, the vessel itself was still a submersible, spending most of its time on the surface and diving only when it was absolutely necessary to do so. Nor could these boats go very deep, and few could dive to a depth greater than their own length.

During World War II the submarine was again a major element in the combat, although the major navies faced differing strategic situations. Thus, German U-boats in 1939-41 in the Atlantic and in 1942 on the North American coast operated in a "target-rich environment" with thousands of enemy merchant ships to be attacked. For the British, there were few enemy merchant ships to be attacked, except in the Mediterranean where surface traffic between Italy and North Africa offered rich pickings. In the Pacific the Japanese depended upon merchant shipping for movement between captured territories and their homeland and this traffic had been virtually brought to a halt by August 1945. The Japanese operated the most numerous fleet of the largest submarines in the world but achieved indifferent success and were fought to a standstill by the Allies. The Germans and Japanese realised that the basic diesel-electric submarine was capable of better underwater performance if it was streamlined and given greater battery power, but fortunately for the Allies the new classes the Axis powers designed never attained service in significant numbers.

In the immediate post-war period, the former Axis powers were deprived of their submarine fleets, while the victorious navies made do with modernised versions of their wartime boats until a totally new generation of true submarines were ready. The greatest advance came about with nuclear power, with USS *Nautilus* (SSN-571) employing it for the first time on 17 January 1955, but this has proved so expensive that its use is confined to the very few, wealthiest navies. Nevertheless, it is the answer to the dream in which a true submarine can travel in the depths with the only restrictions being the physiological limits of the crew and the amount of supplies that can be carried. The first nuclear submarine powers were the USA, the USSR and the UK, followed by France and then China, although India and Brazil both have active programmes which should result in SSNs by 2020 at the latest.

Meanwhile, the first non-nuclear air-independent propulsion (AIP) boats are coming into service, which will give submarines the capability of remaining submerged for about 14-21 days at a time. There are a number of different systems, but all are used for low-speed cruising, depending upon batteries for high-speed operations. But, just as the number of navies with diesel-electric submarines had increased over the past fifty years, so, too, will the numbers of AIP grow, increasing yet again the threat posed by submarines.

Entries in this book
Submarines are grouped by the country of origin in order to show the development of submarine design within a country and also to show the overall picture as a class. Thus, for example, today's German-built Type 209 is in service with some 15 navies; if each navy's holdings were described individually there would be a great deal of duplication and it would be difficult for the reader to get an overall picture of the class. Thus, the Type 209 is described in one consolidated entry under Germany.

Within the country of origin submarine classes are listed in chronological order of the launch of the first-of-class. The specifications given are for the first-of-class, as built, unless otherwise stated in italics at the foot of the specification table. Where a reasonably accurate figure cannot be discovered, that item is omitted. Individual entries are:

Type = description of primary role.
Total built = grand total for all customers.
Completed = in-service dates of first and last of class.
Displacement = surfaced displacement when fully loaded, and submerged.
Dimensions = overall length and beam between extremities; draught is on the surface at standard displacement.
Propulsion = diesels (number, power per engine); electric motors (number, power per motor); battery (number of cells); shafts.
Performance = surface and submerged speeds as designed; surfaced and submerged ranges are expressed as *x* nautical miles (nm) at *y* knots (kt); note that one can be traded against the other; ie, a submarine capable of 11,000nm at 11kt might be capable of 15,000nm at 8kt.
Weapons = torpedoes (tubes by number, location and calibre); guns (by number and calibre). Mines are listed only for specialised minelayers or when special strap-on devices are available; they are not listed where they can be carried in place of torpedoes, as is the case with virtually all modern submarines.
Complement = total crew.

Diesel-Electric Patrol Submarines 1860-1921

There were many attempts during the 19th Century to develop a viable submarine, but one of the major problems preventing complete success was that of underwater propulsion. As described elsewhere in this book, various means were tried, including men turning a crank, and steam, which gave plenty of power but was dangerous in an underwater environment. Compressed air and electric storage batteries were tried as the sole means of propulsion, but both resulted in limited range and the need for the boat to return to harbour to recharge from a shore-based generator. It was the Irish-American inventor, J. P. Holland, who realised that the answer lay in taking an internal combustion engine to sea, where it would both recharge the battery and propel the boat on the surface, thus leaving the battery to provide the power underwater. This battery, which consisted of a large number of individual cells, had to provide power not only for propulsion but also for what is today termed the "hotel load", ie, lighting, heating, operating pumps and valves, raising and lowering the periscopes, operating the cookers, and so on. Thus, the power could rapidly be exhausted and it was one of the captain's many responsibilities to juggle with the problem of speed versus endurance.

Early submarines were powered by gasoline engines, which gave good power for their size but used a fuel which was inherently dangerous, and there were many minor and some major explosions. Realising the danger of gasoline, the Germans used kerosene, but it was extremely pungent and gave off a

Below: German U-38 (U-31-class) under the Turkish flag.

Above: U.S. Navy's first submarine, **Holland, October 1901.**

dense white exhaust. The answer was found in the diesel and by about 1910 this had become the preferred power source, although a few steam-powered boats were still built. The diesel engine itself took some years to perfect. Early models had a poor power output and the Americans, somewhat uncharacteristically, found it difficult to build a reliable diesel. The engine situation became even more complicated when, on the outbreak of World War I, the export of the best diesels – those from M.A.N. of Nuremburg, Germany – suddenly ceased.

In the years following the launch of Holland's submarine, development was rapid, spurred on by the naval races in Europe between Germany and the UK, and in the Far East between Japan and Russia. Then came World War I in which the stand-off between the great battle fleets and the tight trade embargo imposed by Britain and France led to the extremely rapid development of the patrol submarine, partly as an anti-warship weapon but increasingly in its anti-merchant ship role. The latter was of comparatively limited interest to the Western Powers since the Central Powers (Germany and Austria-Hungary) soon had very few merchant ships left, but was of immense interest to Germany.

Despite their name "submarine" these early boats were in reality "submersibles" – ie, they spent most of their time on the surface and submerged only when actually forced to do so. Then, once submerged, their endurance was strictly limited by the life of the battery, and the boats were both slow moving and difficult to manoeuvre.

Torpedoes

The primary weapon of the submarine was the torpedo. Most submarines entered World War I with 18in (457mm) tubes, but during the war there was a steady increase in calibre. The 21in (533mm) torpedo was introduced into Allied submarines from 1917 onwards, while on the German side the calibre rose from 450mm (17.7in) to 500mm (19.7in), although by the end of the war a 600mm (23.6in) torpedo was under development.

This increase in calibre resulted in both larger warheads and more fuel for greater range, but also meant that larger, heavier tubes were required and greater storage space was needed in the submarine. The real problems with torpedoes, however, were aiming, reliability and accuracy. Aiming depended solely upon the captain, since he alone could see out through the periscope and then had to assess the range and the relative speeds, angles and courses of his own boat and the target. In this era there were no computers to help him. Reliability was a function of a number of systems; first, the torpedo's engine had to be started, then the missile had to be driven down the tube, following which it had to run straight and maintain the correct depth. Finally, if all worked properly and it actually did hit the target, the fuze had to function and explode the warhead.

One of the choices open to the captain was that he could trade the torpedo's speed for range, which in the German G6, for example, could be set for either 1,640yd (1,500m) at 34.5kt, or for 3,380yd (3,000m) at 26kt. Generally, however, captains preferred to keep the range very short and the "rule-of-thumb" for British captains prior to the outbreak of war was that they should launch their torpedo at about three times the length of their own submarine, which, in practical terms, was about 300yd (274m).

Country	Torpedo	IOC	Calibre	Warhead	Maximum Speed	Maximum Range
Austria-Hungary	Whitehead	1911	18in (457mm)	220lb (100kg)	44kt	2,200yd (2,012m)
Germany	C/06	1907	17.7in (450mm)	270lb (123kg)	26kt	3,380yd (3,000m)
	G/6	1911	19.7in (500mm)	235lb (160kg)	35kt	5,470yd (5,000m)
UK	18in Mk VI	1909	18in (457mm)	200lb (91kg)	29kt	6,000yd (5,486m)
	Weymouth 21in Mk II	1914	21in (533mm)	225lb (102kg)	29kt	10,000yd (9,144m)
	21in Mk VI	1917	21in (533mm)	515lb (237kg)	40kt	5,000yd (4,572m)
U.S.	21in U.S.	1917	21in (533mm)	385lb (175kg)	27kt	13,500yd (6,124m)

World War I torpedoes. Note that there was a "trade-off" between speed and range and that to achieve maximum range the speed would be reduced and vice versa.

Various means of launching torpedoes were tried, the most obvious being bow tubes. Early submarines had just one such tube, but this gradually increased to two, then to four, and by about 1918 there were even some with six tubes. Such an increase was primarily intended to enable the captain to fire a number of torpedoes at a time, thus greatly increasing the chance of a hit. The British developed the idea of beam tubes, with a pair of tubes rigidly mounted roughly amidships and pointing, one to each side, at 90 degrees to the boat's axis. The beam had to be increased to accommodate these tubes and the idea did not persist beyond a few classes. Some other navies tried using rotating mounts, which were situated on the upper casing and turned by a mechanical linkage; this proved particularly popular with the French, but was eventually discontinued. The idea of the stern tubes was also introduced, sometimes in a tube outside the pressure hull, but more frequently inside the pressure hull and thus reloadable. Such tubes were mainly intended to fire at chasing warships.

Several navies used metal frames known as "drop collars" of which that designed by the Russian, Drzewiecki, was the most widely used. Such frames were mounted on the upper deck, usually in a recess, and held one torpedo. The torpedo was launched by swinging the frame outboard and then releasing the weapon. Reloading at sea was not possible and the device added considerably to the hydrodynamic resistance of the boat. They were especially popular in the French and Russian navies, but little liked anywhere else.

Guns

The first guns were mounted on submarines in about 1912-13, but they did not become commonplace until about 1916-17.The main requirement was to engage and sink merchant ships, since gun ammunition was far more plentiful than torpedoes. There were very few German merchant ships for Allied submarines to attack, but the British found the guns essential for attacking fleeing U-boats. Early guns were of 3in (76mm) calibre, but this soon increased to 88mm in the German case and 4in (102mm) for the British.

German submarines

Where submarines were concerned, there can be no doubt that the most influential navy in the period 1914-18 was that of Germany. The Germans came late to the submarine field, their previous top priority having been the development of the High Seas Fleet. Indeed, despite the ruthless reputation they subsequently earned, they were ill-prepared for submarine warfare and on the outbreak of war in August 1914 there were just 20 operational U-boats, with another 15 either employed in non-operational tasks (for example, training) or under construction. As soon as it became clear that the war would last much longer than expected the naval staff set in hand a "Mobilisation" (Ms) programme in which they sought to achieve a rapid increase in numbers by economies of scale and also by sticking, so far as was possible, to progressive development of existing designs. Their efforts were, however, beset by a number of problems. First, were the frequent changes in strategic direction concerning U-boat warfare by the government and the High Command, which often meant that the type of U-boat required changed also. But there were also a host of production difficulties, one of the most important being the shortage of skilled manpower, particularly as so many shipyard workers were called-up for Army service. This exacerbated the second problem, which was the difficulties the yards experienced in expanding their capacity to meet the great increase in numbers of U-boats required, as well as the rapid advance in U-boat technology. Further problems were caused by shortages of certain items of equipment, particularly diesel engines. Despite these difficulties, the German Navy brought the U-boat to a degree of size, sophistication, complexity and strategic importance which J. P. Holland could barely have dreamt of only a decade earlier.

U-1/-3/-5 classes

AUSTRIA-HUNGARY

Type: coastal, gasoline/kerosene-electric.

Class	U-1*	U-3	U-5
Total built	2	2	3
Completed	1909	1908	1909-11
Displacement surfaced submerged	230 tons 249 tons	240 tons 300 tons	240 tons 273 tons
Dimensions length beam draught	100ft 0in (30.5m) 15ft 9in (4.8m) 12ft 8in (3.9m)	138ft 9in (42.3m) 14ft 0in (4.5m) 12ft 6in (3.8m)	105ft 4in (32.1m) 13ft 9in (4.2m) 12ft 10in (3.9m)
Propulsion main engines power electric motors power shafts	2 x gasoline 720bhp 2 200shp two	2 x kerosene 600bhp 2 320shp two	2 x gasoline 500bhp 2 230shp two
Performance speed, surface submerged range, surfaced submerged	10.3kt 6kt 950nm at 6kt 40nm at 2kt	12kt 8kt 1,200nm at 12kt 40nm at 3kt	10.8kt 8.5kt 800nm at 8.5kt 48nm at 6kt
Weapons TT location torpedoes guns	3 x 17.7in (450mm) bow-2, stern-1 5 1 x 37mm cannon	2 x 17.7in (450mm) bow-2 3 –	2 x 17.7in (450mm) bow-2 4 –
Complement	17	21	19

* Specifications for U-1/U-2, as built.

Above: Holland design, U-6, was built by Whitehead, Fiume.

History: Work on submarines for the Imperial Austro-Hungarian Navy began in 1904. The first effort was not a success, so it was decided to buy two boats from each of three leading builders; the naval staff laid down the outline specifications, but the design was left to the shipyards. The first pair (U-1, U-2) were designed by the American, Simon Lake, but built under licence at the Naval Yard in Pola. Of typical Lake design, they had a diving chamber under the bow, variable pitch propellers and retractable wheels for running along the seabed; it was the only one of the three designs to feature a gun armament. There were a number of unsatisfactory features, of which the worst were the gasoline engines, which did not reach anything near the advertised power; as a result, the Navy refused to pay for the engines, which were subsequently replaced by diesels. They were employed as training boats during World War I and were then ceded to the Italians who scrapped them in the early 1920s.

The second pair (U-3, U-4) were designed and built by Germania at Kiel, Germany, and then towed to the Mediterranean. This was only Germania's third submarine design. It was remarkably sound, although some difficulties were experienced with the diving planes, while, as in the early German U-boats., the kerosene engine emitted a vast plume of white smoke. However, it was judged to be the most reliable and the most comfortable for the crew, and a revised design subsequently won the competition for a new class. Both took part in World War I, during which U-3 was sunk by a French destroyer, while U-4 sank an Italian armoured cruiser in 1915.

U-5 and U-6 were of a Holland design and were partially built in the USA before being shipped to Whitehead, Fiume, for completion. They were single-hulled boats with a "teardrop" hull and two torpedo tubes, which were completed in 1909. Whitehead then went ahead to build a third boat, an improved version of the Holland design; it was offered to and turned down by various navies, but when war broke out it was finally accepted by Austria-Hungary, who commissioned it as U-12. All three were sunk during the war, although U-5 was raised and rebuilt.

Above: U-4 (U-3-class) – built for Austria by Germania, Kiel.

Above: U-12 (U-5-class), sunk by a mine off Venice in 1916.

Havmanden-class AUSTRIA-HUNGARY (DENMARK)

Type: coastal, gasoline/diesel-electric.
Total built: 6.
Completed: 1912-14.
Displacement: surfaced 164 tons; submerged 204 tons.
Dimensions: length 127ft 8in (38.9m); beam 11ft 10in (3.6m); draught 7ft 7in (2.3m).
Propulsion: 2 x FIAT/M.A.N. diesel engines, 450bhp; 2 x electric motors, 275shp; one shaft.
Performance: surface – 12kt; submerged – 13kt; range surfaced 1,400nm at 10kt; submerged 23nm at 8kt.
Weapons: 2 x 18in (457mm) TT (bow); 1 x 8mm MG.
Complement: 10.
Specifications, as built.

History: The Royal Danish Navy had already taken delivery of the *Dykkeren* (qv) in 1909, which was designed and built by Fiat at La Spezia, but it had suffered many teething problems. This led them to look elsewhere for their second class of submarines, which was to be built in some numbers and with some, at least, being built in Denmark. The Austrian firm of Whitehead at Fiume had already established its reputation for the design and manufacture of torpedoes, but in the early years of the 20th Century it also designed and built a number of submarines. Most of these were for the Austro-Hungarian Navy, but a number were for export, including this class for Denmark.

    The original order was for two, of which the first, *Havmanden,* would be built by Whitehead, while the second, *Havfruen,* would be built at the Copenhagen Navy Yard, using plans purchased from Whitehead. While the first

Above: **Havfruen** *and* Najaden *(Havmanden-class) in 1914.*

was still under construction a second order was placed, with another two to be built at Whitehead *(Thetis* and *Triton)* and the Copenhagen Navy Yard *(Najaden* and *Nymfen)*. One of these, *Triton*, was paid for by popular subscription, an event which happened in a number of countries in the years leading up to World War I, and its name was changed to *2den April*, to commemorate Nelson's Battle of Copenhagen, which was fought on 2 April 1801.

In 1913 the boats were given numbers from #2 to #7 *(Dykkeren* became #1) which were painted on their bridges. This was later changed again and they were redesignated the "A-class" becoming *A-2* to *A-7*. They were stricken and scrapped between 1928 and 1932.

U-10 class

Type: patrol, diesel-electric.
Total built: 4.
Completed: 1915.
Displacement: surfaced 126 tons; submerged 140 tons.
Dimensions: length 91ft 6in (27.9m); beam 16ft 10in (5.2m); draught 8ft 11in (2.7m).
Propulsion: 1 x diesel, 60bhp; 1 x electric motor, 120shp; one shaft.
Performance: surface – 6.5kt; submerged – 5.5kt.
Weapons: 2 x 17.7in (450mm) TT (bow), 2 x torpedoes.
Complement: 17.

History: The outcome of the competition among the first three classes (*U-1, U-3, U-5*)was an order to Germania for five 500-ton boats, to be commissioned into the Austro-Hungarian Navy as *U-7* to *U-11*. However, war broke out before they could be delivered and since the long voyage was considered too

U-20 class

Type: coastal, diesel-electric.
Total built: 4.
Completed: 1916-17.
Displacement: surfaced 173 tons; submerged 210 tons.
Dimensions: length 127ft 2in (38.8m); beam 13ft 0in (4.0m); draught 9ft 0in (2.8m).
Propulsion: 1 x diesel, 450bhp; 1 x electric motor, 160shp; one shaft.
Performance: surface – 12kt; submerged – 9kt.
Weapons: 2 x 17.7in (450mm) TT (bow); 2 x torpedoes.
Complement: 18.

dangerous they were sold to the Germany Navy, who commissioned them as *U-66* to *U-70* (see *U-66* entry). An alternative solution was found in the German UB-1-class, for which the German builder, AG Weser, devised a plan to despatch the boats in sections by rail. The first two boats were duly despatched in sections and rivetted together at Pola. They were then commissioned into the Imperial German Navy as *UB-1* and *UB-15* and operated for several months under the Austrian flag, but manned by German crews and with just one Austrian officer aboard each boat. They were then transferred to the Austrian Navy in mid-1915 as *U-10* and *U-11*, respectively, and manned by Austrian crews. The remaining three, *U-15, -16, -17*, were operated from the start as Austrian units.

As built, none had a deck-gun, but in late 1916 all were armed, *U-11* with a 66mm weapon, the others with a 37mm. *U-16* was sunk during the war, while *U-10* was mined but recovered and rebuilt; she with the other survivors was transferred to Italy in 1920 and scrapped.

History: The Austria-Hungary Navy acquired a number of miscellaneous submarines. One was the French *Curie*, which was sunk trying to enter the main naval base at Pola, and then recovered, repaired and commissioned as *U-14*. Commanded by Oberleutnant Georg Ritter von Trapp, it became one of the most successful boats in the Austrian Navy, while the captain was later immortalised as the hero in the film "The Sound of Music". *U-20* had its origins in a design ordered from Whitehead at Fiume in 1911 by the Royal Danish Navy; three were built and delivered between 1911 and 1913 as the Havmanden-class. On the outbreak of war the Austria-Hungarian Navy seized the design and in March 1915 ordered four boats (*U-20* to *U-22*). Such was the inefficiency of the Austrian system, however, that the boats were not actually commissioned until late 1916/early 1917. All took part in operations in the Adriatic; two were sunk and two survived the war to be ceded to the Allies and scrapped in the early 1920s.

Left: **U-14 (French Curie-class). Captured and rebuilt by the Austrian Navy, her captain was von Trapp, later hero of the film "The Sound of Music".**

U-27 class

Type: coastal, diesel-electric.
Total built: 8.
Completed: 1916-17.
Displacement: surfaced 264 tons; submerged 301 tons.
Dimensions: length 121ft 1in (36.9m); beam 14ft 4in (4.4m); draught 12ft 2in (3.7m).
Propulsion: 2 x diesels, 270bhp; 2 x electric motors, 280shp; two shafts.
Performance: surface – 9kt;submerged – 7kt; maximum operational diving depth 164ft (50m).
Weapons: 2 x 17.7in (450mm) TT (bow); 4 x torpedoes.
Complement: 23.

History: This was the most numerous class of submarines built for the Austria-Hungarian Navy and was essentially the German UB-II design built under licence with a few minor modifications to meet Austrian operational requirements. The order was placed in October 1915, with six to be built at the Pola Naval Yard and two by the Danubius Yard at Fiume. All were delivered in 1917, having taken somewhat longer to build than their German counterparts. The only known variation in the design was *U-41,* the last to be completed, whose hull was extended by 30in (762mm) to accommodate two diesel engines of a different design, which had originally been intended for *U-6.* All served in the Adriatic but only one was lost (due to causes unknown, in early April 1917). After the war the surviviving boats were allocated to France and Italy, who scrapped them.

These were the last boats to be built for the Austria-Hungary Navy. Two UB

Aegir/Rota classes

Type: coastal, diesel-electric.

Class	Ægir (B-class)	Rota (C-class)
Total built	5	3
Completed	1915-16	1918-20
Displacement surfaced submerged	185 tons 235 tons	301 tons 369 tons
Dimensions length beam draught	133ft 2in (40.6m) 12ft 2in (3.7m) 7ft 11in (2.4m)	133ft 2in (47.5m) 14ft 5in (4.4m) 8ft 9in (2.7m)
Propulsion main engines power electric motors power shafts	2 x diesel 450bhp 2 340shp one	2 x diesel 900bhp 2 640shp two

Above: Austrian U-27-class, modified German UB-II-class.

II-class submarines were operated locally by the German Navy and then sold to Austria in 1917, who commissioned them as *U-43* and *U-47*. Various other designs were either under construction or on the drawing-boards at the time of the Armistice.

Performance		
speed, surface	13.5kt	14.5kt
submerged	9.8kt	10.5kt
Weapons		
TT	3 x 18in (457mm)	4 x 18in (457mm)
location	bow – 2, stern – 1	bow – 2, stern – 1
guns	1 x 57mm	1 x 57mm
Complement	11	17

Specifications in all cases, as built.

History: The Royal Danish Navy's first submarine was *Dykkeren*, which was designed and built by Fiat at La Spezia (see Italy). Driven by two Fiat gasoline engines, it sailed to Denmark where it was accepted in June 1909. It was later given the Danish pennant number "1" and was sunk in collision with a Norwegian steamer in 1916. This was followed by the Havmanden-class, which was designed by Whitehead at Fiume, with six completed between 1911 and 1914, of which three (*Havmanden, Thetis, Triton*) were built at Fiume and three (*Havfruen, Najaden, Nymfen*) under licence at the Copenhagen Navy Yard (see Havmanden- class under Austria-Hungary).

They were later redesignated the A-class. Denmark was neutral during World War I, and all six boats served until being scrapped between 1928 and 1932.

Next came the Δgir-class of five boats, which were designed and built in the Copenhagen Navy Yard. This was the class in production when

Below: C-class submarine, **Rota,** *launched August 1918.*

Below right: Danish-built **Neptun** *(B-class) launched in 1915.*

Aigrette-class

FRANCE

Type: harbour-defence, diesel-electric.
Total built: 2.
Completed: 1904.
Displacement: surfaced 178 tons; submerged 253 tons.
Dimensions: length 117ft 7in (35.9m); beam 13ft 3in (4.0m); draught 8ft 7in (2.6m).
Propulsion: 1 x diesel engine, 150bhp; 1 x electric motor, 130shp; one shaft.
Performance: surface – 9.3kt; submerged – 6.2kt; range surfaced 1,300nm at 8kt, submerged 65nm at 3.8kt.
Weapons: 4 x 17.7in (450mm) (2 x Drzwiecki launch cradles, 2 x external cradles).
Complement: 14.

History: The history of French submarine development in the 1890s and early 1900s is one of a bewildering succession of classes, most consisting of one, sometimes two boats, before the Navy and technology moved on. The number of designers in the field can be judged by the fact that when the Navy ran an open competition in 1896 for a 200-ton boat it attracted no fewer than 29 submissions. One of the well-known designers of the day, Maxime Laubeuf (1864-1939), was responsible for a number of sound designs starting with the steam-driven Narval- and Sirène-class (see "Steam" section), which were, in essence, submersible torpedo boats, with twin hulls and ballast tanks between them. Laubeuf's next step was the Aigrette-class, which was based on the Sirène design, but with diesel-electric

Dykkeren was sunk in 1916, and plans were made to build an additional boat to replace it, but although the materials were acquired it was never built.

Fourth in this Danish series was the Rota- or C-class of three boats, designed and built in Denmark. It was originally planned to have a fifth torpedo tube on the upper casing but this could not be made to work properly on the first-of-class and the idea was shelved. All three were scuttled in Danish ports on 29 August 1943 and were later raised and scrapped in the 1950s.

rather than steam power. One feature, typical of the time, was that all four torpedoes were mounted in external launching frames and not in internal tubes. As completed, *Aigrette* had two large girders mounted at an angle, one at the bow, the second above the bridge; they appear to have been intended to deflect the cables used to protect harbour entrances.

It was originally planned to build a total of 13 boats, but in the event only two were completed, *Aigrette* and *Cigogne*. Both served in a harbour defence role in World War I and were scrapped in 1919.

Below: **Aigrette*, with cable-cutters and torpedo in drop-collar.*

Émeraude/Mariotte-classes   FRANCE

Type: coastal, diesel-electric.
Total built: 6.
Completed: 1906-08.
Displacement: surfaced 392 tons; submerged 425 tons.
Dimensions: length 147ft 4in (44.9m); beam 12ft 10in (3.9m); draught 12ft 0in (3.6m).
Propulsion: 2 x Sautter-Harlé diesel engines, 600bhp; 2 x electric motors; two shafts.
Performance: surface – 11.5kt; submerged – 9.2kt; range surfaced 2,000nm at 7.3kt, submerged 100nm at 5kt.
Weapons: 6 x 17.7in (450mm) TT (bow – 4; stern – 2); 6 x torpedoes.
Complement: 21.
Specifications for Émeraude-class, as built.

History: The Émeraude-class introduced the French Navy's custom of naming submarines after precious stones, which continues to this day. With a submerged displacement of 425 tons, these were the largest submarines and their armament of six torpedo tubes the heaviest built in France up to this time. They suffered from a number of problems, mainly related to inadequate surface buoyancy and unreliable diesel engines. As built, they had no guns, but in August 1915, two of the class became the first French boats to be armed in this way, each being fitted with a single 37mm cannon.

There was a plan at one stage to produce two boats to a modified Émeraude design in which the hull would have been lengthened by 32ft 9in (10m). Work was actually started on both at Rochfort Arsenal, but seems to

Circé-class   FRANCE

Type: coastal, diesel-electric.
Total built: 2.
Completed: 1907.
Displacement: surfaced 351 tons; submerged 491 tons.
Dimensions: length 154ft 6in (47.1m); beam 16ft 1in (4.9m); draught 9ft 10in (3.0m).
Propulsion: 2 x M.A.N. diesel engines, 630bhp; 2 x electric motors, 460shp; two shafts.
Performance: surface – 11.9kt; submerged – 7.7kt; range surfaced 2,160nm at 8kt, submerged 98nm at 3.5kt.
Weapons: 6 x 17.7in (450mm) drop-collars/external cradles, 6 x torpedoes.
Complement: 22.

History: Maxime Laubeuf, who had designed the Narval-, Sirène- and Aigrette-classes, next turned to the Circé-class. Two boats, *Circé* and *Calypso*, were ordered in 1904 and launched three years later in September and October 1907, respectively. This was again a twin-hull design, but this time, however, Laubeuf selected the German firm of M.A.N. to supply the diesel engines.

Above: **Saphir (Émeraude-class), as completed in 1908.**

have proceeded very slowly and all work ceased in 1908.

The design was altered yet again to produce *Mariotte,* which was launched in February 1911. This was even longer, with an overall length of 210ft 3in (64.7m) but had the same power train. Armament was, however, different, with four internal torpedo tubes and two in external Drzwiecki drop-collars; a total of eight 17.7in (450mm) torpedoes was carried. During trials she attained an underwater speed of 11.7kt, a remarkable speed for that era, although how long it was sustained is not recorded. *Mariotte* was employed in the Gallipoli campaign.

Calypso collided with *Circé* off Toulon on 7 July 1914 and was sunk; collisions between submarines were not rare, but it was unusual for a boat to be sunk by its own sister-ship. In May 1917, during World War I, *Circé* sank the German minelayer, *UC-24* (see UC II-class), but was later herself sunk by *U-47* (see U 43-class).

Below: **Circé, a twin-hull Laubeuf design, launched in 1907.**

Brumaire-class

Type: coastal, diesel-electric.
Total built: 16.
Completed: 1911-13.
Displacement: surfaced 397 tons; submerged 551 tons.
Dimensions: length 170ft 11in (52.1m); beam 17ft 9in (5.1m); draught 10ft 2in (3.1m).
Propulsion: 2 x M.A.N. 6-cylinder diesel engines, 840bhp; 2 x electric motors 660 shp; two shafts.
Performance: surface – 13kt; submerged – 8.8kt; range surfaced 1,7800nm at 10kt, submerged 84nm at 4kt.
Weapons: 1 x 17.7in (450mm) TT (bow), 2 x torpedoes; 4 x Drzwiecki drop collars, 2 x external cradles, 6 x torpedoes.
Complement: 29.

History: Laubeuf had already been responsible for the 18-strong steam powered Pluviôse-class (see "Steam" section) and this new class of 16 was essentially a diesel-powered alternative. The main engines were M.A.N. designed diesels, but manufactured under licence in France by a variety of companies, including Indret, AC Loire, Normand, Sabathé and Sautter-Harlé. All these boats were involved in World War I where they served in the Mediterranean and, in common with most submarines in most navies, they were fitted with a gun on the foredeck in 1916, in this case either a 75mm or a 47mm.

One of the early losses during the war was *Curie*, which was captured by

---

Clorinde/Amphitrite/
Bellone-classes

Type: coastal, diesel-electric.
Total built: 2.
Completed: 1914.
Displacement: surfaced 413tons; submerged 567 tons.
Dimensions: length 176ft 10in (53.9m); beam 16ft 9in (5.1m); draught 11ft 2in (3.4m).
Propulsion: 2 x M.A.N.-Loire 2-stroke diesels, 800bhp; 2 x electric motors 700shp; two shafts.
Performance: surface – 13kt; submerged – 9kt; range surfaced 1,300nm at 10kt, submerged 100nm at 5kt.
Weapons: 6 x Drzewiecki drop-collars, 2 x external cradles; 8 x 17.7in (450mm) torpedoes.
Complement: 29.
Specifications for Clorinde-class, as built.

History: A product of the designer M. Hutter, the two boats of the Clorinde-class were developed from Laubeuf's Brumaire-class. *Clorinde* and *Cornélie* were slightly larger than the Brumaire-class and had rather more powerful engines with a designed output power of 1,300bhp, but no more than 800bhp was ever obtained in practice, as a result of which the expected

Above: **Curie***, as built and prior to rebuild by Austrian Navy.*

the Austro-Hungarians, modified and put into service as *U-14* (see U-20 entry above). Two were sunk by mines, *Bernoulli* (February 1918) and *Joule* (May 1915), while *Foucault* was sunk by Austro-Hungarian aircraft in May 1915, one of the earliest examples of aircraft sinking a submarine. A 1917 plan to convert the surviviving boats into minelayers was not pursued and they were stricken at a slow rate, starting with *Coulomb* in 1919 and ending with *Brumaire* in 1930.

15kt surface speed was never realised. Like most contemporary French submarines they did not have any torpedo tubes, being fitted instead with a mix of "drop-collars" designed by the Russian engineer Drzwiecki, and simple frames, all of which were mounted on the upper casing. This was much simpler than torpedo tubes, but they could not be reloaded at sea. Both boats were

Below: **French Bellone-class***, with unique free-flood casing.*

employed in the Atlantic during World War I and both were given a 75mm deck gun at some time in 1916-17. They were stricken in 1926.

The Clorinde-class was followed by eight boats of the Amphitrite-class which were virtual repeats, but with slight increases in the beam (17ft 9in/5.4m) and in submerged displacement (609 tons). Authorised in the Navy's 1909 programme, they were not laid down until 1911-13 and completed until 1914-15. Two of the class were completed as minelayers, although they did not become available until 1918.

Three more boats were built to an improved and larger design, also by Hutter. The Bellone-class were 216ft 6in (60.6m) long, with a submerged displacement of 788 tons. Their engines had a theoretical output of 1,800bhp, although, again, this was never achieved and the maximum surface speed was just under 15kt against a designed figure of

Armide/O'Byrne-classes FRANCE

Type: patrol, diesel-electric.

Class	Armide	O'Byrne
Total built	3	3
Completed	1916-17	1919-20
Displacement surfaced submerged	457 tons 670 tons	342 tons 513 tons
Dimensions length beam draught	184ft 5in (56.2m) 17ft 1in (5.2m) 9ft 10in (3.0m)	172ft (52.4m) 15ft 5in (4.7m) 8ft 10in (2.7m)
Propulsion main engines power electric motors power shafts	2 x diesels 2,200bhp 2 900shp two	2 x diesels 1,020bhp 2 400shp two

17kt. *Bellone* was completed in 1915, *Gorgone* in 1916 and *Hermione* in 1917. All three served on in the post-war Navy and all were stricken in July 1935.

Below: **Artemis *(Amphitrite-class)*with Drzwiecki dropcollars.**

Performance		
speed, surface	17.5kt	14kt
submerged	11kt	8kt
range, surfaced	2,600nm at 11kt	1,850nm at 10kt
submerged	160nm at 5kt	55nm at 5kt
Weapons		
TT	6 x 17.7in (450mm)	4 x 17.7in (450mm)
location	bow	bow
torpedoes	8	6
guns	1 x 47mm	1 x 47mm
Complement	31	25

Specifications in all cases, as built.

History: Maritime nations have traditionally considered it their right on a declaration of war to requisition naval vessels under construction for foreign navies in their shipyards, and it is of little concern whether these were ordered by hostile or friendly nations. Thus, the French naval ministry requisitioned six submarines during the course of World War I, all of them being constructed by Schneider, at Chalon-sur-Saône.

Schneider was building four large, long-range boats, two each for Greece and Japan. These were double-hulled boats with a submerged displacement of 670 tons, designed by Maxime Laubeuf and based on his very successful Pluviôse- and Brumaire-classes. The boats intended for Japan were the S1-class and were to be numbered #14 and #15 by the IJN, but the French requisitioned only the former, which was taken over on 3 June 1915, just before its launch, and commissioned into the French Navy as *Armide*. (The second boat was completed and delivered to the IJN as #15). The Greeks had already taken delivery of two Schneider- built boats (see Delfin-class, above) and this second pair were due to be delivered in 1917. They had the temporary Greek designations of "X" and "Ps" but were taken over by the French on 30 May 1917 and commissioned as *Amazone* and *Antigone*. All three boats served well into the post-war period, before being stricken between 1932 and 1935.

The O'Byrne-class originated in an order from the Rumanian Navy (its first for submarines) placed with Schneider in 1916, at a time when that country was allied to the Western powers. When Rumania was defeated by Germany the French requisitioned the three boats, although they were not actually launched until 1919-20, well after the war's end, but by then Rumania was in no position to pay for them. They were a little smaller than the Greek and Japanese boats; one was stricken in 1928, the other two in 1935.

Right: Built for Rumania, **Henri Fournier** *was requisitioned.*

Fulton-class

Type: patrol, diesel-electric.
Total built: 2.
Completed: 1917-19.
Displacement: surfaced 870 tons; submerged 1,247 tons.
Dimensions: length 242ft 9in (74.0m); beam 21ft 0in (6.4m); draught 11ft 10in (3.6m).
Propulsion: 2 x Schneider-Carels diesels, 2,700bhp; 2 x electric motors, 1,640shp; two shafts.
Performance: surface – 16.5kt; submerged – 11kt; range surfaced 4,300nm at 10kt, submerged 125nm at 5kt.
Weapons: 8 x 17.7in (450mm) TT; 10 x torpedoes; 1 x 75mm gun.
Complement: 47.

History: These two submarines were originally intended to have steam propulsion, which would have given them a surface speed of 20kt and a range of 2,400nm at 10kt. Construction was approved under the 1914 funding programme, but *Joessel* was not launched until July 1917 and *Fulton* until April 1919, much of this delay being due to the decision, made in the light of wartime experience but while they were under construction, that they should be powered by diesel engines. As a result, the steam units were reallocated to two sloops and the submarines were completed with a pair of Schneider-Carels diesels instead. Both boats also had internally mounted torpedo tubes, the

Above: Amazone *(Armide-class), originally built for Greece.*

various external drop-collars and frames having at last been abandoned, and both mounted a 75mm gun. After completion, a much higher bridge structure was added. There was to have been a second batch of six boats, with work starting from May 1915 onwards, but the programme was cancelled. *Fulton* and *Joessel* were both stricken in mid-1935.

Below: Meant for steam, Joessel *was completed with diesels.*

La Grange-class

Type: patrol, diesel-electric.
Total built: 4.
Completed: 1918-25.
Displacement: surfaced 920 tons; submerged 1,318 tons.
Dimensions: length 246ft 9in (75.2m); beam 20ft 8in (6.3m); draught 11ft 10in (3.6m).
Propulsion: 2 x Sulzer diesels, 2,600bhp; 2 x electric motors, 1,640shp; two shafts

Performance: surface – 16.5kt; submerged – 11kt; range surfaced 4,300nm at 10kt, submerged 125nm at 5kt.

Weapons: 8 x 17.7in (450mm) TT; 10 x torpedoes; 2 x 75mm guns.
Complement: 47.

History: As with the Fulton-class, these four boats were ordered just before the outbreak of war and were to have steam propulsion plants, but the Navy decided during construction that this should be changed to diesels. As a result, the steam units were reallocated to sloops and the Lagrange-class fitted with Sulzer

---

U1-class

Type: coastal, diesel-electric.
Total built: 1.
Completed: 1906.
Displacement: surfaced 238 tons; submerged 283 tons.
Dimensions: length 138ft 9in (42.3m); beam 12ft 6in (3.8m); draught 10ft 6in (3.2m).
Propulsion: 2 x Körting diesel engines, 400bhp; 2 x electric motors, 400shp; battery 396 cells; two shafts.
Performance: surface – 10.8kt; submerged – 8.7kt; range surfaced 1,500nm at 10kt, submerged 50nm at 5kt; maximum operating diving depth 98ft (30m).
Weapons: 1 x 17.7in (450mm) TT (bow); 2 x torpedoes.
Complement: 22.

History: In 1902 Germaniawerft, newly bought by steelmaker Krupp, started to design submarines, their first product, a 17-ton vessel named *Forelle*, being sold to the

Right: The first of the "U-boats," U-1, commissioned in 1906.

diesels. Also as in the Fulton-class, these boats were reconstructed after the war and among other improvements were given higher bridges and much improved periscopes. The boats were completed in a somewhat erratic order: *La Grange* – 1917; *Romazotti* (the last to be ordered) – 1918; *Laplace* – 1919; and *Regnault* – 1924. *La Grange* was stricken in 1935, the remainder in 1937.

Below: **La Grange**, *following her post-war rebuild.*

Imperial Russian Navy .The firm then sold a further three larger boats (Karp class) to Russia and it was only at this point that the Imperial German Navy began to show interest in this new weapon. The order for the first boat was placed in April 1904, with the design being prepared by a Spanish naval architect, d'Equevilley-Montjustin, and construction taking place at Germaniawerft. The design was based on that of the Russian Karp-class, although the Germany naval staff, aware of numerous accidents with petrol engines, insisted on engines driven by kerosene (paraffin). These were certainly safer, but the fuel was far more pungent and there was a major tactical penalty in that the boats emitted a vast cloud of dense white exhaust, which could be seen for miles. The particular type of engines installed in *U-1* could not be reversed, as a result of which she was fitted

---

Forel/Karp-classes   GERMANY (RUSSIA)

Type: coastal, diesel-electric.
Total built: 3.
Completed: 1907.
Displacement: surfaced 207 tons; submerged 235 tons.
Dimensions: length 130ft 0in (39.6m); beam 9ft 0in (2.7m); draught 8ft 0in (2.5m).
Propulsion: 2 Körting kerosene engines, 400bhp; 2 x electric motors, 200shp; two shafts.
Performance: surface – 10kt; submerged – 8.5kt; range surfaced 1,250nm at 10kt, submerged 50nm at 5kt; maximum operating diving depth 98ft (30m).
Weapons: 1 x 18in (457mm) TT (bow); 2 x Drzwiecki drop-collars.
Complement: 28.

History: The Imperial Russian Navy was among the most enthusiastic of submarine pioneers and initially concentrated on its own designs (see Aleksandrowski, Drzwiecki, Delfin/Kasatka), but the outbreak of the Russo-Japanese war (8 February 1904) led to an emergency expansion. Orders were quickly placed to acquire submarines from the United States (see Holland, Lake) and also from Germany. The first to be purchased was the *Forel*, a midget, electrically powered submarine, which had been designed and built by

with controllable-pitch propellers.

The new boat was commissioned in 1906 as *Unterseeboot-1* (submarine number 1), thereby introducing a new (and ominous) term into the international lexicon. *U-1* was subjected to careful testing and then took part in many trials, including a 1910 exercise with *U-3* and *U-4* in which they practised working together against a surface enemy, a tactic which would become known 30 years later as a "wolf-pack".

U-1 was relegated to training duties before the outbreak of World War I and was stricken in 1920. She was then presented to the Deutsches Museum in Munich, where she remains on display to this day, cut-away to reveal the extraordinary hazards and dire conditions endured by the submarine pioneers.

Germaniawerft, Kiel, as a private venture, intended to interest the German Navy in submarine operations. When this failed to happen they sold the vessel to Russia where it was immediately deployed to Vladivostok, but it proved too small to be of any tactical value. Meanwhile, in June 1904 the Russians placed another order with Germaniawerft for three boats. The yard itself was not very experienced in submarine work, but its chief designer, the Spaniard D'Equevilley had worked with Maxime Laubeuf in France and already had several successful designs to his credit. The Russians became considerably annoyed when the German Navy not only placed an order with Germaniawerft for a boat which was virtually identical to their *Karp*, but also ensured that the yard gave such priority to the German boat that although it had been started later was finished before any of the Russian boats.

The three Karp-class boats were delivered to Russia in 1907 and then transferred to the Black Sea by rail. *Kambala* was accidentally rammed and sunk by the Russian battleship *Rostislav* in June 1909, but the remaining two served until 1917, when they were stricken. They became part of the short-lived Ukrainian Navy in 1918, but were then captured by the Germans, only to be surrendered to the British in November 1918, who ordered them to be scuttled.

Below: Russia's three Karp-class boats, built in Germany.

U-13/U-16/U-17 classes

Type: coastal, diesel-electric.

Class	U-13	U-16	U-17
Total built	3	1	2
Completed	1910-11	1911	1912
Displacement surfaced submerged	516 tons 644 tons	489 tons 627 tons	564 tons 691 tons
Dimensions length beam draught	189ft 11in (57.9m) 19ft 8in (6.0m) 11ft 2in (3.4m)	189ft 8in (57.8m) 19ft 8in (6.0m) 11ft 2in (3.4m)	204ft 9in (62.4m) 19ft 8in (6.0m) 11ft 2in (3.4m)
Propulsion main engines power electric motors power shafts	4 x Körting diesels 2 x 350/2 x 250bhp 2 2 x 600shp two		4 x Körting diesels 4 x 350bhp 2 2 x 600shp two
Performance speed, surface submerged range, surfaced submerged	14.8kt 10.7kt 2000nm/14kt 90nm/5kt	15.6kt 10.7kt 2,100nm/15kt 90nm/5kt	14.9kt 9.5kt 6,700nm/8kt 75nm/5kt
Weapons TT location torpedoes	4 x 17.7in (450mm) bow – 2; stern – 2 6		
Complement	29		

History: The U-1-class was followed by steadily improving designs: U-2-class – one boat; U-3-class – two boats; U-5-class – four 4 boats; and U-9-class – four boats. All were powered by kerosene (paraffin) engines and all were armed with four 17.7in (450mm) torpedo tubes. This first series of boats culminated in the three classes listed here, which were virtually identical, with the U-13-class (three boats) and U-17-class (two boats) built at the Danzig Navy Yard, while the U-16-class (one boat) was built by Germaniawerft. All served during World War I. *U-13, U-14, U-17* and *U-18* were sunk in 1914-15, and of the two survivors *U-16* sank while on tow to England with only *U-17* managing to reach a breaker's yard. *U-16* and *U-17* both had a 2in (50mm) gun added at some time after 1915.

Right: U-17 receives a torpedo at sea; not an easy task.

Above: U-13, lead boat in a class of three completed 1910-11.

Above: U-16; note plume from kerosene-engine exhaust.

U-19/U-23/U-27/ U-31/U-43-classes

Type: patrol, diesel-electric.

Class	U-19	U-23	U-27	U-31	U-43
Total built	4	4	4	11	8
Completed	1912-13	1913	1913	1914	1914-15
Displacement surfaced submerged	650 tons 837 tons	669 tons 864 tons	675 tons 867 tons	685 tons 878 tons	725 tons 940 tons
Dimensions length beam draught	210ft 8in (64.2m) 20ft 0in (6.1m) 11ft 10in (3.6m)	212ft 3in (64.7m) 20ft 8in (6.3m) 11ft 6in (3.5m)	212ft 3in (64.7m) 20ft 8in (6.3m) 11ft 6in (3.5m)	212ft 3in (64.7m) 20ft 8in (6.3m) 11ft 10in (3.6m)	213ft 3in (65.0m) 20ft 4in (6.2m) 12ft 2in (3.7m)
Propulsion main engines power electric motors power shafts	2 x M.A.N. 2 x 850bhp 2 2 x 600shp two	2 x Germania 2 x 900bhp 2 2 x 600shp two	2 x M.A.N. 2 x 1,000bhp 2 2 x 600shp two	2 x Germania 2 x 925bhp 2 2 x 600shp two	2 x M.A.N. 2x1000bhp 2 2x 600shp two
Performance speed, surface submerged range, surfaced submerged maximum operational diving depth	14.8kt 10.7kt 2000nm/14kt 90nm/5kt 164ft (50m)	15.6kt 10.7kt 2,100nm/15kt 90nm/5kt 164ft (50m)	14.9kt 9.5kt 6,700nm/8kt 75nm/5kt 164ft (50m)	16.4kt 9.7kt 7,800nm/8kt 80nm/5kt 164ft (50m)	15.2kt 9.7kt 8100nm/8kt 51nm/5kt 164ft (50m)
Weapons TT location torpedoes guns	4 x 17.7in (450mm) bow – 2; stern – 2 6 1 x 88mm				4 x 19.7in (500mm) bow – 2; stern – 2 6 2 x 88mm
Complement	29			35	36

History: The next five classes were very similar to each other. The first in the series, the U-19-class, introduced two major developments, of which the most significant was that surface power was provided by diesel engines rather than the unsatisfactory kerosene engines. Second, it was armed with four tubes for the new 19.7in (500mm) torpedo, which was both more powerful and more reliable than its predecessor. Each class was constructed by one builder: Danzig Naval Yard built the U-19, U-27 and U-43 classes, which were all powered by M.A.N. diesels, while Germaniawerft built the U-23- and U-31-classes and powered them with its own Germania diesels. The great majority of these boats were given deck-guns in 1915-16, which were of two types, either one (or in some cases, two) 3.9in (88mm), or one 4.1in (105mm) (none was known to have mounted two of these heavier weapons). Further, some of those fitted with 88mm weapons in 1915 had them replaced by 105mm guns in 1916-17. These variations almost certainly stemmed from what was available in dockyards, although the desires and persuasiveness of individual captains may have also played a part.

All served throughout World War I, with two achieving different types of distinction. *U-29* was rammed and sunk by HMS *Dreadnought* on 18 March 1915, the only known occasion on which a submarine has been sunk by a battleship. The other boat was *U-35*, which remains the highest scoring submarine of all time, having sunk no fewer that 224 ships (535,000 gross registered tons) in the course of 25 patrols off the British and West African coasts, and in the Mediterranean. This was achieved under the command of four highly skilled officers, of whom the most famous was Kapitän-Leutnant Lothar von Arnauld de la Perrière, whose personal score was 194 ships sunk (453,716 tons); indeed, in one three-week cruise in *U-35* he sank 54 ships (91,000 tons), which was achieved with the expenditure of 900 rounds of ammunition and four torpedoes. Fifteen of the 31 U-boats were war losses and

Below: U-29, photographed from one of her victims.

the surviving boats were broken up by the European Allies, except for *U-46* which went to Japan, where it served as *O-2* until 1922, when it, too, was scrapped.

The one break in the numerical sequence from *U-19* to *U-50* was *U-42*, which was ordered from the Italian company, Fiat, in order to gain knowledge of foreign submarine and diesel engine technology. However, the war broke out before it could be delivered, the boat was requisitioned by the Italian Navy as *Ballila* (qv), and the number 42 in the first series of German numbering remained unused.

Right: U-35, highest scoring submarine in any navy, ever.

U-51/U-57/U-63/ U-81 classes

GERMANY

Type: patrol, diesel-electric.

Class	U-51	U-57*	U-63	U-81
Total built	6	12	3	6
Completed	1915-15	1916-17	1916	1916
Displacement surfaced submerged	715 tons 902 tons	786 tons 954 tons	810 tons 927 tons	808 tons 946 toms
Dimensions length beam draught	213ft 11in (65.2m) 21ft 0in (6.4m) 11ft 10in (3.6m)	219ft 10in (67.0m) 20ft 8in (6.3m) 12ft 6in (3.8m)	224ft 5in (68.4m) 20ft 8in (6.3m) 13ft 2in (4.0m)	230ft 0in (70.1m) 20ft 8in (6.3m) 13ft 2in (4.0m)
Propulsion main engines power electric motors power shafts	2 x M.A.N. 2 x 1,200bhp 2 2 x 600shp 2	2 x M.A.N. 2 x 900bhp 2 2 x 600shp 2	2 x Germania 2 x 1,000bhp 2 2 x 600shp 2	2 x M.A.N. 2 x 1,200bhp 2 2 x 600shp 2

History: The first "Mobilisation" (Ms) type was the U-51-class, six boats (*U-51* to *U-56*) built by Germania, the design being an improved version of the pre-war U-31-class, which had been built by the same company. There were a number of improvements: for example, two more torpedoes were carried for a total of eight, while the two 88mm deck-guns were mounted during construction (they were later replaced by a single105mm gun in most boats). Two boats were lost in World War I, three survived to be broken up in 1919-22, and the fourth survivor was allocated to Japan where it became *O-3*.

Performance				
speed, surface	17.1kt	14.7kt	16.5kt	16.8kt
submerged	9.1kt	8.4kt	9.0kt	9.1kt
range, surfaced	9,000kt/8nm	7,730nm/8kt	8,100nm/8kt	8,100nm/8kt
submerged	55kt/5nm	55nm/5kt	115nm/5kt	56nm/5kt
maximum operational diving depth	164ft (50m)	164ft (50m)	164ft (50m)	164ft (50m)
Weapons				
TT		4 x 19.7in (500mm)		
location		bow – 2; stern – 2		
torpedoes		8		
guns		2 x 88mm or 1 x 105mm		
Complement		35		

Specifications for U-57 to U-62, as built.

Right:* U-53 *of the U-51-class at sea in 1917.

The U-57-class consisted of two groups, *U-57* to *U-62*, and *U-99* to *U-104*, both built by AG Weser, at Bremen. These were virtually identical except that the second group had more powerful diesels (2 x 1,200bhp) and could stow a total of 12 torpedoes. Seven were lost in the war: three to surface warships, one to mines, one to another submarine, one cause unknown, and one rammed by the liner *Olympic*; the boats that survived were broken up.

The U-63-class was a further batch of three improved U-51-class boats built by Germania, ordered in May 1915. One was lost in the war, one was scuttled, and one survived to be broken-up.

Finally in these first Ms-boats came the U-81-class, a further batch of six from Germania. Torpedo stowage was again increased, this time to 12. Two survived the war, one being broken-up while the other foundered on the way to the breakers' yard; four were lost during the war, one by a submarine and three by surface warships.

Right: U-86 (U-81-class) at an English port, following her surrender. The forward gun was a 105mm, the after gun an 88mm. Torpedo armament was four 500mm (19.7in) tubes (2 bow, 2 stern) and 12 torpedoes.

U-66-class

GERMANY (AUSTRIA)

Type: patrol, diesel-electric.

Class	U-7 (Austria)	U-66 (Germany)
Total built	0	5
Completed	–	1916-17
Displacement surfaced submerged	695 tons 885 tons	791 tons 933 tons
Dimensions length beam draught	228ft 0in (69.5m) 20ft 8in (6.3m) 12ft 5in (3.9m)	228ft 0in (69.5m) 20ft 8in (6.3m) 12ft 6in (3.8m)
Propulsion main engines power electric motors power shafts	2 x diesels 2 x 1,150bhp 2 2 x 620shp 2	2 x Germania 2 x1,1500bhp 2 2 x 615shp 2

Performance		
speed, surface	17kt	16.8kt
submerged	11kt	10.34kt
range, surfaced	–	6,500nm/8kt
submerged	–	115nm/5kt
maximum operational		
diving depth	164ft (50m)	164ft (50m)
Weapons		
TT	6 x 450mm (17.7in)	5 x 17.7in (450mm)
location	bow – 4; stern – 2	bow – 4; stern – 1
torpedoes	9	12
gun	1 x 66mm	1 x 88mm
Complement	36	36

History: The U-66-class was not part of the German "Mobilisation" (Ms) programme, but was an unsought bonus. Following their early experiences, the Austro-Hungarian Navy stated a requirement for a new type, which was essentially an improved version of the Austrian *U-3*. The competition was won by Germaniawerft of Kiel and five boats were ordered in February 1913 (as the

Austrian *U-7* to *U-11*) for delivery in 1916-17. There was to be a powerful armament of six torpedo tubes and a single 66mm gun, and particular emphasis was placed on a high underwater speed, to achieve which there was to be no bridge while a battery of very powerful cells was installed. On the outbreak of World War I, however, it was considered that the proposed delivery voyage from Kiel to Pola in the Adriatic would be far too hazardous and the boats were much too large to be sent by rail, so they were sold, or

U-87/U-93-classes

Type: patrol, diesel-electric.

Class	U-87 (Project 25)	U-93
Total built	6	24
Completed	–	1916-17
Displacement surfaced submerged	757 tons 998 tons	838 tons 1,000 tons
Dimensions length beam draught	224ft 9in (65.8m) 20ft 4in (6.2m) 12ft 9in (3.9m)	234ft 11in (71.6m) 20ft 8in (6.3m) 12ft 9in (3.9m)
Propulsion main engines power electric motors power shafts	2 x M.A.N. 2 x 1,200bhp 2 2 x 620shp 2	2 x M.A.N. 2 x 1,200bhp 2 2 x 620shp 2

he ways, to Germany. The German Navy then had them modified to German standards, for example by replacing the Austrian 66m gun by a German 88mm and increasing the torpedo load-out to 12, and then completed the work. Three were sunk by British ships and two survived the war, to be broken-up in 1919-21.

Below: **U-70** *was built for Austria, but bought by Germany.*

Performance		
speed, surface	16.9kt	16.8kt
submerged	8.6kt	8.6kt
range, surfaced	8,000nm/8kt	8,300nm/8kt
submerged	56nm/5kt	50/5kt
maximum operational		
diving depth	164ft (50m)	
Weapons		
TT	6 x 450mm (17.7in)	6 x 450mm (17.7in)
location	bow – 4; stern – 2	bow – 4; stern – 2
torpedoes	12	12
gun	1 x 105mm	1 x 105mm
Complement	36	36

History: The U-87-class, all built by Danzig Naval Yard, was based on *U-50*, the last of the U-43-class, but with the number of forward torpedo tubes increased to four and the torpedo load-out doubled to 12. In addition, the gun armament was changed from two 88mm guns to one 105mm. Six were built, of which four were war losses. Up till now German U-boats had either vertical

stems or a backward sloping stem, but a noticeable change in the U-93 class
was the adoption of the raked 'clipper' bow. This is generally thought to have
been intended to improve sea-keeping when running on the surface (which was
certainly one of its effects) but the real reason was that, in combination with the
raked and serrated cable-cutter now mounted atop the bow, it was intended to

UB-1-class (Project 34)   GERMAN

Type: coastal, diesel-electric.
Total built: 17.
Completed: 1915.
Displacement: surfaced 127 tons; submerged 142 tons.
Dimensions: length 92ft 2in (28.1m); beam 10ft 6in (3.2m); draught 9ft 10in
(3.0m).
Propulsion: 1 x Daimler 4-cylinder diesel, 60bhp; 1 x Siemens-Schucke
electric motor, 120shp; one shaft.
Performance: surface – 6.5kt; submerged – 5.5kt; range surfaced 1,650nm a
5kt, submerged 45nm at 4kt; maximum operating diving depth 164ft (50m).
Weapons: 2 x 17.7in (450mm) TT (bow); 2 x torpedoes; 1 x 8mm MG.
Complement: 14.

History: The speed of the German advance along the North Sea coast
August-September 1914 took the Imperial German Navy by surprise and
found itself faced with a demand for small coastal submarines, but with r
assets immediately available to meet it. A design was rushed through and c
15 October an order was duly placed for what was, in essence, a submersib
torpedo-boat, with a displacement of about 125 tons and armed with tw
torpedo tubes. An essential element of the requirement was that the boat ha
to be transportable by railroad. The result was a neat little craft, single-hulle
and with a maximum diameter of 10ft 4in (3.15m), which was imposed by th
railway loading limits, and a crew of 14.

The initial order was for eight boats from Germaniawerft (UB-1 to UB-8) ar
seven boats from AG Weser (UB-9 to UB-15); the former were powered b
Daimler diesels, the latter by Körting diesels. This order was, however, quick
increased by two (UB-16 and UB-17) to compensate for the sale of two of th
initial order (UB-1 and UB-15) to the Austro-Hungarian Navy. Several years lat
German ally Bulgaria wanted to buy two of these boats for the defence of i

nable the boat to force its way through anti-submarine nets more effectively.
he cable-cutter and raked bow then became a visual characteristic of German
U-boat design for the next 20 years.

Below: U-96 shows the smooth lines of 1917-18 U-boats.

Above: The UB-1 class boats were built incredibly quickly.

lack Sea port, Varna; *UB-7* was sunk before it could be handed over, but *UB-*
was delivered in May 1918.

Building time was extraordinarily short, the first boat being completed in
ist 75 days and the last of the 17 was handed over in May 1915. All but a few
oats were then despatched by rail, each requiring three low-loader wagons for
le main assemblies (the fore-, centre- and after-sections) plus more for the
ridge, engines and cells. Most went to either Antwerp or Hoboken, but a
umber also went to Pola on the Adriatic coast.

In 1918 four were converted to minelayers, which involved adding a
ection to increase hull length to 105ft (32.0m) and replacing the torpedo
bes by four 39.4in (1,000mm) mine tubes; eight mines could be carried.
total of seven boats were lost during the war, one was demolished by the
ermans as they withdrew from Flanders; the remainder were scrapped in
919-20.

UB-II-class (Project 39)

Type: coastal, diesel-electric.
Total built: 30.
Completed: 1915-16.
Displacement: surfaced 263 tons; submerged 292 tons.
Dimensions: length 118ft 5in (36.1m); beam 14ft 5in (4.4m); draught 12ft 2 (3.7m).
Propulsion: 2 x Daimler, Körting or Benz diesels, 2 x 140bhp; 2 x electr motors, 280shp; two shafts.
Performance: surface – 9.2kt; submerged – 5.8kt; range surfaced 6,500nm 5kt, submerged 45nm at 4kt; maximum operating diving depth 164ft (50m).
Weapons: 2 x 19.7in (500mm) TT (bow); 4 torpedoes; 1 x 50mm gun.
Complement: 22.
Specifications for UB-18, as built.

History: The first batch of coastal submarines (see UB-I-class above) wa produced remarkably quickly and did all that had been asked of it in th operational requirement, but that was soon out-of-date. Even as the first boat were running trials in early 1915, it was realised that they were too slow an too small. Once they were in service, however, a further problem wa revealed; in the current state of development of diesel engines a singl engine/single propeller drive system was woefully inadequate and mechanical problem anywhere in the power-train left the boats wallowin helplessly and very vulnerable. So, the UB-II (Project 39) was developed a a matter urgency, with a larger hull, more powerful electrical cells and

---

UB-III-class (Project 44)

Type: coastal, diesel-electric.
Total built: 93.
Completed: 1917-18.
Displacement: surfaced 516 tons; submerged 651 tons.
Dimensions: length 181ft 5in (55.3m); beam 19ft 0in (5.8m); draught 12ft 2 (3.7m).
Propulsion: 2 x A.E.G., M.A.N., Körting or Benz diesels, 2 x 550bhp; 2 x electr motors, 2 x 296shp; two shafts.
Performance: surface – 13.5kt; submerged – 7.5kt; range surfaced 9,040nm 6kt, submerged 55nm at 4kt; maximum operating diving depth 164ft (50m).
Weapons: 5 x 19.7in (500mm) TT (bow – 4; stern – 1); 10 torpedoes; 1 105mm gun.
Complement: 34.
Specifications for UB-48, as built.

History: By mid-1915 one of the major problems facing the German Navy wa the maintenance of the blockade around the British Isles. There was also need for boats to carry out patrols in the Mediterranean The large U-boats we in short supply and new ones were taking a long time to build, while the muc smaller UB-I and UB-II boats were simply inadequate for the job; the endurance was insufficient, the armament poor and the crew too few number for protracted patrols in such a harsh environment. A requirement wa therefore stated for a U-boat of simple design, displacing some 600 tons an most importantly, which could be designed and built quickly.
    The new design was based upon that of the UC-II minelayer (qv), but wi

Above: UB-40, one of 30 coastal boats of the UB-II-class.

econd power-train, all of which added some 270 tons to the surface
displacement. Initially, it was accept-ed that these boats could not be moved
by rail, although this was actually achieved, even though it entailed cutting
the hull sections longitudinally.

A total of 30 boats were built, 12 by AG Weser in two blocks of six, the
remaining 18 by Blohm + Voss. This was Blohm + Voss's first U-boat
construction programme. Two were sold to Austria-Hungary in 1917; *UB-43* and
UB-47 kept the same numbers, becoming *U-43* and *U-47*, respectively. Despite
their small size and limited capabilities, some of these boats were very
successful: *UB-18* sank 126 merchant ships (128,555 tons) while *UB-40* sank
fewer ships but with a greater tonnage – 99 ships (131,680 tons). Some 20
boats were lost during the war (surface warships – 10; mines – 7; aircraft – 2;
scuttled – 1), leaving 10 which were broken up in 1919-22.

Above: Nine Blue Maxes were won aboard UB-III-class boats.

totally new forward section and a torpedo compartment in place of the vertical
minelaying shafts. This enabled the boats to mount a forward battery of four
19.7in (500mm) torpedo tubes, with a fifth tube in the stern. The deck gun was
a naval pattern 88mm gun on a U-boat mounting. The initial orders were issued
in May 1916 and a total of 93 boats were built in four yards: Blohm + Voss,
Hamburg; AG Weser, Bremen; Vulkan, Hamburg; and Germaniawerft, Kiel, and
more were under construction at the war's end. There were many minor
differences between the various production batches and by 1918 boats were
just over 2ft (0.6m) longer and had increased in displacement by some 5 tons.

UB-III boats served in the waters around the British Isles, as well as the
Mediterranean, and of the 29 awards of *Pour le Merite* made to U-boat officers
during World War I, no fewer than nine went to men serving aboard UB-III-class
boats. Many of these boats were lost in the war, and the relatively small
number that survived were handed over to the Allies and broken up.

Kobben/A-2-classes GERMANY (NORWAY)

Type: patrol, kerosene/diesel-electric.

Class	Kobben (A-1)	A-2
Total built	1	3
Completed	1909	1913
Displacement surfaced submerged	206 tons 259 tons	268 tons 353 tons
Dimensions length beam draught	128ft 11in (39.3m) 12ft 2in (3.7m) 9ft 10in (3.0m)	152ft 7in (46.5m) 15ft 9in (4.8m) 8ft 10in (2.7m)

History: The Royal Norwegian Navy (RNorN) was one of the first to show an interest in submarines and sent an officer to watch the trials of USS *Holland* (SS-1) in 1901. Norway's first proposal to build submarines was made in 1902, but it was not until 1907 that the parliament endorsed the Navy's plans. An order was then placed with Germania and the first boat was delivered on 28 November 1909. It was named *Kobben*, but this was changed in 1913 to *A-1*. This boat was generally similar to Germany's *U-1* (qv) and like that boat was powered by two Körting kerosene engines, but had an oval cross-section and an external torpedo tube aft. *Kobben* was used for trials and training, but was used operationally in World War I in defence of Norway's neutrality. She was stricken in 1926 and scrapped in 1933.

In May 1911 Norway next ordered a further three boats to a new design, and these, the A-2-class, were again built by Germania, being launched in 1913 and delivered in early 1914. Norway also placed a further order for a fourth boat in 1912, but this was not launched until May 1914 and was still fitting out when war was declared in August 1914; she was immediately requisitioned by the German Navy and commissioned as *UA*. These four boats had a gyroscopic compass, a wireless installation, and a transverse propeller in the bow for precise positioning when launching torpedoes while the boat was stationary.

The RNorN employed *A-2*, *A-3* and *A-4* as operational boats and they were still in service when Germany invaded Norway in April 1940. Two were unab

Propulsion		
engines	2 x Körting gasoline	2 x Germania diesels
power	2 x 225bhp	2 x 350bhp
electric motor	2	2
power	2 x 150shp	2 x 190shp
shafts	two	two
Performance		
speed, surface	11.9kt	14.5kt
submerged	8.9kt	9.0kt
range, surfaced	1,450nm/9kt	900nm/10kt
submerged	45nm/6.5t	76nm/3.3kt
diving depth	164ft (50m)	164ft (50m)
Weapons		
TT	3 x 18.0in (457mm)	3 x 18.0in (457mm)
location	bow – 2; deck – 1	bow – 2; stern – 1
torpedoes	4	5
Complement	14	17

bove: Norwegian A2, built by Germania, captured by Germany.

attack the invaders and were scuttled by their crews, but *A-2* was forced to e surface by German ships. She changed hands several times before being roken up. *UA* was employed briefly by the Germans as an operational boat, ut was transferred to training in 1916 and was scrapped in the UK in 1919.

Holland-class

Type: harbour defence, gasoline-electric.
Total built: 5.
Completed: 1901-02.
Displacement: surfaced 113 tons; submerged 122 tons.
Dimensions: length 63ft 10in (19.5m); beam 11ft 10in (3.6m); draught 9ft 11 (3.0m).
Propulsion: Wolseley gasoline engine, 160hp; 1 x electric motor, 70hp; or shaft.
Performance: surface – 7.4kt; submerged – 6kt; range surfaced 235nm at 7k submerged 20nm at 5kt; maximum operating diving depth 50ft (15m).
Weapons: 1 x 18in (457mm) TT (bow); 3 x torpedoes.
Complement: 8.

History: The Royal Navy watched the development of submarines abroad wi growing concern, especially those immediately across the Channel in Franc but it was not until the success of the Holland boats in the United States th they decided to take positive action. Thus, when the Electric Boat Co. let th British know that they would be interested in a deal, negotiations were quick concluded and a contract signed for the construction of a Holland design at th Vickers yard at Barrow-in-Furness. The design was virtually the same as that the U.S. Navy's Adder-class (qv) and progress was rapid, HMS *No 1* being la down in February 1901 and launched in October, and all five were in service k 1903. They were to standard Holland pattern, single-hulled, with one torpe tube in the bows and a gasoline engine for surface propulsion and rechargir

---

A-class

Type: harbour defence, gasoline-electric.
Total built: 13.
Completed: 1902-05.
Displacement: surfaced 190 tons; submerged 207 tons.
Dimensions: length 103ft 3in (31.5m); beam 11ft 10in (3.6m); draught 10ft 1 (3.1m).
Propulsion: 1 x 16-cylinder Wolseley gasoline engine, 350bhp; 1 x elect engine, 125hp; battery 120 cells; one shaft.
Performance: surface – 9.5kt; submerged – 6kt; range surfaced 500nm at 9 submerged 20nm at 5kt; maximum operating diving depth 50ft (15m).
Weapons: 1 x 18in (457mm) TT (bow); 3 x torpedoes.
Complement: 11.
Specifications for A-1, as built.

History: The rapid progress made by both Vickers and the Admiralty meant th the sixth of the Holland-class was built to a revised design and became HM *A-1*, the first of the A-class. She was 40ft (12m) longer and had a much mo powerful gasoline engine, but there were numerous changes made to the cla during construction. Thus, all boats from *A-2* to *A-13* had a larger hull, 105ft C (32.0m) in length, with a 12ft 9in (3.9m) beam and a surface draught of 10ft 8 (3.3m). The output power of the Wolseley gasoline engine was als progressively improved: *A-1* – 350bhp; *A-2* to *A-4* – 450bhp; *A-5* to *A-7* 550bhp; and *A-8* to *A-12* – 600bhp. The electric motor was also improve giving 125shp in *A-1* and 150shp in all later boats. Armament was given significant increase in *A-5* onwards, which had two torpedo tubes, both in t

Above: British Holland inadvertantly displays its lines.

ne batteries. They were used to gain experience in the design and operation of uch novel warships, but despite the fact that they were worked hard and used or many trials, not one was lost in service. The original intention was to build ix units, but progress was so rapid that the sixth was altered while under onstruction and became the first unit of the British A-class (qv).

All the boats were commissioned in 1902-03 and served for some 10 years. Il were sold in 1912-13 and two were broken up. The other three, however, all ank whilet on tow to the breaker's yard, including *No 1* whose wreck was ound in April 1981. She was then raised and is now on display at the RN ubmarine Museum in Gosport, the only original Holland design to have urvived.

Above: Pre-1914 picture of British submarine A-11.

ow, and carried a total of four torpedoes. The last boat, *A-13*, was powered by Hornsby-Ackroyd six-cylinder, vertical, heavy-oil engine, an interim step in the rogress towards a true diesel engine. Other changes included increases in the eight of the conning-tower and the introduction of an embryonic bridge.

The A-class was a success and provided a major advance in the Royal avy's build-up of a submarine arm. Three out of the first four suffered a fate hich was all too common in the early days of submarines (and which is by no eans unknown today), namely accidental ramming by a surface ship. Thus, *A-* was lost on 18 March 1904, *A-4* on 16 October 1`905 and *A-3* on 2 February 912, and although all three were raised, none was ever returned to service. *A-* foundered and was lost in January 1914, but nine boats survived until 1919-) when they were sold for breaking up, although *A-2* sank en route to the eaker's yard.

B/C-classes

Type: coastal defence, gasoline-electric.
Total built: 11.
Completed: 1904-06.
Displacement: surfaced 287 tons; submerged 316 tons.
Dimensions: length 142ft 2in (43.3m); beam 13ft 7in (4.1m); draught 11ft 7 (3.4m).
Propulsion: 1 x 16-cylinder Vickers gasoline engine, 600bhp; 1 x electric motor 290shp; battery 166 cells; one shaft.
Performance: surface – 12kt; submerged – 6kt; range surfaced 1,300nm at 9k submerged 50nm at 4.5kt; maximum operating diving depth 50ft (15m).
Weapons: 2 x 18in (457mm) TT (bow); 4 x torpedoes.
Complement: 15.
Specifications for B-class, as built.

History: The C-class was a virtual repeat of the B-class, all major characteristic being identical, so the two are treated here together. A total of 11 B-class wer launched between 1904 and 1906 and were generally similar in layout to the A class but appreciably longer and with a much more substantial deck casing improve surface performance and to make life easier for the crew. The A-class had a single pair of hydroplanes aft, but the B-class had an additional pa mounted on the conning tower in order to improve underwater manoeuvrabilit but this was never repeated in a British design.

Six boats (*B-6* to *B-11*) were sent to the Mediterranean and one of thes *B-11*, managed to penetrate the Dardanelles defences and sink the Turkis coastal guardship *Messudieh* (9,120 tons) on 13 December 1914. These s boats became unemployable after 1915 due to lack of essential spares in th theatre, so they were converted at the Italian Navy's Venice dockyard in surface patrol boats. One was, however, destroyed in an Austrian bombir

D-class

Type: coastal, diesel-electric.
Total built: 8.
Completed: 1908-11.
Displacement: surfaced 483 tons; submerged 595 tons.
Dimensions: length 163ft 0in (49.7m); beam 20ft 6in (6.2m); draught 10ft 5 (3.2m).
Propulsion: 2 x 6-cylinder diesels, 2 x 600bhp; 2 x electric motors, 2 x 277sh battery 210 cells.
Performance: surface – 14kt; submerged – 9kt; range surfaced 1,750nm 11.2kt, submerged 50nm at 5kt; maximum operating diving depth 10C (30.5m).
Weapons: 3 x 18in (457mm) TT (bow – 2, stern – 1); 6 x torpedoes.
Complement: 25.
Specifications for D-1, as completed.

History: The D-class incorporated three substantial improvements in Briti submarine design: the introduction of diesel engines, which resulted in substantial enhancement in safety for the crews; the first use of saddle tank which gave a much higher reserve of buoyancy; and the use of transver watertight bulkheads, greatly improving survivability in the event of an accider They were also the first with twin propellers and two engines, the latter bein

bove: **C-37** *shows the continuous upper casing now fitted.*

tack while being rebuilt, leaving only five to be employed in the Adriatic. *B-2* as sunk in a collision with a merchant ship, *B-10* was sunk during the war and the remainder were sold for breaking-up in 1919-21.

No fewer than 38 C-class boats were built, six in the Royal Dockyard at hatham and all the rest by Vickers, in what was the largest submarine oduction run up to that time, launches being from July 1906 to February 1910. ey were identical to the B-class in most respects, but lacked the amidships vdroplanes and had many detailed improvements.

C-11 was sunk in a peacetime collision with a merchant ship in 1909, it the remainder, although built for coastal work, all had a very busy war. lost were based in the UK, but three (*C-26, C-28, C-35)* were sent to help ussia in 1916, being sent to Archangel by ship, and then by canal barge d rail to the Baltic; all three were scuttled in April 1918 to prevent capture the Germans.

bove: **D-8***; note the upper rudder.*

iportant at a time when engines were none too reliable. All this led to an crease in length – 163ft (49.7m) compared to 142ft (43m) in the B/C-classes iut this meant that a crew of 25 could be accommodated, the extra numbers ing needed for the longer operations. The boats were armed with twin 18in 57mm) torpedo tubes in the bows, which were in an "over-and-under" infiguration to ensure that the bow was as fine as possible. Only one, *D-4,* er mounted a gun, a 12-pounder on a "disappearing" mount, which proved imsy and complicated and was later fixed; as far as can be ascertained this as the first gun to be mounted during construction in any submarine, in any vy. There were marginal differences in length – *D-1* was 163ft (49.7m) long, iile *D-2* was slightly shorter at 162ft 1in (49.4m), and *D-3* to *D-9* longer at 7ft 7in (50.2m).

E-class

Type: attack, diesel-electric.

Class	E-1 group	E-9 group
Total built	10*	41**
Completed	1912-13	1913-16
Displacement surfaced submerged	655 tons 796 tons	667 tons 807 tons
Dimensions length beam draught	178ft 1in (54.2m) 22ft 8in (6.9m) 12ft 6in (3.8m)	181ft 0in (55.2m) 15ft 2in (4.6m) 12ft 6in (3.8m)
Propulsion engines power electric motor power shafts	2 x Vickers-Admiralty diesels 2 x 800bhp 2 2 x 420shp two	
Performance speed, surface submerged range, surfaced submerged maximum diving depth	15.25kt 9.25kt 3,000nm/10kt 65nm/5kt 200ft (61m)	
Weapons TT location torpedoes gun	4 x 18in (457m) bow – 1, stern – 1, beam – 2 8 1 x 12pdr (76mm)	5 x 18in (457mm) bow - 2; stern -1; beam - 10 1 x 12pdr
Complement	30	34

* Includes two for RAN.

** Does not include six completed as minelayers.

History: The E-class were enlarged and improved versions of the D-class, b
the main operational difference resulted from a request by the officers of t
Submarine Service, who asked for beam torpedo tubes to be fitted. T
problem was that the torpedoes of the time had to be fired at very short range
indeed, the teaching was that the boat had to approach to a distance from t
target of some three times the length of the submarine – and this meant th
in an "end-on" attack the boat then had great difficulty in getting away witho
colliding with its victim. Some submarine officers held this opinion so strong
that they wanted to do away with bow tubes altogether, but this view did n
prevail. The first eight boats (E-1-class) were therefore completed with just o

Above: E-class boat with 12pdr (76mm) on foredeck.

ow tube, one stern tube and two of the new lateral tubes, one on each beam.
xercises, later reinforced by wartime experience, showed that this was not
ne answer and from *E-9* onwards there were two tubes in the bow, but, unlike
ne "over-and-under" in the D-class, these were side-by-side.

Although not fitted during construction in the early boats, from 1915
nwards all E- class had a single gun, usually the 12-pdr (76mm), although a
pdr and the heavier 4in (102mm) was fitted in some boats, a few of them on
"disappearing mount". The E-1 group had two watertight bulkheads, but from
-9 onwards this was increased to three, but it should be noted that
ontemporary Italian designs, eg, Fiat-Laurenti, had 10 such bulkheads. The
oats were originally classified as having an operational depth of 100ft (31m)
ut this failed to take account of the stronger hull and the internal bulkheads
nd was later increased to 200ft (61m). In fact, *E-40* once struck bottom at
18ft (97m) and the only damage was minor leaks at the engine hatch and stern
ubes.

The original plan was for the E-class to be succeeded by the larger G-class,
ut these took longer to build and on the outbreak of war in August 1914 it was
ecided to order more E-class boats to build up the British submarine force as
uickly as possible.

*Below: E-31, one of 35 E-class Group III boats
built 1915-17.*

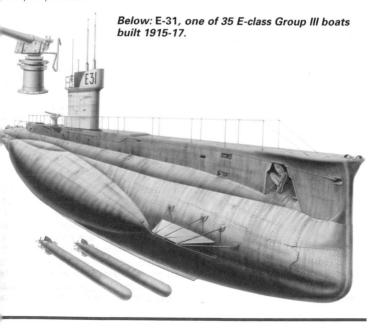

V-class

Type: attack, diesel-electric.
Total built: 4.
Completed: 1914-15.
Displacement: surfaced 386 tons; submerged 453 tons.
Dimensions: length 144ft 0in (43.9m); beam 16ft 6in (5.0m); draught 11ft 6
(3.5m).
Propulsion: 2 x Vickers-Admiralty 8-cylinder diesels, 2 x 450bhp; 2 x electr
motors, 2 x 150shp; battery 132 Exide cells; two shafts.
Performance: surface – 14kt; submerged – 8.5kt; range surfaced 3,000nm
9kt, submerged 50nm at 5kt; maximum operating diving depth 150ft (46m).
Weapons: 2 x 18in (457mm) TT (bow); 4 x torpedoes; 1 x 12pdr (76mm) gur
Complement: 20.
Specifications for V-1, as built.

History: In 1912 the Admiralty sought two coastal types displacing 250-30
tons, and a committee recommended the Italian Fiat-Laurenti design which w
then built by Fiat's UK agents, Scott's of Greenock (see S-type, below). Bi
despite having plenty of other work on hand, Vickers produced a design of the
own, and, somewhat surprisingly, this was accepted.

The V-class had a partial double-hull, which extended over about 75 ft (23r
amidships, and a well designed hull which gave the boats a good underwat
speed, although submerged endurance was limited by the electrical capacity
the cells in the battery. There were minor variations between *V-1* and tl
remaining boats *V-2* to *V-4*, mainly because the latter had two additional 21

F-class

Type: coastal, diesel-electric.
Total built: 3.
Completed: 1915-16.
Displacement: surfaced 353 tons; submerged 525 tons.
Dimensions: length 151ft 0in (46.0m); beam 16ft 1in (4.9m); draught 10ft 7
(3.2m).
Propulsion: 2 x Vickers diesels, 2 x 450bhp; 2 x electric motors, 2 x 200sh
battery 128 New Exide cells; two shafts.
Performance: surface – 14.5kt; submerged – 9kt; range surfaced 3,000nm
9kt, submerged 90nm at 3kt.
Weapons: 3 x 18in (475mm) TT (bow – 2; stern – 1); 6 x torpedoes; 1 x 2pdr gu
Complement: 19.

History: The Admiralty placed orders for three different types of coas
submarines in 1912 and early 1913 – S-, V- and W-classes – but despite this
was decided to order yet another class, this time to the Admiralty's own desig
resulting in the F-class. The design was based on that of the V-class, but w
a number of improvements, including a third (stern) torpedo tube and tv
additional torpedoes, with a partial double-hull.

The three boats were built at different yards, with long intervals betwee
them, the builders and launch dates being: *F-1* – Chatham Navy Yard, Mar
1915; *F-2* – J. Samuel White, July 1917; and *F-3* – Thornycroft, February 191
The three boats were identical except that *F-1* and *F-3* were powered
standard Vickers diesels, while *F-2* was powered by M.A.N. diesels built und
licence by J. Samuel White. A further five boats were planned but we

bove: British V-class coastal submarine; four were built.

).53m) frames inserted in the centre of the hull and two shorter frames
moved forward, which resulted in a net increase in length of 3ft 6in (1.1m)
nd an increase in submerged displacement of 4 tons. A further difference was
hat *V-1* had two Laurence Scott electric motors (2 x 150shp) whereas the
thers had Don Works motors (2 x 190shp).

Two boats served in the English Channel in 1915-16, following which all four
perated in the North Sea, being based at Harwich and Great Yarmouth. Two
oats were transferred to training duties in 1918, but all four were placed in
serve as soon as the war ended and were sold for scrapping in 1920-21.

bove: F-2 on builder's trials in 1917.

ncelled by Admiral Fisher on his return to the Admiralty as First Sea Lord on
e outbreak of war. The three boats served in harbour defence and training
ties during the war and were scrapped in the early 1920s.

Nautilus-class

Type: overseas, diesel-electric.
Total built: 1.
Completed: 1915.
Displacement: surfaced 1,441 tons; submerged 2,026 tons.
Dimensions: length 258ft 5in (78.8m); beam 26ft 0in (7.9m); draught 17ft 9in (5.4m).
Propulsion: 2 x Vickers 12-cylinder diesels, 2 x 1,850hp; 2 x electric motors, 2 500shp; battery 2 x 176 Exide cells; two shafts.
Performance: surface – 17kt; submerged – 10kt; range surfaced 5,300nm at 11k submerged 72nm at 5kt; maximum operating diving depth 200ft (61m).
Weapons: 8 x 18in (457mm) TT (bow – 2; stern – 2; beam – 4), 16 x torpedoes; 1 12pdr (76mm) gun.
Complement: 42.

History: The origin of this design lay in a 1912 Admiralty requirement for what wa then termed an "overseas submarine" (ie, with longer range and greater endurand than the coastal types), which would have double-hull construction, displace son 1,000 tons and be capable of a surface speed of 20kt. This speed was of gre significance, since 20kt was the current speed of the battlefleet and th requirement was to lead in due course to the attempt in many navies to produce "fleet submarine" capable of moving and cooperating closely with surface ship Diesel-electric submarines were never able to meet this requirement, stear electric submarines came a little closer but introduced all sorts of other problem and it was only the advent of nuclear propulsion that produced the answer.

The requirement went to Vickers, at that time not only Britain's mo

---

G-class

Type: attack, diesel-electric.
Total built: 14.
Completed: 1916-17.
Displacement: surfaced 703 tons; submerged 837 tons.
Dimensions: length 187ft 1in (57.0m); beam 22ft 8in (6.9m); draught 13ft 4 (4.1m).
Propulsion: 2 x Vickers 8-cylinder diesels, 2 x 800bhp; 2 x electric motors, 2 420shp; battery 2 x 100 Exide cells; two shafts.
Performance: surface – 14.3kt; submerged – 9kt; range surfaced 2,400nm 12.5kt, submerged 99nm at 3kt.
Weapons: 1 x 21in (533mm) TT (stern), 2 x torpedoes; 4 x 18in (457mm) TT (bc – 2, beam – 2), 8 x torpedoes; 1 x 3in (76mm) AA gun.
Complement: 30.

History: In 1913 naval intelligence reported that there was a large-scale programm in Germany to build long-range, double-hulled submarines, which would produce very clear threat to British naval interests. In a somewhat panicked response t Admiralty issued a requirement for a new type with a displacement similar to the class (ie, about 800 tons submerged), a partial double-hull, one of the very new 21 (533mm) torpedo tubes forward, and two 18in (457mm) tubes, one on each bean This resulted in the G-class and between June and November 1914 orders we placed for a total of 15 boats with Chatham Dockyard (five), Armstrong Whitwo (two), Vickers (six), Scott's (one) and White (one). Some of these firms were giv permission to install their own choice of suitable diesel, with a view to expandi the knowledge-base on this relatively new type of engine. However, on t

*Above: Intended for "overseas" duties, **Nautilus** was a failure.*

experienced submarine builders, but also the most experienced with diesel engines. They responded with a design powered by a new type of 12-cylinder diesel, which, with an output of 1,850bhp, would be capable of driving the boat at 17kt on a displacement of 1,270 tons.

The Admiralty placed an order with Vickers and the *Nautilus* was launched on 31 December 1914, but development of the very advanced big diesel took much longer, especially under wartime conditions, and the boat was not completed until October 1917, by which time she had been re-named *N-1*.

Nautilus was quickly relegated to other uses, first as an instructional ship and then as a floating generator. Although the exercise was an apparent failure the experience gained in building such an advanced and (for the time) large boat and its diesel engines proved invaluable experience for the future. *N-1* was sold for scrap in 1922.

*Above: **G-10**; note gun and large masts for HF radio antenna.*

outbreak of war the supply of M.A.N. engines from Germany stopped immediately, while the main alternative came from Sulzer in neutral Switzerland; obtaining the latter might have been possible but could not be guaranteed. The outcome was that all these boats were completed with Vickers engines, except for *G-13*, built by Scott's, which had two Fiat diesels (800bhp each), and even those were unsatisfactory and were later replaced by Vickers engines.

It was originally planned to install the single 21in (533mm) tube in the bows but war experience showed that a minimum of two tubes were needed to secure a good probability of a hit, but for weight reasons it was impossible to install a second of the larger tubes, so the 21in tube was moved to the stern and replaced by two 18in tubes. The gun was a 3in (76mm) weapon on a "disappearing " mount.

One boat was cancelled, so only 14 were completed, 13 in 1916 and one in 1917. All operated in the North Sea, where they sank two U-boats for the loss of three of their own.

J-class

Type: overseas, diesel-electric.
Total built: 7.
Completed: 1916.
Displacement: surfaced 1,204 tons; submerged 1,820 tons.
Dimensions: length 275ft 6in (84.0m); beam 23ft 0in (7.0m); draught 14ft 0in (4.3m).
Propulsion: 3 x Vickers 12-cylinder diesels, 3 x 1,200bhp; 2 x electric motors 2 x 675shp; battery 232 cells; three shafts.
Performance: surface – 19.5kt; submerged – 9.5kt; range surfaced 5,000nm at 12.5kt, submerged 55nm at 5kt.
Weapons: 6 x 18in (457mm) TT (bow – 4, beam – 2), 12 x torpedoes; 1 x 12pdr (76mm) gun, 1 x 3in (76mm) AA gun.
Complement: 44.

History: In late 1914 the Admiralty received reports that the German Navy was developing U-boats with a surface speed of 22kt, which coincided with yet another request from Admiral Jellicoe, CinC Grand Fleet, for a submarine capable of operating with the main fleet. As a result, Admiral Fisher, who had recently returned to duty as First Sea Lord and had a fascination with speed, determined that the Royal Navy must produce something even faster. At the time Vickers was still trying to get their new, big 1,850hp diesels to run properly (see Nautilus-class) and steam was briefly considered for this new project and then rejected. The only apparent option remaining was to produce a more powerful engine by adding another four cylinders to the existing eight-cylinder

H-class

Type: coastal, diesel-electric.

History: Shortly after the outbreak of war in 1914 the president of Bethlehem Steel visited the UK and secured a contract to supply the Royal Navy with 20 coastal submarines, identical in all respects to the U.S. Navy's H-class (qv). In view of the United States' neutrality, it was arranged that all the parts for the first 10 boats would be delivered to Canadian-Vickers who would then assemble them. The next 10 of the order, however, would be built entirely in the United States, since it was considered at that time that the war would have ended by the time of delivery, so that the question of U.S. neutrality would no longer be relevant. Despite the complexities of manufacturing components all over the USA, sending them to Canada and then assembling them in a yard with no previous submarine experience, the Canadian-assembled boats (H-1 to H-10) were completed in record time, the first being delivered on 26 May 1915, the last on 29 June 1915, and they were immediately commissioned into the RN. H-1 to H-4 made the first ever crossing of the Atlantic by submarines, proceeding via the Azores and Gibraltar to the eastern Mediterranean, where they took part in the Gallipoli operations. H-5 to H-10 crossed in July but went to the UK where they operated in the North Sea. The U.S.-built boats, numbered H-11 to H-20, were also completed very quickly but the planners prediction of an early end to the war proved to be hopelessly optimistic and the boats were then held in Boston Navy Yard. Six (H-13 and H-16 to H-20) were released in January 1917 and transferred to Chile in partial compensation for the British having requisitioned a Chilean battleship in 1914. The remaining four did not leave the USA until August 1918; two reached the UK and the other two were

Above: J-class, the first to have the raised gun platform.

Vickers diesel and to install three of these in the new J-class. This gave a maximum surface speed of 19.5kt and also resulted in the only three-shaft submarine ever to be built for the RN. For submerged propulsion there was a battery of 232 cells, driving two electric motors, one on each of the outer shafts; there was no motor on the central shaft. All this resulted in a large hull.

There boats had no stern torpedo tubes, but did have four tubes in the bow, one of the first British boats to do so, which resulted in a great increase in the hit probability in a single salvo. There was one reload torpedo for every tube. The main gun was a 3in (76mm) mounted on the foredeck, but when the boats were transferred to Australia in 1919 a raised gun platform immediately before the bridge was fitted to enable the gun to be fought when proceeding into a head sea.

Above: H-class, one of the most popular to serve in the RN.

presented to the RCN.

The H-class boats were popular in the RN. They were excellent sea-boats, very stable and easy to control, and dived quickly. They had four watertight compartments, their machinery was reliable and the bow battery of four tubes gave them impressive firepower. The first 10 worked hard during the war. Four spent the entire war in the Mediterranean where *H-4* sank the German *UB-52* (23 May 1918), while *H-1* sank numerous Turkish vessels, but then accidentally sank the Italian submarine *H-5* (16 April 1918), ironically also an H-class boat and also built by Canadian Vickers. The only one of the four to be lost was *H-3*, mined on 15 July 1916. Of the remaining six, the British *H-5* was lost in a collision (2 March 1918), *H-6* was stran-ded on the coast of the neutral Nether-lands who later ac-quired it and

Class	H-class	H-21 (Improved H)-class
Total built	20*	23
Completed	1912-13	1917-19
Displacement surfaced submerged	364 tons 434 tons	423 tons 510 tons
Dimensions length beam draught	150ft 3in (45.8m) 15ft 4in (4.7m) 12t 6in (3.8m)	171ft 9in (52.4m) 15ft 4in (4.8m) 13ft 3in (4.0m)
Propulsion engines power electric motors power battery shafts	2 x NLSE diesels 2 x 240bhp 2 2 x 310shp 2 x 60 Gould cells two	

com-missioned it into the RNethN as *O-8*, while *H-10* was lost in the North Sea cause un-known (19 January 1918).

Popular as the original H-class was, the Improved H-class was even better. This

R-class

GREAT BRITAIN

Type: hunter-killer, diesel-electric.
Total built: 10.
Completed: 1918-19.
Displacement: surfaced 410 tons; submerged 503 tons.
Dimensions: length 163ft 9in (49.9m); beam 15ft 3in (4.7m); draught 11ft 6in (3.5m).
Propulsion: 1 x 8-cylinder diesel, 240bhp; 2 x electric motors, 2 x 600shp; 1 auxiliary motor, 1x 25bhp; battery 4 x 55 Chloride cells; one shaft.
Performance: surface – 9.5kt; submerged – 15kt; range surfaced 2,000nm at 9kt, submerged 15nm at 14kt; maximum operating diving depth 250ft (76m).
Weapons: 6 x 18in (457mm) TT (bow), 12 x torpedoes.
Complement: 22

History: This was one of the most significant and imaginative submarine designs of World War I, being the first "hunter-killer" in any navy and with an underwater speed not equalled until the mid-1940s. The design resulted from wartime experience which showed the RN that a submarine at periscope depth had a reasonable chance of detecting a German U-boat, but that it was then very difficult to actually catch and sink it, with luck frequently being the decisive factor. So, a requirement was prepared for a submarine purpose-built to find, track and destroy enemy U-boats, for which it would need good detection apparatus, high underwater speed and an effective anti-submarine battery. The result of this extremely perceptive analysis was the R-class, single-hulled boats with a "body-of-revolution" hull – ie, a spindle form symmetrical about the main axis. There was a minimal superstructure, essentially a bow casing, and

Performance		
speed, surface	13kt	11.5kt
submerged	11kt	10.5kt
range, surfaced	2,000nm/130kt	2,000nm/13kt
submerged	30nm/5kt	70nm/3kt
maximum diving depth	150ft (46m)	150ft (46m)
Weapons		
TT	4 x 18in (457m)	4 x 21in (533mm)
location	bow	bow
torpedoes	8	6
Complement	22	22

All built for RN, but 2 given to Canada and 6 to Chile (see text)

was the result of a 1917 Admiralty requirement for more of these coastal boats. These incorporated a number of improvements as the result of operational experience, principally four 21in (533mm) tubes for the new, larger and much more powerful torpedoes, as well as a much more powerful radio. The boats had to be some 21ft (6.4m) longer to accommodate the larger torpedoes, and orders were placed for 34, but 10 were cancelled prior to completion as a result of the Armistice. One of the others (*H-41*) sank while fitting out and, although raised, was never completed; thus the number joining the fleet was actually 23. Many of these were sold in the 1930s, but nine served in World War II, during which two were lost; the remainder were scrapped in 1944-45.

Above: **R-10**, *one of the first hunter-killers in any navy.*

streamlined fairing around the bridge, with a single propeller and two spade rudders to ensure good manoeuverability. Propulsion was provided by a single diesel engine, identical to that used in the H-class (ie, NLSE design, licence-built in the UK), with two electric motors and – another innovation – a 25hp engine, mounted on the main shaft, for slow speed underwater (what would later be termed a "creep motor"). There were six torpedo tubes, a very heavy battery for this size of submarine, but necessary for its mission. It was originally intended to mount a gun, and a gun platform was actually installed in some boats, but no weapon was ever mounted since it would have reduced the underwater speed. In yet another innovation, five sensitive hydrophones were mounted in the bows in order to detect an enemy submarine while both hunter and hunted were submerged.

L-class

Type: attack, diesel-electric.

Class	L-class	L-9-class	L-50-class
Total built	8	13	7
Completed	1917-18	1918-24	1918-25
Displacement surfaced submerged	891 tons 1,074 tons	890 tons 1,080 tons	960 tons 1150 tons
Dimensions length beam draught	231ft 1in (70.4m) 23ft 6in (7.2m) 13ft 3in (4.0m)	238ft 7in (72.7m) 23ft 6in (7.2m) 13ft 3in (4.0m)	235ft 0in (71.6m) 23ft 6in (7.2m) 13ft 2in (4.0m)
Propulsion main engines power electric motors power shafts	2 x diesels 2 x 1,200bhp 2 2 x 800shp two	2 x diesels 2 x 1,200bhp 2 2 x 800shp two	2 x diesels 2 x 1,200bhp 2 2 x 800shp two
Performance speed, surface submerged range, surfaced	17kt 10.5kt 3,800nm at 10kt	17kt 10.5kt 3,800nm at 10kt	17kt 10.5kt 4,500nm at 8t
Weapons TT - bow torpedoes TT - beam torpedoes guns	4 x 18in (457mm) 8 2 x 18in (457mm) 2 1 x 4in (102mm)	4 x 21in (533mm) 8 2 x 18in (457mm) 2 –	6 x 21in (533mm) 12 – – 2 x 4in (102mm)
Complement	35	38	44

History: The L-class originated as a slightly larger development of the E-class but the first pair, originally designated *E-57* and *E-58*, proved to be sufficiently different to be redesignated the L-class and renumbered as *L-1* and *L-2*. These were followed by an order for six more, and the type then underwent several more major developments. The class can be divided into four groups, the first being the basic design, *L-1* to *L-8*, armed with 18in (457mm) bow and beam torpedo tubes. Like the E-class, these were saddle-tank boats, but 50ft (15.3m) longer, the increase being mainly due to the addition of a further two 18in (457mm) torpedo tubes in the bow battery. This resulted in an increase in displacement of 267 tons but considerable improvements in the diesel engines and electric motors resulted in a better performance. Like the E-class, the L-1 class boats had two beam torpedo tubes, but the stern tubes were deleted.

Next came *L-9* to *L-33*, with the omission of *L-13*, which was never ordered (presumably for reasons of superstition), and six minelayers. The major change

bove: L-21, *one of 28 in this very successful class.*

this group were that the forward armament was upgraded to the new 21in 33mm) tubes (but the 18in/457mm beam tubes were retained), an additional atertight bulkhead was fitted, the length of the pressure hull was increased, nd fuel capacity was enlarged. The third group, comprising *L- 14, L-17* and *L- 4* to *L-27*, is described separately in the Minelayer section.

Finally came the L-50-class, which was developed before *L-1* had even een launched. The hull and machinery were virtually the same as in the earlier oats, but the major change was that the number of bow tubes, all 21in 33mm), was increased to six, with one reload for each tube, and the beam bes were deleted. *L-50* to *L-55* were ordered in early 1917 (before *L-1* had

been launched), followed by an order for a further 19 (*L-56* to *L-74*) two month
later. With the end of the war, most were cancelled and only seven wer
actually completed.

All of the L-1-class, six of the L-9-class and none of the L-50-class wer
completed before the end of the war, and work then continued at a muc
slower pace to complete the remainder, the last being *L-23*, which had been lai
down at Vickers on 29 August 1917 and launched by them on 1 July 1919, bu
was later towed to the Naval Dockyard at Chatham, where it was final
completed on 31 October 1924.

The gun armament varied widely. Some of the early boats had no guns
all while others were completed with a single 3in (76mm) deck gun on
disappearing mounting on the deck casing. However, the guns (one in earlie
boats, two in the L-50-class) were then mounted at bridge level, resulting in
long bridge structure, with separate trunks for the gun crews and ammunitio
supply. Although such an arrangement seriously affected the topweight, th
reason was that it enable the gun crew to get their weapon into action ver
much faster – usually before the boat was fully surfaced – than
if it was mounted at deck level, which was of particular
importance in anti-U-boat engagements. This arrangement,
accompanied by a breastwork integrated into the mounting
and revolving with it, also enabled the crew to fight the gun
more effectively in rough weather than was the possible with
a deck gun.

Some of the L-class saw war service in the North Sea and
English Channel, during which *L-10* sank a German destroyer (3
October 1918) and *L-12* sank *UB-90* (16 October). The only war
loss was *L-10* (3 October 1918), although *L-2* was nearly sunk by

Delfino-class

Type: patrol, gasoline-electric.
Total built: 1.
Completed: 1892 (?).
Displacement: surfaced 102 tons; submerged 113 tons.
Dimensions: length 78ft 9in (24.0m); beam 9ft 5in
(2.8m); draught 8ft 4in (2.5m).
Propulsion: 1 x gasoline, 130bhp; 1 x electric motor,
65hp; one shaft.
Performance: surface – 6kt; submerged – 5kt.
Weapons: 2 x 14in (356mm) TT.
Complement: 8.

History: Designed by a naval engineer, Giacinto
Pullino, this was the Italian Navy's first submarine
and the first of very many to be built at La Spezia
Navy Yard. There is some uncertainty about the dates
of her launch and completion, but it seems that she
was at sea by 1892. There was clearly a degree of
experimentation, since as built she was powered by
batteries, which drove three propellers, one for
normal propulsion on the horizontal plane, and two
for vertical movement, either to dive or to surface.
She was completely rebuilt in 1902, during which the
bridge was enlarged, the two 14in (356mm) torpedo
tubes were replaced by a single 17.7in (450mm) tube

.S. warships in February 1918. Three of the class were sent to the Baltic during the "Intervention War" in 1919, during which *L-55* hit a British mine and was lost with all hands (4 June 1919). She was salvaged by the Soviet Navy in 1928, the dead were treated with meticulous correctness, and she was then refitted and returned to service, still bearing the same number. The boats provided the backbone of the submarine service in the 1920s when, since the type had been specifically designed for service in the North Sea, the Admiralty naturally despatched a number to serve on the China Station.

The first of the L-9 group was scrapped in 1927, followed by the majority of the L-1s and L-9s in 1931-32, but with the last of these two early groups holding out until 1937. Four of the L-50s were scrapped in the late 1930s, but three continued to serve throughout World War II when they were employed in either training submarine crews or, in 1944-45, providing targets for ASW frigate crews of the Royal Canadian Navy.

Below: Another view of **L-21**; *note the high gun position.*

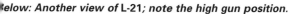

nd a gasoline engine added for surface propulsion. Despite her age, Delfino saw service in World War I, but was stricken immediately afterwards.

elow: **Delfino**, *first of many submarines to be built in Italy.*

Glauco/Foca-classes

Type: patrol, gasoline-electric.
Total built: 5.
Completed: 1905-09.
Displacement: surfaced 157 tons; submerged 240 tons.
Dimensions: length 120ft 9in (38.8m); beam 14ft 1in (4.3m); draught 8ft 8
(2.6m).
Propulsion: 2 x Fiat gasoline engines, 600bhp; 2 x Savigliano electric motor
170shp; two shafts.
Performance: surface – 13kt; submerged – 6kt; range surfaced 900nm at 8
submerged 40nm at 5kt.
Weapons: 3 x 17.7in (450mm) TT (bow).
Complement: 15.
Specifications for Glauco, as built.

History: The Glauco-class was the first design from the drawing board
Cesare Laurenti, an engineering lieutenant who was subsequently to
responsible for many important submarines. This was also the first Itali
design to be produced in quantity and there were some differences betwe
the boats: *Glauco* was built with three torpedo tubes, while the remainder h
only two; and three had Fiat gasoline engines, while the other two h
Thornycroft engines. All served in World War I, providing local defence f
Brindisi and Venice, but *Glauco* was stricken in 1916 followed by the remaind
in 1918.
 Foca, designed and built by Fiat at La Spezia, was a slightly larg

---

Dykkeren-class

Type: patrol, diesel-electric.
Total built: 1.
Completed: 1909.
Displacement: surfaced 105 tons; submerged 132 tons.
Dimensions: length 113ft 10in (34.7m); beam 10ft 10in (3.3m); draught 7ft 3
(2.2m).
Propulsion: 2 x Fiat gasoline engines; 2 x electric motors, 210hp; two shaft
Performance: surface – 12kt; submerged – 7.5kt; range surfaced 100nm at 8
Weapons: 2 x 18in (457mm) TT (bow).
Complement: 9.

History: In the early 1900s the Royal Danish Navy decided to add the fi
submarines to its small fleet and, like a number of other navies, it turned
Italy, whose designers enjoyed a considerable reputation at this time. One
these was Engineer Lieutenant-Commander Cesare Laurenti, whose desig
had certain common characteristics, including a double hull for about thre
quarters of their length and a high reserve of buoyancy, which made the
somewhat skittish in a seaway. They also took a long time to dive, but in tho
pre-radar days that was not too much of a disadvantage. They also had
remarkable number of internal bulkheads; as many as 10 in some.
 The *Dykkeren* design was based on the Italian Glauco- and Foca-class
(qv) and in common with them, the gasoline engines were unreliable and t
fuel positively dangerous. *Dykkeren* was armed with two 18in (4567m
torpedo tubes, but never carried a gun.
 Dykkeren was commissioned into the Royal Danish Navy in June 1909 b

*ght: Glauco
lass, the first
esign of
eutenant
ngineer)
esare
aurenti.*

velopment of the *Glauco,* being 19ft 8in (6m) longer and with a 40-ton crease in submerged displacement. As built, it had three shafts, each wered by a Fiat gasoline engine or a Siemens electric motor. However, the at suffered an internal explosion in April 1909 while in harbour at Naples, hich ignited her fuel and to save the boat she was immediately scuttled. She as later raised and returned to La Spezia, where she was rebuilt, but without e central shaft and gasoline engine/electric motor. This explosion convinced e Italian Navy that gasoline was an inherently dangerous fuel and all later signs were powered by diesel engines. Launched in 1908, *Foca* was stricken 1918.

bove: Danish **Dykkeren** *was built by Fiat-Laurenti, Italy.*

perienced many mechanical problems which led to her spending a great deal time in the Royal Dockyard in Copenhagen. She was sunk on 9 October 1916 a collision with a Norwegian merchant ship. She was raised in 1917 but did t return to service, being scrapped in 1918. The next class of Danish omarine, the Havmanden-class (qv) was ordered from Whitehead in Fiume.

Medusa-class

Type: harbour defence, diesel-electric.
Total built: 8.
Completed: 1911-13.
Displacement: surfaced 248 tons; submerged 252 tons.
Dimensions: length 147ft 8in (45.1m); beam 13ft 9in (4.2m); draught 9ft 6 (3.0m).
Propulsion: 2 x Fiat/M.A.N. diesels, 650bhp; 2 x Savigliano-Siemens elect motors, 300shp; two shafts.
Performance: surface – 12kt; submerged – 8kt.
Weapons: 2 x 17.7in (450mm) TT (bow); 4 x torpedoes.
Complement: 22.

History: These eight boats were the Italian Navy's first class of diesel-power submarines, all being driven by Fiat engines and Savigliano electric motor except for *Velella*, which had M.A.N. engines and Siemens motors. Four we built by Fiat, La Spezia, and two each by Orlando and Riuniti Yard, both Leghorn. They were well thought-of and considered to have particularly go underwater stability and control.

Two were lost to enemy action: *Medusa* by German U-boat, *UB-1* disguised as Austrian *U-11* (10 June 1915), and *Jalea* by an Austrian-la mine (17 August 1915). *Zoea* was driven ashore in a storm in 1917 an although recovered, was not returned to service. At the war's end one bo *Argo*, was undergoing conversion to an assault transport to carry troops a frogmen in an attack on the Austro-Hungarian naval base at Pola, but t

Below: The Medusa-class had fine lines for their time.

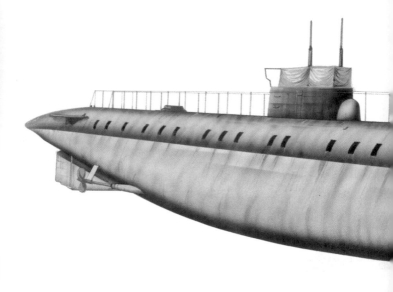

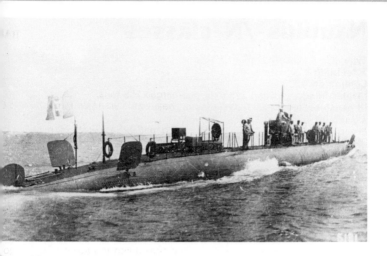

bove: **Medusa** *was Italy's first diesel-powered submarine.*

tack was cancelled. The six surviving boats were stricken in 1918 and rapped.

Three other types of small submarine were designed and built for the lian Navy at this time. One, *Atropo*, was designed and built in Germany and pears to have been an attempt to discover what progress Germany was aking in submarine technology. The other two were the two-boat Nautilus-ss and six-boat N-class; see next entry.

Nautilus-/N-classes

Type: patrol, diesel-electric.
Total built: 2.
Completed: 1913.
Displacement: surfaced 225 tons; submerged 320 tons.
Dimensions: length 134ft 4in (40.9m); beam 14ft 1in (4.3m); draught 9ft 4in (2.8m).
Propulsion: 2 x Sulzer diesels, 600bhp; 2 x Ansaldo electric motors, 320shp; two shafts.
Performance: surface – 13.2kt; submerged – 8kt; maximum operational diving depth 164ft (50m).
Weapons: 2 x 17.7in (450mm) TT (bow); 4 x torpedoes.
Complement: 19.
Specifications for Nautilus, as built.

History: The Nautilus-class, which entered service just before the outbreak of World War I was the first to be designed by Lieutenant-Commander (Engineer) Curio Bernardis, who went on to became a noted naval architect. The two boats were built in the Venice Navy Yard. Both classes displaced 320 tons and were armed with two 17.7in (450mm) torpedo tubes. Both also had high surface speeds, *Atropo* being capable of just under 15 knots, and all three seem to have been used as submersible torpedo-boats. *Neride* was sunk by Austrian submarine *U-5* (Agust 1915); the other two were stricken in 1919.

Svatoy Georgi/S/
F1-classes ITALY (BRAZIL, PORTUGAL, RUSSIA, SPAIN, U

Type: patrol, diesel-electric.

History: The F-1 design was a major success for Italian designer Cesa Laurenti and shipbuilders Fiat-San Giorgio, with a total of 34 built for six navi including a very prestigious order of three for Britain's Royal Navy. The desi originated with the *Svatoy Georgi*, which was ordered by the Imperial Russ Navy in 1912 to a design which was essentially an improved *Medusa* (qv). T improvements included more powerful electric motors, a second perisco retractable hydroplanes and new signalling equipment. The boat w completed shortly after the outbreak of World War I but before it could delivered, it was illegally taken over by an impetuous Italian lieutenant who w so desperate to end his country's neutrality that he tried to sail it to the Adria where he intended to attack Austrian targets, thus creating a *cassus belli*. T boat was intercepted by the French in Corsica and returned to Italy, who boug the boat from Russia and took it into Italian service as the *Argonauta*. It serv until 1928 when it was scrapped, but the Italians also built a replacement the Russians, which was also named *Svatoi Georgi;* it was handed over in 19 and delivered to the Arctic Fleet in a voyage lasting two months, calling Gibraltar, Lisbon and Plymouth en route. It was beached in 1918 and scrapp in 1925.

Meanwhile, the Brazilian Navy decided to buy its first submarine flotilla a placed an order with Fiat-San Giorgio for three boats, together with a speci

elow: N-3 of the six N-class: 277 tons displacement; length 150ft '5.8m); beam 14ft (4.2m); draught 10ft 2in (3.1m); two TT; one gun.

bove: F1-class submarine of the Royal Italian Navy.

*signed submarine depot ship, *Ceara* (6,400 tons). These boats were signated the F1-class, were delivered in 1913-14 and served until 1933.

When Italy joined the Allies the Navy was short of small submarines for use the restricted waters of the Adriatic against the powerful Austro-Hungarian *vy*. An order was placed in 1915 for F-class boats, which were again based the Medusa-class, but incorporating many of the improvements already *ade* in the Russian and Brazilian designs, such as a second periscope, duced diving time and Fessenden signalling equipment, but with the addition, sulting from wartime experience, of a 76mm (3in) gun. The initial Italian order *as* for 24 boats but three were sold to Portugal (F-19 to F-21 as *Foca, Goldino,* *d Hidra*) and a further three were sold to Spain (F-22 to F-24 as *Narciso* *onturiol, Cosme Garcia* and *A-3*). These were taken from the Italian order to *eed* delivery and a further three were then ordered for the Italian Navy, *aving* it with 21 boats, plus the virtually identical *Argonauta*.

The British order resulted from a visit by a group of RN officers a Admiralty officials to La Spezia in 1911, when they were impressed by *Medu* and *Velilla*. Thus, when Fiat's British agent, Scott's Shipyard, offered to buil similar boat for £70,000 the offer was accepted, followed by an order for tw more. *S-1* was completed in August 1914, followed by *S-2* in May and *S-3* September 1915; the designation as "S"-class was out of sequence with t RN's normal system and simply stood for Scott's, the name of the builders few changes made to suit British practices, for example in the number a layout of the battery. These boats were unpopular for a variety of reason including their slowness in diving, but most probably due to prejudice agai foreign ships, and as soon as Italy joined the Allies the RN sold all three to t

Class	Svatoy Georgi	F1	S	F1
Country	Russia	Brazil	UK	Italy, Portugal, Spa
Total built	2	3	3	27 (Italy – 21 Portugal – 3; Spain – 3)
Completed Displacement surfaced submerged	1914 255 tons 306 tons	1913 250 tons 305 tons	1914 265 tons 324 tons	1916-18 262 tons 319 tons
Dimensions length beam draught	148ft 0in (45.1m) 13ft 9in (4.2m) 9ft 10in (3.0m)	150ft 11in (46.0m) 14ft 6in (4.4m) 12ft 2in (3.7m)	148ft 2in (45.1m) 14ft 5in (4.4m) 10ft 4in (3.2m)	149ft 7in (45.6 13ft 8in (4.2m) 10ft 2in (3.1m)

Micca-class

Type: patrol, diesel-electric.
Total built: 6.
Completed: 1917-19.
Displacement: surfaced 842 tons; submerged 1,244 tons.
Dimensions: length 207ft 6in (63.2m); beam 20ft 4in (6.2m); draught 14ft (4.2m).
Propulsion: 2 x Fiat diesels, 2 x 1,300bhp; 2 x Ansaldo electric motors, 2,300shp; two shafts.
Performance: surface – 11kt; submerged – 10kt.
Weapons: 6 x 17.7in (450mm) TT (bow – 4, stern – 2), 8 x torpedoes; 2 x (76mm) guns.
Complement: 40.

History: These were the largest submarines built for the Royal Italian Na during World War I and suffered from the disadvantage of being designed b committee, in this case the Navy's Committee for New Ships, although a na constructor, Lieutenant Virginio Cavalinni, seems to have kept design matt under reasonable control. The order was originally placed with the Venice Na Yard which actually laid down the first three boats and worked on them about four months, but the entire order was then passed to the La Spezia Na Yard. This did not, however, involve the work already done, and the incompl

lian Navy, where they retained their "S" numbers. They did not mount a gun
ile in British service, but appear to have done so when serving with the
lian Navy.

The Japanese F1-class was also a Fiat-Laurenti design, but was
nsiderably larger and the choice of an identical designation appears to have
en sheer coincidence – see F1 (Japan).

opulsion				
esel engines	2 x Fiat	2 x Fiat	2 x Scott-Fiat	2 x Fiat
wer	700bhp	700bhp	2 x 325bhp	670bhp
ectric motors	2 x Savigliano	2 x Savigliano	2 x Scott	2 x Savigliano
wer	450shp	500shp	2 x 200hp	500shp
afts	two	two	two	two
rformance				
eed, surface	13.5kt	13.5kt	13.3kt	12kt
bmerged	8.8kt	8kt	8.5kt	8.2kt
nge, surfaced	950nm/12kt	800nm/13.5kt	1,600nm/8.5kt	1,600nm/8.5kt
bmerged	100nm/4kt	18nm/8kt	75nm/5kt	80/4kt
aximum				
ving depth	130ft (40m)	130ft (40m)	130ft (40m)	130ft (40m)
eapons				
	2x7.7in (450mm)	2 x 18in (457mm)	2 x 18in (457mm)	2 x 17.7in (450mm)
cation	bow	bow	bow	bow
rpedoes	4	4	4	4
n	–	–	–	1 x 3in (76mm)
mplement	24	20	18	26

ove: Angelo Emo, laid down in 1914, launched in 1919.

ls were simply dismantled. Even now, the building process was so drawn
that although the order was placed in 1914, the first-of-class was not
nched until 1917 followed by three in 1918 and two in 1919. As built, these
ats had six torpedo tubes and the original intention was to mount a further
r in a rotating mount on the casing, but this was never done. They proved to
unreliable in service and all underwent a partial rebuild in 1923-25. One was
cken in 1928, three in 1930 and the remainder in 1937-38.

Provana-class

Type: patrol, diesel-electric.
Total built: 4.
Completed: 1918-19.
Displacement: surfaced 762 tons; submerged 924 tons.
Dimensions: length 219ft 10in (67.0m); beam 19ft 4in (5.9m); draught 12ft
(3.8m).
Propulsion: 2 Fiat diesels, 2,600bhp; 2 x Ansaldo electric motors, 1,400sh
two shafts.
Performance: surface – 16kt; submerged – 9.6kt; maximum operating div
depth 164ft (50m).
Weapons: 6 x 17.7in (450mm) TT (bow – 4, stern – 2), 8 x torpedoes; 2 x
(76mm) guns.
Complement: 40.

History: As with the Micca-class, so also with the Provana-class – progre
in construction was very slow and even though they were laid down in la
1915, the first boat was not actually launched until November 19
followed by the other three in January, July and September 1918, and n
one actually entered service before the war's end. The design was prepar
by Cesare Laurenti and Virginio Cavallini and was very sound, as evidenced
the surface speed of 16kt, the highest of any Italian World War I submari
although the submerged speed was no more than 9.8kt, rather less than th
claimed for the Micca-, Balilla- and Pacinotti-classes. They proved good s
boats and handled well, but as with virtually all Italian boats of this period th

F1-/F2-classes

Type: patrol, diesel-electric.
Total built: 2.
Completed: 1920.
Displacement: surfaced 689 tons; submerged 1,047 tons.
Dimensions: length 215ft 1in (65.6m); beam 19ft 11in (6.1m); draught 13ft
(4.2m).
Propulsion: 2 x Fiat diesels, 2,800bhp; 2 x Savigliano electric moto
1,200shp; two shafts.
Performance: surface – 13kt; submerged – 8kt; range surfaced 3,500nm
10kt, submerged 75nm at 4kt; maximum operating diving depth 130ft (40m
Weapons: 5 x 18in (457mm) TT (bow – 3, stern – 2), 8 x torpedoes; 1 x 7.7mm M
Complement: 43.
Specifications are for F1-class, as built.

History: The F1-class were the first Italian-designed submarines to be orde
by the Imperial Japanese Navy (IJN), being designed by Fiat-Laurenti and b
in Japan by Kawasaki at Kobe. Confusingly, the Japanese designated them
F1-class, but the boats had little, if any, relationship with the Italian F1-cla
(see page 74), being considerably larger and much more heavily armed.
first two, *No 18* and *No 19* were ordered in 1915 and completed in 1920, wh
they became the first Japanese submarines with an ocean-going capability.
designed, the cross-section of their pressure hulls was not cylindrical, wh
was intended to give extra volume, but this was, quite correctly, considered
the IJN to compromise the integrity of the structure, so they added scantlin
during construction to provide added strength. The three reload torped

ove: **Andrea Provana,** *nameship of a class of four.*

re very slow to dive and their maximum depth was only 164ft (50m),
newhat less than their overall length.

One boat, *Sebastiano Veniero*, was sunk in a collision with an Italian
rchant ship (August 1925) an all too frequent occurrence in the early days
submarines. Two were stricken in 1928, but the fourth, *Giacomo Nani*,
vived until 1935.

ove: **Italian F1-class submarine.**

re all forward; the stern tubes were "one-shot" devices. A 3in (76mm) gun
s added in the early 1920s.

The three boats of the F2-class (*Nos 31, 32, 33*) were virtual repeats of the
class, except that a different model of Fiat diesel was installed, which
ually produced less power and thus reduced the maximum speed to 14kt.
e diesels were also notoriously unreliable. This group was especially
opular in the IJN and had a very short service life. All five boats were
ected by the IJN's renumbering exercise in the early 1920s, being
egorised as medium (Ro) submarines and numbered *Ro-1* (ex-*No 18*) to *Ro-*
x-*No 33*). All were stricken in 1930.

Espadarte/Foca-classes ITALY (PORTUGA

Type: patrol, diesel-electric.
Total built: 3.
Completed: 1920.
Displacement: surfaced 260 tons; submerged 389 tons.
Dimensions: length 147ft 9in (45.0m); beam 13ft 10in (4.2m); draught 10ft 6in (3.2
Propulsion: 2 x Fiat diesels, 2 x 275shp; 2 x Savigliano electric motors, :
200shp; two shafts.
Performance: surface – 14.2kt; submerged – 8.2kt; range surfaced 3,500nm
8.5kt, submerged 100nm at 4kt.
Weapons: 2 x 18in (457mm) TT (bow), 4 x torpedoes.
Complement: 21.
Specifications are for Foca-class, as built.

History: Portugal's first submarine was the *Plongeur*, which was built in
early 1890s and scrapped in 1910. The second submarine was *Espadarte*
Laurenti-Fiat boat, built at La Spezia, launched in December 1912 and hand
over in 1913. This boat displaced 300 tons submerged and was 148ft (45.1
long, powered by two Fiat diesels and armed with two 18in (475mm) torpe
tubes, both in the bows. It was identical, in virtually all respects, to
submarine then building for Russia (see *Svatoy Georgi*). Next came the Fc
class, again designed and built by Fiat-San Giorgio at La Spezia, with three bo
delivered in 1917. They were *Foca*, *Golfinho* and *Hidra*, which were essenti
repeats of the earlier *Espadarte*, with the same measurements and propuls
system, but with somewhat greater endurance.

K1/-2/-3/-4/KT-classes JAP,

Type: patrol, diesel-electric.

Class	K-1	K-2/K-3	K-4	KT
Total built	2	9	3	4
Completed	1919	1920-23	1923-24	1923-24
Displacement surfaced submerged	735 tons 1,030 tons	755 tons 1,050 tons	770 tons 1,080 tons	665 tons 1,000 tons
Dimensions length beam draught	227ft 0in (69.2m) 20ft 10in (6.4m) 11ft 3in (3.4m)	230ft 0in (70.1m) 20ft 0in (6.1m) 12ft 1in (3.7m)	243ft 6in (74.2m) 20ft 0in (6.1m) 12ft 1in (3.7m)	243ft 6in (74.2 20ft 0in (6.1m) 12ft 1in (3.7m)
Propulsion diesel engines power electric motors power shafts	2 x Sulzer 2,600bhp 2 x Savigliano 1,200shp two	2 x Sulzer 2,600bhp 2 x Savigliano 1,200shp two	2 x Sulzer 2,600bhp 2 x Savigliano 1,200shp two	2 x Sulzer 1,200bhp 2 x Savigliar 1,200shp two

*ove: **Espadarte**, Italian Laurenti-Fiat design built for Portugal.*

rformance				
eed, surface	18kt	17kt	17kt	13kt
bmerged	9kt	9kt	9kt	8kt
nge, surfaced	4,000nm/10kt	6,000nm/10kt	6,000nm/10kt	8,000nm/10kt
bmerged	85nm/4kt	85nm/4kt	85nm/4kt	85nm/4kt
eapons				
cation	6 x 18in (457mm)	6 x 18in (457mm)	4 x 21in (533mm)	4 x 21in (533mm)
rpedoes	bow – 4; deck – 2	bow – 4; deck – 2	bow	bow
n	10	10	8	8
	1 x 3in (76mm)	1 x 3in (76mm)	1 x 3in (76mm)	1 x 4.7in (120mm)
			1 x 7.7mm MG	1 x 7.7mm MG
mplement	44	45	45	43

tory: For the first decade of its existence the IJN's submarine arm
pended upon foreign designs, which were originally built overseas, but then
lt in increasing numbers in Japanese yards. The IJN became increasingly
satisfied with these foreign designs, which they considered, with good
son, to be designed to meet very different conditions from those facing the
anese. In particular, the Japanese found them to have insufficient range for
vast distances of the Pacific, to have hulls lacking the strength to take
antage of the much greater depths of Asian seas, and to have insufficiently
cise depth control. This gave rise to a series of K-class (K = *kaigun-chu* =
dium, Navy type) designs, which were progressively improved. First in the
es, the K1 design was based on the Schneider-Laubeuf S-class, but with a

much wider beam (20ft 10in/6.4m compared to 17ft 1in/5.2m) and a stron⟨g⟩
hull, consisting of heavy plates and frames reinforced by an exceptional degr⟨ee⟩
(by Western standards) of internal sub-division. The outcome was a hull wh⟨ich⟩
could withstand heavy punishment, either from depthcharges or collisions.

The K2 design was essentially a progressive development of the K1 wit⟨h a⟩
slightly longer hull and 10in (0.25m) less beam. Most importantly, fuel
bunkerage was increased from 60 tons to 75 tons, giving a 2,000nm incre⟨ase⟩
in range. The K3 had the same hull and characteristics as the K2, but wit⟨h⟩

Below: K1-class, No 19, was
armed with four bow 18in
(457mm) torpedo tubes and
two drop-collars.

O-classes

NETHERLAN⟨DS⟩

Type: patrol, diesel-electric.

Class	O-1	O-2	O-6	O-7
Total built	1	4	1	1
Completed	1906	1911-14	1916	1916
Displacement surfaced submerged	105 tons 124 tons	134 tons 149 tons	192 tons 233 tons	176 tons 206 tons
Dimensions length beam draught	677ft 0in (20.4m) 16ft 0in (4.96.4m) 9ft 23in (2.8m)	105ft 3in (32.1m) 10ft 9in (3.3m) 9ft 10in (2.7m)	117ft 0in (35.7m) 13ft 6in (4.1m) 10ft 2in (3.1m)	112ft 2in (34.2⟨m⟩ 12ft 9in (3.9m) 9ft 6in (2.9m)
Propulsion engines power electric motors power shafts battery	1 x Otto gasoline 160bhp 1 65shp one 60 cells	1 x M.A.N. diesel 280bhp 1 145shp one 60 cells	1 x M.A.N. 375bhp 1 210shp one 60 cells	1 x M.A.N. 350bhp 1 210shp one 60 cells

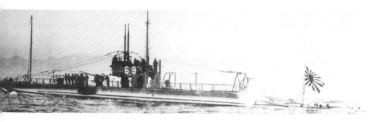

ove: KT-class, **No 69;** *similar to K4-class but better range.*

...mber of internal improvements; nine were built, making it the most ...merous class of IJN submarine up to that time. The K4 had a yet longer hull, ...3ft 6in (74.2m) compared to 230ft 0in (70.1m), which was mainly attributable ...the introduction of the internationally standard 21in (533mm) torpedo tubes. The 3in (76mm) gun was also moved forward of the bridge.

The KT (*kai-toku-chu* = medium special, Navy type) was dimensionally identical to the K4-class, but had less powerful Sulzer diesels, which reduced maximum surfaced speed to 13kt; however, bunkerage increased to 116 tons, resulting in an increase in range to 8,000nm at 10kt.

All these boats were renumbered in the "Ro" series in 1923. Most of the K1-, K2- and K3-classes were stricken in 1931-32; a few were retained until 1936. Two of the K4-class were stricken in 1940 but one survived World War II. Only one KT-class survived the war.

...rformance				
...eed, surface	8.5kt	11kt	12kt	11.5kt
...bmerged	8kt	8kt	8.5kt	8.5kt
...nge, surfaced	200nm/8kt	500nm/10kt	750nm/10kt	750nm/10kt
...bmerged	24nm/6kt	35nm/7kt	42nm/7kt	42nm/7kt
...ing depth	82ft (25m)	82ft (25m)	131ft (40m)	131ft (40m)
...eapons				
	1 x 9in (250mm)	2 x 17.7in (450mm)	3 x 17.7in (450mm)	3 x 17.7in (450mm)
...cation	bow	bow	bow – 2; stern – 1	bow – 2; stern – 1
...rpedoes	3	4	5	5
...mplement	10	10	15	15

...story: For many years the Dutch had a unique arrangement. Under this ...stem the Ministry of Defence paid for submarines for use in European waters ...d these classes were designated "*Onderzeeboot*" (undersea boat = ...bmarine) followed by an Arabic numeral – eg, O-2. But submarines intended ...r deployment in the Dutch East Indies were paid for by the Colonial Ministry ...d were designated "*Koloniën*" (colonial), followed by a Roman numeral – eg, ...l. In both cases, however, the procurement policy was the same, with ...duction licences for foreign designs being purchased and all construction ...ing place in Dutch yards, either De Schelde at Vlissingen or Fijenoord in ...tterdam. There were two sources for the designs in both the "O-" and "K-" ...ies: Hay-Whitehead in Austria (transferred to Hay-Denny, Scotland, after the ...break of World War I) and the Electric Boat Co., in Groton, Connecticut,

whose designs were known as "Holland-type" after the inventor, J. P. Hollar
In addition, the preferred source of diesel engines was the German compar
M.A.N., but, due to its commitments to the German U-boat programme, th
company was unable to supply any more after 1917, after which the Dut
sourced their diesels from the Austrian company, Sulzer.

The first of the O-boats was foisted on a reluctant Navy by the I
Schelde yard, which purchased a licence to produce a Holland design frc
the Electric Boat Co. This private venture, named *Luctor et Energo*, w
launched in July 1905 and failed the first round of naval trials, but, d
mainly to the persistence of a naval officer, Lt. Koster, and the
builder, De Schelde, the boat underwent a second round of
trials, which proved successful and she was bought by the
Navy in December 1907. Originally powered by a gasoline
engine, she was given a 200hp M.A.N. diesel in 1914, and was
scrapped in 1920.

This was followed by four boats of the O-2-class built by De
Schelde, but to a design by Hay-Whitehead of Fiume in Austria,
the only non-Electric Boat design this yard was to build. These
were somewhat larger and armed with two 17.7in (450mm)
torpedo tubes mounted one above the other in the bows. They
also featured the first ever rudimentary air-supply tube that
enabled the diesels to be run while the boat was partially
submerged – a device which eventually led to the schnorkel
("snort"). They entered service in 1911-13 and were stricken in
1931-35.

The next two boats, *O-6* and *O-7*, are usually described as a
two-boat class but, although their armament and machinery were

K-classes (Dutch overseas) NETHERLAN

Type: patrol, diesel-electric.

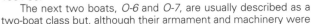

Class	K-I	K-II/K-V	K-III/K-VIII
Total built	1	4	4
Completed	1914	1919-21	1919-23
Displacement surfaced submerged	333 tons 358 tons	569 tons 649 tons	649 tons 721 tons
Dimensions length beam draught	159ft 5in (48.6m) 15ft 5in (4.7m) 10ft 2in (3.1m)	188ft 0in (57.3m) 17ft 5in (5.3m) 12ft 6in (3.8m)	211ft 3in (64.4r 18ft 4in (5.6m) 11ft 10in (3.6m
Propulsion diesel engines power electric motors power shafts battery	2 x M.A.N. 2 x 850bhp 2 2 x 157shp two 130 cells	2 x Sulzer* 2 x 600bhp 2 2 x 250shp two 120 cells	2 x M.A.N.** 2 x 900bhp 2 2 x 210shp two 132 cells

he same, there were many differences between them. In fact, *0-6,* the larger of the two, was a Holland design built by De Schelde, armed with three torpedo ubes, two in the bows and one mounted externally on the after casing. *O-7,* designed by William Denny & Bros of Dumbarton Scotland, and built by ijenoord, was slightly smaller, had a quite different hull form and included one very unusual feature, a steering propeller which operated in a transverse duct ocated just forward of the main propeller. It was stricken in 1939.

Below: Dutch submarine O-5 *during World War I.*

Performance			
speed, surface	17kt	13.5kt	16.5kt
submerged	10.5kt	8kt	8.5kt
range, surfaced	3,500nm/11kt	3,500nm/11kt	3,500nm/11kt
submerged	30nm/8kt	25.5nm/8.5kt	25nm/8.5kt
diving depth	131ft (40m)	131ft (40m)	131ft (40m)
Weapons			
TT	3 x 17.7in (450mm)	4 x 17.7in (450mm)	6 x 17.7in (450mm)
location	bow – 2; stern – 1	bow – 2; deck – 2	bow – 2; stern – 2; deck – 2
torpedoes	6	12	12
gun	–	1 x 75mm; 1 x MG	1 x 75mm
Complement	17	29	31

K-II was powered by two 900hp M.A.N. diesels and was 2kt faster – see notes.
* *K-VII* was powered by two 900hp M.A.N. diesels, *K-IX* and *K-X* by 600hp Sulzers, making them 1kt slower.

History: For several centuries the Netherlands ruled a large colonial empire in the Far East: the Dutch East Indies, modern Indonesia. This huge, sprawling erritory required a large naval force, which in turn needed ships and, later, submarines with great range and the ability to operate in conditions of tropical heat. Submarines for the Dutch East Indies were paid for by the Colonial Ministry, and were given "K" (*Koloniën* = colonial) designation, followed by the ull number using Roman numerals.

The first of the overseas boats, *K-I,* was built by De Schelde, Vlissingen to a Hay-Whitehead design, being laid down in September 1911, launched in May 1913 and commissioned in July 1914. She was powered by two M.A.N. diesels and armed with three torpedo tubes, two in the bows and one in the stern. This boat had little reserve buoyancy and tended to be very uncomfortable when on the surface. It was stricken in 1928.

After this first "colonial" design there were two more classes built by De Schelde to Electric Boat Co. designs. The KIII-class *(K-III, K-IV)* were much larger boats, but there were delays caused by World War I, particularly with the diesels, since M.A.N. could supply only two of the required four 900hp diesels which were installed in *K-III.* As a result, *K-IV* was powered by two 600hp Sulzers, the loss of power resulting in a 1.5kt reduction in speed. Armament was four torpedo tubes, two in the bows, and two mounted externally on the after casing.

Next from De Schelde/Electric Boat Co. came the K-VIII-class *(K-VIII, K IX, K-X)* which were to have been armed with six torpedo tubes; two in the bows and two externally on the upper casing abaft the sail, as in the K-III class, but with two more reloadable tubes aft. However, war experience by other navies had shown that externally mounted tubes were vulnerable in depth-charge attacks, and these were deleted. It had also been planned to mount a 75mm gun but, again, war experience showed a more powerful gun was required and an 88mm was mounted instead. Only *K-VIII* was powered by the planned M.A.N diesels, the other two having 600hp Sulzers. These were also the first Dutch colonial boats to be of double-hull construction and had a much larger sail than earlier boats.

The two other classes of "colonial" boats were built by Fijenoord to a Hay-Denny design. The first, the single-boat K-II-class was laid down in

---

Toro-/Ferre-classes

Type: patrol, diesel-electric.
Total built: 2.
Completed: 1912-13.
Displacement: surfaced ca300 tons; submerged ca400 tons.
Dimensions: length 170ft 11in (52.1m); beam 17ft 9in (5.1m); draught 10ft 2in (3.1m).
Propulsion: 2 x Schneider-Carels 6-cylinder diesel engines; 2 x electric motors two shafts.
Performance: surface – 13kt; submerged – 8kt; range surfaced 2,000nm at 10kt, submerged ca 80nm at 4kt.
Weapons: 4 x 17.7in (450mm) TT (bow), 6 x torpedoes.
Complement: 21.
Specification for Ferre-class, as built.

History: A submarine pioneer who has received less recognition than his due is the Peruvian Federico Blume (1831-1901), a railroad engineer who prepared his first submarine design in 1864 during the war against Spain. The conflict ended before Blume could complete his boat and nothing more was done until the outbreak of the War of the Pacific (1879-1883), this time against Chile, when Blume, at his own expense, completed a submersible, which he named *Toro* (bull). This vessel was cylindrical in shape with pointed ends and was based on a boiler some 48ft (14.6m) long and constructed from 0.3in (6mm) iron plate, which was then reinforced by appliqué sheets of iron, the whole device being jointed by rivets. Propulsion was by means of a single propeller operated by a long hand crank, which was turned by eight of the 11-man crew

1915 and launched in 1919, but was not completed until 1922, after the supposedly later K-III-class. This was because M.A.N. was unable to complete the engines, which therefore had to be transported to Vlissingen to be finished by Fijenoord; not surprisingly, this took much more time than had been planned. The very similar K-V-class (*K-V, K-VI, K-VII*) were all powered by Sulzer diesels.

Most of these boats were stricken in the 1930s but the K-VIII-class served on into World War II. *K-X* was scuttled off Soerabaya, but the other two reached Australia, where *K-VIII* was stricken. *K-IX* served for a time as a unit of the Royal Australian Navy (RAN) and then reverted to Dutch control as an oiler. She was stricken in 1946.

Below: **K-III, designed for operations in the Dutch East Indies.**

Right: Model of the Peruvian Toro *of 1864, an ingenious design.*

The vessel submerged by flooding the ballast tanks and surfaced by expelling the water using a manual pump. There was a watertight entrance hatch and there were two hollow retractable masts made of brass to admit air and expel the fumes. Trials started in October 1879 with Blume conducting three weeks of tests and demonstrations; he successfully reached a depth of 72ft (22m) and a submerged speed of 4kt and remained submerged for up to 30 minutes at a time. *Toro* was taken to Callao to attack the Chilean fleet but, warned of this impending attack, the enemy fleet withdrew out of range and *Toro* was later sunk to avoid capture.

There was then a gap of some years. Then, in the early 1900s there was a particularly active French naval mission, which managed to persuade the Peruvian Navy to buy a destroyer and two submarines. The latter were Laubeuf designs and were delivered in 1913, the first modern submarines in any South American navy. These had a rather short operational life, being stricken in 1919, which was primarily due to the difficulty of obtaining spare parts and new cells.

Delfin/Kasatka-classes

Type: harbour defence, gasoline/kerosene.
Total built: 6.
Completed: 1904.
Displacement: surfaced 140 tons; submerged 170 tons.
Dimensions: length 110ft 0in (33.5m); beam 11ft 6in (3.5m); draught 11ft 3i
(3.4m).
Propulsion: 1 x kerosene engine, 200bhp; 1 x electric motor, 100shp; on
shaft.
Performance: surface – 8.5kt; submerged – 5.5kt; range surfaced 700nm a
8kt, submerged 50nm at 3kt; maximum operational diving depth 150ft (46m)
Weapons: 4 x Drzwiecki drop collars, 4 x torpedoes.
Complement: 24.
Specifications for Kasatka-class, as built.

History: *Delfin*, designed by I. G. Bubnov, ordered in 1901 and completed i
1903, was the Imperial Russian Navy's first operational submarine. It displace
124 tons, was 64ft (19.6m) long and was armed with two torpedoes i
Drzwiecki drop-collars. It was a saddle-tank design. It sank in harbour in Jun
1904 when grossly overloaded with no fewer than 33 people aboard,
combination of indiscipline and a failure to understand the significance o
excess weight in a submarine; no fewer than 21 died and those who survive
did so through sheer luck rather than skilled rescue. The boat was raised
refitted and sent to Vladivostock.

Delfin's designer, Bubnov, next produced the Kasatka-class. There wer

Osetr (Lake)/Kaiman-classes

Type: patrol, gasoline-electric.

Class	Osetr (Lake)	Kaiman
Total built	6	4
Completed	1905	1907-08
Displacement surfaced submerged	153 tons 187 tons	409 tons 482 tons
Dimensions length beam draught	72ft 0in (22.0m) 12ft 0in (3.6m) 12ft 3in (3.7m)	132ft 0in (40.2m) 14ft 0in (4.3m) 16ft 0in (4.9m)
Propulsion engines power electric motor power shafts	2 x gasoline 2 x 120bhp 2 2 x 60shp two	2 x gasoline 2 x 600bhp 2 2 x 200shp two

Above: **Kasatka** *saw service in the Russo-Japanese War.*

delays in the supply of the engines so the design was recast for a single propeller and engine; this used kerosene which was very smelly and emitted dense white fumes, but was safer than the gasoline used in *Delfin*. Initially, the type showed some unsatisfactory characteristics, in particular trimming stern-down when submerged, but these were solved by installing floats in the after casing. Four were sent to the Far East for the Russo-Japanese War.

Performance		
speed, surface	8.5kt	10.5kt
submerged	4.5kt	7.0kt
range, surfaced	385nm	1,050nm/8kt
submerged	35nm	40nm/5kt
maximum		
diving depth	96ft (30m)	–
Weapons		
TT	3 x 15in (381mm)	4 x 18in(457mm)
location	bow – 2; stern – 1	bow – 2; stern – 2
Complement	24	34

Specifications apply to first-of-class, as built

History: In its rush to purchase new equipment for the war against Japan, the Imperial Russian Navy bought as many submarines as possible, the basic criterion being that they should reach the theatre of war as rapidly as possible. One element of these orders was the building of six boats designed by the American, Simon Lake, whose company contracted to provide one complete example as a pattern for the construction of a further five in Russia. Several countries showed interest in Lake's *Protector*, which had been built in the United States and was unusual for two reasons: it was the first submarine designed to operate on an even keel when both surfacing and submerging, and it had hydraulically extended wheels for running on the seabed. It arrived in Russia in June 1904 and the other five

boats were completed in 1905. *Protector* was renamed *Osetr* and all si
were then sent to the Far East as quickly as possible. All were scrapped i
1913-15.

For the Russians the main drawback of the *Osetr* (Lake) boats was that the
lacked the range to enable them to operate off the coast of Japan, so a
improved-Protector design was prepared and four were built in St. Petersbur
as the Kaiman-class. They were completed in 1910, but immediately becam
the subject of controversy, their shortcomings including failure to meet th
performance criteria in various respects (diving time was 10 minutes) an
excess weight, and the Russian Navy refused to pay the full contract price

Below: **Paltus***, an Osetr/Lake-class boat, in about 1907.*

Minoga/Akula/Morzh-class

RUSSIA

Type: patrol, diesel-electric.

Class	Minoga	Akula	Morzh
Total built	1	1	3
Completed	1908	1907	1914-15
Displacement surfaced submerged	117 tons 142 tons	370 tons 475 tons	630 tons 760 tons
Dimensions length beam draught	105ft 9in (32,2m) 9ft 2in (2.8m) 8ft 2in (2.5m)	184ft 0in (56.0m) 12ft 0in (3.7m) 11ft 0in (3.4m)	219ft 8in (67.0m) 14ft 7in (4.5m) 12ft 8in (3.9m)
Propulsion engines power electric motor power shafts	2 x diesel 2 x 120bhp 1 70shp two	3 x diesel 3 x 300bhp 1 225shp three	2 x diesel 2 x 250bhp 2 2 x 400shp two

though they did insist on taking delivery in order to prevent the boats being
sold to a third party. The boats were then modified to improve their
performance and eventually entered service in the Baltic in late 1911; they
carried out some operations in the early part of World War I, but were stricken
1916 and scuttled in 1918.

Below: Kaiman-class Krokodil; note gap for torpedo drop-collar.

Performance			
Speed, surface	11kt	10.6kt	10.8kt
Submerged	5kt	6.6kt	8kt
Range, surfaced	600nm/10kt	1,900nm	2,500nm
Submerged	50nm/3.5kt	38nm/4.8kt	120nm
Maximum diving depth	96ft (30m)	150ft (46m)	150ft (46m)
Weapons			
TT	2 x 17.7in (450mm)	4 x 18in (457mm)	4 x 18in (457mm)
Location	bow	bow – 2; stern – 2	bow – 2; stern – 2
Drop collars	–	4	8
Torpedoes	2	1 x 47mm	1 x 57mm; 1 x 47mm
Complement	22	34	47

Specifications apply to first-of-class, as built

History: The submarine designer I. G. Bubnov was one of the first to
produce a submarine based on the lessons of the Russo-Japanese War
(1904-5) and his *Minoga,* launched in October 1908, was a small (155 ton
displacement), single-hulled boat. Its significance, however, was that it was
the first Russian submarine powered by diesel engines, with two 120hp
units driving a single propeller. Unfortunately, this required complicated
mechanical control linkages and the boat was not a success, although it did
see several years' service.

   Bubnov's next design, *Akula*, was essentially an enlarged and improved

Minoga, but with three shafts; indeed, Bubnov seems to have been fascinated by complicated power systems. This system was as fault-prone as the others and all three propellers had to be changed three times and the electric motor once before a satisfactory solution was found. Despite these problems she was considered the most successful of the pre-World War I Russian designs. She was sunk by a mine on 28 November 1915.

Bubnov's next design was the Morzh-class, with three being completed in 1914-15. The design was based on that of the *Akula,* but was not a great success and included a number of inherent faults. The hull design was more like that of a surface ship than that of a submarine, creating even more hydrodynamic drag than usual with submarines of the period and thus reducing submerged speed well below the intended 12 knots. The problems were exacerbated when the outbreak of World War I prevented the German firm of Krupps from delivering the promised diesel engines and the only suitable substitutes which could be found had to be removed from gunboats of the Russian Navy's Amur River flotilla. Despite all these problems the boats were quite successful in service with the Black Sea Fleet, claiming 16 merchantmen sunk and a near miss against *Goeben,* the German/Turkish battlecruiser. *Morzh* failed to return from patrol in May 1917, while *Tyulam* was captured in harbour by the Germans, then handed over to the British and finally taken by the White Russians to Bizerta where she was sold in 1924. *Nerpa* was taken over by the Soviet Navy and was operational from 1922 to 1931, when she was scrapped.

Holland/Narval/AG-classes   RUSSIA

Type: patrol, diesel-electric.

History: In its rush to make good the deficiencies shown up by the Russo-Japanese War, the Imperial Russian Navy ordered submarines from Germany and from both the Electric Boat Co. (Holland) and Simon Lake in the USA. J.

Class	Beluga (Holland)	Narval	AG
Total built	7	3	11
Completed	1904-07	1915	1916-21
Displacement surfaced submerged	105 tons 122 tons	673 tons 1,045 tons	355 tons 433 tons
Dimensions length beam draught	65ft 6in (20.0m) 11ft 6in (3.5m) 9ft 6in (2.9m)	230ft 3in (70.2m) 21ft 3in (6.5m) 11ft 8 in (3.6m)	151ft 0in (46.0m) 16ft 0in (4.9m) 12ft 6in (3.8m)
Propulsion engines power electric motor power shafts battery	1 x gasoline 1 x 160bhp 1 70shp one n.k	4 x diesel 4 x 160bhp 2 2 x 225shp two n.k	2 x NLSE diesels 2 x 480bhp 2 2 x 320shp two 2 x 60 cells

bove: Akula *looked more like a ship design than a submarine.*

erformance			
peed, surface	8.5kt	10.5kt	12kt
ubmerged	6kt	11.5kt	10kt
ange, surfaced	585nm	1250nm/8.5kt	1,600nm/10kt
ubmerged	42nm	120nm/7kt	100nm/2kt
aximum			
ving depth	96ft (30m)	150ft (46m)	180ft (55m)
Veapons			
T	1 x 15.0in (381mm)	4 x 18in (457mm)	4 x 18in (457mm)
cation	bow	bow – 2; stern – 2	bow
rop collars	–	4	–
orpedoes	–	–	8
un	–	1 x 75mm;1 x 63mm	1 x 47mm
omplement	22	47	30

ecifications apply to first-of-class, as built

olland had a design ready for export with the demonstrator, the *Fulton*, mediately available. A contract was quickly signed and *Fulton* was broken wn into sections and despatched to Russia under the guise of a "steam iler". On arrival it was reassembled, renamed *Som* (catfish) and then used as e pattern for another six which were built at the Nevski Yard in St. Petersburg. ly *Som* and one of the Russian-built boats reached Vladivostok in time to ke part in the war against the Japanese; two were sent to the Black Sea and e others served in the Baltic. *Som* was sunk in a collision with a merchant ip in the Baltic, the remainder were stricken in 1916 and scuttled in 1918-19.

The next Holland design to be built for Russia was the three-strong Narval- ass, which were built at the Nevski Yard in Nikolayev and launched in 1914, d were by far the largest submarines built for the Tsarist Navy. The specifications for *Narwal* are given in the table but the other two boats had slightly lower displacement (994 tons) and were more heavily armed, with fo additional Drzwiecki drop-collars making a total of eight. It was origina intended that they should be powered by two 850bhp diesels, but these we not available (there was an international shortage of these engines in th period) and four much less powerful units had to be installed instead. All thr served in the Black Sea throughout World War I, sinking some 80 enemy ship and all were scuttled in April 1919.

The last of these three classes was known in the Tsarist Navy Amerikanskji Golland (AG) (American Holland). They were ordered in 1915 fro the Electric Boat Co. at a time when the USA was neutral, and to circumve this political predicament all parts of the submarines were manufactured in th USA in 1915-16 and then sent by railroad to the Vickers Yard at Montreal Canada, where an American work-force assembled the boats. The boats we then broken down again into major assemblies and sent by rail to the Canad West Coast where they were transferred to ships for the voyage to Vladivost There they were transferred to rail yet again and sent via the Trans-Siber railroad to the West for final assembly; five boats were assembled at the Ba yard, St. Petersburg, and six boats at the Nikolayev Navy Yard. These Russ boats were identical in every respect to those delivered to the U.S. Navy (S 28 to *SS-30*), the British Royal Navy (*H-1* to *H-10*) and the navies of Chile a

Below: This Holland design from the Electric Boat Company served in five navies and was one of the most successful types of World War I.

*ove: **AG-14**, one of the successful boats designed in the USA.*

dia. The original Russian order was for 18 boats, but only 11 were delivered
fore the Revolution and the U.S. Navy requisitioned the remaining six, but
nat happened to the last of the boats, *AG-17*, has never been established.
Main armament comprised four 18in (457mm) torpedo tubes, all in the bow; there were no stern tubes or drop-collars. The Baltic boats took part in operations in World War I: one was sunk and the remainder scuttled in April 1918. The AG-class was the last to enter service with the Imperial Russian Navy and although other types were under construction the Revolution overtook them and they were cancelled.

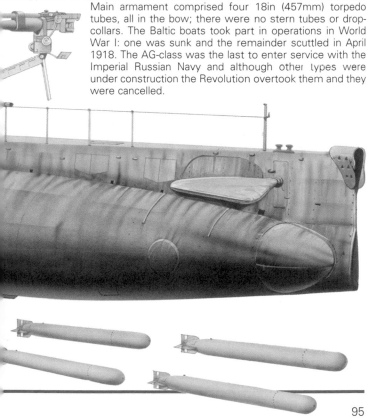

Bars-class

Type: patrol diesel-electric.
Total built: 18.
Completed: 1915-17.
Displacement: surfaced 650 tons; submerged 782 tons.
Dimensions: length 223ft 0in (68.0m); beam 15ft 0in (4.5m); draught 13ft 0in (3.9r
Propulsion: 2 x diesel engines, 2 x 1,320bhp; 2 x electric motors, 2 x 450sł
two shafts.
Performance: surface – 18kt; submerged – 10kt; range surfaced 400nm
17kt, submerged 25nm at 9kt; maximum operating diving depth 150ft (46m)
Weapons: 4 x 18in (457mm) TT (bow – 2, stern – 2); 8 x Drzwiecki drop-colla
1 x 63mm gun, 1 x 37mm AA gun.
Complement: 33.

History: This was the last and most numerous of I. G. Bubnov's designs
enter service in World War I, with orders for 24 being placed in 1912-13. In t
event, only 18 were completed as patrol submarines, two were converted
minelayers during construction, and four were never completed due to t
Revolution. The design, which was essentially that of the Morzh-class (qv) w
an added centre section, promised a powerful armament, high speed both
the surface and submerged, and a long range, but, for a variety of reasor
failed to deliver in all three areas and repeated many of the failings of previc
Bubnov designs. A matter outside Bubnov's control was the non-availability
the 1,320hp diesels ordered from Germany, which were replaced from a varie
of sources, including new engines from the USA. Some boats us
powerplants from Russian patrol boats on the Amur River, but all we
considerably less powerful than the German diesels, with the result that t
planned surface speed of 18kt was never achieved, few ever exceeding 8
and range was also considerably less. There were also problems with t
Russian-made (Jevetsky) torpedo tubes, while the Drzwiecki drop-collars we
mounted too close to the waterline in the original boats, resulting in an increa

Isaac Peral-/A-/B-classes

Type: patrol, diesel-electric.
Total built: 6.
Completed: 1922-23.
Displacement: surfaced 556 tons; submerged 730 tons.
Dimensions: length 210ft 4in (64.1m); beam 17ft 4in (5.6m); draught 11ft
(3.4m).
Propulsion: 2 x NLSE diesels, 2 x 700bhp; 2 x electric motors, 2 x 210shp; t
shafts.
Performance: surface – 16kt; submerged – 10kt; range surfaced 8,000nm
10.5kt, submerged 125nm at 4.5kt; maximum operating diving depth 20
(60m).
Weapons: 4 x 18in (475mm) TT, 8 x torpedoes; 1 x 3in (76mm) gun.
Complement: 28.

History: After the shelving the *Peral* (qv) the Spanish Navy did not order a
more submarines until 1915, when one Holland design was built by the Fe
River Co. Named *Isaac Peral*, this was very similar to USS *M-1* (SS-47), the U
Navy's first double-hulled submarine, which was also built by Fore River a
launched in 1915 (see USA M-1-class). The gun was a 3in (76mm) cali

ove: Bars; inefficient design caused great underwater drag.

drag and a liability to damage (these devices were later removed altogether
most boats and the recesses plated over).

Other problems were, however, of Bubnov's own making. The hull generated
siderable hydrodynamic drag so that the underwater speed of 10kt was never
ieved, while the lack of internal watertight bulkheads meant that any penetration
the hull was fatal. Less serious, but tactically unsound, was the use of pumps to
de the ballast tanks and the large plumes of water which were generated, which
de submerging both slow and easy to spot from a distance.

Most boats saw service during World War I in which four were lost: *Mars*
ed (May 1917); two to unknown causes, *Guepard* (October) and *Lvitsa* (June);
ile *Yedinorog* sank under tow (February 1918). The boats also achieved some
:cesses, sinking eight German transports in the Baltic, of which *Volk* accounted
four. During the Revolution a number were scuttled, but the surviving boats
re taken over by the Communists and *Pantera* sank the British HMS *Vittoria*
490 tons) on 31 August 1919; the latter was a modern V-class destroyer and
nains the largest warship ever sunk by a Russian submarine. The remaining
ats served on and were gradually scrapped, except for *Pantera*, which served as
attery hulk until 1955.

ove: The Spanish Isaac Peral *shortly after completion.*

weapon and was on a "disappearing mount" – ie, when not in use the wh
apparatus folded back into a cavity in the casing. When boats were given let
designations, *Isaac Peral* became *A-0*. It was scrapped in 1930. Next ca
three Fiat-Laurenti boats, which were classified as the "A-class" in Span
service: *Narciso Monturiol* (*A-1*), *Cosme Garcia* (*A-2*) and *A-3* (which did
have a name) – see F-1-class (Italy).

It had always been intended to start submarine construction in Spain a
this was achieved with the B-class, construction of which began in 19
although they were not launched until 1921-23. The design was essentiall

Hajen-/UB-2-/Delfinen-/
Laxen-/Abborren-classes   SWED

Type: patrol, diesel-electric.

Class	Hajen	UB-2	Delfinen	Laxen	Abborren
Total built	1	3	1	2	2
Completed	1904	1909	1914	1914-15	1915-16
Displacement					
surfaced	107 tons	138 tons	260 tons	140 tons	174 tons
submerged	127 tons	230 tons	370 tons	170 tons	310 tons
Dimensions					
length	70ft 10in (21.6m)	87ft 8in (26.8m)	139ft 5in (42.5m)	87ft 11in (26.8m)	101ft 8in (31.0
beam	11ft 10in (3.6m)	11ft 10in (3.6m)	14ft 1in (4.3m)	11ft 10in (3.6m)	11ft 10in (3.6
draught	9ft 10in (3.0m)	9ft 10in (3.0m)	n.k.	n.k.	10ft 2in (3.1m
Propulsion					
engines	1 x kerosene	1 x diesel	2 x diesels	2 x diesels	2 x diesels
power	1 x 200bhp	4 x 420bhp	2 x 500bhp	2 x 350bhp	2 x 460bhp
electric motor	1	1	2	2	2
power	70shp	1 x 200shp	2 x 150shp	2 x 100shp	2 x 140shp
shafts	one	one	two	two	two
Performance					
speed, surface	9.5t	8.8kt	13.6kt	8.8.kt	9.5kt
submerged	7kt	6.6kt	9.4kt	6.6kt	7.4kt
Weapons					
TT	1 x 18.0in (457mm)	1 x 18in (457mm)	2 x 18in (457mm)	1 x 18in (457mm)	2 x 18in (457n
location	bow	bow	bow	bow	bow
torpedoes	n.k	3	n.k.	n.k.	4
Complement	11	12	21	10	

Specifications apply to first-of-class, as built

History: Two submarines were constructed in Sweden by A. B. Sandah
1869 and S. V. Zethelius in 1870, although without apparent success, an

ghtly larger and improved version of the *Isaac Peral* (*A-0*) and like the earlier
at were powered by NLSE diesels, which were M.A.N. designs
anufactured under licence in the United States.

All were either sunk or scuttled during the Spanish Civil War. Two were lost
combat in 1936, of which one, *B-5*, was sunk by Nationalist aircraft in June,
hile the other, *B-6*, was lost to unknown causes, in September. The
mainder were scuttled at the end of the Civil War; all were raised and
ee were scrapped, while the fourth, *B-2*, was used as a battery charging
lk until 1948.

ove: **Delfinen** *photographed while on trials in 1915.*

s left to the arms manufacturer, T. Nordenfelt, to build the nation's first
ble submarine in 1883. Like many submarine pioneers he failed to
erest his own navy, but did manage to sell one to Greece and two smaller
ats to Turkey. The development of the Holland boats in the United States
I, however, engage the Navy's interest: they saw the submarine as an
ective component in the defence of Sweden's neutrality and in 1900
spatched Commander (Engineer) Carl Richson to see what was going on.
his return parliament voted the funds for the construction of one
omarine, *Hajen*, which was designed by Richson based on the Holland
nciples. It displaced 127 tons and was powered by an Avance kerosene
gine, with a Luth & Rosen electric motor for submerged propulsion.
jen was reclassified as a 2nd class submarine in 1909 and in 1916 its
ance engine, which had never been really satisfactory, was replaced by a
5bhp diesel. It was stricken in 1922, but remains on display in Sweden as
nuseum exhibit.

Following experience with *Hajen* the RSwedN diversified by ordering
e submarine from Fiat-Laurenti (see *Hvalen*, below) and three of a
veloped versions of *Hajen*, which were designated *Underwattensbåten*
s 2-4 (*Hajen* having been retrospectively designated No 1). They were
signed by Carl Richson and built by Motala verkstad, all being launched in
09. They were somewhat longer than *Hajen*, were better equipped and
d a more reliable engine, but had the same armament of one 18in
37mm) torpedo tube and three torpedoes. They were stricken in 1929-30.

Delfinen was a further Richson design, but was much larger, had twin
gines/propellers, and was armed with two torpedo tubes. Launched in
14, it served until 1930 and was then stricken. *Delfinen* was a "one-off"
d this development line then reverted to smaller boats. First came the
o-boat Laxen-class, which were virtually the same size and layout as the
derwattensbåten No 2-class, retaining the single 18in (457mm) torpedo
e, but with twin engines and propellers. The Abborren-class, which

followed a year later, was larger, again had twin engines/propellers, but in this case had two torpedo tubes, both in the bows.

Right: **Hajen** *was designed on the* **USS** Holland *principles.*

Hvalen/Svårdvisken-classes   SWED

Type: patrol, diesel-electric.

Class	Hvalen	Svårdvisken
Total built	1	2
Completed	1909	1914
Displacement surfaced submerged	186 tons 230 tons	252 tons 370 tons
Dimensions length beam draught	139ft 1in (42.4m) 8ft 10in (2.7m) 13ft 9in (4.2m)	14ft 1in (4.3m) 149ft 3in (45.5m) n.k.
Propulsion engines power electric motor power shafts	3 x gasolene 3 x 250bhp 1 150shp one	2 x diesel 4 x 500bhp 2 1 x 150shp three
Performance speed, surface submerged	14.8kt 6.3kt	14.2kt 8.5kt
Weapons TT location torpedoes gun	2 x 18.0in (457mm) bow 4 –	2 x 18in (457mm) bow 4 1 x 37mm
Complement	17	12

Specifications apply to first-of-class, as built

ove: Svårdvisken, *the first Swedish-built submarine.*

story: In the early years of the 20th century a number of navies sought to quire the latest submarine technology by buying a very small number of boats m foreign companies. They then absorbed the lessons and either abandoned t particular avenue or decided to set up their own submarine design and nstruction facilities based on licence production of a development of the ginal design. Thus, although Sweden had found the American Holland design :isfactory (see previous entry) they purchased a single boat from Italian mpany, Fiat-San Giorgio, which had established a good reputation at that e. Named *Hvalen*, this was virtually identical to the Italian Navy's Foca-class) and the boat was soon in the world's Press when it sailed from Le Spezia Stockholm without any accompanying escorts. She served in the RSwedN til 1919 when she was sunk as a target.

In 1910 the Swedish company Kockums of Malmo purchased the Swedish nce from Fiat-San Giorgio, which enabled it to win the next contract for what s now designated a first-class sub-marine. The new class com-prised two ts, *Svårdvisken* and *Tumlaren,* and were slightly larger than *Hvalen*, mainly order to accommodate two Hesselman six-cylinder diesels in place of the lier boat's gasoline engines. As com-pleted, both boats mounted a single mm gun, which was later replaced by a 57mm weapon. They were both cken in 1936 but served on as anti-aircraft gun platforms until 1946 when y were scrapped.

Hajen-/Bävern-classes

Type: patrol, diesel-electric.

Class	Hajen	Bävern
Total built	3	3
Completed	1917-18	1921
Displacement surfaced submerged	422 tons 600 tons	472 tons 650 tons
Dimensions length beam draught	177ft 2in (54.0m) 17ft 1in (5.2m) 11ft 6in (3.1m)	187ft 0in (57.0m) 19ft 0n (5.8m) n.k.
Propulsion engines power electric motor power shafts	2 x diesel 3 x 1,000bhp 2 350shp two	2 x diesel 2 x 1,050bhp 2 260shp two

rformance		
eed, surface	15.5kt	15.2kt
bmerged	9kt	8.2kt
eapons		
ation	4 x 18in (457mm) bow	4 x 18in (457mm) bow
pedoes	8	n.k.
n	–	1 x 75mm
mplement	30	31

cifications apply to first-of-class, as built

tory: By the middle of World War I the successes of German U-boats had placed ir designers in a pre-eminent position which, coupled with the proximity of many just across the Baltic, meant that Sweden looked to that country for its t design. The result was that Kockums bought the licence for a design from one he most successful German shipyards, Weser AG of Bremen, later to become schimag. This was altered to meet Swedish require-ments and the outcome was Hajen-class, a double-hull design, armed with four 18in (457mm) torpedo tubes l a single 75mm gun. This was followed in 1921 by the improved Bävern-class, of three boats, which was some 10ft (3m) longer. The Hajen-class was stricken 942-43 and the Bävern-class in 1944, except for *Illern*, which was rammed by a rchant ship on 12 August 1944 and sank.

ow: Valrossen*, one of three boats in the Hajen-class.*

Holland-class

Type: harbour defence, gasoline-electric.
Total built: 1.
Completed: 1897.
Displacement: surfaced 64 tons; submerged 74tons.
Dimensions: length 53ft 10in (16.4m); beam 10ft 3in (3.1m); draught 8ft (2.6m).
Propulsion: 1 x Otto gasoline engine, 45bhp; 1 x Electro-Dynamics elec motor, 50shp; battery 50 cells; one shaft.
Performance: surface – 8kt; submerged – 5kt; maximum operating div depth 100ft (31m).
Weapons: 1 x 18in (457mm) TT (bow); 3 x torpedoes; one 8in (203m pneumatic gun.
Complement: 7.

History: J. P. Holland was an Irish inventor who produced a series of desi for submarines from 1878 onwards, eventually having that for the *Plur* accepted by the U.S. Navy in 1895. This was, however, a steam-powe design and Holland, believing that steam would never be suitable, abando construction, returned the money to the Navy, and built *Holland Numbe* using his own funds instead. This was by no means the first submarine, bu was certainly the first successful underwater weapons system and inclu many design features that are still in use today. The design was optimised underwater performance, with a streamlined "teardrop" hull and a sin propeller. Also, she dived with her ballast tanks full, relying for control on aft-mounted hydroplanes, unlike most contemporary submersibles, wh varied the amount of water in their tanks to change depth and, as a res suffered from instability due to the free-surface effect in their ballast tanks.

Below: USS Holland *1 (SS-1) in Long Island Sound in 1899.*

ove: USS Holland *under repair; note the very clean lines.*

An air-breathing, gasoline-powered drive system provided propulsion on the face and also charged the batteries, which provided an air-independent pulsion system for submerged operations. Other features, too, have stood test of time, including the controls and clutches which enabled the petrol jine either to drive the propeller directly, or to recharge the batteries using motor as a generator, with or without turning the propeller – ie, the batteries ild be recharged either while moving at sea or while at rest alongside.

Holland Number VI was constructed at the Crescent Shipyard, abethport, New Jersey, and was launched on 17 May 1897. Trials went well spite a hitch in October that year when a shipyard worker left a valve open ile the boat was on the slip, which resulted in her being flooded when the e came in. Fortunately, actual damage to the electrical system was vented and the boat passed all her tests.

Main armament was an 18in (457mm) torpedo tube, covered by a tertight cap which was raised for firing by a worm gear. Compensation to intain the trim when a torpedo was launched was extremely effective. She o mounted a single 8in (203mm) pneumatic gun (also known as a ynamite" gun) on the bow above the torpedo tube. This was a fixed mount ended to be fired with the muzzle just clear of the water, but, as far as is wn, it was never fired.

The boat was purchased by the U.S. Government on 11 April 1900 and ned USS *Holland,* subsequently also being allocated the historic number SS- She was commissioned on 1 October 1900, the commander being utenant Harry H. Caldwell, USN. *Holland* was used mainly for trials and was o employed as a training boat at the U.S. Naval Academy, Annapolis, until 17 y 1905. She was stricken on 21 November 1910 and sold to a breaker's yard June 1930. Unfortunately, no trace of this historic boat remains.

A-class

Type: harbour defence, gasoline-electric.

Class	A-class	Holland-class	Holland (Beluga)-class	Holland-cla
Country	USA	Japan	Russia	UK
Total built	7	5	7	5
Completed	1901-03	1905	1904-05	1901-02
Displacement surfaced submerged	107 tons 123 tons	103 tons 124 tons	105 tons 122 tons	113 tons 122 tons
Dimensions length beam draught	63ft 10in (19.4m) 11ft 11in (3.6m) 10ft 7in (3.2m)	67ft 0in (20.4m) 11ft 11in (3.6m) 10ft 3in (3.1m)	65ft 6in (20.0m) 11ft 6in (3.5m) 9ft 6in (2.9m)	63ft 10in (19.5 11ft 10in (3.6m 9ft 11in (3.0m
Propulsion main engines power electric motors power battery shafts	1 x Otto gasoline 160bhp 1 150shp 60 cells one	1 x Otto gasoline 180bhp 1 70shp 60 cells one	1 x gasoline 160bhp 1 70hp 60 cells one	1 x gasoline 160bhp 1 70shp 60 cells one
Performance speed, surface submerged range, surfaced submerged	8kt 7kt – –	8kt 7kt 184nm at 8kt 21nm at 7kt	8.5kt 6kt 585nm 42nm	7.5kt 6kt 500nm at 7 –
Weapons TT location torpedoes	1x 18in (457mm) bow 3	1 x 18in (457mm) bow 2	1 x 15in (381mm) bow –	1x 18in (457m bow 3
Complement	7	13	22	8

History: Following the success of *Holland* (SS-1) four navies built versions o
P. Holland's next design, a slightly larger development. In the U.S. Navy
new design was known as the A-class (Adder-class), but the British, Japan
and Russian navies gave them the generic title of "Holland-type" boats.
last three are described in their own national entries, but are also included h
to show their relationship to the Adder-class. The U.S. Navy's boats w
specifically intended for harbour defence, with the crew living either ashore
aboard a tender. Seven were built and were given names as well as
numbers (SS-2 to SS-8) and class numbers (A-1 to A-7), and to add to
confusion first-of-class *Adder*, which was launched on 22 July 1901, was gi
hull number SS-3, while the fifth to be launched, *Plunger*, was given

ove: A-class boat USS Porpoise (SS-7) alongside in 1902.

enior" numbers of SS-2 and A-1.

The design of the A-class was generally similar to that of *Holland* (SS-1), but th a deck casing stretching from just before the conning tower to the stern. e 8in (203mm) dynamite gun was deleted and the number of torpedoes creased to five. All boats in the class except *Plunger* were shipped to the ilippines in pairs in 1908, 1909 and 1915, where they formed the 1st bmarine Division of the Asiatic Torpedo Fleet, based at the U.S. Navy's major cility at Cavite. *Plunger*'s career was marked by two memorable episodes: st, President Theodore Roosevelt spent several hours submerged in her on March 1905, which he immensely enjoyed; and, second, her last mmanding officer was Ensign Chester Nimitz, who was to earn undying ne in World War II. After a period in reserve, *Plunger* was stricken in 1913 d sold for scrap in 1922, while the Philippines-based boats served during orld War I, but without seeing any actual combat and were later used as gets; all six were then stricken on 16 January 1922.

The British Holland-class (qv) were built to virtually the same design, but der licence in the ckers shipyard. Both e Japanese and ssian boats, how- er, were built in the ited States and en broken down into ctions and taken ross the USA by rail fore being shipped ross the Pacific to eir respective destin- ons.

ght: Porpoise and ark in 1905. Note e sailor in the rpedo tube.

B-/C-/D-classes   UNITED STATES OF AMERIC

Type: harbour defence/coastal patrol, gasoline-electric.

Class	B-class	C-class	D-class
Total built	3	5	3
Completed	1906-07	1908-10	1909-10
Displacement surfaced submerged	145 tons 173 tons	238 tons 275 tons	288 tons 337 tons
Dimensions length beam draught	82ft 5in (25.1m) 12ft 6in (3.8m) 10ft 7in (3.2m)	105ft 4in (32.1m) 13ft 11in (4.2m) 10ft 0in (3.0m)	134ft 10in (41.1 13ft 11in (4.2m) 12ft 6in (3.8m)

History: These three small classes followed each other, each representing
increase in size and displacement on the original gasoline-engined Holland-cl

until the D-class. The B-class, like the
Holland and A-classes had a single
propeller, but the C-class introduce a
second shaft and propeller, which
arrangement was to endure in U.S.
submarines until the *Albacore* in the
1950s. The second power-train made
greater horsepower available and
improved manoeuvrability, but above
all in an era when mechanical reliability
was not great, it provided redundancy
and ensured that a single fault did not
immobilise the submarine at sea.

The B-class were designated
"harbor defense" submarines and all
three were transferred to the
Philippines in 1912, where they joined
the A-class. Also like the A-class, they
were stricken in 1922. The C-class
was actually built in parallel to the B-
class, but were larger and had greater
range, leading to them being
designated coastal defence submarines. In World War I they were
deployed in defence of the Panama
Canal, and all were stricken in 1920.
The D-class followed on from the C-
class, being slightly larger and with
greater range. All were stricken in
1922.

Right: **Cuttlefish *(SS-11),* second of
the B-class.**

Propulsion			
main engines	1 x Craig gasoline	1 x Craig gasoline	2 x NLSE gasoline
power	250bhp	500bhp	2 x 300bhp
electric motors	1	1	2
power	150shp	300shp	2 x 260shp
battery	60 cells	120 cells	120 cells
shafts	one	one	two
Performance			
speed, surface	9kt	10.5kt	13kt
submerged	8kt	9kt	9.5kt
range, surfaced	800nm/8kt	800nm/8kt	1,240nm/9kt
submerged	12nm/4kt	80nm/5kt	–
maximum operational diving depth	150ft (46m)	200ft (61m)	200 (61m)
Weapons			
TT	2x 18in (457mm)	2 x 18in (457mm)	4 x 18in (457mm)
location	bow	bow	bow
torpedoes	4	4	4
Complement	10	15	15

E-/F-/H-/K-classes

Type: coastal patrol, diesel-electric.

Class	E-class	F-class	H-class	K-class
Total built	2	4	9	8
Completed	1911	1911-12	1913-18	1913-14
Displacement surfaced submerged	287 tons 342 tons	330 tons 400 tons	358 tons 467 tons	329 tons 521 tons
Dimensions length beam draught	135ft 3in (41.2m) 14ft 7in (4.4m) 11ft 8in (3.6)	142ft 7in (43.5m) 15ft 5in (4.7m) 12ft 2in (3.7m)	150ft 4in (45.8m) 15ft 10in (4.8m) 12ft 5in (3.8m)	153ft 7in (46.9r 16ft 8in (5.1m) 13ft 1in (4.0m)

History: These four classes represent a steady increase in the refinement ar effectiveness of the Holland-type submarine. The E-class was the first in th U.S. Navy to be powered by diesel engines, thus doing away with the inhere danger of the gasoline engines. Even so, these early diesels proved to be a source of constant trouble, which was so severe in the E- and F-classes that the boats had to be withdrawn from service in 1915 and given completely new engines. The E-class were the first U.S. submarines to have bow planes and also the first to have radio equipment and antennas installed in construction.

The F-class was developed and built in parallel with the E-class and was slightly larger. The development train finally came together with the H-class, although only three were actually ordered for the U.S. Navy – *H-1* (SS-28) to *H-3* (SS-30). The type did, however, attract great foreign interest, with large numbers being built for Britain's Royal Navy (see H-class, UK) and the Imperial Russian Navy (see AG-class). At the time of the Russian Revolution six boats remained in the United States awaiting delivery and these were purchased by the U.S. Navy in 1918, being designated *H-4* (SS-147) to *H-9* (SS-152). The K-class succeeded the H-class and was slightly larger.

The two E-class boats both survived World War I, to be stricken in 1922, but the four F-class boats were not so fortunate. *F-4* was the first to be lost, sinking during a diving exercise off Honolulu on 25 March 1915, with the loss of all hands. That was followed by a collision between *F-3* and *F-1* on 17 December 1917 in which the latter sank with the loss of 19 lives. The remaining two boats were stricken and scrapped in 1922. One H-class boat was lost, *Seawolf* (SS-28), which suffered an onboard fire off the Pacific coast and was deliberately run ashore; four men, including the commanding officer were drowned trying to reach the shore and the boat then sank while being hauled off by a repair ship. One of the remaining two original boats was stricken in 1922, while the other boat plus all those from the Russian order were scrapped in 1931.

Right: USS K-5 (SS-36), launched in 1914, scrapped in 1931.

Propulsion				
main engines	2 x NLSE diesels	2 x NLSE diesels	2 x NLSE diesels	2 x NLSE diesels
power	2 x 350bhp	2 x 390bhp	2 x 475bhp	2 x 475bhp
electric motors	2	2	2	2
power	2 x 300shp	2 x 300shp	2 x 300shp	2 x 340shp
battery	120 cells	120 cells	120 cells	120 cells
shafts	two	two	two	two
Performance				
speed, surface	13.5kt	13.5kt	14kt	14kt
submerged	11.5kt	11.5kt	10.5kt	10.5kt
range, surfaced	2,100nm/11kt	2,300nm/11kt	2,300nm/11kt	4,500nm/10kt
submerged	100nm/5kt	100nm/5kt	100nm/5kt	120nm/5kt
maximum operational diving depth	200ft (61m)	200ft (61m)	200ft (61m)	200ft (61m)
Weapons				
TT	4x 18in (457mm)	4 x 18in (457mm)	4 x 18in (457mm)	4 x 18in (457mm)
location	bow	bow	bow	bow
torpedoes	4	4	8	8
Complement	20	22	28	28

G-class

UNITED STATES OF AMERIC

Type: coastal patrol, gasoline/diesel-electric.

Class	Seal (G-1)	Tuna (G-2)	Turbot (G-3)	Thrasher (G-4
Pennant No	SS-191/2	SS-27	SS-31	SS-26
Total built	1	1	1	1
Completed	1911	1915	1915	1914
Displacement surfaced submerged	288 tons 337 tons	400 tons 516 tons	393 tons 460 tons	360 tons 475 tons
Dimensions length beam draught	161ft 0in (49.1m) 13ft 1in (4.0m) 12ft 6in (3.8m)	161ft 7in (49.3m) 13ft 1in (4.0m) 12ft 6in (3.8m)	161ft 0in (49.1m) 13ft 1in (4.0m) 12ft 10in (3.9m)	157ft 6in (48.0m 17ft 6in (5.3m) 10ft 11in (3.3m

History: These four boats were actually individual designs and were groupe together as the G-class for administrative convenience. Three of them – G-1, 2 and G-3 – were designed by Simon Lake. G-1 and G-2 were each powered four gasoline engines, which caused a lot of problems and both spent a gre deal of time in maintenance and refits. G-1 was the first design by Simon La to be accepted by the U.S. Navy, being constructed by Newport News (the fir submarine to be built there) and commissioned on 28 October 1912, and w unique in the U.S. Navy's numbering system, being given a fractional numbe SS-19½. Her only notable achievement was to carry out a dive of 256ft (78m

Propulsion				
main engines	4 x gasoline	4 x gasoline	2 x diesels	2 x gasoline
power	4 x 300bhp	4 x 600bhp	2 x 600bhp	2 x 500bhp
electric motors	2	2	2	2
power	2 x 260shp	2 x 260shp	2 x 300shp	2 x 220shp
battery	120 cells	120 cells	120 cells	164 cells
shafts	two	two	two	two
Performance				
speed, surface	14kt	14kt	14kt	14kt
submerged	10kt	10.5kt	95kt	95kt
range, surfaced	2,500nm/8kt	2,500nm/8kt	2,500nm/8kt	2,500nm/8kt
submerged	70nm/5kt	70nm/5kt	70nm/5kt	70nm/5kt
maximum				
operational				
diving depth	200ft (61m)	120ft (61m)	200ft (61m)	200ft (61m)
Weapons				
TT	6 x 18in (457mm)	4 x 18in (457mm)	6 x 18in (457mm)	4 x 18in (457mm)
location	bow – 4; deck – 2	bow	bow	bow
torpedoes	8	4	10	8
Complement	24	24	25	24

record at the time. From 1915 onwards she was used in training and ended her days as an aerial target, being sunk by bombs on 21 June 1920. At one time she was commanded by Lieutenant Charles Lockwood, who as Commander Submarines Pacific (COMSUBPAC) in World War II would mastermind the submarine war against Japan. G-2 (SS-27), another Lake design, had a relatively short career, being launched in 1911, commissioned in February 1915 and stricken 1919, which included a lengthy overhaul from March 1916 to June 1917. Most of her career was devoted to experimental and training duties and she then became a target for depth-charges. She was undergoing maintenance on 30 July 1919 when she suddenly sank, drowning three of her crew. G-3 (SS-31) was the only one of this group of Lake boats to be powered by diesels and served from completion in December 1913 until being stricken in 1922.

G-4 (SS-31), originally named Thrasher, was built by Cramp in the USA under licence from Fiat-Laurenti, the only submarine ever to be built for the U.S. Navy to a foreign design. The craft was delivered some three years late and proved generally unsatisfactory, with poor surface range (1,680nm at 8kt), a lack of stability, a very small conning tower and a particularly heavy hull, the latter a consequence of the Laurenti practice of using non-circular frames, which then needed extra bracing.

Left: Seal (SS-19½), Lake's first boat for the U.S. Navy.

L-/M-classes

Type: coastal, diesel-electric.
Total built: 11.
Completed: 1915-17.
Displacement: surfaced 450 tons; submerged 548 tons.
Dimensions: length 167ft 4in (51.0m); beam 17ft 5in (5.3m); draught 13ft 5
(4.1m).
Propulsion: 2 x NLSE diesels, 2 x 600bhp; 2 x electric motors, 2 x 400sh
battery 120 cell; two shafts.
Performance: surface – 14kt; submerged – 10.5kt; range surfaced 3,300nm
11kt, submerged 150nm at 5kt; maximum operating diving depth 200ft (61m
Weapons: 4 x 18in (457mm) TT (bow), 8 x torpedoes; 1 x 3in (76mm) gun.
Complement: 28.
Specifications for L-class, as built.

History: There were 11 L-class boats, seven (*L-1* to *L-4*, *L-9* to *L-11*) to i
Electric Boat design, which were built by Fore River at Qunicy, and four to
Lake design, of which three (*L-5* to *L-7*) were built by Lake at Bridgeport ar
one (*L-8*) at Portsmouth Navy Yard, the latter being the first submarine to k

Right: First of her class, L-1 (SS-40) puts to sea.

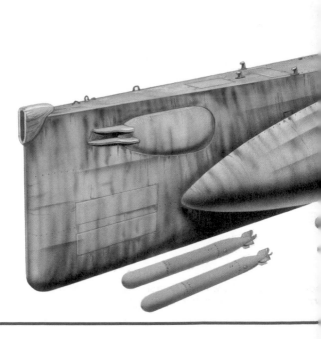

ove: USS L-11. Note the "disappearing" mount which left part of the rel barrel protruding vertically from the foredeck.

built in any U.S. Navy yard. The four Lake boats were marginally smaller th the others, being 165 ft (50.3m) long and with a submerged displacement 524 tons. These submarines were the first in the U.S. Navy to mount a de gun, as built, the 3in (76mm) weapon being on a "disappearing" mount, wh was unique to the U.S. Navy. To "disappear", the entire mounting swu backwards through 90deg and then lowered into a recess, but leaving forward 3ft (0.9m) of the barrel protruding vertically above the deck, the muz being closed off with a tampion.

L-8 (SS-48), the fourth of the Lake boats, had an unusual history. Dur World War I it was used in a secret deception scheme, which also involved four-masted schooner, USS *Charles Whittemore*. The idea was that *Whittemore* towed the submerged L-8, which thus remained hidden but sti close contact with the surface ship by telephone, while the apparen defenceless sailing ship was supposed to attract the attention of a maraud enemy U-boat, whereupon L-8, alerted by telephone, would carry out an atta The British tried a similar idea, but neither navy scored any successes. In 1§

AA (T)-class

Type: fleet, diesel-electric.
Total built: 3.
Completed: 1920-22.
Displacement: surfaced 1,106 tons; submerged 1,486 tons.
Dimensions: length 268ft 9in (81.9m); beam 22ft 10in (6.9m); draught 14ft 2in (4.3
Propulsion: 4 x NLSE diesels, 4 x 1,000bhp; 2 x electric motors, 2 x 675shp; batt 2 x 60 cells; two shafts.
Performance: surface – 20kt; submerged – 10.5kt; range surfaced 3,000nm 14kt, submerged 100nm at 5kt; maximum operating diving depth 150ft (46m).
Weapons: 6 x 21in (533mm) TT (bow – 4, deck – 2), 16 x torpedoes; 2 x 3in (76m guns.
Complement: 38.
Specifications for T-1 (SS-52), as built.

History: This class was the first of several attempts by the U.S. Navy to prod that ideal sought by a number of the world's largest navies – the "fleet" subman which could operate with the battle fleet. The first-of-class was authorised in 19 followed by two more in 1915. The designations require an explanation. The fi of-class was given the class number *SF-1* (SF = Submarine, Fleet-type); the seco and third boats were simply given numbers – *SF-2* and *SF-3*. The class designat was then changed to the AA-class, with the boats renumbered *AA-1* to *AA-3*, and finally in 1920 it changed yet again, becoming the T-class (*T-1* to *T-3*). The first-of-class bore the name *Schley* (SS-52), but the other two only ever carried numbers.

The boat had a partial double-hull, with single-hull compartments at each end. *Schley* was one of the first boats in any navy to have trainable torpedo-tube mountings on the upper deck. These had twin 18in (457mm) tubes and the entire mount was

3 was deliberately sunk to become a target for magnetic exploders.

During 1917-18 seven boats deployed to Bantry Bay in Ireland, where their dge dodgers were prominently marked with the letters "AL-" to differentiate em from the British L-class. Although involved in several actions with U-boats, ey scored no successes. The Lake-designed boats were scrapped in 1925, ile two of the others were stricken in 1922 and the remainder in 1930-32.

The sole M-class submarine, *M-1* (SS-47), had the same weapons as the L-ss, but was the first U.S. Navy double-hull submarine and, with an overall gth of 196ft 3in (59.8m), she was the longest built for the U.S. Navy up to s time. However, she also had a very narrow beam – 14ft 9in (4.5m) – and s considered to be very crowded and certainly less habitable than ntemporary single-hull boats. She also had a habit of taking up a large list en diving or submerging, which, not surprisingly, caused some anxiety ong her crew. *M-1* was commissioned on 16 February 1916 and spent ost all of her relatively brief career as a training boat. She was stricken on March 1922 and sold for scrap six months later.

ned from inside the boat by means of handwheels and mechanical linkages on ers from the captain at the periscope. Trials showed this to be not worth the nplications and first one and then the other deck mounts were removed from *hley* and none was ever mounted on the other two boats. *Schley* also initially unted two 3in (76mm) guns, but this was later changed to a single 4in (102mm). th the deck tubes *Schley* carried the very impressive load of 16 torpedoes and en when the deck tubes were removed all three boats carried 12 torpedoes, ich was considerably more than most contemporary submarines, apart from ne of the very large U-boats of the German Navy.

To obtain the necessary power, there were four NLSE diesel engines, each with ower output of 1,000bhp, which were mounted in tandem on each shaft, but this sed a great deal of vibration, which, despite many changes of clutches and mping, was never overcome. The third boat, *T-3*, was re-engined with two large A.N. diesels, but this proved to be of little benefit.

The boats proved to be just capable of reaching their design speed under al conditions, but had so many shortcomings, especially in hull design and pulsion systems, that they were put into reserve in 1922 and scrapped in 30.

ow: **Schley** *(formerly AA-1), the first "fleet" submarine.*

N-class

Type: attack, diesel-electric.
Total built: 7.
Completed: 1916-17.
Displacement: surfaced 348 tons; submerged 414 tons.
Dimensions: length 147ft 4in (44.9m); beam 15ft 9in (4.8m); draught 12ft (3.8m).
Propulsion: 2 x NLSE diesels, 2 x 300bhp; 2 x electric motors, 2 x 150s battery 120 cells; two shafts.
Performance: surface – 13kt; submerged – 11kt; range surfaced 3,500r submerged 30nm at 5kt; maximum operating diving depth 200ft (61m).
Weapons: 4 x 18in (457mm) TT (bow), 8 x torpedoes.
Complement: 25.
Specifications for N-1 (SS-53), as built.

History: For some years U.S. submarines had suffered from problems v their diesel engines and in the N-class it was decided that, instead of seek to obtain the greatest possible power from a unit, the designers wo deliberately reduce power in order to enhance reliability and reduce maintenance load. This was tested in the N-class and proved to be suc success that more modest power outputs were adopted in the succeec classes, while many existing boats were re-engined. Also, for about a deca U.S. submarines had been given an embryonic bridge, which consisted c platform mounted on top of the conning tower, usually with a canvas dodge give some protection to the watchkeepers. The N-class, however, was the 1

O-class

Type: attack, diesel-electric.
Total built: 16.
Completed: 1918.
Displacement: surfaced 521 tons; submerged 629 tons.
Dimensions: length 172ft 3in (52.2m); beam 18ft 1in (5.5m); draught 14ft (4.4m).
Propulsion: 2 x NLSE diesels, 2 x 440bhp; 2 x electric motors, 2 x 370s battery 120 cells; two shafts.
Performance: surface – 14kt; submerged – 10.5kt; range surfaced 5,500nn 11.5kt; maximum operating diving depth 200ft (61m).
Weapons: 4 x 18in (457mm) TT (bow), 8 x torpedoes.
Complement: 29.

History: The O-class consisted of 16 boats which were built at five differ yards. Those built at Portsmouth Navy Yard (1), Puget Sound Navy Y Bremerton (1), Fore River, Quincy (7), and California Shipbuilding, Long Be (3), were identical, but the three from Lake, Bridgeport, were, as usual with company, different in many minor details. The details of the Lake boats, C (SS-72) to O-13 (SS-74), were: length 175ft 3in (52.4m), beam 16ft 9in (5. and submerged displacement 629 tons. A further difference in the last six bc (ie, Lake and California Shipbuilding) was that they were powered by Su diesels, produced in the United States by Busch-Sulzer.

Two were peacetime losses: O-5 (SS-66) was in collision with a merch ship on 28 October 1923 and O-9 (SS-70) foundered in 1941. Most boats w employed in the training role from 1928 onwards, although six were stricke

...ght: N-1 (SS-53).
...e N-class were
...e first U.S.
...bmarines to have
...-metal bridges.

...follow foreign example and have an all-steel bridge. The N-boats were the
... U.S. submarine class to be built without a deck gun until the late 1940s.
   Three N-boats were built by Seattle Construction and four by Lake. The
...er were 155ft (47.2m) long, and had a 14ft 6in (4.4m) beam, with a
...bmerged displacement of 415 tons. The Lake boats were commissioned in
...18 and decommissioned and sold for scrap in 1922, a remarkably brief
...vice life, whereas the Seattle boats were commissioned in 1917 and served
...il 1926, after which they were held in reserve until 1930. *N-2* (SS-54) was
...dified to test the Neff air-independent propulsion system and while the
...tem worked it was considered to offer no significant advances over
...nventional diesel-electric systems and was not pursued further.

...ht: O-12 as
...verted for the
...empt to reach the
...rth Pole under the

...30 and one in 1938.
...ven served through
...rld War II and
...re scrapped in
...5-46.
   O-12 (SS-73), one
...those stricken in
...30, was leased by
...   Australian ex-
...rer, Sir Hubert
...kins (1888-1958),
...the sum of $1 per
...r for five years in

...er to lead a submarine expedition to the North Pole. *O-12* was converted
...Brooklyn Navy Yard, the changes including the addition of a long, curved
...per deck, a collapsible bowsprit, and two air-drills capable of drilling holes
...ugh up to 100ft (30.5m) of ice. She was renamed *Nautilus* after Jules
...ne's fictional submarine and the boat, now with civilian status, was
...ved across the Atlantic by a U.S. Navy battleship. She set out from
...way in late 1931 and did actually go under the ice, but Wilkins was forced
...urn back when still some 450nm (724km) from the Pole. It was a very brave
...empt.

R-class

Type: attack, diesel-electric.
Total built: 27.
Completed: 1918-19.
Displacement: surfaced 569 tons; submerged 680 tons.
Dimensions: length 186ft 5in (56.8m); beam 18ft 1in (5.5m); draught 14ft 5in (4.4
Propulsion: 2 x NLSE diesels, 2 x 600bhp; 2 x electric motors, 2 x 467s
battery 120 cells; two shafts.
Performance: surface – 13.5kt; submerged – 10.5kt; range surfaced 4,700
at 6.2kt; maximum operating diving depth 200ft (61m).
Weapons: 4 x 21in (533mm) TT (bow), 8 x torpedoes; 1 x 3in (76mm) gun.
Complement: 29.
Specifications are for R-1 (SS-78), as built.

History: The 27 R-class boats were built in three yards, Fore River (14), Union
Works (6) and Lake (7), and as usual the Lake boats were different. This time t
were dimensionally identical to the others, but had a lesser displacement: 510 t
surfaced, 583 tons submerged. Of greater significance was that they had diffe
engines, Busch-Sulzer diesels (2 x 500bhp), and they retained the 18in (457r
torpedo tubes, whereas all the rest mounted four of the new 21in (533mm) tul
the first U.S. submarines to do so.

As in the L- and N-classes, the Lake-built boats were the first to be scrapp
in this case in 1930. Three R-boats, *R-3, R-17* and *R-19*, were transferred to Brita
Royal Navy in 1941-42. Of these, the latter, then designated HMS *P-514*, was s
in a collision with the minesweeper USS *Georgian*, off Cape Race (21 June 19

S-class

Type: patrol, diesel-electric.

History: The S-class started with the first submarine-design competition e
run by the U.S. Navy, which resulted in three prototypes: two comp
designs, *S-1* (SS-105) from the Electric Boat Company and *S-2* (SS-106) fr
Simon Lake, and a government-designed boat, *S-3* (SS-107), built
Portsmouth Navy Yard. The result of the competition was that the Lake de
was considered unsatisfactory and orders were placed for two grou
followed by two separate repeat orders.

Group 1, the Electric Boat design, comprised 25 boats: the
prototype, *S-1* (SS105), plus 12 boats each from Fore River (*S-18*
to *S-29*) and Union Iron Works (*S-30* to *S-41*). These were single-
hulled boats, powered by NLSE diesels, completed between 1919
and 1922.

Group 2, the official Bureau of Ships design, comprised 15
boats, the first of which was the prototype, *S-3*, the production
boats being completed by Portsmouth Navy Yard (*S-4* to *S-13*) and
Lake (*S-14* to *S-17*). This group shared the major characteristics of
the Group I design, but was double-hulled and was always
considered to be much more crowded. Unusually among U.S.
submarines of the period, these boats were built with non-folding
bow hydroplanes, although they were given folding mechanisms in
1922-24 refits. These boats were powered by a variety of main
engines, from NLSE, M.A.N. or Busch-Sulzer.

Group 3 was a development of the Electric Boat design, with

ove: Peruvian **R-1**, *export version of the U.S. Navy's R-class.*

only other loss was USS *R-12* (SS-89) which sank during a torpedo exercise off
West, Florida. The boat was on the surface, preparing to dive, when it suddenly
ted to flood forward; a warning was sounded but she went down extremely
kly and the only survivors were five men of the bridge crew. The number crew
was 42, which suggests that she was seriously overmanned, possibly with
ees. The initial cause of the disaster was never determined. *R-12* was one of
two U.S. submarines lost in the Atlantic during World War II.

R-14 (SS-91) was involved in a famous incident when it ran out of fuel while
ching for a missing tugboat south-east of Hawaii in May 1921. Rather than wait
e found the crew sewed blankets and mattress covers together to make a
ber of square-rigged sails and then proceeded back to Hawaii, an epic voyage
took five days and remains unique in submarine history.

oats (*S-42* to *S-47*) completed at Fore River in 1923-24.

Group 4 comprised four boats (*S-48* to *S-51*) completed by Lake in 1922. They
e to a C&R design, were longer than the three earlier groups, and had a stern
edo tube, bringing the number of tubes to five and torpedoes carried to 14.

The first Lake type, *S-2*, was the original Lake prototype which displaced
tons (submerged), was 207ft (63.1m) long, and had speeds of 15kt on the
ace and 11.5kt submerged. Although this design was rejected in favour of

ow: **S-1** *conducting aircraft-carrying trials in the 1920s.*

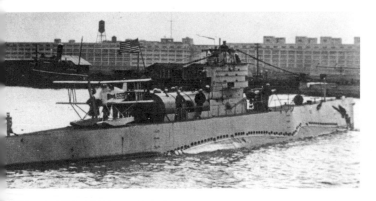

	Group 1	Group 2	Group 3	Group 4
Total built	25	15	6	4
Hull Nos	S-1, S-18 – S-41	S-3, S-4 – S-17	S-42 – S-47	S-48 – S-51
Completed	1920-24	1919-23	1924-25	1922
Displacement surfaced submerged	854 tons 1,062 tons	876 tons 1.092 tons	906 tons 1,126 tons	903 tons 1,230 tons
Dimensions length beam draught	219ft 3in (66.9m) 20ft 8in (6.3m) 15ft 9in (4.8m)	231ft 07in (70.4m) 22ft 0in (6.7m) 13ft 1in (4.0m)	225ft 5in (68.7m) 20ft 8in (6.3m) 16ft 1in (4.0m)	240ft 2in (73.2 21ft 8in (6.6m 13ft 5in (4.1m

the Electric Boat design, and despite its "one-off" status, *S-2* v
commissioned into the U.S. Navy and served in the Asiatic Fleet from 192
1929, not being scrapped until 1931.

A total of 51 S-boats entered service between 1918 and 1924, and th
were three peacetime losses. *S-4* was rammed by a USCG cutter as she v
surfacing and sank with loss of all hands. She was later raised, repaired
returned to service, being stricken in 1931. *S-5* was flooded and sank (1 Aug
1920) coming to rest on the bottom. The crew managed to raise the stern u
it was above the water and then cut a hole through which they all escaped.
hulk was recovered but was not returned to service. The third loss was S
which was rammed by the merchant ship, *City of Rome*, off Block Island, N
York (25 September 1925); only three out of the 36 aboard were rescued.
hulk was raised but never returned to service. Two boats of Group 4 and
sole Lake prototype were scrapped in 1931 and a further one Group 1 and
Group 2 boats were stricken and scrapped in 1936-37. The remaining 3

opulsion				
ain engines	2 x NLSE diesels	2 x NLSE diesels	2 x BS diesels	2 x BS diesels
wer	2 x 600bhp	2 x 1,00bhp	2 x 600bhp	2 x 900bhp
ectric motors	2	2	2	2
wer	2 x 750shp	2 x 600shp	2 x 600shp	2 x 750shp
afts	two	two	two	two
ttery	120 cells	120 cells	120 cells	120 cells
rformance				
eed, surface	14kt	15kt	14.5kt	14l.5kt
bmerged	11kt	11kt	11kt	11kt
ge, surfaced	3,420nm/6.5kt	5,000nm/10kt	2,510nm/6.5kt	5,900nm/10kt
bmerged	–	–	–	–
aximum				
erational				
ing depth	200ft (61m)	200ft (61m)	200ft (61m)	200ft (61m)
eapons				
	4 x 21in (533mm)	4 x 21in (533mm)	4 x 21in (533mm)	5 x 21in (533mm)
cation	bow	bow	bow	bow – 4, stern – 1
rpedoes	12	12	12	14
n	1 x 4in (102mm)	1 x 4in (102mm)	1 x 4in (102mm)	1 x 4in (102mm)
mplement	38	22	38	38

ts all saw service in World War II, six of which (all Group 1) were supplied
oreign navies: Poland – 1 (1941) and UK – 5 (1942). Seven in U.S. service
re lost during the war, six Group 1 (*S-26*, *S-27*, *S-28*, *S-36*, *S-37*, *S-39*) and
e Group 3 (*S-44*). The remaining boats survived the war and were then either
apped or expended as targets in 1945-46.

*iow: **S-48**, 2nd Lake Type. Fifty-one S-class were built.*

Diesel-Electric Patrol Submarines 1922-1946

World War I transformed the submarine from an interesting novelty into a m
weapon of war. Indeed, the manner in which German U-boats had brought
mighty British Royal Navy to the verge of defeat showed clearly how submarin
properly used, could exert a strategic influence out of all proportion to t
numbers. Despite the German defeat, the U-boats had established a reputation
effectiveness and sound design, and many Allied navies seized the opportunit
obtain examples in the post-war share-out of U-boat prizes, which were t
examined in the most minute detail. In fact, the British were so shaken by t
experiences that when they attended the Washington Naval Conference in 1921
they proposed the total abolition of the submarine, but this received little sup
from other navies, although limits were agreed on total tonnage and gun calibre

Submarine construction continued during the 1920s, albeit at a slow p
partly due to the Washington limits, but also as a consequence of the increasi
severe financial situation. Thus, most navies built a number of small classes
"patrol" submarines, while some of the larger navies also tried to produce a "f
submarine" which would be capable of steaming at the same speed as the sur
battlefleet. In the 1920s this meant a sustained speed of 20kt, but such a
proved very elusive, requiring ever larger submarines with increasingly powe
diesels. Then, when the 20kt speed was achieved, it was discovered that the sp
of the battlefleet had increased to 28-30kt and by the early 1930s it was apprecia
that the concept was flawed and designers' turned to more productive fields.

The technical advances made during the inter-war period were steady ra
than spectacular. New steels were introduced, which, coupled with the us
welding in place of riveting, enabled diving limits to be increased and impro
watertightness, particularly in fuel tanks. Designs became more sophistica
although many navies encountered control and stability problems when
classes were introduced.

The 1930s also saw the first attempts to make revolutionary improvemen
the submerged performance of submarines. Speed and range had improved
marginally since before World War I, apart, of course, from the British R-clas
1918. The problem was attacked in the 1930s by German and Japanese design
acting quite independently of each other. The Japanese appear to have been
their No 71 was launched in 1938 and achieved an underwater speed of 2
although they seem not to have tried to find a new air-independent propulsion (
system to take full advantage of these new capabilities. The German inventor
Walter, produced equally revolutionary prototypes in the late 1920s, although
work also included propulsion systems; however, when he was nearing
operational design which was both streamlined and air-independent, his design
adapted for the diesel-electric Type XXI.

During World War II the Germans fought their Atlantic campaign with the
VII and Type IX, neither of which was outstanding in any way. However, they w
sound designs, and capable of being produced in large numbers; by May 1945 s
705 Type VIIs had been produced, of which 437 were lost in action, while of
Type IXs as many as 150 were lost. The U-boats sank large amounts of A
shipping but they were eventually defeated by a combination of surface
airborne anti-submarine warfare (ASW), coupled with the electronic wa
systems which broke the Enigma code upon which the Germans were so rel
Two other factors were also of great importance: Allied scientists stayed one

*Right: Loading a torpedo aboard a German Type VIIC which, because
limited space, could carry only 14.*

ahead of Axis scientists throughout the war, and the shipyards, particularly thos the United States, built new ships faster than the Germans could sink them.

The second great campaign was fought in the Pacific, where the Japan started with a large fleet, mainly of very large boats, of which much was expec Their overall performance, however, was disappointing, their big submarines be slow to dive, difficult to manoeuvre underwater and easy for Allied ASW force find. Their primary mission was to sink Allied warships and they certainly sar number, including 2 carriers, 10 cruisers and 10 destroyers, but never enoug cause the Americans significant concern.

The United States' submarine force was based on the excellent "fleet" bo which were large, capable, comfortable, and available in large numbers. They w ideally suited for conditions in the Pacific and by August 1945 had virtually stop movements by Japanese surface shipping. A total of 53 U.S. submarines were during the war, 45 of them in action.

British submarines also fought a hard war, but of quite a different type, s Axis merchant shipping quickly disappeared and by 1942 there were very few s targets left. The British had, therefore, to concentrate on warships and sank cruisers, 16 destroyers, 35 U-boats and many other smaller vessels.

The table shows the distribution of the world's submarine fleets at the s of World War II and makes it clear that, despite the attention paid to German U-boat fleet, the largest submarine fleets were actually operated by Soviet and Italian navies. The latter was by far the more effective, although Soviets suffered from the perennial Russian maritime problem of having operate four totally separate fleets, none of which was in a position to su another. Next came the United States, followed by France, with the Br Royal Navy ranking fifth, only just ahead of Japan. Like the Soviets, howe

British position was worse than the numbers suggest, since it had global
commitments in defence of the Empire and colonies, which meant that its
submarine fleet was spread very thinly.

World Submarine Fleets: September 1939			
Europe		United Kingdom	69
Denmark	11	USSR (approx)	150
Estonia	2	Yugoslavia	4
Finland	5		
France	77	**North America**	
Germany	65	United States	100
Greece	6		
Italy	107	**South America**	
Latvia	2	Argentina	3
Netherlands	24	Brazil	4
Norway	9	Chile	9
Poland	5	Peru	4
Portugal	4		
Romania	1	**Asia**	
Spain	9	Japan	65
Sweden	24	Siam	4
Turkey	9		

Below: Precursor of a massive fleet; Japanese No 69 built in the 1920s.

Daphne/ Havmanden-classes

DENMA

Type: patrol.

Class	Daphne-class	Havmanden-class
Total built	2	4
Completed	1926-27	1938-42
Displacement surfaced submerged	308 tons 381 tons	320 tons 402 tons
Dimensions length beam draught	160ft 9in (49.0m) 17ft 1in (5.2m) 8ft 2in (2.5m)	157ft 6in (48.0m) 15ft 5in (4.7m) 9ft 2in (2.8m)
Propulsion main engines power electric motors power shafts	2 x Burmeister & Wain 2 x 600bhp 2 x Titan 2 x 200shp two	2 x Burmeister & Wa 2 x 600bhp 2 x Brown-Boveri 2 x 225shp two
Performance speed: surface submerged	13.4kt 6.8kt	15kt 8kt
Weapons TT location guns	63 x 18in (457mm) bow – 4, stern – 2 1 x 75mm gun 1 x 20mm AA cannon	5 x 18in (450mm) bow – 3, stern – 2 2 x 40mm AA 2 x 8mm MG
Complement	25	20

History: The Royal Danish Navy was one of the smallest to maintain its submarine design and construction capabilities, having done so since 1 when the Ægir-class of 5 boats was designed and built by the R Copenhagen Dockyard in 1915-16. That was followed by the Rota-class class) three boats launched in 1918-20.

Building of the Daphne-class (D-class) started in 1924 and two were be Daphne, completed in 1926 and Dryaden completed in 1927. This wa medium-sized design and rather surprisingly carried 18in (457mm) torp tubes. It was powered by diesel engines built by a Danish company, Burme & Wain. Both boats were scuttled with the rest of the Danish submarine when the occupying German forces took control of the country on 29 Au 1943. They were raised by the Germans but did not return to service and v scrapped in 1943.

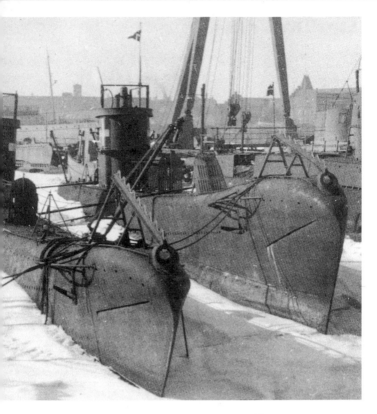

ove: Two boats of the Havmanden-class; note cable cutters.

ove: Dryaden, a Daphné-class boat, built in the 1920s.

Despite the indifference of Danish politicians to defence matters, the ·manden-class (H-class) of four submarines were completed between 1938 1940, while a fifth boat (known only as H-5) was cancelled. Two unusual tures of this design were that they had three bow tubes and they were the in any navy to be built with the outmoded 18in (457mm) tubes. Like the ·hne-class, all four were scuttled on 29 August 1943, but were later raised. scrapped.

Saukko-class

Type: inshore, patrol.
Total built: 1.
Completed: 1930
Displacement: surfaced 114 tons; submerged 142 tons.
Dimensions: length 107ft 10in (32.9m); beam 10ft 6in (3.2m); draught 9ft (2.9m).
Propulsion: 1 x Germaniawerft diesel, 200bhp; 1 x electric motor, 120shp; shaft.
Performance: surface – 10kt; submerged – 6.3kt; range surfaced 500nm at submerged 50nm at 4kt.
Weapons: 2 x 18in (457mm) TT (bow); 9 x 176lb (80kg) mines; 1 x 12.7mm r
Complement: 15.

History: The Finnish Saukko is unique among the world's submarines in ha been designed specifically to operate in a lake. Lake Ladoga (known as *Laatokk* the Finns and *Ladozhskoye Ozero* to the Russians) is the largest lake in Europe, is located northeast of St. Petersburg; it covers some 7,000 square miles (18,1C km), and is approximately 130 miles (210km) long and 80 miles (130km) w with a maximum depth of 738ft (225m). Traditionally, the northern part of lake belonged to the Grand Duchy of Finland which had been part of Russian Empire since the Napoleonic Wars but regained her independe while the Russians were preoccupied with the revolution in 1917-18. A pe treaty was later signed between Finland and the Soviet Union (Treaty of Ta 14 October 1920),one of whose conditions was that neither side could ope

---

Vesikko-class

Type: coastal.
Total built: 1.
Completed: 1933.
Displacement: surfaced 250 tons; submerged 300 tons.
Dimensions: length 134ft 2in (40.9m); beam 13ft 6in (4.1m); draught 13ft (4.2m).
Propulsion: 2 x M.W.M. diesels, 2 x 350bhp; 2 x electric motors, 2 x 180s battery 62 Tudor cells; two shafts.
Performance: surface – 13kt; submerged – 7kt; range surfaced 1,500nn 13kt, submerged 50nm at 5kt; maximum operating diving depth 300ft (91r
Weapons: 3 x 21in (533mm) TT (bow – 3); 6 x torpedoes;1 x 20mm canno
Complement: 30.

History: As early as 1930 German naval planners were considering the ty of U-boat that would be needed for rapid construction in a future war and of them, designated Project Lilliput, was a 200-250 ton boat which coulc built rapidly and in large numbers when the time came. The Germans nee a foreign navy to order one and, having tried and failed with Estonia, t suggested to the Finnish Navy that such a boat would complement t planned submarine arm, although without, of course, letting on that it merely a device for trialling a boat for the German Navy. The Finns insistec waiting until they had trialled the *Vetehinen*, but then did place an order.

The new boat was built by Crichton-Vulcan at Abo, Finland, and launched in 1932. It had three torpedo tubes, all in the bow, and was powe by two diesels from Motoren-Werke Mannheim (M.W.M.), which were alre

ove: Saukko, the only submarine designed to operate in a lake.

rships with a displacement exceeding 100 tonnes (98.4 tons) on Lake
doga.
S. produced a submarine design but the Finns did not place an order,
ssibly because they considered her to be too small to justify the
ablishment of a submarine arm. In 1929, however, the Finns placed an order
several sea-going boats and decided to include one of these smaller boats
heir plans. Thus an order was placed for one boat to an improved design now
signated Pu-110, which was built by Hietelahden Laivatelakka in Helsinfors
d launched in July 1930. She was commissioned in late 1930 and named
ukko, being the smallest true submarine in any navy at the time.

Once built, it transpired that the displacement of *Saukko* was actually 116
nes surfaced and 144 tonnes submerged, so much in excess of the limit that
Finns decided not to annoy their far larger neighbour and Saukko never
nt to the lake, but she found plenty of employment in the Baltic, being
nstantly employed against Soviet forces between 1939 and 1944. She was
cken in 1947 and scrapped in 1953.

*ght: The
nish
ssikko
s the
ototype*

*rmany's
e IIA.*

roduction for the R-class motor-minesweepers. The Germans provided the
trials team and took the boat to Germany for its "designers' testing" which
ed some two years. Indeed, they even went so far as to prolong the trial
iod in order that the boat could be used to instruct officers attending the
rman Navy's first submarine engineering course since 1918. There were two
ults of this subterfuge, the first being that *Vesikko* was not commissioned
the Finnish Navy until 1936. The longer term outcome, however, was that
design for what was to become the new German Navy's Type IIA had been
d and tested and was ready as soon as Hitler gave the go-ahead for U-boat
struction to restart.

Vesikko was employed in the Baltic throughout World War II and was
cken in 1947 when, in the peace treaty with Russia, Finland was banned
m operating any submarines at all. However, the boat was retained as a
morial and remains on display in Finland.

Requin-class

Type: ocean-going attack/reconnaissance.
Total built: 9.
Completed: 1925-28.
Displacement: surfaced 947 tons; submerged 1,441 tons.
Dimensions: length 256ft 8in (78.25m); beam 22ft 5in (6.8m); draught 16ft 8in (5.1
Propulsion: 2 x Sulzer/Schneider diesels, 2 x 1,450bhp; 2 x electric motors
x 900shp;
Performance: surface – 15kt; submerged – 9kt; range surfaced 6,400nm
12kt, submerged 70nm at 5kt; maximum operating diving depth 250ft (80m
Weapons: 10 x 21.7in (550mm) TT (bow – 4, stern – 2, external 2 x 2); 1
torpedoes; 1 x 3.9in (100mm) gun, 2 x 8mm MG.
Complement: 51.

History: This was the French Navy's first post-World War I subma
programme and took advantage not only of the staff studies of the war but a
of detailed physical examination of the 10 German U-boats handed over
France in 1920 as reparations. With this class three missions appeared wh
were to recur in the French Navy in the inter-war years: scouting for the ba
fleet, long-range anti-shipping attacks, and colonial service.

These double-hulled boats were large by the standards of the time, and
a particularly heavy torpedo armament consisting of no fewer than 10 torp
tubes and 16 torpedoes. There were four tubes in the bow, two in the st
and two pairs in rotating mounts on the upper casing. The latter, which wer
be fitted in most French submarines over the following 20 years, could

600-tonnes type

Type: patrol (*sous-marins de moyenne patrouille*).

Class	Sirene-class	Ariane-class	Circe-class
Total built	4	4	4
Completed	1926-27	1926-2	1926-28
Displacement surfaced submerged	609 tons 757 tons	626 tons 787 tons	615 tons 776 tons
Dimensions length beam draught	209ft 11in (64.0m) 17ft 1in (5.2m) 14ft 1in (4.3m)	216 ft 6in (66.0m) 20ft 4in (6.2m) 13ft 6in (4.1m)	204ft 11in (62.5 20ft 4in (6.2m) 13ft 1in (4.0m)
Propulsion main engines power electric motors power shafts	2 x Sulzer 2 x 650bhp 2 2 x 500shp two	2 x Normand 2 x 625bhp 2 2 x 500shp two	2 x Schneider 2 x 625bhp 2 2 x 500shp two

*ight: Narval,
*ne of the first
*ubmarines
*uilt by France
fter the war.

tated by mechanical linkages from inside the pressure hull, whether on the
rface or submerged. In effect, they gave the beam-launching capability the
itish had sought in their fixed tubes (see E-class) but without the excessive
am, although they could not, of course, be reloaded at sea. Once in service
e Requin-class proved to have poor handling characteristics and also suffered
om the problem which afflicted so many submarines intended to cooperate
th the battle fleet – a lack of speed. They also suffered from unreliable
achinery and cramped bridges, both problems being addressed in major refits
the mid-1930s.

Narval and *Morse* were sunk by mines in 1940, and *Souffleur* was sunk by
e British submarine HMS *Parthian* (25 June 1941). *Caiman*, having been
uttled and recovered, was finally sunk in a USAAF bombing raid on Toulon on
March 1944. Four were seized by the Germans on 8 December 1942 and
ere handed over to the Italians, who commissioned them as *FR-111* (ex-
oque), *FR-113* (ex-Requin), *FR-114* (ex-Espadon) and *FR-115* (ex-Dauphin)
d set about converting them to the transport role. The only one of these to
completed was *FR-111*, which was sunk by Allied aircraft while on a
supply run to the Italian island of Lampedusa (28 February 1943) while the
her three were scuttled on 9 September 1943. *Marsouin* survived the war to
scrapped in 1946.

erformance			
eed: surface		14kt	
ubmerged		7.5kt	
nge: surfaced		2,300nm/3kt	
ubmerged		75nm/5kt	
aximum			
ving depth		256ft (80m)	
eapons			
cation		7 x 21.7in (550mm) bow – 1, external fixed, forward – 2, external fixed, aft – 2, external rotating – 2,	
rpedoes		8	
uns		1 x 3in (76mm) 2 x 8mm AA MG	
omplement	41	41	41

story: The French Navy tried a procurement experiment with the 600
nne-class by issuing an operational requirement and a set of general
ecifications to three shipbuilders and leaving it to them to design and
ild four boats each. All three designs were considered to be reasonably
tisfactory, being manoeuvrable both on the surface and when
bmerged, but with a curiously dispersed torpedo armament. This
nsisted of one internal tube in the bow and two fixed tubes on the upper
sing, facing forward. There were also two fixed external tubes in the

stern and a pair of tubes on a rotating, external mount. Thus, there we
seven tubes with torpedoes immediately available to launch, but on
one reload (for the bow tube). Armament was a single deck gun; th
was 3in (76mm) in most boats, but 4in (102mm) in some.

All three designs were based on that of the German UB-III and each ye
employed a well-known submarine designer as a consultant: AC de la Loi
Nantes (Sirene-class) – Simonot; Augustin-Normand (Ariane-class)
Fenaux; and Schneider (Circe-class) – Laubeuf. The double-hull, a featu
inherited from the UB-III, resulted in cramped working conditions for t
crew and slow diving characteristics, while although the machinery w

Katsonis/
Proteus classes

FRANCE (GREEC

Type: medium-range, patrol.

History: These six submarines represented a major expansion of the Gre
Navy's submarine arm, which since 1912 had consisted of just two sm
boats, *Delfin* and *Xiphias*. The first order was for two boats, Schneid
Laubeuf designs, based on that of the 600-ton Circe-class (see previo
entry). These were fairly conventional designs, but with the unusual Fren
combination of internal and external torpedo tubes which prevailed in t
1920s and 1930s. In this case, the Greek boats (*Katsonis, Papamicolis*) h
four externally mounted tubes, two in the bows and two in the stern, whi
could not be reloaded at sea, and only two internal tubes in the bows
which just one reload was carried. The design differed from that of t
French boats in having a rather large bridge tower, with the 3.9in (100m
gun mounted on a rotating platform at its forward end, a design featu
which appears to have originated with the British Royal Navy and wh
was intended to enable the gun-crew to get the weapon into action wit
minimum of delay after surfacing.

The four-strong Proteus-class (*Glavkos, Nereus, Proteus, Triton*) we
ordered about a year after the two Katsonis-class. These new boats wer
Loire-Simonot design, and were slightly larger, which enabled a much mo
operationally effective armament to be carried, consisting of eight torpe
tubes, six in the bow and two in the stern, all mounted internally, with tv

fferent in each of the types it was generally unreliable.

Ondine was sunk by a merchant ship in 1928 and *Nymphe* was paid off 1938, but the remainder were refitted in 1937-38 and on the outbreak of orld War II the 10 boats formed the largest single group of medium-range bmarines in the French Navy. *Doris* was torpedoed and sunk by *U-9* (9 ay 1940). Most of the remainder were scuttled at Toulon on 27 November 42; a few of these were then raised, only to be bombed by the Allies. ne survived the war.

elow: Sirene, the first of 12 French "600-tonne" types.

ove: French-built Papamicolis; note high gun position.

oads. Also, the 3.9in gun mounting was brought down from the forward d of the bridge tower and mounted on the casing.

During World War II all six submarines escaped from Greece and

Class	Katsonis	Proteus
Total built	2	4
Completed	1927	1927-28
Displacement surfaced submerged	605 tons 778 tons	750 tons 960 tons
Dimensions length beam draught	204ft 9in (62.4m) 17ft 6in (5.3m) 11ft 0in (3.4m)	225ft 0in (68.6m) 18ft 10in (5.7m) 13ft 8in (4.2m)

thereafter operated under British direction. *Katsonis* was rammed and su
in the Aegean by a German submarine-chaser (14 September 1943), b
Papamicolis survived the war, only to be stricken in 1946. Three of t
Proteus-class were war losses: two were sunk by Axis surface warship
Proteus (19 December 1940) and *Triton* (16 November 1942) – wł
Glavkos was sunk by bombs in Malta harbour (4 April 1942). *Nere*
survived, but was stricken immediately after the war.

1,500-tonnes type

FRAN

Type: ocean-going (*sous-marins de grand patrouille*).
Total built: 31.Series 1 – 19; Series 2 – 6; Series 3 – 6.
Completed: Series 1 – 1928-31; Series 2 – 1931-35; Series 3 – 1934-37.
Displacement: surfaced 1,570 tons; submerged 2,084 tons.
Dimensions: length 302ft 10in (92.3m); beam 26ft 11in (8.2m); draught 15ft 5in (4.7m).
Propulsion: 2 x Schneider/Sulzer diesels, 2 x 3,00bhp; 2 x electric motors, 2 x 1,000shp; two shafts.
Performance: surface – 17kt; submerged – 10kt; range surfaced 10,000nm at 10kt, submerged 100nm at 5kt; maximum operating diving depth 250ft (76m).
Weapons: 9 x 21.7in (550mm) TT, 11 x torpedoes; 2 x 15.7in (400mm), 2 x torpedoes; 1 x 3.9in (100mm) gun, 2 x 13.2mm AA MG (1 x 2) (see text).
Complement: 61.
Specifications for Series 1, as built.

History: Like the American and British navies, the French Navy (*Mar*

ropulsion		
main engines	2 x Schneider-Carels	2 x Sulzer
ower	2 x 650bhp	2 x 710bhp
ectric motors	2	2
ower	2 x 500shp	2 x 600shp
hafts	two	two
erformance		
peed: surface	14kt	14kt
ubmerged	9.5kt	9.5kt
nge: surfaced	1,500nm/10kt	1,500nm/10kt
ubmerged	100nm/5kt	100nm/5kt
aximum		
vingdepth	2,760ft (850m)	270ft (85m)
Veapons		
T	6 x 21in (533mm)	8 x 21in (533mm)
cation	bow – 4, stern – 2	bow – 6, stern – 2
rpedoes	7	10
uns	1 x 3.9in (100mm)	1 x 3.9in (100mm)
	1 x 3pdr (76mm) AA	1 x 3pdr (76mm) AA
omplement	39	41

ove: 1,500-tonnes type submarine of the **Marine Nationale.**

Nationale) was fascinated by the idea of a "fleet submarine" (*sous-ma d'escadre*), which would be able to keep pace with the battle fleet, act scouts and, if the opportunity arose, attack units of the enemy battle fle The project began in 1914, but became of greater importance in the 192 when the most likely enemy was perceived as being Italy and the possibil of a clash between the two nations' battle fleets was something for whi French naval planners had to prepare. As with the other navies, the targ speed for the submarine was 20kt and the problem lay in obtaini sufficient power from the propulsion system; the British had used steam their K-class (qv) but the French, despite their own long experience w steam submarines, decided to turn instead to the diesel. It was known th the German company M.A.N. had been planning a 3,000bhp diesel at t end of World War I and various French manufacturers were tasked w achieving similar power levels.

The outcome was the 1,500-tonnes-type, which was produced in thr versions: Series 1 – Redoutable-class, 19 boats; Series 2 – L'Espoire-cla 6 boats; and Series 3 – Agosta-class (6 boats). The later two series had t same hull and weapons as Series 1, but differed in their power systems the designers struggled to attain the magic figure of 20kt. Thus, in Series two 3,000bhp diesels produced a speed of 17kt and in Series 2 this w increased to 3,600bhp and 19kt, while in Series 3 power output w 4,000bhp. Thus, the figure of 20kt was reached at last, although the Fren knew that stretching an engine to its limits reduced its overall life a increased the unreliability problem, so a peacetime limit of 75 per ce power was set, which reduced speed to a maximum of 15kt.

Armament comprised 11 torpedo tubes. There were four 21.

630-tonnes type

FRAN

Type: patrol (*sous-marins de deuxième classe*).

History: These 22 boats belonged to four distinct groups, the first three Argonaute-, Diane- and Orion-classes – being further examples of the policy issuing a specification to private yards and then allowing them to produce th own designs. The fourth was the Minerve-class, which was designed to same specification by the official French Navy design bureau, S.T.C.N.; her its alternative name, the Amirauté-type (admiralty-type). These were outcome of a specification for a slightly larger and improved successor to 600-tonnes type, and three yards were awarded contracts. Hulls and armame were essentially similar, but propulsion was different. The Argonaute-class w a Schneider-Laubeuf design and consisted of six boats, all built by Schneid and powered by two-stroke Schneider-Carels diesels. The Diane-class wa Normand-Feneux design, powered by four-stroke Normand-Vickers diese nine boats were built at two different yards. The Orion-class consisted of j two boats; it was a Loire-Dubigeon design, powered by two-stroke Sul diesels; two were built at different yards.

Armament comprised six 21.7in (550mm) torpedo tubes, with three in the bows, one internal with a single reload, and two outside the pressure hull. There were a further two tubes in a trainable mounting on the upper deck, immediately abaft the tower. Finally, there was a second trainable mounting at the stern, which carried one 21in tube in the centre, flanked by two 15.7in (400mm) tubes.

50mm) tubes forward, mounted internally, with another three 21.7in 50mm) tubes in a rotating mount on the upper deck immediately abaft the er gun position. As in other French classes, this could be trained from ide the boat, but could not be reloaded at sea. There was a second ating mount right aft which contained four torpedo tubes, two for the avyweight 20.7in (550mm) torpedoes, and two for the new 15.7in 0mm) torpedo. This had been developed because naval planners nsidered that a 550mm torpedo would provide an unnnecessary degree overkill against small surface targets, although wartime experience would ow that it was a most unreliable system and in 1943-44 surviving boats d their stern quadruple mount replaced by a triple 21.7in (550mm) mount.

Two boats, *Prométhée* and *Phénix*, were lost in pre-war accidents, ving 29 at the outbreak of war, but their story is a sad one. Four were uttled at Brest on 18 June 1940 and 10 were destroyed during Allied acks on French colonial possessions under Vichy control. Seven were uttled at Toulon on 27 November 1942, although some were later covered, only to be destroyed by Allied bombing. *Sfax* was torpedoed in or by a German U-boat (19 December 1940) and *Protée* was sunk by rman patrol boats in December 1943. The remainder survived the war d were broken up in the early 1950s.

A much improved, successor class was under construction at the start the war. First-of-class *Roland Morillot* was ordered in 1934, followed by econd in 1937 and three more in 1938, with another 11 planned, but such s the slow pace of submarine construction that only three were laid wn by the time of the German attack in June 1940 and all were destroyed the ways.

e boats also included many minor improvements, including hydraulically erated (as opposed to electric) control surfaces, enhanced underwater bility, and a general tidying up of the exterior which resulted in an increase underwater speed to 9kt.

The French Admiralty's own design, the Minerve-class, brought together e best points of the three earlier 630-tonnes designs. In addition, the nament was considerably improved. In the bows the number of tubes was reased from three to four, and all were internal. The stern trainable mounting s deleted and replaced by two internally mounted 21.7in (550mm) tubes. ally, the midships trainable mounting was retained, but all tubes were of the nter 14.7in (450mm) type. The Minerve-class was powered by four-stroke rmand-Vickers diesels, which had proved better than the two-stroke Sulzer d Schneider-Carels types.

All were in service at the time of the outbreak of war. In the Argonaute-

low: Junon, after post-war refit; the gun has been removed.

Class	Argonaute-class	Diane-class	Orion-class	Minerve-clas
Total built	5	9	2	6
Completed	1930-33	1930-33	1931	1935-39
Displacement surfaced submerged	630 tons 798 tons	571 tons 809 tons	558 tons 787 tons	662 tons 856 tons
Dimensions length beam draught	208ft 0in (63.4m) 21ft 0in (6.4m) 13ft 10in (42m)	211 ft 4in (64.4m) 20ft 4in (6.2m) 14ft 1in (4.3m)	219ft 0in(66.8m) 20ft 4in (6.2m) 14ft 5in (4.0m)	223ft 5in (68.1 18ft 5in (5.6m 13ft 3in (4.0m
Propulsion main engines power electric motors power shafts	2 x Schneider-Carels 2 x 650bhp 2 2 x 500shp two	2 x Normand 2 x 700bhp 2 2 x 500shp two	2 x Sulzer 2 x 700bhp 2 2 x 500shp two	2 x Norman 2 x 900bhp 2 2 x 615shp two

class, the nameship was sunk by depth charges (8 November 1942) and remainder survived, only to be broken-up in 1946. In the Diana-class La Sib was believed to have been sunk in error by a German U-boat, four were scutt and one beached itself during the Allied invasion of North Africa, and th survived, to be scrapped in 1946. The two boats of the Orion-class both join the Free French Navy in Britain and were cannibalised for spares for Junon a Minerve, and then scrapped in 1943. In the Minerve-class, three were scutt

Type IA-class

Type: ocean-going patrol.
Total built: 2.
Completed: 1937.
Displacement: surfaced 862 tons; submerged 983 tons.
Dimensions: length 237ft 6in (72.4m); beam 20ft 5in (6.2m); draught 14ft (4.3m).
Propulsion: 2 x 8-cylinder, 4-stroke M.A.N. diesels, 2 x 1,400bhp; 2 x B electric motors, 2 x 500shp; battery 2 x 62 cells; two shafts.
Performance: surface – 17.8kt; submerged – 8.3kt; range surfaced 6,700nm 12kt, submerged 78nm at 4kt; maximum operating diving depth 328ft (100r
Weapons: 6 x 21in (533mm) TT (bow – 4, stern – 2), 14 x torpedoes; 105mm gun, 1 x 20mm AA cannon.
Complement: 43.

History: The decision to rebuild the U-boat arm was taken in late 1932 and designs were designated Motorenversuchsboote (M.W.B. = experimer

Performance	
Speed: surface	14kt
submerged	9kt
Range: surfaced	4,000nm/10kt
submerged	85nm/5kt
Maximum	
diving depth	256ft (80m)
Weapons	
Location	6 x 21.7in (550mm)
Torpedoes	(see notes)
Guns	1 x 3in (76mm)
	1 x MG (Minerve-class – 2)
Complement	41

November 1942, one was wrecked in September 1945, and two survived to broken up in the early 1950s.

The Aurore-class was the culmination of the 600/630-tonne series, being a much improved version of the Minerve-class, and it was planned to build a total of 15, but the war intervened. Only *Aurore* had been completed the time of France's capitulation in June 1940 and she was scuttled at Toulon.

La Creole was fitting out and was towed to the UK where she lay incomplete until 1946 when she was returned to France and completed. Four were captured incomplete by the Germans; three of these were given German naval numbers, but only one, *UF-2* (ex-*La Favorite*), was commissioned into the *Kriegsmarine* on 5 November 1940; she was decommissioned in June 1944 and scuttled at Gotenhafen in May 1945. Post-war, the five surviving boats were completed to a revised design and served until the 1960s when they were scrapped. The Aurore-class was larger than the Minerve-class, with a 1,170 ton submerged displacement, an overall length of 241ft 2in (73.5m) and nine 21.7in (550mm) torpedo tubes.

Above: Type IA-class **U-25** *sank six ships before being lost with all hands 3 August 1940, possibly after hitting a mine.*

motor boats).The larger of the two original designs, the Type I was based on the *E1* built for Spain and later sold to Turkey (see Gür-class). With a displacement of 983 tons, the Type I was considered large by the German

Navy, although it was modest compared to contemporary boats such as the British T-class (1,575 tons) and the U.S. Salmon-class (2,210 tons). Externally, the design showed evidence of German World War I practice, including the serrated cablecutter in the bows, the large bridge and the single 4.1in (105mm) gun, but there were major advances internally, including an all-welded pressure hull and 21in (533mm) torpedo tubes, thus adopting the *de facto* international standard for the first time in a U-boat.

U-25 and *U-26* entered service in 1937 and were soon relegated to training duties, but they were reinstated as *frontboote* (operational boats) as soon as war broke out. *U-25* carried out one successful Atlantic voyage, which included refuelling at supposedly neutral Cadiz; five merchant ships were sunk. She later took part in the invasion of Norway but was lost with all hands on 3 August 1940, possibly to a mine. *U-26* also went into the Atlantic, but after sinking three merchant ships and damaging a fourth it was attacked by British ASW forces. She surfaced and, the crew having abandoned ship, the boat was scuttled; all 48 crew members were rescued.

Type II-class

GERMA

Type: coastal patrol.

	Type IIA	Type IIB	Type IIC	Type IID
Total built	6	20	8	16
Completed	1936	1936-40	1938-39	1940
Displacement surfaced submerged	259 tons 301 tons	279 tons 329 tons	291 tons 341 tons	314 tons 364 tons
Dimensions length beam draught	134ft 2in (40.9m) 13ft 4in (4.1m) 12ft 6in (3.8m)	140 ft 1in (42.7m) 13ft 5in (4.1m) 12ft 9in (4.0m)	144ft 0in (43.9m) 13ft 5in (4.1m) 12ft 6in (3.8m)	144ft 4in (44.0 16ft 5in (5.0m 12ft 9in (3.9m
Propulsion main engines power electric motors power battery shafts	2 x M.W.M. 350bhp 2 x S.S.W. 2 x 180shp 62 cells two	2 x M.W.M. 350bhp 2 x S.S.W. 2 x 180shp 62 cells two	2 x M.W.M. 350bhp 2 x S.S.W. 2 x 205shp 62 cells two	2 x M.W.M 350bhp 2 x S.S.W. 2 x 205shp 62 cells two

ove: U-26, second of two Type IAs commissioned in 1937.

rformance				
eed: surface	13kt	13kt	12kt	13kt
omerged	6.9kt	7kt	7kt	7.4kt
ge: surfaced	2,000nm/8kt	3,900nm/8kt	4,200nm/8kt	3,200nm/12.7kt
omerged	35nm/4kt	35nm/4kt	35nm/4kt	56nm/4kt
ximum				
ing depth	328ft (100m)	328ft (100m)	328ft (100m)	256ft (80m)
eapons				
ation		3 x 21in (533mm)		
pedoes		bow		
ns		6		
		1 x 20mm AA twin		
mplement		25		

tory: The Type IIA was virtually identical to the Vesikko-class (qv) built for Finland , although designated the second of the two new designs, the Type II was ally the first to be built. This was done in great secrecy and the programme was ealed only with the signing of the Anglo-German Naval Treaty. The Type IIA was ngle hull boat, but had an all-welded hull (unlike the Vessiko-class which had a ted hull) and was fitted internally to launch the latest G7a and G7e 21in (533mm) edoes. Work started on the Type IIB before the first Type IIA was launched, the n aim being to increase the range by adding three new frames in the hull and ing a new oil bunker beneath the control room. The Type IIC had a further two nes to improve facilities in the radio room and to accommodate a second scope. The Type IID was generally similar to the Type IIC but had saddle tanks, which were used as self-compensating fuel tanks, thus increasing range yet ag and enabling these boats to operate around the Western coast of the British Is Kort nozzles (a shroud around the propellers) were also fitted and although t seem to have worked well enough they were not adopted on other U-boat class Two Type IIBs were being built for the Chinese Navy when war broke out and w immediately seized and incorporated into the German Navy.

These boats were nicknamed *Einbäume* (dug-out canoes) by their crews, f their small size and very heavy rolling on the surface. They were primarily inten to train the many crews needed for the resurrected U-boat arm, but had to

Below: U-22, Type IIB, with 20mm mounted from 1943 .

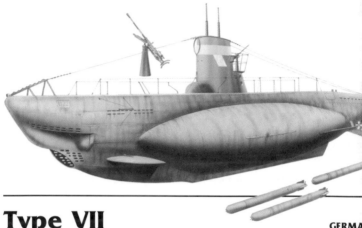

Type VII

GERMA

Type: ocean-going attack.

History: The Type VII is one of the most important designs in the history of the submarine, a total of 709 of all sub-types having been built between *U-27* (commissioned 12 August 1936) and *U-1308* (commissioned 17 January 1945). Although produced in such large numbers, and despite its great influence on the war at sea, the Type VII was by no means the best submarine of its era, nor was any aspect of its performance truly outstanding. Instead, it was an adequate compromise and its greatest attribute was that it could take the trade war well out into the Atlantic, having adequate range, armament and seaworthiness. It was also relatively easy to build and required a fairly small crew, although it should be noted that they lived in very cramped conditions, which became increasingly unpleasant as each voyage progressed.

Type VIIA. All Type VIIs followed the general pattern of the Type VIIA, a single-hull design with saddle-tanks,

Right: U-402, Type VIIC, before launch. Note saddle-tanks, twin rudders, canoe stern.

ove: Type IIBs were known as "dug-out canoes".

ssed into service in 1939-40 to overcome the desperate shortage of *frontboote* erational boats). Six Type IIBs were transferred to the Black Sea in 1942, which olved them being dismantled and mounted on pontoons, enabling them to move river and canal to Dresden in southern Germany. From there they went by road ngolstadt in Austria, where they were again loaded onto pontoons and moved vn the Danube to Galati in Romania. Here they were reassembled and handed r to their crews, who took them on the final leg to Constanza on the Black Sea. vas an epic achievement by any standard.

Fifty Type IIs were built, of which 11 were lost in combat: aircraft – two, marines – 2; mines – 2; surface ships – 5. Four were lost in training accidents, were stricken in 1944, and five were scuttled in the Black Sea. That left 25 in vice at the end of the war, of which 21 were scuttled in German waters and four nt to the UK where they were sunk in Operation Deadlight.

Class	Type VIIA	Type VIIB	Type VIIC	Type VIIC/
Total built	6	20	8	16
Completed	10	24	577	88
Displacement surfaced submerged	626 tons 745 tons	753 tons 857 tons	761 tons 865 tons	759 tons 860 tons
Dimensions length beam draught	211ft 7in (64.5m) 19ft 0in (5.8m) 14ft 4in (4.4m)	218ft 2in (66.5m) 20ft 3in (6.2m) 15ft 5in (4.7m)	220ft 1in (67.1m) 20ft 4in (6.2m) 15ft 8in (4.8m)	220ft 5in (67.2 20ft 4in (6.2m 15ft 8in (4.8m
Propulsion main engines power electric motors power battery shafts	2 2 x 1,160bhp 2 2 x 375shp 2 x 62 cells two	2 2 x 1,400bhp 2 2 x 375shp 2 x 62 cells two	2 2 x 1,400bhp 2 2 x 375shp 2 x 62 cells two	2 2 x 1,400bh 2 2 x 375shp 2 x 62 cells two

Below: U-55, a Type VIIB, slightly longer than Type VIIA.

rformance				
eed: surface	16kt	17.2kt	17.2kt	13kt
bmerged	8kt	8kt	7.6kt	7.4kt
ge: surfaced	4,300nm/8kt	6,500nm/12kt	6,500nm/12kt	6,500nm/12kt
bmerged	90nm/4kt	90nm/4kt	80nm/4kt	80nm/4kt
aximum				
ving depth	328ft (100m)	328ft (100m)	328ft (100m)	394ft (120m)
eapons				
:ation	5 x 21in (533mm)	5 x 21in (533mm)	5 x 21in (533mm)	5 x 21in (533mm)
	bow – 4, stern – 1	bow – 4, stern – 1	bow – 4, stern – 1	bow – 4, stern – 1
pedoes	11	14	14	14
ns	1 x 88mm	1 x 88mm	1 x 88mm	1 x 88mm
	1 x 20mm AA	1 x 20mm AA	1 x 20mm AA	1 x 20mm AA
mplement	44			

h six internal watertight compartments, and specially strengthened kheads at each end of the control room. There were five torpedo tubes, four he bows and one, externally mounted, aft. Ten of these boats were built by Weser (6) and Germania (4), being commissioned between July 1936 and il 1937.

e VIIB. The first Type VIIA was tested against the first Type IA (qv) and was clear winner, although various improvements were suggested, which led to Type VIIB. These included lengthening the hull by 6.6ft (2m), increasing the

capacity of the saddle tanks in order to give more fuel and thus greater ran and fitting superchargers to the engines. The single rudder was replaced twin rudders, one behind each propeller, which not only improv manoeuverability but also enabled the stern torpedo tube to be resited wit the pressure hull, a much more satisfactory arrangement. The torpedo load v also increased by three, a most important advance since many wartime patr were to be ended due to running out of torpedoes.

Type VIIC. The VIIB solved most of the shortcomings of the VIIA, but sim did not have the space for new electronic devices coming into service, so hull was lengthened yet again, the space inside the conning-tower v increased, and more fuel tanks were added. Other changes included a n diesel-oil filtration system, a new air compressor and an updated electr control system. As there was no increase in engine power, the result was t the Type VIIC was slightly slower and had less range than the VIIB.

Type VIIC/41. Once combat experience began to be gained it became clear that Type VIIC had a number of shortcomings and, in particular, that it did not have speed and seakeeping ability to catch up with fleeing targets, while increased de would enable the boats to escape from more ASW attacks. A major we reduction programme pared some 11.5 tons off the weight, although 10 of th tons saved was immediately lost when it was decided to increase the thicknes the pressure hull, but this enabled the normal operating depth to be increase 394ft (120m), a very significant operational gain. The seakeeping requirement v met by lengthening the bow by 5in (13cm) and widening the foredeck. Th changes did not warrant a new sub-type designation, so the modified boat v termed the Type VIIC/41, the figures indicating that the decision to procure modified boat had been made in 1941.

Others. There were several more projects which never reached product including the Type VIIC/42 which would have had a longer hull, more powe engines and a greater diameter pressure hull. The Type VIIC/43 was a T VIIC/42 but with much heavier armament. Two types that did reach product were the Type VIID minelayer and the Type VIIF transport; the Type VIIE v

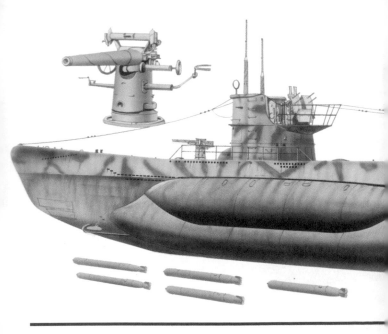

ended to test an experimental lightweight diesel, but never got beyond the wing-board.

nversions. Inevitably in a type produced in such vast numbers, there were merous in-service conversions and modifications. One of the most serious eats facing the Type VIICs was air attack by the increasingly aggressive Allied and naval forces, to which one answer was improved AA protection. Thus ere were at least eight "bridge conversions" which mounted a variety of AA apons on or around the bridge. Such additional platforms and weapons sulted in longer diving times and a loss in submerged speed and noeuvrability. These bridge conversions were intended to improve individual boats' self-defence, but there were also *flak* U-boats, which were intended provide an aggressive air defence umbrella for a group of U-boats (eg, when dezvousing with a supply boat) and involved several extensive platforms for quadruple 20mm mounts and a single 37mm. Two boats were converted d one was sent to sea but it quickly became apparent that the concept of ghting it out on the surface" was flawed and work on five more ceased and boats were returned to normal duties.

The Type VII was at the forefront of the U-boat battle in the North and central antic, in the Mediterranean, and in the Arctic, and sank by far the greatest portion of Allied shipping. *U-30* (Lemp) sank the liner *Athenia* on 3 September 39, the first day of the war, in which 118 people, including 28 U.S. citizens, were d. *U-48,* a Type VIIB, was the most successful submarine of World War II. tween September 1939 and June 1941 (when it was transferred to training ies) it undertook 13 operations, spending 291 days at sea under three captains, ing which it sank 51 ships with a total tonnage of 310,407.

The Type VII remained in production until the final months of the war, but it d been gradually phased out in favour of the new *electroboote,* the Types XXI d XXIII. In retrospect, it is surprising that the Germans did not consider a ically modernised version of the Type VII, as the U.S. Navy did with its

ow: Type VIIC with naval 88mm gun and quad 20mm flak.

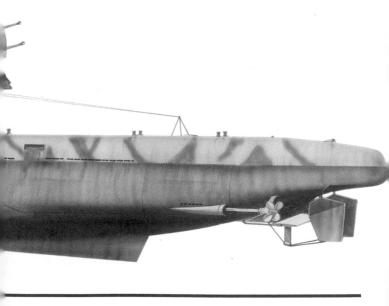

Guppy-series boats (qv) and the British with their modernised A- and T-classes (qqv). Both these navies showed how, by increasing battery power, deleting drag-creating protuberances and generally streamlining the hull, a much faster and more efficient boat could be produced at relatively small expense and with little technical risk. One particular shortcoming of the Garman design was its small size and as Admiral Dönitz sent his boats further across the Atlantic resupply of fuel, torpedoes and food became an increasingly severe problem; they left port literally stuffed solid, but resupply became inevitable and as this was a time-consuming process which could only be done on the surface they laid themselves open to attacks by Allied aircraft and ships.

No fewer than 437 Type VIIs were lost in action and a further number were lost in accidents or during Allied bombing of ports and harbours. At the end of the war a large number were scuttled, but even so there were a many surviving boats, of which a small number were transferred to Allied navies and the others were sunk in the British Operation Deadlight.

Right: Type VIIC returns to Narvik, Norway, after a series of attacks on Convoy PQ-17.

Type IX

Type: long-range attack.

History: The origin of the Type IX lay in a 1935 requirement for a long-range boat capable of fast transits to and from distant operational areas, with g endurance and a substantial load of weapons, fuel and supplies. The result Germany's second most numerous class of U-boat, with 236 built in seven s types. Start point for the Type IX design was the Type IA (qv), which itself been based on the World War I *U-81* design (qv). It was a fully double-hu boat with a wide, flat upper deck, one of whose benefits was that it g storage space for 10 torpedoes in watertight containers. There were four n variants.

Type IXA. The original version, of which eight were built in two four-b batches.

Type IXB. This had fuel bunkerage increased from 154 to 165 tons, wh increased range to 12,000nm. 14 were built.

Type IXC. Further evolutionary development with increased fuel bunkerag 208 tons. A total of 54 were built.

Type IXC/40. A variant of the -C sub-type and by far the most numerous to into service, the Type IXC/40 resulted from the designers managing to cre yet further space for fuel bunkers, increasing the total to 214 tons and rang 11,400nm at 12kt. This led to orders for 163, but only 95 were laid down which 87 were actually commissioned.

Type IXD. Very long-range, with IXD1 maximised for speed and IXD2 for rar All IXDs had a longer pressure hull than earlier versions. IXD1 was built a cargo boat with six fast diesels. Two were built but were unsuccessful, b

above: U-532, Type IXC, surrenders at Liverpool, England.

Class	Type IXA/B*	Type IXC - C/40**	Type IXD2 -IXD/42*
Total built	22	141	29
Completed	1938-40	1940-44	1941-44
Displacement surfaced submerged	1,032 tons 1,153 tons	1,120 tons 1,232 tons	1,616 tons 1,804 tons
Dimensions length beam draught	251ft 0in (76.5m) 21ft40in (6.5m) 15ft 5in (4.7m)	252ft 0in (76.8m) 22ft 4in (6.8m) 15ft 5in (4.7m)	287ft 5in (87.6m) 24ft 7in (7.5m) 17ft 8in (5.4m)
Propulsion main engines power cruise engines power electric motors power battery shafts	2 x M.A.N. 2 x 2,200bhp 2 x S.S.W. 2 x 500shp 2 x 62 cells two	2 x M.A.N. 2 x 2,200bhp 2 x .S.S.W. 2 x 500shp 2 x 62 cells two	2 x M.A.N. 2 x 2,200bhp 2 x M.W.M. 2 x 580bhp 2 x M.W.M. 2 x 580shp 2 x 62 cells two

Below: Type IXC with 105mm deck gun forward, 37mm aft.

rformance			
eed: surface	18.2kt	18.3kt	19.2kt
bmerged	7.7kt	7.3kt	6.9kt
nge: surfaced	8,100nm/12kt	11,000nm/12kt	23,700nm/12kt
bmerged	65nm/4kt	63nm/4kt	57nm/4kt
aximum			
ving depth	492ft (150m)	492ft (150m)	492ft (150m)
eapons			
	6 x 21in (533mm)	6 x 21in (533mm)	6 x 21in (533mm)
cation	bow – 4, stern – 2	bow – 4, stern – 2	bow – 4, stern – 2
rpedoes	22	22	24
ns	1 x 105mm	1 x 105mm	1 x 105mm
	1 x 37mm	1 x 37mm	1 x 37mm
	1 x 20mm AA	1 x 20mm AA	1 x 20mm AA
rcraft	–	–	1 x Focke-Achgelis Fa-330
mplement	48	48	57

etails are for Type IXA
Details are for Type IXC
Details are for Type IXD2

converted to normal diesels. The Type IXD2 had the same hull as Type IXD1
the propulsion system comprised two supercharged M.A.N. 9-cylinder, 4-str
diesels, as in Type IXC, but with two additional M.W.M. 6-cylinder, 4-str
unsupercharged diesels. The normal arrangement on the surface was to
the larger M.A.N. diesels to recharge the battery or for high-speed, and
smaller M.W.M. engines to power the boat in the cruise regime. Type IXD
incorporated minor changes from Type IXD2 but only one was comple
before production switched to Type XXI. The Type IXD2 carried a single Foc
Achgelis Fa-330 rotary kite, which was stored in a cylinder on the bridge
was used to extend the observation range, particularly in the southern Atla
and Indian Oceans, but it proved of very limited value.

Variations. Most of the later boats were fitted with *schnorchels* and some
extra radio masts. The Type IX's diving speed was slow by later war standa
and in an effort to overcome this some Type IXC/40s had the forward sec
of the upper casing narrowed; this reduced the crash-dive time but also
down the number of reload torpedoes that could be carried.

A total of 145 Type Is were lost at sea due to enemy action: aircraft –
surface ships – 58, submarines – five, mines – eight, and captured – one
further five were lost at sea, one as a result of a collision with another U-b
and the other four from causes unknown. Five were passed to Japan, two
presents from Hitler and three taken over in Far Eastern ports when Germ
surrendered. Six were stricken during the war and the remainder survived to
passed to the Allies; a few served in Allied navies but most were sunl
Operation Deadlight.

Type IXs had many achievements to their credit, one of the m
remarkable being the Far Eastern cruise of *Kapitänleutnant* Lüdden in *U-18*
Type IXC/40. Lüdden took his boat from France to Penang and Singapore

Ay-class

Type: ocean-going patrol.
Total built: 3.
Completed: 1938-39.
Displacement: surfaced 934 tons; submerged 1,210 tons.
Dimensions: length 262ft 6in (80.0m); beam 21ft 0in (6.4m); draught 14ft (4.3m).
Propulsion: 2 x Burmeister & Wain diesels, 2 x 1,750bhp; 2 x electric motors, 2 x 500bhp; two shafts.
Performance: surface – 20kt; submerged – 9kt; maximum operating diving depth 300ft (100m).
Weapons: 6 x 21in (533mm) TT (bow – 2; stern – 2); 1 x 3.9in (100mm) gun; 1 x 20mm AA cannon.
Complement: 44.

History: These three boats were part of a
substantial modernisation. of the Turkish Navy
which took place in the late 1930s, the other
submarines involved including the German-built
Batiray minelayer and the British-built Oruc Reis-
class (qqv). The Ay-class was closely based on the
German Navy's Type IXA, but with major
modifications to comply with Turkish requirements,
the most visually obvious being that the 3.9in
(100mm) gun was mounted in a raised platform

*ove: **U-110, Type IXB, sinks in the Atlantic, 10 May 1941.***

en back to France in a voyage lasting 354 days, during which time they were sea for 297 days and covered 39,792 miles, of which 2,866 were submerged. ring this voyage Lüdden sank eight merchant ships and damaged another, d sank seven dhows. He also made six successful high-seas rendezvous with er U-boats, each one highly hazardous, but survived all of them.

Another significant voyage was made by *Korvetten-Kapitän* Timm in mmand of *U-862*, a Type IXD2. Timm left Brest in June 1945 and arrived ely in Batavia, in the Dutch East Indies, in September 1944, during which yage he sank five merchantmen (28,018grt). He and his men left Batavia on November 1944 and headed south, sailing down the west coast of Australia d then eastwards, circumnavigating Australia and returning to Batavia on 15 bruary 1945. The only traces the Australians ever found of his presence were en he damaged one ship and two sank two others.

mediately forward of the bridge, as was the practice in contemporary British ats. *Atilay* was lost during a training exercise in July 1942 and the other two re scrapped in 1957.

*low: **Ex-Turkish** Batiray, serving in German Navy as UA.*

Type XXI

Type: long-range attack *electroboot*.
Total built: 120.
Completed: 1944-45.
Displacement: surfaced 1,621 tons; submerged 1,819 tons.
Dimensions: length 251ft 7in (76.7m); beam 21ft 7in (6.6m); draught 20ft
(6.3m).
Propulsion: 2 x M.A.N. diesels, 2 x 2,200bhp; 2 x S.S.G. main electric motc
2 x 2,500shp; 2 x S.S.W. "creep" electric motors, 2 x 323shp; battery 3 x 1
cells; two shafts.
Performance: surfaced – 15.7kt; submerged – 17.2kt; range surfac
11,150nm at 12kt, submerged 285nm at 6kt; maximum operating diving de
656ft (200m).
Weapons: 6 x 21in (533mm) TT (bow), 23 x torpedoes; 2 x twin 20mm
cannon.
Complement: 57.

History: The Type XXI represented a major step forward in submar
technology but, although the concept and the design were brilliant, the ac
story was by no means as successful as is often made out. Before the Type >
the vessels were properly called submersibles, since they spent most of th
time on the surface and submerged only for strictly limited periods, dur
which they were slow and relatively unmanoeuvrable. The Type XXI w
however, designed from the start as a submarine whose natural habitat wa
the depths. Its design originated in late 1942 when the *Kriegsmarine* realis
that the Allies were winning the war against the U-boats and that the balar
could only be restored if the Type VIIs and IXs could be replaced by someth
greatly superior. Since the early 1930s Professor Walter, a distinguish
engineer and inventor, had been working on a series of submarine projects w
innovative hull shapes and powered by a revolutionary hydrogen-perox

*Below: Type XXI had six bow
torpedo tubes (no stern
tubes), and carried 23 G7e
torpedoes. Also carried two
twin 20mm cannon for air
defence. Note single rudder,
twin propellers.*

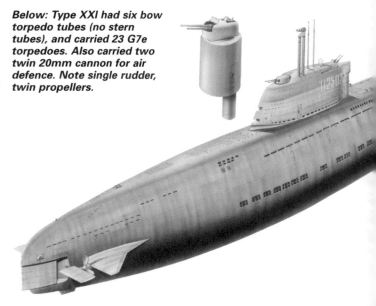

ove: **Wilhelm Bauer** *(ex-U-2540), now a German museum.*

pulsion system. His most recent project was the Type XVIII and in May 1943
vas suggested that the best way to get a major new design into service
ckly would be to modify this hull design, which showed excellent
rodynamic properties, to take conventional diesel engines and batteries.
s proposal was seized upon and in some areas progress was rapid. Admiral
nitz approved the design on 19 June 1943 and the entire programme was
en the go-ahead on 20 August. The first completed module was ready in
:ember and the first boat was launched on 19 April 1944. Some 120 had
:n launched by the war's end, but the cold fact is that no more than a handful
reached an operational state and just two Type XXIs carried
out a combat patrol.

Everything about the Type XXI was new. It had a
streamlined hull optimised for submerged operation, there
were no deck guns and the two twin 20mm cannon were
mounted in streamlined housings at each end of the bridge.
On the bridge all extending devices such as the *schnorchel*,
radar/radio masts and periscopes withdrew into the structure
when not in use and the traditional open bridge was replaced
by three small individual openings for the watchkeeper and
lookouts.

Internally, the longer and better designed figure-of-eight
pressure-hull gave much greater volume. Thus, the battery
size was tripled (372 cells compared to the Type IX's 124),
which in combination with the much more efficient hull
design gave an underwater speed of 16kt and an underwater
endurance of 72 hours at 5kt. Armament was greatly
increased with six bow tubes for which 23 torpedoes were
carried, but not so obvious was that there was a totally new
rapid loading device, enabling the Type XXI to launch three full
six-round salvoes in 20 minutes.

Allied with the revolutionary design was an equally
ambitious plan for rapid construction in large numbers. The
boat was assembled from 10 modules whose fabrication was
dispersed over much of the Third Reich. This optimised the

use of resources, reduced the time each hull would occupy space at
shipyards, and enabled groups of workers to accumulate considerable exper
in their particular area. Also, such wide dispersal would, it was thought, m
the task of Allied bombers much more difficult. Finally, assembly of comple
outfitted modules meant that it would no longer be necessary to install lar
heavy items of equipment (eg, electrical cells, diesel engines) through s
patches. In theory, all this reduced the labour requirement per boat fr
460,000 man-hours on a Type XB to some 300,000 on a Type XXI.

All did not go to plan, with transportation being one area that presen
severe problems. Most movement was done using Germany's very effici
inland waterway system, but some works were up to six miles from the nea
canal or river and specially designed transporters were necessary to m
sections from one to the other. Then, when the completed sections w
moved long distances along the waterways, it was discovered that they wo
warp, with disastrous consequences when trying to align them with ot
sections, which necessitated them being fitted with complicated inte
frames to ensure absolute rigidity.

There was immense pressure to get these boats into service; older m
died from exhaustion and sections were despatched with parts missing in or
to meet the rigidly imposed deadlines – such components then had to be ad
later, exacerbating the confusion. Allied bombing played a significant part, w
many delays being caused by destruction, for example, at the M.A.N.
Siemens-Schukert works, and on the waterway systems. The bombing also
secondary effects such as lengthy power failures and workers taking time
to look after or rehouse their families.

All the completed Type XXIs worked up in the Baltic, where several w
sunk by Allied aircraft. A number eventually sailed for the U-boat bases
Norway – with some being sunk en route – where deep-diving tests show
that yet further modifications were required, and this was done in lo
workshops. Two boats, *U-2511* and *U-3008*, carried out brief patrols before
war's end, but without scoring any successes. After the war, the French, So
British and U.S. navies were all eager to test these boats and they undoubt
learnt many lessons from them which were then incorporated into their c

Type XXIII

GERMA

Type: coastal.
Total built: 62.
Completed: 1944-45.
Displacement: surfaced 234 tons; submerged 275 tons.
Dimensions: length 113ft 10in (34.7m); beam 9ft 10in (3.0m); draught 2
4in (7.7m).
Propulsion: 1 x M.W.M. 6-cylinder diesel, 630bhp; 1 x A.E.G. elect
motor, 580shp; 1 x "creep" motor, 35shp; battery 62 cells; one shaft.
Performance: surface – 9.7kt; submerged – 12.5kt; range surfa
4,450nm at 12kt, submerged 285nm at 6kt).
Weapons: 2 x 21in (533mm) TT (bow), 2 x torpedoes.
Complement: 14.

History: The idea of a replacement coastal U-boat was mooted in 1942
it was decided to produce a new design, using many of the ideas from
Type XXI, such as modular construction, streamlining, and high underw
performance. Admiral Dönitz approved the design in early 1943 but,
senior officers often do, he threw two spanners in the works by demand
that it be rail-transportable and that its torpedo tubes should be 23ft (

ove: Type XXIs lying at Bergen, Norway, May 1945.

>igns. Very few of the Type XXIs were put into service, however, except by
 French and Soviet navies, and then only for a limited period. One sunken
»e XXI was raised by the West German Navy in the 1950s and employed for
years as an experimental boat named *Wilhelm Bauer*. It is now preserved as
nonument in Germany, the last of a remarkable breed.

ove: Type XXIII U-2325 at speed in the Baltic in 1945.

long, rather than the shorter 16.4ft (5m) tubes originally planned. The des
was duly modified to meet the commander-in-chief's requirements,
every effort was made to use in-service components to ease production
was decided that final assembly should be as near to the intenc
operational area as possible, which meant:Atlantic/North Sea – Hambu
Mediterranean – Toulon and Genoa; and Black Sea – Nikolayev. A lot
effort was expended in preparing the foreign facilities, but by the time
project was ready for production Allied advances meant that none of
foreign yards was available, and the only yards involved were in Germa
Assembly of first-of-class U-2321 started on 10 March 1944; it v
launched on 17 April and commissioned on 12 June 1944.

The Type XXIII had an all-welded single hull, with no superstruct
apart from the bridge and a small "hump" housing the diesel exha
silencer. In line with Dönitz's requirements, the hull could be broken do
into four sections, with the bridge making a fifth. In addition, the lon
torpedo tubes were installed, as demanded by Dönitz, although this me
not only that no reloads could be carried, but also that the torpedoes w
loaded by ballasting down the stern until the mouths of the tubes w
above water-level, and then installing the torpedoes backwards fr
outside.

By the time war ended (8 May 1945) some 62 Type XXIIIs had be
completed, of which 18 were stationed in Norway, the remainder in Germ
ports. Ten boats carried out patrols which resulted in five Allied ships be
sunk but without any loss to the U-boats, although seven Type XXIIIs w
lost either in training or during transits between Germany and Norway.

Right: The Allies judged Type XXIIIs to be particularly dangerous.

Oberon/Oxley/Odin-classes GREAT BRIT/
and Capitan O'Brien-class GREAT BRITAIN (CHI

Type: overseas patrol.

History: When the Anglo-Japanese friendship and cooperation treaty v
ended in 1922, the British Admiralty was required to introduce a new type,
"overseas patrol" submarine, primarily for service in Far Eastern waters
which the main advances over existing types were to be much gre
endurance, increased diving depth and improved habitability. A prototype, H
Oberon, was laid down in 1924, followed shortly afterwards by two boats
the Royal Australian Navy, *Otway* and *Oxley*, which were designed by Vick
and were marginally larger, had better lines and were thus faster, but with
same armament. Next came the Odin-class of six boats, which incorpora
lessons learnt from experience with *Oberon*. Finally, in this "O-group" ca
three boats for the Chilean Navy: *Capitan O'Brien*, *Capitan Thompson*
Almirante Simpson. The design was generally similar to that of the Oxley-cl
and on the surface they were easily recognised by their huge bridge. Th
were the only boats in the group to mount the 4.7in (120mm) gun, which
originally been proposed for all the British O-class boats as well, but was
fitted due to a change in Admiralty policy.

Oberon had a vertical stem, but the remainder, including the Chilean bo
had a "ram" bow (ie, sloping back towards the upper casing), whose curve
directly into a net-cutter mounted on the foredeck. Two requirements, gre
depth and increased fuel bunkerage, proved to be mutually incompatible. F

ove: **Capitan O'Brien**, *built by Vickers for the Chilean Navy.*

fuel oil was carried in external tanks, which "as built" were riveted, but the
ater depth gave rise to oil leaks, creating a tell-tale track on the surface and
se tanks had to be replaced by new welded tanks during refits. Second, the
at amount of fuel needed made the boats very heavy for their size, with the
ult that they tended to dive very rapidly, which was frequently difficult to control.
All these class were armed with eight 21in (533mm) torpedo tubes, six in

the bow and two in the stern. *Oberon* carried a total of 16 torpedoes, but all others had 14. All mounted a single 4in (102mm) main gun, which v mounted on a trainable mount at the forward end of the bridge structure, wh was characteristic of most British submarines of the time. This ever longer a higher bridge tower became so massive that it was easily visible when on surface and caused considerable hydrodynamic drag when submerged.

Oberon was some 14 years old when World War II started and served u 1944 when she was stricken and scrapped. *Oxley* and *Otway* were delivered the RAN in 1927, but defence cutbacks resulted in them being put into rese in 1930 and transferred to the RN in 1931. *Triton*, a British T-class bo accidentally torpedoed *Oxley* on 10 September 1939, making her the f British submarine casualty of the war, but *Otway* survived the war to scrapped in 1945. In the Odin-class, four boats were wartime losses: *O Orpheus* and *Oswald* were all sunk by Italian destroyers in 1940, w *Olympus* was sunk by a mine (8 May 1942). The remaining two sere stricke 1946, *Osiris* being scrapped and *Otus* scuttled. The Chilean boats served u the late 1950s, when they were scrapped.

Class	Oberon	Oxley	Odin	Capitan O'Bri
Total built	1	2	6	3
Completed	1927	1927	1929-30	1929
Displacement surfaced submerged	1,598 tons 1,831 tons	1,354 tons 1,872 tons	1,475 tons 2,038 tons	1,540 tons 2,020 tons
Dimensions length beam draught	269ft 8in (82.2m) 28ft 0in (8.5m) 15ft 6in (4.7m)	275ft 0in (83.8m) 27ft 8in (8.4m) 15ft 9in (4.8m)	283ft 6in (86.4m) 29ft 11in (9.1m) 16ft 1in (4.9m)	260ft 0in (79.3 28ft 0in (8.5m 13ft 6in (4.2m
Propulsion main engines power electric motors power battery shafts	2 x Admiralty 2 x 1,350bhp 2 2 x 650shp 3 x 112 cells two	2 x Vickers 2 x 1,550bhp 2 2 x 675shp 3 x 112 cells two	2 x Admiralty 2 x 2,200bhp 2 2 x 660shp 3 x 112 cells two	2 x diesels 2 x 2, 375b 2 650shp 3 x 112 cell two
Performance speed: surface submerged range: surfaced submerged maximum diving depth	13.8kt 7.5kt 12,000nm/8kt 60nm/4kt 300ft (91.4m)	15kt 8.5kt 12,300nm/8kt 60nm/4kt 300ft (91.4m)	17.5kt 8kt 11,400nm/8kt 52nm/34kt 300ft (91.4m)	15kt 9kt 12,300nm/8 60nm/4kt 300ft (91.4
Weapons TT location torpedoes guns	8 x 21in (533mm) bow – 6, stern – 2 16 1 x 4in (102mm)	8 x 21in (533mm) bow – 6, stern – 2 14 1 x 4.in (102mm)	8 x 21in (533mm) bow – 6, stern – 2 14 1 x 4.0in (102mm)	8 x 21in (533n bow – 6, stern 16 1 x 4.7in (120n
Complement	54	55	53	54

ove: One of the Chilean O'Brien-class at the Vickers yard.

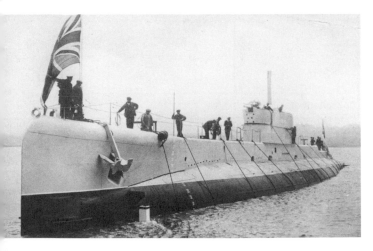

ove: Oberon, the only one in the class with a vertical stem.

Parthian/Rainbow-classes GREAT BRIT

Type: overseas patrol.

Class	Parthian	Rainbow
Total built	6	4
Completed	1928-31	1931-32
Displacement surfaced submerged	1,760 tons 2,040 tons	1,763 tons 2,030 tons
Dimensions length beam draught	289ft 2in (88.1m) 29ft 11in (9.1m) 15ft 11in (4.9m)	287ft 2in (87.5m) 29ft 11in (9.1m) 16ft 1in (4.9m)
Propulsion main engines power electric motors power battery shafts	2 x Admiralty 2 x 2,320bhp 2 2 x 817shp 3 x 112 cells two	2 x Admiralty 2 x 2,320bhp 2 2 x 835shp 3 x 112 cells two
Performance speed: surface submerged range: surfaced submerged maximum diving depth	17.5kt 8.6kt 7,050nm/9kt 62nm/4kt 300ft (91m)	17.5kt 8.8kt 7,050nm/9kt 70nm/4kt 300ft (91m)
Weapons TT location torpedoes guns	8 x 21in (533mm) bow – 6, stern – 2 14 1 x 4in (102mm)	8 x 21in (533mm) bow – 6, stern – 2 14 1 x 4.7in (120mm)
Complement	53	55

History: The P-class was designed as a lineal follow-on to the O-class, v
six boats laid down in 1928 and launched in 1929. It was proposed to fo
these with a further six boats in the R-class, but budgetary constra
reduced this to four, which were laid down in 1929 and launched in 1$
The O-class had not been totally satisfactory and unfortunately
shortcomings of that class were not resolved such that the P-class
proved less manoeuvrable than was required when submerged. There v
minor differences with the previous class. The ram bow which had b
such an obvious feature of the all the O-class (except *Oberon*)
discontinued and the P-class adopted the more conventional clipper k
although not so sharply raked as in most foreign boats. In the P-class

n gun was at bridge level, but in the R-class it was located one deck
l lower. In both classes the bridge was lower and the forward edge
ved back to provide watchkeepers with some shelter.

A rearrangement of some of the internal spaces and equipment in the
ass enabled the pressure hull, and thus the overall length, to be
rtened by some 2ft (0.61m). All boats had the standard battery fit of 336
s, but one boat in each class (*Parthian* and *Rainbow*) had a new type of
n capacity cell, the Exide HCSS 41/4750, which delivered 5,500
peres/hour compared to 3,500 for cells in rest of the two classes.
seus was fitted for a short period with an experimental 4.9in (125mm)
, an unusual calibre for the Royal Navy.

One boat in this class was due to be named *Python* until it was observed
several RN ships with snake names had suffered disasters. *Serpent* was
in 1890 with the loss of 173 lives, while both *Viper* and *Cobra* were
cked within weeks of being commissioned in 1901, the latter breaking in
off the Yorkshire coast with the loss of 67 of her crew. As a result *Python*
renamed *Pandora*.

The loss rate in these classes was very high. In the P-class, the first to be
was *Poseidon*, which was sunk in a peacetime collision off the China coast
June 1931. During the war, two were lost to mines, *Perseus* (6 December
1) and *Parthian* (10 August 1943), *Phoenix* was sunk on 16 July 1940 by an
an MAS boat (equivalent to British MTB or U.S. PT-boat) and *Pandora* was
bed at Malta (1 April 1942). The sole survivor, *Proteus,* was scrapped in
6. In the R-class, *Rainbow* was sunk in the Adriatic (15 October 1940), while
were lost to unknown causes, probably mines: *Regent* (18 April 1943) and
ulus (6 December 1940).

ve: *Parthian-class patrol submarine,* **Perseus.**

Thames-class

Type: fleet submarine.
Total built: 3.
Completed: 1932-35.
Displacement: surfaced 1,830 tons; submerged 2,680 tons.
Dimensions: length 345ft 0in (105.2m); beam 28ft 3in (8.6m); draught 15f
(4.8m).
Propulsion: 2 x Admiralty supercharged diesels, 2 x 5,000bhp; 2 x ele
motors, 2 x 1,250shp; 2 x Ricardo auxiliary engines, 2 x 400bhp; battery 2 x
cells; two shafts.
Performance: surface – 22.5kt; submerged – 10kt; range surfaced 13,200n
8kt, submerged 118nm at 4kt; maximum operating diving depth 200ft (60r
Weapons: 6 x 21in (533mm) TT (bow), 12 x torpedoes; 1 x 4.7in (120mm)
0.303in MG.
Complement: 61.
Specifications are for Thames, as built.

History: The design for the Thames-class (sometimes known as the R
class) started as a replacement for the steam-driven K-class fleet submari
but it was later decided to merge this role with that of the overseas p
submarine (ie, O-/P-/R-classes). The first result was the Thames-class, I
boats for their time, displacing 1,830 tons and with a design speed of 2
although 21.5kt was achieved on trials. Despite their large size, the high sp
and long range could be achieved only at the expense of armament, which
not particularly heavy: six bow torpedo tubes (there were no stern tubes) a

S-class

Type: short-range patrol.

Class	Swordfish	Shark	S-class War Programmes*
Total built	4	8	50
Completed	1932-33	1934-38	1942-45
Displacement surfaced submerged	730 tons 927 tons	761 tons 960 tons	715 tons 990 tons
Dimensions length beam draught	202ft 6in (61.7m) 24ft 11in (7.3m) 11ft 11in (3.6m)	208ft 8in (63.6m) 24ft 0in (7.3m) 11ft 10in (3.6m)	217ft 0in (66.1 23ft 9in (7.2m) 13ft 10in (4.2m)

* There were minor differences between batches. 1941 programme boats had 7 torpedo tubes, 19
and 1943 programme boats had 6 (see notes).

History: The S-class was a replacement for the obsolete H-class (qv) an
boats were built in four groups, which were completed between 1932
1945. First came the Swordfish-class, followed by the Shark-class, which w

...ve: Severn, *one of the three-strong Thames-class.*

...l of 12 torpedoes. *Thames* was armed with a 4.7in (120mm) gun, but this
later changed to 4in (102mm), and the other two had the smaller gun from
...start, which saved 6 tons in topweight.
...The maximum speed of 21kt (22.5kt in *Severn* and *Clyde*) was faster than
...other European boat of the time, and exceeded only by a very few
...nese boats. Such a speed would have guaranteed a place with the
...efleet of the early 1920s, but by the time the Thames-class appeared in the
...-1930s capital ship speed had increased to some 30kt, and it was at last
...pted that the concept of the fleet submarine could no longer be realised.
...*Thames* was laid down in January 1931, followed by *Severn*, which was
...ginally larger, and then *Clyde* which was identical to *Severn*.

...pulsion			
...n engines	2 x Admiralty	2 x Admiralty	2 x Admiralty
...ver	2 x 775bhp	2 x 775bhp	2 x 950bhp
...ctric motors	2	2	2
...ver	2 x 720shp	2 x 720shp	2 x 650shp
...fts	two	two	two
...formance			
...ed: surface	13.8kt	15kt	14.8kt
...merged	10kt	10kt	9kt
...ge: surfaced	5,750nm/8kt	5,750nm/8kt	
...merged	.60nm/23kt	60nm/2kt.	
...ximum			
...ng depth	300ft (90m)	300ft (90m)	300ft (90m)
...apons			
...tion	6 x 21in (533mm)	6 x 21in (533mm)	7 x 21in (533mm)
...edoes	bow	bow	bow – 6, stern – 1
...s	12	12	13
	1 x 3in (76mm)	1 x 3in (76mm)	1 x 4in (102mm)
...mplement	38	39	48

...ntly larger and had greatly simplified internal arrangements; they were
...pleted between 1933 and 1938. On the outbreak of war the War
...rgency and 1941 programmes were rushed into production, comprising a

series of 33 boats, which were a larger version of the Shark-class, with we frames and other improvements, and also included a single, external s torpedo tube. Finally came the 1942/43 programmes, which were vi repeats of the War Emergency programme, but without the external torp tube (except in a few cases) and these were completed between 1943 1945.

All groups in the S-class were intended for short-range operation enclosed waters such as the North Sea and Mediterranean, with a secon role in training. They were double-hulled, saddle-tank boats and carrie relatively heavy armament of six torpedo tubes (all forward) with one reload per tube. One of the features of the initial Swordfish-class was a long additional casing ahead of the bridge, which housed a small boat and a disappearing mount for the 3in (76mm) gun. This casing proved heavy and the mount was over-complicated, so the greater part of the extension was removed, leaving a rump that was used as an ammunition store for the main gun, which was now mounted directly on the upper casing, as in virtually every other submarine. Like all other large classes, there were differences not only between the groups, but also minor variations between different boats in the same group.

All boats fought hard throughout the war, mainly in their planned operational areas of the North Sea and Mediterranean, and 18 were lost.

T-class

Type: patrol submarine.

History: The Oberon-, Parthian- and Rainbow-classes, while adequate, v never really successful and in the mid-1930s the British Admiralty decide embark on the development of a replacement. A major design constraint that the recently concluded London Naval Treaty stipulated that the perm maximum submarine tonnage was 16,500, so the Admiralty decided displacement of 1,000 tons, which would enable 16 to be built. displacement was some 400 tons less than the boats to be replaced and limited the length, which in turn limited the size of the diesel engines, and result the surface speed was less. This apart, the resulting design was sup in almost every other respect, with more powerful armament, better hand both on the surface and when submerged, better habitability, and incre submerged speed. *Triton* and Group I had a unique armament with six int torpedo tubes, two in the raised bow casing, and yet another two amids all 10 tubes launching their torpedoes ahead. This gave the boats a impressive salvo, which was intended to provide a high probability of a long ranges, although only the six internal tubes were reloadable. Underpin all this was greatly simplified construction, thus reducing building time, great attention to ease of operation and maintainability, which resulted technically very efficient and reliable submarine.

First-of-class was *Triton*, laid down at Vickers, Barrow, in August 1 launched in October 1937 and commissioned in December 1938. She followed by a further 21 boats, in which the dimensions and displacement v all reduced slightly, and which entered service between 1940 and 1

the 44 that survived, two were sunk in peacetime accidents, three were
ended as targets, five were sold to friendly navies (Israel – 2, Portugal – 3),
le the remainder were stricken between 1946 and 1960. A number of those
t survived the war were converted to high-speed targets for ASW training,
ch involved streamlining the hull, casing and bridge tower, and fitting more
verful cells; as a result, submerged speeds of up to 17kt could be achieved
short periods.

ow: Scorcher, *one of the S-class 1943 programme boats.*

ve: A T-class Group II boat.

Class	Triton	Group I	Group II
Total built	1	21	31
Completed	1938-39	1941-43	1943-46
Displacement surfaced submerged	1,095 tons 1,585 tons	1,090 tons 1,575 tons	1,090 tons 1,575 tons
Dimensions length beam draught	277ft 6in (84.4m) 26ft 7in (8.1m) 15ft 0in (4.6m)	275ft 0in (83.8m) 26ft 6in (8.1m) 14ft 10in (4.5m)	273ft 6in (83.4 26ft 7in (8.1m) 14ft 10in (4.5m
Propulsion main engines power electric motors power shafts	2 x Vickers 2 x 1,250bhp 2 2 x 725shp two	2 x Vickers 2 x 1,250bhp 2 2 x 725shp two	2 x Vickers 2 x 1,250bhp 2 2 x 725shp two

Experience of operating these new boats led to a requirement for more
slightly modified design, which then became known as Group II. These b
had an all-welded hull with slightly modified lines, but the only change
substance were to the armament. The Group I boats lacked the stern tu
which were carried by most contemporary submarines, so one tube
installed in the after casing, while the two forward launching tubes s
amidships were moved aft of the bridge tower and turned to face aft, an
out at about 20 degrees. Although primarily intended to provide an adeq
salvo, this had a coincidental advantage in that when running on the surfac
at periscope depth the forward-facing midships tubes created a substa
wave which had not only interfered with visibility, but also cau
hydrodynamic drag and trim problems. The Group II boats were also fitted
a 20mm Oerlikon cannon on a platform at the after end of the bridge struc
A total of 40 Group II boats were ordered but the last seven were cancelle
favour of the even more advanced A-class (qv).

As always, there were many modifications. Once the
addition of the stern tubes and the rearrangement of the
midships tubes had been proved a success in the Group II boats,
most Group I boats were modified to the same standard at their
next refit. They were also given a 20mm Oerlikon. Later in the
war many T-boats were required for service in the Far East and
these had a number of ballast tanks converted into fuel tanks,
increasing range to some 11,000nm at 8kt.

One tragic incident was the loss of *Thetis*, which sank in
Liverpool Bay on 1 June 1939 while carrying not only her crew of
69 but also an additional 50 men from the shipyard and the
Admiralty. A faulty indicator resulted in the boat being flooded
and she sank. This tragedy apart, the T-boats operated with great
success, although their heavy involvement in operations in every
theatre brought with it the inevitable heavy losses. The T-class
achieved particularly good results against enemy submarines,
and they sank four German, six Italian and three Japanese boats.
They also achieved some major successes against enemy
surface warships, sinking one German and two Japanese

rformance			
ed: surface	15.3kt	15.3kt	15.3kt
omerged	9kt	9kt	9kt
ge: surfaced	8,000nm/10kt	8,000nm/10kt	8,000nm/10kt
omerged	80nm/4kt	80nm/4kt	80nm/4kt
ximum			
ing depth	300ft (91m)	300ft (91m)	350ft (107m)
eapons			
ation	10 x 21in (533mm)	10 x 21in (533mm)	11 x 21in (533mm)
	bow – 6, external – 4	bow – 6, external – 4	bow – 6, external – 5
oedoes	16	16	17
ns	1 x 4in (102mm)	1 x 4in (102mm)	1 x 4in (102mm)
	3 x 0.303in MG*	3 x 0.303in MG*	1 x 20mm AA
			3 x 0.303in MG
mplement	59	56	61

er replaced or supplemented by 1 x 20mm Oerlikon AA.

sers, and seriously damaging three others. In another success, *Thunderbolt*
ich had originally been named *Thetis* and had been recovered and renamed
r her sinking) carried some chariots (human torpedoes) which entered
ermo harbour and sank the almost completed cruiser, *Triano*. These
cesses were offset by 17 losses, plus another which was so badly damaged
it was consider irreparable.

The remaining 35 boats survived the war, of which *Truant* was wrecked in
6 and *Truculent* was lost following a collision (12 January 1950). Six boats
e transferred to foreign navies, three each to Israel and the Netherlands. Of
remainder, five riveted boats were given partial conversions, while five with
ded hulls were given full conversions, equivalent to the U.S. Navy's Guppy
gramme, which extended their lives until 1965-60, while the others were
en up, some of them immediately after the war, although others lasted into
mid-1960s.

ow: **Truculent***, lost in a collision in the Thames in 1950.*

U/V-class

Type: coastal.

Class	U-class Group I	U-class Group II	V-class
Total built	15	34	22
Completed	1938-39	1941-43	1943-46
Displacement surfaced submerged	630 tons 730 tons	648 tons 732 tons	660 tons 740 tons
Dimensions length beam draught	190ft 7in (58.1m) 15ft 9in (4.8m) 15ft 9in (4.8m)	195ft 6n (59.6m) 15ft 9in (4.8m) 15ft 10in (4.8m)	203ft 5in (62.0 15ft 9in (4.8m) 15ft 10in (4.8m
Propulsion main engines power electric motors power battery shafts	2 x Paxman-Ricardo 615hp 2 2 x 825shp 2 x 112 cells two	2 x Paxman-Ricardo 615hp 2 2 x 825shp 2 x 112 cells two	2 x Paxman 615hp 2 2 x 825shp 2 x 112 cells two
Performance speed: surface submerged range: surfaced submerged maximum diving depth	11.5kt 9kt 4,050nm/10kt 23nm/8kt 200ft (61m)	11.5kt 9kt 4,050nm/10kt 23nm/8kt. 200ft (61m)	12.5kt 9kt 4,700nm/10kt 30nm/9kt 300ft (91m)
Weapons TT location torpedoes guns	6 x 21in (533mm) bow – 4, external – 2 8 3 x 0.303in MG (see notes)	4 x 21in (533mm) bow 8 1 x 3in (76mm) 3 x 0.303in MG	41 x 21in (533r bow 8 1 x 3in (76mm 3 x 0.303in M
Complement	27	33	33

History: The U-class had its origins in a 1936 Admiralty requirement for t
small, unarmed submarines to be used as targets in anti-submarine wa
(ASW) training, which were to be easy and cheap to build, and to require a s
crew. After the hulls had been laid down in February 1937 it was realised
they could also be suitable for short-range operational missions, so they v
modified during construction to take six 21in (533mm) torpedo tubes, all in
bows, and with four inside the pressure hull, and two externally-mounted
raised bow casing. The outcome of this somewhat piecemeal approach wa
outstanding single-hulled design (the first since the R-class [qv]) which pr
to have first-class handling, to be very manoeuvrable both on the surface

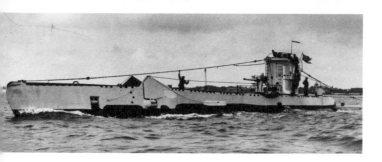

...ove. Norwegian **Ula** *in 1949, formerly HMS* **Varne.**

...merged, easy to produce and comparatively cheap to build, maintain ... man. As a result 12 more were ordered, which were initially intended ... be identical to the first three, but after four had been completed it was ...ided that the raised bow casing containing two external torpedo tubes ... no longer required, so they were completed with just four tubes. These ...boats constituted Group I and they were followed by 34 Group II boats, ...ch were identical to the four-tube Group I boats except that the stern ... extended by some 5ft (1.5m) in order to improve the flow of water over ... propellers.

The first two boats to be completed, *Undine* and *Unity*, did not have a ...n gun and carried a 27-man crew, but from the third, *Ursula,* onwards, ...oats mounted a 3in (76mm) gun, raising the crew to 33. As the gun was ...trospective modification there was no separate hatch for the gun crew ... ammunition, which caused delays in getting into action on surfacing ... prevented rapid crash-dives, one of the few shortcomings in this ...ign.

...It was decided in 1941 to develop a modified version of the U-class with ...lar characteristics and armament, but which would be even stronger, while ...g still easier and cheaper to build. This resulted in the V-class which were ...11in (2.4m) longer (they are sometimes referred to as the "long-hull ...nt") and had a partly-welded pressure hull. It was slightly faster.

The U-class saw service mainly in the North and Mediterranean Seas, ...re they achieved some outstanding successes. Twenty were lost in the war ... a number were supplied to Allied navies; the remainder were broken up in ...late 1940s and early 1950s. The V-class entered service between 1943 and ...5 and there were no war losses. A number were passed to Allied navies ...mark – 2, France – 2, Greece – 3 and Norway – 4) both during and after the ... and the remainder served on with the Royal Navy, being progressively ...ken between 1946 and 1961. One of this class, HMS *Venturer,* holds the ...ue distinction of being the only submarine ever to have sunk another ...marine with both boats remaining submerged throughout the engagement ...n she sank *U-864,* a Type IXD2 off the Norwegian coast on 9 February ...5.

...A brief note on names is required. The 15 Group I boats had names ...nning with the letter "U." When Group II boats were launched it was ...iralty policy for new boats to be given a letter "P" (= patrol) followed by a ...ber, but this was changed to names on the personal order of the Prime ...ster, Winston Churchill. As a result, *P-44* became *United,* and so on, but ...e that had already been lost were never renamed and are thus recorded ...y by their number – eg, *P-33.* One further complication is that the last five ...he U-class Group II had names beginning with the letter "V" but were ...rt-hull" boats and not part of the "long-hulled V-class."

A-class

Type: long-range patrol.
Total built: 16.
Completed: 1945-48.
Displacement: surfaced 1,385 tons; submerged 1,620 tons.
Dimensions: length 279ft 3in (85.1m); beam 22ft 3in (6.8m); draught 17ft (5.2m).
Propulsion: 2 x Vickers/Admiralty supercharged diesels, 2 x 2,150bhp; English Electric electric motors, 2 x 625shp; two shafts.
Performance: surface – 18.5kt; submerged – 8kt; range surfaced 10,500nr 11kt, submerged 90nm at 3kt; maximum operating diving depth 350ft (107
Weapons: 10 x 21in (533mm) TT (bow – 6, stern – 4); 1 x 4in (102mm) gu x 20mm Oerlikon AA, 3 x 0.303in MG.
Complement: 61.

History: The great majority of British submarine production during World W was either repeats or modifications of designs produced in the 1930s. The exception (apart from the very small X-craft) was the A-class and even this essentially an enlarged and greatly modified version of the T-class. The de was prepared in response to a requirement for boats for the war against Ja for which the main requisites were very long range, heavy armament and pl of reload torpedoes, and good habitability for long patrols in tropical conditi The result was an excellent design, with an all-welded hull, simpl construction and a substantial armament of 10 torpedo tubes, six in the (two of which were external) and four aft (two external) and a total load o

Balilla/Calvi-classes and Humaita-class

Type: long-range cruiser.

Class	Balilla	Humaita	Calvi
Total built	4	1	3
Completed	1928-29	1929	1935-6
Displacement surfaced submerged	1,450 tons 1,904 tons	1,390 tons 1,884 tons	1,550 tons 2,060 tons
Dimensions length beam draught	282ft 09in (86.8m) 25ft 7in (7.8m) 15ft 3in (4.7m)	285ft 5in (87.0m) 25ft 7in (7.8m) 13ft 2in (4.0m)	276ft 7in (84.3 25ft 3in (7.7m 17ft 1in (5.2m

History: In the inter-war years the Italians had considerable col commitments on the east coast of Africa and the Balilla-class was desig to provide long-range patrol submarines for operations in the Indian O

ove: A-class, HMS *Affray, lost on 17 April 1951.*

edoes. Range was 11,500nm at 11kt and an efficient air-conditioning
tem was installed for better crew comfort. Major efforts were made to
uce underwater noise levels and, after some initial problems with rolling,
keeping was excellent. The class was also one of the first to be fitted with
ir-warning radar antenna mounted on a hydraulic mast, which could be used
e running at periscope depth. As built, the A-class did not have schnorkels;
se were added after the war.

A total of 46 boats were ordered and the first to be launched was *Amphion* (31
ust 1944); eight were launched and two completed before VJ-day, but none
ame operational in time to see combat. Meanwhile, the orders had been cut
< and the total completed was only 16. One boat, *Affray*, was lost in a peacetime
dent (17 April 1951). Of the remaining 15, all except one were given a Guppy-
e conversion in the 1950s and then served into the 1970s.

pulsion			
n engines	2 x Fiat	2 x Ansaldo	2 x Fiat
ver	2 x 2,450bhp	2 x 2,450bhp	2 x 2,200bhp
ise	1 x Fiat diesel	–	–
ver	425bhp	–	–
ctric motors	2 x Savigliano	2 x electric motors	2 x San Giorgio
ver	2 x 1,100shp	2 x 450shp	2 x 900shp
fts	two	two	two
formance			
ed: surface	16kt	18.5kt	17kt
merged	7kt	9.5kt	7.4kt
ge: surfaced	12,000nm/7kt	12,000nm/7kt	11,400nm/8kt
merged	110nm/3kt	110nm/3kt	80nm/4kt
ximum			
ng depth	288ft (90m)	288ft (90m)	288ft (90m)
apons			
	6 x 21in (533mm)	6 x 21in (533mm)	8 x 21in (533mm)
tion	bow – 4, stern – 2	bow – 4 stern – 4	bow – 4, stern – 4
edoes	12	12	16
s	1 x 4.7in (120mm)	1 x 4in (102mm)	2 x 4.7in (120mm)
	1 x 13mm AAMG	–	4 x 20mm AA
es	–	16	–
nplement	77	61	72

and Red Sea. This required a good endurance and surface speed, ar
heavy torpedo armament with reloads. The resulting Balilla-class was ba
on detailed examination of *U-120*, a German U-117-class minelayer, wh
had been allocated to Italy at the end of the World War I and was a stron
built, double-hulled design; the Balillas were also the largest submarines
far built for the Italian Navy.

The hull design was not as good as in later Italian submarines and
designed surface speed of 17.5kt and submerged speed of 8.9kt w
never achieved in practice. There were six torpedo tubes, four in the b
two in the stern, with one reload for each tube and one boat, *Ant*
Sciesa, also had a tube for four mines. The 4.7in (120mm) gun was origin
built into the foot of the tower, but was later moved forward onto the o
deck. One unusual feature was a 450bhp diesel which was intended
either very long-range cruising or for charging the battery when the n
engines were being used for propulsion; this was never repeated in
successor classes.

The Calvi-class was an improved version of the Balilla-class, wi
better hull form for increased stability, but less powerful machin
Considerable extra space was gained by redesign, which enabled two n
torpedo tubes and reloads to be carried aft. A second 4.7in (120mm)
was also carried on the after deck.

The Brazilian Navy ordered a modified version of the Balilla-class, w
was delivered in March 1929. The modifications were extensive
included siting the propulsion system well forward, eleminating di
planes, and the installation of a minelaying system which enabled 16 m
to be delivered.

All the Italian boats of both classes participated in the Spanish Civil \

Pisani- and related classes

n

Type: short-range patrol.

History: These 13 single-hull boats were designed by Bernadis for operat
in the Mediterranean, the original Pisani-class being laid down in 1925-26
launched in 1927-28. Once in service they proved to lack lateral stability

Class	Pisani	Bandiera	Squalo	Fieramosc
Total built	4	4	4	1
Completed	1928	1930	1930-31	1930
Displacement surfaced submerged	866 tons 1,040 tons	925 tons 1,080 tons	920 tons 1,125 tons	1,530 tons 2,094 tons
Dimensions length beam draught	223ft 9in (68.2m) 20ft 0in (6.1m) 16ft 2in (4.9m)	212ft 9in (69.8m) 22ft 3in (7.3m) 16ft 0in (5.3m)	212ft 9in (69.8m) 22ft 0in (7.2m) 15ft 10in (5.2m)	275ft 6in (84 27ft 3in (8.3 16ft 9in (5.1

ove: Balilla, *launched in 1927, laid up in 1941.*

the time World War II broke out the Balilla-class was somewhat dated,
nough *Enrico Toti* sank two British submarines, *Rainbow* (15 October
0) and *Perseus* (1 December 1941). Two others were used as fuel
rage tanks from April 1941, while *Toti* and *Sciesa* were used to transport
plies to North Africa. All three of the Calvi-class, *Calvi, Finzi* and *Tazzoli*,
re employed in the Atlantic during the war, operating from the Italian
e at Bordeaux, where *Tazzoli* became the most successful Italian
marine of the war, sinking 19 merchant ships (96,533grt). *Calvi* was sunk
he Atlantic (1942) and the other two were then modified for use as
sport boats to the Far East, *Tazzoli* being lost on her first voyage to
gapore. *Finzi* was still at Bordeaux when Italy surrendered to the
mans and was taken over by the German Navy as *UIT-21*, but was
troyed in port on 25 August 1944.

opulsion				
in engines	2 x Tosi	2 x Fiat or Tosi	2 x Fiat	2 x Tosi
ver	2 x 1,500bhp	2 x 1,500bhp	2 x 1,500bhp	2 x 2,600bhp
ctric motors	2 x C.G.E.	2 x Savigliano	2 x C.R.D.A.	2 x .Marelli
ver	2 x 500shp	2 x 650shp	2 x 650shp	2 x 1,000 shp
afts	two	two	two	two
rformance				
ed: surface	15kt	15kt	15.1kt	15kt
merged	8.2kt	8kt	8kt	8kt
ge: surfaced	4,230nm/9.3kt	4,750nm/8.5kt	5,650nm/8kt	5,300nm/8kt
merged	70nm/4kt	60nm/4kt	100nm/3kt	90nm/3kt
ximum				
ng depth	288ft (90m)	288ft (90m)	288ft (90m)	288ft (90m)
apons				
ation	6 x 21in (533mm)	8 x 21in (533mm)	8 x 21in (533mm)	8 x 21in (533mm)
	bow – 4, stern 2	bow 4, stern 4	bow – 4, stern – 4	bow – 4, stern – 4
pedoes	9	12	12	14
ns	1 x 4in (102mm)	1 x 4in (102mm)	1 x 4in (102m)	1 x 4.7in (120mm)
	2 x 13.2mm MG	2 x 13.2mm MG	2 x 13.2 AAMG	4 x 20mm AA
mplement	49	52	53	78

e fitted with external bulges, which resulted in a loss of speed of about 2kt
he surface and 1kt submerged. Next came the Bandiera-class, which not
also required additional bulges once in service, but also needed a raised

bow to improve performance when steaming into a head sea. The Squalo-c
was a virtual repeat of the Bandiera-class, but with additional bunkerage gi
increased range; like the Bandieras they also need extra bulges and a rai
bow. The sole Fieramosca-class boat was a much modified version of the Pi
design, and was originally intended to be a submarine cruiser, armed with n
torpedo tubes and a heavy gun (4.7in/120mm) and with a hangar for a sn
reconnaissance floatplane. At the time, similar concepts were being teste
other navies, but the Italian Navy changed its mind while the boat was un
construction. As a result, the aircraft was cancelled, and the design of
submarine radically altered, with one torpedo tube and the hangar be
deleted, and *Fieramosca* was completed as a normal patrol submarine.

By the outbreak of war the Pisani-class boats were old and had p
performance by contemporary standards, so after a few limited operations t
were put to other uses, one becoming a floating oil tank and another a bat
charger. Only one, *Vettor Pisani*, remained in service and was stricken in 1S

The Bandiera-class were also inadequate for World War II operations
were used to transport supplies to North Africa; three were transferrec
training duties in 1942, but *Samarosa* continued as a transport until it groun
and was then torpedoed by a British MTB (20 January 1943). The Squalo-c
had a more active war, but with little success. *Tricheco* was sunk by the Bri
submarine *Upholder* (18 March 1942), while *Narvalo* was scuttled to a
capture by British ASW forces (14 January 1943) and *Deffino* was lost in
accident (23 March 1943). That left just one boat, *Squalo*, which survived
war and was broken up in 1948. *Fieramosca* was slow to dive and when
suffered a battery explosion in 1940 the opportunity was taken to lay her up

In 1929, the Turkish Navy placed a large contract with Italy for the de
and construction of four destroyers and two submarines. Both the latter w

Mameli/Settembrini/
Archimede-classes

IT.

Type: short-range patrol.

History: The Mamelli-class was designed by Cavallini and built by Tos
Taranto. Like other Italian designs of the early/mid-1920s, they benefited gr
from the examination of their national share of the German U-boats which w

Class	Mamelli	Settembrini	Archimede
Total built	4	2	4
Completed	1928-29	1932	1934
Displacement surfaced submerged	830 tons 1,010 tons	953 tons 1,153 tons	985 tons 1,259 tons
Dimensions length beam draught	213ft 3in (64.6m) 21ft 4in (6.5m) 14ft 1in (4.3m)	226ft 8in (69.1m) 21ft 7in (6.6m) 14ft 7in (4.5m)	231ft 4in (70.5 22ft 6in (6.9m) 13ft 6in (4.1m)

ove: **Giovanni Bausan**, *one of the four-strong Pisani-class.*

down in February 1930, launched one year later and after the usual builder's
's arrived in Istanbul at the begining of November 1931. The two boats were
erent from each other, but both were designed by Bernadis and built by CNT,
r designs being based on Italian boats. *Dumlupinar* was based on the Pisani-
ss, but with slightly different hull lines and a submerged displacement of
50 tons, and was powered by M.A.N. engines, which combined to give her
additional 2kt in surface speed. *Sakarya* was a little smaller, with a
merged displacement of 940 tons, her design being based on that of the
an Navy's Argonauta-class. Like *Dumlupinar*, *Sakarya*, too, was powered by
.N. engines. Both were stricken about 1950.

pulsion			
in engines	2 x Tosi	2 x Tosi	2 x Tosi
wer	2 x 1,500bhp	2 x 1,500bhp	2 x 1,500bhp
ctric motors	2 x C.G.E.	2 x Ansaldo	2 x Marelli
wer	2 x 550shp	2 x 700shp	2 x 550shp
fts	two	two	two
formance			
ed: surface	15kt	17.5kt	17kt
merged	7.5kt	7.7kt	8kt
ge: surfaced	4,360nm/8kt	9,000nm/8kt	10,300nm/8kt
merged	110nm/3kt	80nm/4kt	105nm/3kt
ximum			
ng depth	288ft (90m)	288ft (90m)	288ft (90m)
apons			
ation	6 x 21in (533mm)	8 x 21in (533mm)	8 x 21in (533mm)
	bow – 4, stern – 2	bow – 4, stern – 4	bow – 4, stern – 4
edoes	10	12	16
s	1 x 4in (102mm)	1 x 4in (102mm)	2 x 3.9in (100m)
	2 x 13.2mm MG	2 x 13.2mm MG	2 x 13.2mm MG
mplement	49	56	55

ributed to the victorious allies. They had partial double-hulls and were
icularly strong, and although their normal diving depth was 288ft (90m) one

boat reached 380ft (116m) during trials. As with so many Italian submarines this period they proved to suffer from lateral instability and external bulges to be added after completion, which reduced their speed, both on the surf and submerged. They mounted six 21in (533mm) torpedo tubes and relo were provided only for the four bow tubes. The Settembrini-class, a designed by Cavallini and built by Tosi, were based on the Mamelli-class with modifications to improve stability. The Archimede-class was a slig enlarged version of the Settembrini-class, one specific improvement being increase in torpedo load from 12 to 16.

The Mamelli-class took part in the Spanish Civil War and then spent W War II up to the Italian surrender in the Mediterranean where *Capponi* was s by the British submarine minelayer *Rorqual* (31 March 1941). In 1943 the th survivors were refitted with more powerful diesels, raising their surface sp to 17kt. After the surrender they were used in the Atlantic to train U.S. N ASW crews and all were scrapped in February 1948. The Settembrini-c spent most of the 1930s in the Red Sea and during the war they alterna between combat patrols, transporting supplies to North Africa and serving the Submarine School. After the surrender they served as targets for U.S. N ASW crews, during which *Settembrini* was accidentally rammed and sunk Buckley-class destroyer-escort USS *Frament* (DE-677) on 15 November 19:

The Archimede-class were good boats and popular with their crews, and all took part in the Spanish Civil War. During World War II, two of the boats v covertly sold to Spain, for which they served until scrapped in 1959. *Galileo* was on her first patrol, being forced to surface and then being captured, following w she was commissioned into the Royal Navy as HMS *X-2*. She was scrapped in 1 The only other boat was *Ferraris* which operated in the Indian Ocean until 1 when she transferred to the Atlantic, where she was sunk on 25 October 1941

Argonauta/Sirena/Perla/ Adua/Acciaio-classes   IT.

Type: short-range patrol.

History: This series of submarines was known after their designer as "Bernardis 600-tonners" . They were not particularly fast, but were strong manoeuvrable. The first in the series, the Argonauta-class, were laid dow

Class	Argonauta	Sirena	Perla/Adua	Acciaio
Total built	7	12	10 + 17	13
Completed	1932	1933-34	1936-38	1942
Displacement surfaced submerged	650 tons 810 tons	679 tons 842 tons	696 tons 825 tons	715 tons 870 tons
Dimensions length beam draught	201ft 0in (61.5m) 18ft 6in (5.7m) 14ft 6in (4.6m)	197ft 6in (73.0m) 21ft 0in (6.5m) 15ft 0in (4.6m)	197ft 6in (60.2m) 21ft 0in (6.5m) 15ft 0in (4.6m)	197ft 0in (60.: 21ft 4in (6.4m 14ft 9in (4.8m

ove: Tito Speri, the last of four in the Mameli-class.

opulsion				
ain engines	2 x Fiat/Tosi	2 x Fiat /Tosi	2 x Fiat/C.R.D.A.	2 x Fiat/Tosi
wer	2 x 750bhp	2 x 675bhp	2 x 700bhp	2 x 700bhp
ctric motors	2 x C.R.D.A.	2 x C.R.D.A.	2 x C.R.D.A.	2 x C.R.D.A.
wer	2 x 400shp	2 x 400shp	2 x 400shp	2 x 400shp
afts	two	two	two	two
rformance				
eed: surface	14kt	14kt	14kt	14kt
omerged	8kt	7.5kt	7.5kt	7.3kt
ge: surfaced	4,960nm/9.5kt	2,280nm/12kt	2,5000nm/12kt	5,000nm/8.5kt
omerged	110nm/3kt	72nm/4kt	740nm/4kt	80nm/3kt
aximum				
ing depth	256ft (80m)	256ft (80m)	256ft (80m)	256ft (80m)
eapons				
	6 x 21in (533mm)	6 x 21in (533mm)	6 x 21in (533mm)	6 x 21in (533mm)*
ation	bow – 4, stern – 2	bow – 4, stern – 2	bow – 4, stern – 2	bow – 4, stern – 2*
pedoes	12	12	12	10*
ns	1 x 4in (102mm)	1 x 3.9in (100mm)	1 x 3.9in (100mm)	1 x 3.9in (100mm)
	2 x 13.2mm MG	2 x 13.2mm MG	4 x 13.2mm MG	4 x 13.2mm MG
mplement	44	45	45	48

me had 8 x 21in (533mm) TT, bow – 4, stern – 4

1929, the design being based on that of the Squalo-class (qv) but with deta`
improvements, although it reverted to a long flat forecastle ending in a vert
stem, as opposed to the rather bulbous bow which had been found necess
in the Squalo-class. The Sirena-class (12 built) had detailed improvements
somewhat less engine power resulted in lower speed and a reduced ran
However, it proved necessary to restore the Squalo-type bow once again.

Next came two groups which, although usually shown as separate class
were virtually identical: 10 Perla-class (C.R.D.A., Monfalcone – 6, OTO,
Spezia – 4), and 17 Adua-class (C.R.D.A. – 4; OTO, Muggiano – 9; Tosi, Tara
– 4). There were minor differences between boats from the various yards;
example, the profile of the C.R.D.A. bridge was different from that of the O`
built boats. Finally, came the Acciaio-class, the last in the 600-ton series, wh
was virtually identical to the Perla-class, but with minor increases
displacement, an increase in range, improvements in equipment and
reduction in the size of the bridge structure.

During the war the seven Argonautas were used exclusively in
Mediterranean, where *Serpente* sank the British destroyer *Hyperion* (Decem
1940) but six out of seven in the class were war losses. The only survivor v
Jalea, scrapped in 1948. The same applied to the Sirena-clas; all were emplo
in the Mediterranean and just one survived.

The Perla-class took part in the Spanish Civil War, during which *Iride*
Onice were lent to the Nationalist Navy for a period of several months. On
outbreak of World War II *Perla* was in the Red Sea and after operating in
area sailed around Africa to Bordeaux and thence back to Italy. One of the m
successful boats in the class was *Ambra* which sank the British cru
Bonaventure (31 March 1941) and also delivered the assault craft which s
20,000 tons of shipping in Algiers harbour in December 1942. There were `

Glauco/Marcello/
Marconi-classes   IT`

Type: long-range patrol.

History: In 1931 the Portuguese Navy ordered a number of submarines fr
abroad, including four from Italy, of which two were long-range, ocean-go
patrol boats, to be designed by Bernadis and built by C.R.D.A., Monfalco
they were to be named *Delfin* and *Espadarte*. Work was started on the bo

Class	Glauco	Marcello	Marconi
Total built	2	11	6
Completed	1935-36	1938-39	1940
Displacement surfaced submerged	1,055 tons 1,325 tons	1,060 tons 1,313 tons	1,195 tons 1,490 tons
Dimensions length beam draught	239ft 6in (73.0m) 23ft 6in (7.2m) 16ft 10in (5.1m)	236ft 6in (73.0m) 23ft 7in (7.2m) 16ft 8in (5.1m)	251ft 0in (76.5r 22ft 4in (6.8m) 15ft 6in (4.7m)

ove: **Nichelio** *(Acciaio-class) surrenders in 1943.*

losses. *Perla* was captured (9 July 1942) by the British who passed her to
Greek Navy, *Ambra* was scuttled and the remainder survived.

opulsion			
ain engines	2 x Fiat	2 x C.R.D.A./Fiat	2 x C.R.D.A.
wer	2 x 1,500bhp	2 x 1,800bhp	2 x 1,800bhp
ctric motors	2 x C.R.D.A.	2 x C.R.D.A.	2 x Marelli
wer	2 x 600shp	2 x 550shp	2 x 750shp
afts	two	two	two
rformance			
eed: surface	17kt	17.4kt	17.8kt
omerged	8kt	8kt	8.2kt
ge: surfaced	9,760nm/8kt	7,500nm/9.4kt	10,500nm/8kt
omerged	110nm/3kt	120nm/3kt	110nm/34kt
aximum			
ing depth	288ft (90m)	328ft (100m)	288ft (90m)
eapons	8 x 21in (533mm)	8 x 21in (533mm)	8 x 21in (533mm)
ation	bow – 4, stern – 4	bow – 4, stern – 4	bow – 4, stern – 4
pedoes	14	16	12
ns	2 x 3.9in (100mm)	2 x 3.9in (100mm)	1 x 3.9in (100mm)
	2 x 13.2mm MG	4 x 13.2mm MG	4 x 13.2mm MG
mplement	57	57	57

Portugal then cancelled both Italian contracts. Fortunately for the builder,
design was so promising that the boats were ordered by the Italian Navy in

1932 as *Glauco* and *Otaria*. They were considered to be fast, stro
comfortable for the crew, and manoeuvrable both on the surface and wl
submerged. The Marcello-class, which followed on from the Glaucos, v
almost identical and, with 11 built, was a surprisingly large class for the Ita
Navy. Like the Glaucos, the Marcellos were considered to be v
manoeuvrable, but were even faster, with one boat achieving 18.24kt on tri
The six-strong Marconi-class followed the same basic design, but the hull v
lengthened, the beam reduced, the bunkers enlarged, and more powe
electric motors installed, while the bridge superstructure was reduced and
after gun removed. The result was an increase in speed, both on the surf
and submerged, much greater range and better stability in a design that v
considered the best of all the long-range submarines in the pre-war Royal Ita
Navy.

Once World War II started, the two Glauco-class boats were emplo
for a short period in the North Atlantic, but *Glauco* had to be scuttled a
being severely damaged by a British destroyer (27 June 1941). *Otaria* t
undertook supply runs to North Africa and survived the war, to be stric
in 1948.

Of the Marcello-class, no fewer than nine were lost in the war, wh
included four sunk by enemy ASW forces, four lost due to causes unkno
and one sunk by bombs while in harbour. The remaining two were fitted
as Far east transports in 1943, but *Barbarigo* was sunk in the Bay of Bisc
soon after starting the outward voyage. The other, *Capellini*, reached
Dutch East Indies, but on the Italian surrender in September 1943
Japanese seized the crew and handed the boat to the Germans, v
commissioned her as *UIT-24*. When Germany surrendered in May 1945
was seized once again by the Japanese who renumbered her as *I-504*,

Argo/Flutto
(Series 1, 2)-classes
ITA

Type: medium-displacement patrol boats.

History: In the early 1930s the Portuguese Navy ordered four boats fr
Monfalcone-based C.R.D.A. (Cantieri Riuniti dell'Adriatico) and work l
already begun when the order was cancelled. However, C.R.D.A. mana

Class	Argo	Flutto Series I	Flutto Series 2
Total built	2	9	3
Completed	1937	1942-43	1944
Displacement surfaced submerged	780 tons 1,000 tons	930 tons 1,093 tons	913 tons 1,113 tons
Dimensions length beam draught	207ft 4in (63.2m) 22ft 9in (6.9m) 14ft 7in (4.5m)	207ft 4in (63.2m) 22ft 11in (7.0m) 16ft 0in (4.9m)	210ft 7in (64.2m 22ft 11in (7.0m 16ft 2in (4.9m)

ove: **Glauco** *photographed in 1935.*

en, in their turn, the Japanese surrendered she was seized by the Americans o scuttled her on 15 April 1946.

opulsion			
ain engines	2 x Fiat	2 x Fiat	2 x Fiat
wer	2 x 750bhp	2 x 1,200bhp	2 x 1,200bhp
ctric motors	2 x C.R.D.A.	2 x C.R.D.A.	2 x CRDA/Marelli
wer	2 x 400shp	2 x 400shp	2 x 400shp
afts	two	two	two
rformance			
eed: surface	14kt	16kt	16kt
omerged	8kt	8kt	8kt
ge: surfaced	5,300nm/14kt	5,400nm/8kt	5,400nm/8kt
omerged	100m/3kt	80nm/4kt	80nm/4kt
ximum			
ing depth	288ft (90m)	400ft (120m)	400ft (120m)
eapons			
	6 x 21in (533mm)	6 x 21in (533mm)	6 x 21in (533mm)
ation	bow – 4, stern – 2	bow – 4, stern – 2	bow – 4, stern – 2
pedoes	10	12	12
ns	1 x 3.9in (100mm)	1 x 3.9in (100mm)	1 x 3.9in (100mm)
	4 x 13.2mm (4 x 1) MG	2 x 20mm (2 x 1) MG	4 x 13.2mm MG
mplement	46	50	50

ersuade the Italian Navy to take over the order, as a result of which the er pair, *Delfim* and *Espadarte,* became the Italian *Glauco* and *Otaria* (see

Glauco-class), and the slightly smaller and less heavily armed pair beca
the Italian Argo-class (it should be noted that another three submarin
ordered by Portugal from Vickers, UK, were not cancelled and w
delivered in 1936). Designed by Cavallini, the Argo-class boats w
generally similar to the Italian Navy's 600-ton series, albeit slightly larg
and were of saddle-tank design. Once in service they were considered to
one of the best of the Italian Navy's medium-displacement boats, being
strong construction and possessing good range and excell
manoeuvrability.

The Italian Navy's high opinion of the Argo-class was reinforced by com
experience in 1940-41, as a result of which an improved design was ordered
the Flutto-class. These boats had marginally larger, but much stronger hu
which led to a significant increase in maximum depth. More powerful dies
gave an increase of 2kt in surface speed and greater range, while a reductio
the size of the tower resulted in increased sub-surface manoeuvrability.
Flutto-class was also armed with two 20mm cannon, replacing the 13.2m
machine guns used in virtually all previous Italian submarines. A total of 12 w
planned, but only nine were actually completed, two of them, *Grongo*
Murena, with large, deck-mounted cylinders for human torpedoes in place
their deck guns.

The initial order became the Series I. A further group was ordered; th
being 3ft 3in (1m) longer to overcome some trim problems. Designated Flu
class Series II, 24 were ordered, of which nine were actually laid down but o
three were actually completed. It was planned to order a further 12, designa
Flutto-class Series III; these would have been identical in all respects to
Series II, but none was ever laid down.

Neither of the two Argo-class survived the war: *Vellella* was sunk

Brin/Liuzzi-classes   IT/

Type: short-range patrol.

Class	Brin	Liuzzi
Total built	5	4
Completed	1938-39	1940
Displacement surfaced submerged	1,000 tons 1,245 tons	1,148 tons 1,460 tons
Dimensions length beam draught	237ft 8in (72.5m) 21ft 11in (6.7m) 14ft 11in (4.5m)	249ft 8in (76.1m) 22ft 11in (7.0m) 14ft 11in (4.6m)
Propulsion main engines power electric motors power shafts	2 x Tosi 2 x 1,700bhp 2 x Ansaldo 2 x 650shp two	2 x Tosi 2 x 1,750bhp 2 x Ansaldo 2 x 750shp two

*ght: Flutto-class Marea was
en to Soviets in 1949.*

:ish submarine *Shakespeare* on
August 1943, and *Argo* was
ttled on the Italian surrender on
September 1943. Twelve Flutto
ies I were laid down but three
not been completed by the time
the Italian surrender and the
inished hulls were scrapped.
ee of the nine boats completed
e lost during the war, all to Allied
face warships: *Flutto* (11 July
3), *Gorgo* (21 May 1943) and
one (19 January 1943). Four were
ttled in September 1943 but
re raised by the Germans,
aired and recommissioned with
T" hull numbers: *Grongo* (UIT-
Murena (UIT-16), Sparide (*UIT-
and Nautilo* (*UIT-19*). All four
e then sunk in Allied air raids.
-19 (ex-*Nautilo*) was raised after
war by the Yugoslavs, refitted
recommissioned under its third
as *Sava*.

rformance		
ied: surface	17.3kt	18kt
omerged	8kt	8kt
ge: surfaced	9,000nm/7.8kt	13,000nm/8kt
omerged	90nm/4kt	110nm/4kt
ximum operational		
ing depth	288ft (90m)	288ft (90m)
eapons		
	8 x 21in (533mm)	8 x 21in (533mm)
ation	bow – 4, stern – 4	bow – 4, stern — 4
oedoes	14 torpedoes	12 torpedoes
ns	1 x 3.9in (100mm)	1 x 3.9in (100mm)
	4 x 13.2mm MG	4 x 13.2mm MG
mplement	54	58

tory: During the Spanish Civil War the Italian Navy, although supposedly
tral, provided a great deal of assistance to the Republican Navy, the most
ificant being the clandestine transfer in 1937 of two submarines –
himede and *Torricelli* of the Archimede-class (see page 180) – which were
nediately given Spanish names. In an attempt to conceal this from foreign
lligence two new submarines were built for the Italian Navy and given the
nes of the transferred boats. These two new boats, plus three others, were
t to a modified Archimede-class design and named after the first to be
npleted, becoming the Brin-class. Compared with the Archimede-class,

these had the same dimensions but the hull was much better shaped, resul
in a higher speed for the same installed power. Like the Foca-class minelay
the Brin-class was built with its 3.9in (100mm) gun at the after end of
bridge, an arrangement somewhat lacking in tactical logic, and this was recti
in 1942 when the gun was moved to the foredeck.

The four-boat Liuzzi-class was designed and built by Tosi at Taranto,
was, in essence, a slightly enlarged and improved version of the Brin-class,
changes including further modifications to the hull-shape and mounting
main gun on the foredeck. Like many Italian designs of the period they
unnecessarily large bridge structures, which were modified and reduced in
in 1942. They were popular with their crews and were particularly fast, one b
achieving a surface speed of 17.9kt on trials.

On the outbreak of war four of the Brin-class were stationed in the
Sea/Indian Ocean area and two – Torricelli and Calvi – were lost within days,
former being scuttled after a major battle in which she set fire to the Bri
destroyer Khartoum, which subsequently sank. The two remaining bo
Archimede and Guglielmotti, continued to operate in the area until May 1
when, in company with other Italian boats in the area, they sailed around At
to Bordeaux, being refuelled en route by a German supply ship. On arrival, t
joined the Italian squadron supporting the German U-boat campaign in
Atlantic. Archimede was lost off the coast of Brazil and Guglielmotti was s
in the Mediterranean, leaving only Brin, which, following the Italian surren
ended her days as a training ship for British ASW crews in Colombo, Ceylo

At the start of the war the Liuzzi-class was in the Mediterranean, wh
Liuzzi herself was sunk by British destroyers (27 June 1940) and Bagnolini s
a British C-class cruiser (12 June 1940). The remaining three boats were t
redeployed to Bordeaux and operated in the Atlantic, where Tarantini was s

Cagni-class

IT/

Type: long-range commerce raiders.
Total built: 4.
Completed: 1941.
Displacement: surfaced 1,708 tons; submerged 2,190 tons.
Dimensions: length 228ft 0in (87.9m); beam 25ft 6in (7.8m); draught 17ft
(5.7m).
Propulsion: 2 x C.R.D.A. diesels, 2 x 2,685bhp; 2 x C.R.D.A. electric motor
x 900shp; two shafts.
Performance: surface – 16.5kt; submerged – 8.5kt; range surfaced 10,700
at 12kt, submerged 107nm at 3.5kt; maximum operating diving depth 3
(100m).
Weapons: 14 x 17.7in (450mm) TT (bow – 8, stern – 6), 36 x torpedoes;
3.9in (100mm), 4 x 13.2mm MG.
Complement: 78.

History: This class had an exceptional armament, which was the direct re
of a very unusual decision by the Italian Naval Staff. The Cagni-class
designed to operate in distant waters against merchant shipping and the N
Staff considered that the boats needed the heaviest possible torpedo batter
increase the probability of a hit and a large number of reloads to ease
resupply problems. Careful analysis indicated that the 18in (457mm) torp
was perfectly adequate for destroying merchant shipping and by adopting
weapon the designers were able to mount eight tubes in the bows and s
the stern, and to carry a total of 36 torpedoes; no operational submarine
ever carried a greater load. It is highly unusual for new ships to incorporate

ove: **Torricelli** *was built to replace a boat given surreptitiously to* *...*ain. *She was scuttled on 23 June 1940 following a short engagement* *...*h *four British ships (the destroyers* **Kandahar, Khartoum** *and* *...*gston, *and the sloop* **Shoreham***) in the Red Sea.*

...e returning from her first patrol. The final pair were both converted into ...sports and both were taken over by the Germans on the Italian surrender ... given "UIT" numbers. *UIT-23* (ex-*Giulani*) was sunk while returning from ...ang (February 1944) and *UIT-22* (ex-*Bagnolini*) was sunk in March 1944 ...e en route to the Far East.

...ht: **Ammiraglio** *...ni, nameship of a* *...s of four.*

...er, less powerful ...pon system, but in ... case the decision ...ms to have been ... justified. These ...ts also carried two ...n (100mm) guns ... four 13.2mm ...chine guns in two ... mounts. The

...s' large size made them relatively comfortable for the crew but, somewhat ...prisingly, did not make them less manoeuvrable, and they were good ...keepers.

...The four boats became operational in mid-1941 and were immediately ...ssed into service as transports, taking supplies to Axis forces in North Africa, ...e course of which they moved a total of 2,370 tons of supplies during 15 ...ages. Three boats – *Caracciolo, Millo* and *Saint Bon* – were sunk in the ...rse of these activities; the first named was scuttled after being severely ...aged, while the other two were both sunk by British submarine HMS ...*olander*. Only *Cagni* survived and she was sent to the Atlantic, departing from ...Maddalena on 6 October 1942 and arriving at Bordeaux on 20 February ...3, having sailed out of the Mediterranean, then south as far as the Cape of ...d Hope, before returning to France; she sank two merchant ships on the way, ...ongest voyage undertaken by any Italian submarine during World War II.

Japanese Attack Submarine Designations

During the period 1922-45 the Imperial Japanese Navy (IJN) employe
complicated system of designations for submarine classes. Originally e
submarine was numbered in a single sequence in the order of launch but
system changed on 1 November 1924 when all submarines were divided
three groups, each given a letter prefix: large ocean-going boats (over 1
tons displacement) – I; coastal (500-1,000 tons) – Ro; and small (less than
tons) – Ha. Within these groups individual boats were allocated a new per
number; thus No 51 became *I-52*, No 84 became *Ro-63*, No 17 became *H*
and so on. In addition to this, the system of class designations was chan
with each class being given a descriptor, such as "*kaigun-dai*" (= large
design) which was then abbreviated, in this case to "KD." Successive cla
of the same type were then numbered in sequence (KD1, KD2, etc) and m
variations indicated by letter suffixes (KD3a, KD3b, etc). The result was th
pennant number prefixed "I-" simply meant a long-range submarine
included attack boats, scouting boats, minelayers and aircraft-carr
submarines.

As a final complication, in May 1942 all surviving I-class boats had
number 100 added to their pennant numbers, *I-68* becoming *I-168*, and so
This did not apply to the "Ro-" series boats, nor was it applied retrospect
to I-boats which had been lost prior to May 1942.

KD1/2/3-classes
JA

Type: long-range patrol.

Class	KD1	KD2	KD3a/b
Total built	1	1	KD3a S 4, KD3b
Completed	1924	1925	1927-31
Displacement surfaced submerged	1,500 tons 2,430 tons	1,500 tons 2,500 tons	1,800 tons 2,300 tons
Dimensions length beam draught	300ft 0in (91.4m) 28ft 10in (8.8m) 15ft 1in (4.6m)	330ft 10in (100.9m) 25ft 1in (7.6m) 16ft 10in (5.1m)	330ft 0in (100. 26ft 2in (8.0m 15ft 10in (4.8r
Propulsion main engines power electric motors power shafts	4 x Sulzer 4 x 1,300bhp 4 4 x 500shp four	2 x Sulzer 2 x 3,400bhp 2 2 x 1,000shp two	2 x Kanpon 2 x 3,400bhp 2 2 x 1,400shp two

breviated ignator	Japanese meaning	Literal translation	Pennant prefix	Japanese class
	hei-gata	C-model	I	1st
	jun(yo) sen (suikan)	cruiser submarine	I	1st
	kai(gun)-chu	Admiralty design, medium	Ro	2nd
	kaigun-dai	Admiralty design, large	I	1st
	kai(gun)-sho	Admiralty design, small	Ro	2nd
	–	–	Ro	2nd
	sen(suikan)-taka	fast submarine	I	1st
	sen(suikan) taka-sho	small fast submarine	Ha	3rd

formance			
ed: surfaced	20kt	22kt	20kt
merged	10kt	10kt	8kt
ge: surfaced	20,000nm/10kt	10,000nm/10kt	10,000nm/10kt
merged	100nm/4kt	100nm/4kt	90nm/3kt
ximum			
ng depth	200ft (61m)	200ft (61m)	200ft (60m)
apons			
tion	8 x 21in (533mm) bow	8 x 21in (533mm) bow – 6, stern – 2	8 x 21in (533mm) bow
edoes	24	16	16
s	1 x 4.7in (120mm) 1 x 3in (76mm)	1 x 4.7in (120mm) 1 x 3in (76mm)	1 x 4.7in (120mm)
mplement	60	60	63

ory: In the post-World War I era the Imperial Japanese Navy (IJN) was en by two perceived imperatives: building more submarines to redress the alance of capital ships imposed by the Washington Naval Conference, and requirement for such submarines to achieve trans-Pacific ranges. The KD1 KD2 classes represented two early attempts in this area, the start of a es which would continue in production from 1921 to 1943. KD1 was based ritish design practice, but with a very long range, and a heavy armament of t torpedo tubes and two guns, one 4.7in (120mm) and one 3in (76mm). She four propellers, each powered by a 1,300bhp Sulzer diesel, one of the very

few submarines in any navy to be driven in this way, but enabling two die
to be used for very long range cruising, and all four to be engaged to ach
maximum speed. Two complete power trains (diesel engine, electric m
shafts and propeller) were removed in 1932 and no further four-s
submarines were built. The 3in gun was also removed in the 1932 refit.

The KD2-class also consisted of one boat, *I-52* (ex- *No 51*) similar in size
identically armed to the KD1-class, but the design was based on that of
German *U-139,* which had been given to Japan as post World War I reparati
Despite having only half the power, maximum speed was a remarkable 22kt, s
2kt faster than the KD1, but surface range was reduced by some 50 per cent.

It was planned to build five more of the KD2-class, but the order
cancelled in favour of the KD3a, which was the first totally Japanese-desig
long-range cruiser submarine, although the design incorporated lessons le
with the KD2 and (to a lesser extent) KD1 designs. Four were built: *I-53* (e
64), *I-54* (ex-No 77), *I-55* (ex-No 78) and *I-58* (the last-named did not ha
previous number as it was ordered after the introduction of the new syst
These were followed by the five-strong KD3b-class, which was virt
identical to the KD3a, differing only in the shape of the bow and stern, w
resulted in a 6in (127mm) increase in overall length. The shape of the br
tower was also altered, giving a sloping leading edge.

I-51 (KD1-class) served as an operational boat from 1924 to 1930, but
then employed as a training boat until 1939, being stricken in 1941. *I-52* (
class) served long enough to be renumbered *I-152* in May 1942, but was
put into reserve and cannibalised for spares.

Of the KD3a/b-classes, *I-63* was lost in peacetime, when she collided
I-60 in the Bungo Strait on 2 February 1939, which resulted in 81 deaths. N
boats in both groups were transferred to the training role in March 1942 ar

KD4/5/6/7-classes

JA

Type: long-range patrol boats.

Class	KD4/5	KD6a/b	KD7
Total built	KD4 – 3, KD5 – 3	KD6a – 6, KD6b – 2	10
Completed	1930	1934-38	1943
Displacement surfaced submerged	1,720 tons 2,330 tons	1,785 tons 2,440 tons	1,833 tons 2,603 tons
Dimensions length beam draught	310ft 6in (94.6m) 25ft 7in (7.8m) 15ft 10in (4.8m)	342ft 6in (104.7m) 26ft 11in (8.2m) 15ft 0in (4.6m)	346ft 2in (105. 27ft 1in (8.3m, 15ft 1in (4.6m,
Propulsion main engines power electric motors power shafts	2 x M.A.N. 2 x 3,000bhp 2 2 x 900shp two	2 x Kanpon 2 x 4,500bhp 2 2 x 900shp two	2 x Kanpon 2 x 4,000bhp 2 2 x 900shp two

ove: **I-58** *lies outboard of* **I-53** *at the war's end.*

e renumbered by the addition of "1" before their old numbers on 20 May
2. One wartime loss, *I-60* was sunk by British destroyer *Jupiter* on 17
uary 1942. Four of the KD3a-class were laid up in reserve in early 1944, but
KD3a and three KD3bs were converted into *Kaiten* carriers in early 1945;
our survived the war and were scuttled in 1946.

formance			
ed: surface	20kt	23kt	23.1kt
merged	8.5kt	8.2kt	8kt
ge: surfaced	10,800nm/10kt	14,000nm/10kt	8,000nm/16kt
merged	60nm/3kt	65nm/3kt	50nm/5kt
ximum			
ng depth	230ft (70m)	250ft (76m)	260ft (80m)
apons			
tion	6 x 21in (533mm)	6 x 21in (533mm)	6 x 21in (533mm)
	bow – 4, stern – 2	bow	bow
edoes	14	14	12
s	1 x 4.7in (120mm)	1 x 3.9in (100mm)	1 x 5.0in (127mm)
	1 x 0.303in MG	1 x 13.2mm AA	2 x 25mm AA
mplement	58	60-84	88

:ory: The *kaidai* series continued with a number of further classes, each of
:h represented a small improvement on its predecessor. The KD4-class
:e units) was some 10ft 8in (3.3m) shorter than the KD3b and mounted six
:ad of eight torpedo tubes (four tubes in the bows and two in the stern) and
had an increase in range. Next came the KD5-class (three units), which
e very similar to the KD4 but were armed with one 3.9in (100mm) in place
ne KD3b's 4.7in (120mm), although the secondary weapon was a 13.2mm
hine gun in place of the earlier, and much lighter) 0.303in (7.7mm) weapon.
KD6a boats (six units) were larger versions of the KD4; in effect, the

designers returned to the size of the KD3b, the extra size being used
increased bunkerage, thus increasing range to 14,000nm at 10kt. These w
among the first Japanese submarines to be powered by the all-Japanese di
engine designed by the Naval Technical Bureau (*kansei honbu*) and which
generally known by that bureau's acronym of "Kanpon." The KD6b-class (
units) were virtually identical to KD6a. Finally, came the KD7-class (10 boat
which, once again, the great majority of the changes were very small, exe
for the armament. The original intention was for each boat not to hav
medium calibre main gun, but to mount four 25mm cannon in two twin mou
However, the weapon was new and suffered from production problems,
only half the number required were available. As a result, a 4.7in (102mm) n
gun was retained and a single twin 20mm mount was installed at the after
of the bridge. It should also be noted that the torpedo load was reduced f
14 to 12. Endurance of these long-range cruisers was 75 days.

Those boats that survived into 1942-43 were relegated to the training
or converted to transports to carry men and supplies to the Japanese-occu
outposts. Most of the latter received only minimal conversion for this new
but *I-171* (ex-*I-71*) was refitted to carry *Daihatsu* amphibious landing craft o
deck. Of these, those that remained in service in mid-1944 were
converted into *kaiten* carriers.

There were three KD4s, of which *I-61* was lost in a pre-war
collision with a Japanese gunboat (2
October 1941), *I-164* (ex-*I-64*) was
sunk by submarine USS *Triton* (17

***Right: I-70. The KD6a-class had
long range and high speed.***

J1-class   JA

Type: long-range cruiser.
Total built: 4.
Completed: 1929.
Displacement: surfaced 2,135 tons; submerged 2,791tons.
Dimensions: length 319ft 11in (97.5m); beam 30ft 3in (9.22m); draught 16f
(5.0m).
Propulsion: 2 x M.A.N diesels, 2 x 3,000bhp; 2 x electric motors, 2 x 1,300
two shafts.
Performance: surface – 18kt; submerged – 8kt; range surfaced 24,400n
10kt, submerged 60nm at 3kt; maximum operating diving depth 260ft (80
Weapons: 6 x 21in (533mm) TT (bow – 4, stern – 2), 20 torpedoes; 2 x !
(140mm) guns; 1 x 0.303in (7.7mm) MG.
Complement: 92.

History: These four boats were the first to be designated *junsen* (= cruise
the IJN and also the first to wear I-series pennants, being numbered *I-1* to
respectively. The programme came under strong German influence, the de
being based on that of the proposed U-142-class and powered by the la
M.A.N. diesels obtained from Germany. More than that, however, a promi
submarine designer/engineer, Dr. Ing. Techel, who had worked at the Kr
owned Germaniawerft throughout the late war, was brought to Japan to ac
during the final phase of the design process and the first month
construction (December 1924 to April 1925). They were double-hulled b
and were designed for a surface range of 24,000nm at 10kt, which
satisfactorily demonstrated during an early trial, although, like all boats of

ɔve: *Unknown KD7-class submarine under attack, 1944.*

ʋ 1942) and *I-162* (ex-*I-62*) survived the war. There were also three KD5s: *I-67*
lost in a pre-war accident (29 August 1940) and the other two, *I-165* (ex-*I-65*)
I-66 (ex- *I-66*), were lost in the war. There were eight KD6a/b boats, not one of
ɔh survived the war: three were sunk by surface warships; two were sunk by
marines; one was sunk by carrier-borne aircraft; one was lost when it was
ɔentally flooded during an air raid; and one was lost on operations, cause
ɔown.

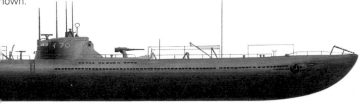

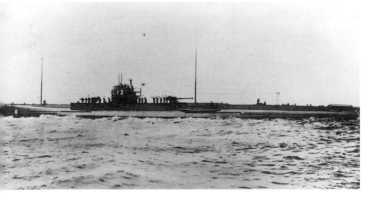

ʋe: *I-3 (J1-class); note the two 5.5in (140mm) guns.*

submerged range was very poor, in this case 60nm at 3kt.
I-3 was sunk by the U.S. *PT-59* (10 December 1942) and *I-4* by USS
dragon (20 December 1942), and the two remaining boats were then
ʋerted for use as transports, with the after gun removed, torpedo-carrying
ɔcity reduced, and fittings installed on the upper casing for carrying *daihatsu*
ɔng craft. *I-1* was damaged by two New Zealand ships and scuttled (29
ɔary 1943) and *I-2* was sunk by a U.S. destroyer (7 April 1944).
The J1 design was continued, but with facilities for carrying a small
ɔhibious aircraft

C1/C2/C3-classes

Type: long-range attack boats.

History: Designed in the mid-1930s and launched in 1938-39, the C1-c
were specialised long-range attack boats, their design being develo
from that of the KD6-class (qv). They were generally similar in size
capability to the A1-class and B1-class, but without the aircraft facili
Instead, the C1-class was fitted to carry one Type A midget submarine
the after casing. The C2-class, laid down in 1942 and completed in 1
was a repeat of the C1-class, with some modern equipment, with sli
less powerful diesels (5,500bhp each, as opposed to 6,200bhp), but wit

Class	C1/C2	C3
Total built	C1 – 5, C2 – 3	3
Completed	1941-44	1944
Displacement surfaced submerged	2,554 tons 3,561 tons	2,564 tons 3,644 tons
Dimensions length beam draught	358ft 7in (109.3m) 29ft 10in (9.1m) 17ft 7in (5.4m)	356ft 7in (108.7m) 30ft 6in (9.3m) 16ft 10in (5.1m)
Propulsion main engines power electric motors power shafts	2 x diesels 2 x 6,200bhp 2 2 x 1,000shp two	2 x diesels 2 x 2,350bhp 2 2 x 600shp two
Performance speed: surface submerged range: surfaced submerged maximum diving depth	23.6kt 8kt 14,000nm/16kt 60nm/3kt 330ft (100m)	17.7kt 6.5kt 21,000nm/16kt 105nm/3kt 330ft (100m)
Weapons TT location torpedoes guns	8 x 21in (533mm) bow 20 1 x 5.5in (140mm) 2 x 25mm AA	6 x 21in (533mm) bow 19 2 x 5.5in (140mm) 2 x 25mm AA
Complement	101	101

fittings for the midget submarines. Next in this series was the C3-class, ch had the same hull as the C2-class, but the main difference was that y had much less powerful main machinery (2,350bhp per engine) which e a dramatic 50 per cent increase in range, albeit with a reduction in ed from 23.6kt to 17.7kt.

All the C1-class took part in the Pearl Harbor operation, in which they ied their midget submarines, but every one of them was subsequently k during the Pacific War by U.S. forces: *I-22* in 1942, *I-18*, *I-20* and *I-24* 943. *I-16* was converted into a transport submarine in 1943, and was k while carrying out a resupply operation in 1944.

The C2-class did not join the fleet until 1944 and *I-47* and *I-48* were ediately converted to suicide-submarine carriers, first for four *kaiten* later for six. Two were sunk in the war, *I-46* (27 October 1944) and *I-48* January 1945), but *I-47* survived, to be scuttled in 1946. Similar fates ll the C3-class, with two war losses, one of them *I-55* in the Pacific (28 1944), while the other was sunk in the Atlantic, while sailing as a sport to Brest. The third, *I-53* was scuttled in 1946.

Plans to build 17 more C3-class and 25 of a modified C4-class were both born.

ɔw: **I-22***, along with the other four C1-class boats, took part in the* *ck on Pearl Harbor. She was sunk on either 5 October or 4* *ember 1942.*

No 71/ST-classes

Type: experimental fast attack.

Class	No 71	ST
Total built	1	6
Completed	1938	1945
Displacement surfaced submerged	213 tons 240 tons	1,291 tons 1,450 tons
Dimensions length beam draught	140ft 5in (42.8m) 10ft 10in (3.3m) 10ft 2in (3.1m)	259ft 2in (79.0m) 19ft 0in (5.8m) 17ft 11in (5.5m)
Propulsion main engines power electric motors power shafts	1 x diesel 1 x 1,200bhp 1 1 x 1,800shp one	2 x diesel 2 x 1,325bhp 2 2 x 2,500shp two
Performance speed: surface submerged range: surfaced submerged maximum diving depth	18kt 25kt 3,830nm/12.5kt 33nm/7kt 280ft (85m)	15.8kt 19kt 5,800nm/14kt 135nm/3kt 360ft (110m)
Weapons TT location torpedoes guns	3 x 18in (457mm) bow 3 –	4 x 21in (533mm) bow 10 2 x 25mm AA
Complement	11	31

History: The German high-speed submarine programme which culminate the development of the Types XXI and XXIII "*electroboats*" is well-known the equally daring Japanese programme has been largely overlooke historians. As allies during World War II, there was a certain amour exchange of information between Japan and Germany; in particular, Japanese Naval Attaché in Berlin obtained a great deal of information abou German Type XXI and Type XXIII U-boats from late 1943 onwards. Japanese high-speed submarine programme, however, started experimental *No 71,* which was laid down in December 1937 and launche August 1938 and was thus well ahead of the German programme. Giver name *No 71* for security reasons, the only boat in the programme was inte solely as what would be described in modern terms a "techno

ove: **No 71**, *fastest submarine since the British R-class.*

nonstrator." Despite its experimetnal status, the design incorporated three
า (457mm) torpedo tubes, a calibre which had not been used by the IJN for
าy years. *No 71*'s hull design appears modern, even by today's standards,
า its exceptionally clean lines broken only by the sail (itself of very
amlined design) and two small platforms, which were presumably
essary for ship-handling in port, and may well have been detachable. There
; a single propeller with cruciform after controls, and no forward
roplanes. *No 71* carried out a series of intensive tests over the period 1938-
and was then scrapped, but her value was derived from the lessons learned,
ch were then incorporated into two operational classes: the ST- and STS-
ses.

The first of the ST-class was launched in 1944 and with a length of 259ft
(79.0m) and submerged displacement of 1,450 tons it was of a similar size
he German Type XXI. The STS was armed with four 21in (533mm) torpedo
es and there were two deck-mounted 25mm AA cannon on fully
ppearing mounts. There was a long, very clean, all-welded hull but, as with
German Type XXI programme, the Japanese naval staff insisted on twin
ellers with twin diesels and electric motors. Surface speed was nearly
;, but this was not so important as the submerged speed, which was
gned as 19kt, although only 17kt was achieved in practice; this was,
ever, considerably in excess of any other contemporary submarine except
he German Types XXI and XXIII. The STS design was optimised for rapid
s-production although, in the event, only three were completed out of a
ned 100.

The hulls were very careful streamlined with an absolute minimum of drag-
cing protrusions, and items such as cleats and capstans were retractable.
other element necessary for high underwater speed was greater battery
er, but while the German solution was to use more cells the Japanese
d instead for a new type of battery, which had a much higher capacity but
e price of a short life. As in other navies, the designers wanted to do away
forward hydroplanes, which were considered unnecessary, but the
nariners insisted on them being fitted. They were needed for low-speed
rol and to avoid broaching during the period immediately following the
ch of a torpedo. The STS also had a Japanese-designed schnorkel, which
raised vertically to a height of about 10ft (3m).

A total of 100 STs were planned in the initial order, but just three were
pleted before the surrender; two of which went to the USA while the third
scuttled in Japanese waters in 1946. Another three were near completion
were broken up on the stocks.

One of the most surprising aspects of this story is that throughout
1920s and 1930s the Japanese produced a series of boats which, ap
from sheer size and aircraft-carrying capability, did very little to extend
boundaries of submarine technology. Their streamlined programr
however, was revolutionary and there is no doubt that the Japanese sho

*Below: **No 71** predated the German Walter boats by four years.*

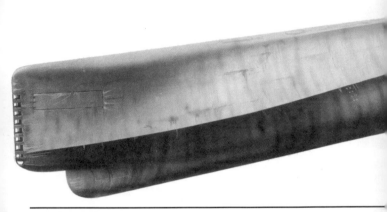

L4-class

JA

Type: coastal (second class).
Total built: 9.
Completed: 1923-27.
Displacement: surfaced 996 tons; submerged 1,322 tons.
Dimensions: length 256ft 0in (76.2m); beam 24ft 3in (7.4m); draught 12f
(3.8m).
Propulsion: 2 x Vickers diesels, 2 x 1,200bhp; 2 x electric motors, 2 x 80C
two shafts.
Performance: surface – 16kt; submerged – 8kt; range surfaced 7,000n
10kt, submerged 85nm at 4kt; maximum operating diving depth 200ft (61
Weapons: 6 x 21in (533mm) TT (bow), 10 x torpedoes; 1 x 3in 76mm) gur
MG.
Complement: 60.

History: Japan built a series of medium submarines based on the Britis
class (qv), starting with the L1-class, two of which were built by Mitsu
to Vickers' plans in 1919-20. These were virtually identical to the British-
L-class, with six 18in (457mm) torpedo tubes, four in the bows and tv
the beam. The IJN quickly established that these beam tubes had
practical value and the next four boats – the L-2-class – were simply
with only four torpedo tubes, all in the bows. These were followed by t
L3-class, which were virtual repeats of the L2-class and then by the
class, which were the last submarines to be built for the IJN base
British plans. These were externally very similar to the L3s but

ve given higher priority to this programme. However, in the early years
the war their entire attention was devoted to attacking the Americans as
across the Pacific as possible. The STS did not fit in with this plan as it
s a relatively short-range boat; nevertheless, it was a remarkable
ievement.

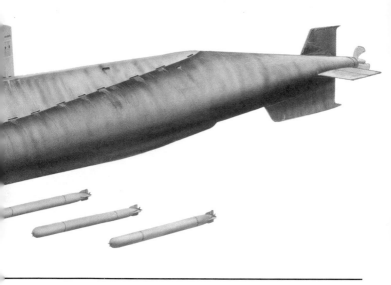

ve: **Ro-68**, one of many medium submarines in the IJN.

ificant internal improvements and two major changes in armament. The
st important of these was that there were now six torpedo tubes, all in
bows, and the calibre was increased to 21in (533mm), giving a major
ase in offensive capability. Also, a 3in (76mm) gun was mounted
ard of the bridge tower. The change to the new numbering system took
e during the construction of the L4-class, with the result that the first
were launched as Nos *59, 72, 73* and *74* and the remaining five as Ro-
o Ro-68; following the change the first four were renumbered as Ro-60
o-63.
All nine boats were still in service on the outbreak of war, but two were
n lost: *Ro-66* sunk after colliding with *Ro-62* (17 December 1941) and
50 was shipwrecked (29 December 1941). The remainder were
gated to training duties in mid-1942, but *Ro-61* was sunk by U.S. ships
aircraft (31 August 1942), and *Ro-65* dived onto a reef while under air
:k (4 November 1942). *Ro-64* was in service as a training boat when
: by a mine (12 April 1945) with the loss of 50 crew plus 30 trainees.
remaining boats surrendered in August 1945 and were then scrapped.

STS-class

Type: high performance, coastal defence.
Total built: 10.
Completed: 1945.
Displacement: surfaced 320 tons; submerged 440 tons.
Dimensions: length 173ft 11in (53.0m); beam 13ft 1in (4.0m); draught 11ft 3in (3.4
Propulsion: 1 x diesel, 1 x 400bhp; 1 x electric motor, 1 x 1,250shp; one sh
Performance: surface – 10.5kt; submerged – 13kt; range surfaced 3,000nr
10kt, submerged 100nm at 2kt; maximum operating diving depth 500ft (152
Weapons: 2 x 21in (533mm) TT (bow); 1 x 7.7mm MG.
Complement: 22.

History: The STS (*sensuikan) taka-sho* = small
fast submarine) were the second outcome of
the *No 71* experimental programme (qv), and
were directly comparable with the German
Type XXIII. The Japanese boats were designed
specifically for homeland defence against the
inexorable advance of the U.S. forces. They
were designed for simple, mass production,
using prefabricated, all-welded, highly
streamlined hulls and a single propeller. Items
such as bollards were retractable, but they
were fitted with both a search radar and a
Japanese-developed schnorkel. Range was

K-XI/O-9-classes

Type: East Indies, patrol; European waters, patrol.

Class	K-XI	O-9
Total built	3	3
Completed	1925	1931-32
Displacement surfaced submerged	670 tons 815 tons	515 tons 647 tons
Dimensions length beam draught	218ft 10in (66.9m) 20ft 2in (6.2m) 12ft 2in (3.7m)	179ft 6in (54.7m) 18ft 8in (5.7m) 11ft 6in (2.5m)
Propulsion main engines power electric motors power battery shafts	2 x M.A.N. diesels 2 x 1,200bhp 2 2 x 360shp 132 cells two	2 x Sulzer 2 x 450bhp 2 2 x 305shp 120 cells two

ne 3,000nm at 10kt and endurance was about 15 days. Like other 3rd class
ats, they were numbered in the "Ha-" series.

The first was not laid down until March 1945 and the production plans were
y ambitious, calling for 13 to be completed every month. However, as with
e Germans, the planners were living in a fantasy world, and just 10 were
mpleted before the end of the war, all of which were still working up when
war ended, and not one was employed operationally. All completed boats
d the incomplete boats on the ways were captured by the Americans.

low: Like the Type XXI, not one STS became operational.

Performance		
eed: surface	15kt	12kt
merged	8kt	8kt
ge: surfaced	3.500nm/12kt	3,500nm/8kt
merged	13nm/8kt	11nm/7.5kt
ximum		
ng depth	200ft (60m)	280ft (85m)
apons		
ation	2 x 21in (533mm)	2 x 21in (533mm)
	bow	bow
ation	4 x 17.7in (450mm)	3 x 17.7in (450mm)
	bow – 2, stern – 2	bow – 2, stern – 1
pedoes	4 x 21in; 8 x 17.7in	4 x 21in, 6 x 17.7in
s	1 x 3.4in (88mm) AA	1 x 3.4in (88mm) AA
	1 x 12.7mm AAMG	1 x 12.7mm AAMG
mplement	31	29

ory: Starting in the early 1900s, the Dutch system was that submarines for
in European waters were paid for out of the naval budget, whereas those
nded for use in the East Indies were paid for by the Colonial Ministry. The
ner were designated "*Onderzeeboot*" (undersea boat = submarine)
wed by an Arabic numeral, and the latter "*Koloniën*" (colonial) , followed by
man numeral. This system continued throughout the 1920s, the first post-
rd War I boats being the K-XI-class, which was a development of the K-VIII-

class (qv), but the torpedo armament consisted of a mix of two calibres. In bow there were four tubes, two of them 21in (533mm) with one reload for e tube, the first time that tubes of this calibre had been fitted into Du submarines. The bow torpedo room also contained two 17.7in (450mm) tut with two reloads for each tube. This mix of two calibres was a most unusual arrangement, which must have casued logistic difficulties in supplying two different types of torpedo and practical complications within the boat, especially over settings and fire control arrangements. The remaining two tubes were aft, but in this case were both 17.7in plus two reloads.

The O-9-class was developed from the K-XI design, but was slightly smaller and slower, although range was still the same. The O-9-class also retained the mix of 21in and 17.7in in the forward torpedo room, but there was only one tube aft.

At the outbreak of war the three O-9-class were all in Dutch waters; 0-11 was captured by the Germans and eventually scuttled as a blockship, while O-9 and O-10 escaped to Britain, where they operated with the British Royal Navy until stricken in 1944. The three K-XI-class boats were in Far Eastern waters at the time of the Japanese attack; K-XII was sunk in

K-XIV/O-12-classes

NETHERLA

Type: East Indies, patrol; European waters, patrol.

Class	K-XIV	O-12
Total built	5	3
Completed	1933-34	1931-32
Displacement surfaced submerged	771 tons 1,008 tons	568 tons 715 tons
Dimensions length beam draught	242ft 9in (74.0m) 25ft 0in (7.6m) 12ft 10in (3.9m)	198ft 6in (60.5m) 18ft 4in (5.6m) 11ft 10in (3.6m)
Propulsion main engines power electric motors power battery shafts	2 x M.A.N. diesels 2 x 1,600bhp 2 x W. Schmitt motors 2 x 50360shp 120 cells two	2 x Sulzer/M.A.N. 2 x 900bhp 2 2 x 310shp 192 cells two

Japanese air attack, while the other two went to Australia where they erated as part of the Allied naval force until 1944 when they were stricken.

low: K-XI, a class of three boats developed from the K-VIII.

erformance		
eed: surface	17kt	15kt
bmerged	9kt	8kt
nge: surfaced	3.500nm/11kt	3,500nm/10kt
bmerged	26nm/8.5kt	12nm/8kt
aximum		
ving depth	260ft (80m)	280ft (85m)
eapons		
	8 x 21in (533mm)	5 x 21in (533mm)
cation	bow – 4, stern – 2, rotating – 2	bow – 4, stern – 1
rpedoes	14	10
ns	1 x 3.4in (88mm) AA	2 x 40mm AA
	2 x 40mm AA	1 x 12.7mm MG
omplement	38	31

story: Starting in the early 1900s, the Dutch system was that submarines use in European waters were paid for out of the naval budget, whereas ose intended for use in the East Indies were paid for by the Colonial nistry. The former were designated "*Onderzeeboot*" (undersea boat = omarine) followed by an Arabic numeral, and the latter "*Koloniën*" lonial), followed by a Roman numeral. This system continued throughout e 1920s, the first post-Wolrd War I boats being the K-XI-class, which was evelopment of the K-VIII-class (qv), but the torpedo armament consisted a mix of two calibres. In the bow there were four tubes, two of them 21in

(533mm) with one reload for each tube, the first time that tubes of 1
calibre had been fitted into Dutch submarines. The bow torpedo room a
contained two 17.7in (450mm) tubes, with two reloads for each tube. T
mix of two calibres was a most unusual arrangement, which must ha
casued logistic difficulties in supplying two different types of torpedo a
practical complications within the boat, especially over settings and
control arrangements. The remaining two tubes were aft, but in this ca
were both 17.7in plus two reloads.

The O-9-class was developed from the K-XI design, but was sligl
smaller and slower, although range was still the same. The O-9-class a
retained the mix of 21in and 17.7in in the forward torpedo room, but th
was only one tube aft.

At the outbreak of war the three O-9-class were all in Dutch waters
11 was captured by the Germans and eventually scuttled as a blocksl
while O-9 and O-10 escaped to Britain, where they operated with the Brit
Royal Navy until stricken in 1944. The three K-XI-class boats were in
Eastern waters at the time of the Japanese attack; K-XII was sunk ii
Japanese air attack, while the other two went to Australia where th
operated as part of the Allied naval force until 1944 when they w
stricken.

*Above right: O-12-class O-13, seen in 1931. She was sunk in error in tH
North Sea by the Polish submarine Wilk shortly after escaping to Brita
in 1940.*

*Right: K-XIV class K-XVI, which sank the Japanese destroyer Sagiri, 24
December 1941, but was sunk a day later by IJN submarine I-66 off Kunchir*

O-16/O-21-classes ·   NETHERLAN

Type: European waters, patrol; ocean patrol.

Class	O-16	O-21
Total built	1	7
Completed	1936	1940-41
Displacement surfaced submerged	896 tons 1,170 tons	990 tons 1,205 tons
Dimensions length beam draught	251ft 0in (76.5m) 21ft 9in (6.6m) 13ft 3in (4.0m)	255ft 0in (77.7m) 22ft 3in (6.8m) 13ft 1in (4.0m)
Propulsion main engines power electric motors power battery shafts	2 x M.A.N. diesels 2 x 1,600bhp 2 x W. Schmitt motors 2 x 500shp 2 x 96 cells two	2 x Sulzer diesels 2 x 2,600bhp 2 2 x 500shp 2 x 96 cells two

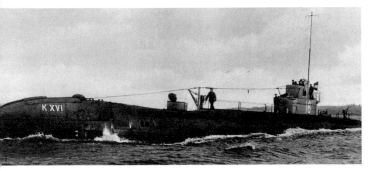

formance		
eed: surface	18kt	19.5kt
bmerged	9kt	9kt
nge: surfaced	10,000nm/12kt	10,000nm/12kt
bmerged	26nm/8.5kt	28NM/8.5KT
aximum		
ving depth	262ft (80m)	328ft (100m)
eapons		
cation	8 x 21in (533mm) bow – 4, stern – 2, rotating – 2	8 x 21in (533mm) bow – 4, stern – 4
pedoes	14	14
ns	1 x 3.4in (88mm) AA 2 x 40mm AA	1 x 3.4in (88mm) AA 1 x 12.7mm MG
mplement	38	39

tory: The sole O-16-class boat was the last Dutch submarine to be designed cifically for employment in European waters, and was slightly larger than the ceding O-12-class. The torpedo armament was increased from five to eight es, the latter including a twin-tube rotating mounting inside the upper casing, as t installed in the K-XIV-class. The O-21-class was the first Dutch submarine ign to be intended for use in any theatre and proved to be outstanding design. 940 was one of the best general-purpose boats in any navy. It was generally ilar to the O-19-class but, since it did not carry mines, was slightly smaller. The

hull was fabricated from high yield (HY-52) steel giving the boats an excel‹
dividng depth for the time of 328ft (100m). As with all Dutch submarines of the ‹
they were very well equipped, and included a schnorkel.

O-16 was, in fact, in the Far East at the time of the Japanese attack,
was sunk when she blundered into a British-laid minefield off Singapore isl‹
(16 December 1941). Five of the O-21-class had been launched at the time‹

the German invasion, four of
which managed to reach the UK.
O-25, which was fitting out, was
scuttled by the Dutch but raised
by the Germans, refitted and
commissioned in 1942 as *UD-3*. A
further two hulls (*O-26* and *O-27*)
were completed by the Germans
and commissioned as *UD-4* and
UD-5. The Germans made various
modifications, including the
removal of the external rotating
torpedo mounting, replacing the
40mm weapons with German
20mm AA, and replacing the
bridge tower with a German-
pattern device. *UD-3* and *UD-4*
were scutlled in May 1945, but
UD-5 was returned to the Dutch
who commissioned her under her
original number of *O-27*.

Orzel-class

NETHERLANDS (POLAN‹

Type: ocean-going patrol.
Total built: 2.
Completed: 1939.
Displacement: surfaced 1,473 tons; submerged 1,650 tons.
Dimensions: length 275ft 7in (84.0m); beam 22ft 0in (6.7m); draught 13ft
(4.2m).
Propulsion: 2 x Sulzer diesels, 2 x 2,370bhp; 2 x Brown-Boveri electric mot‹
2 x 550shp; battery 100 cells; two shafts.
Performance: surface – 20kt; submerged – 9kt; range surfaced 7,000nm‹
10kt, submerged 100nm at 5kt; maximum operating diving depth 260ft (80‹
Weapons: 12 x 21.7in (550mm) TT (bow – 4, stern – 4, rotating mount –
20 x torpedoes; 1 x 4.1in (105mm) Bofors gun, 2 x 40mm Bofors AA,
13.2mm MG.
Complement: 60.

History: With the prospect of war with Germany growing ever nearer, ‹
Polish Navy was forced to expand, and national feeling was so strong that ‹
cost of the first of a new class of submarine was raised by popular subscript‹
The selected design was from RDM in The Netherlands and was an adapta‹
of the impressive O-19-class but without the minelaying capability. It wa‹
double-hull design and equipment came from all over Europe: the boats w‹
powered by Sulzer diesels from Switzerland and Brown-Boveri electric mot‹
from Germany, and both the 4.1in (105mm) and 40mm guns were from ‹
Swedish company, Bofors. The torpedo tubes were French and were 21‹
(550mm) calibre, which was not used before outside the French Navy. Inde‹

The four boats which reached England had to be put into dockyard hands [for] completion, but were then all put into service, under British command, but [with] Dutch crews. *O-22* was sunk by a German minesweeper (8 November [19]40) but the other three – and the returned *O-27* – served on until the 1950s.

[Bel]ow: O-21-class O-24 *survived the war, to be stricken in 1956.*

[Rig]ht: Polish Orzel-
[cla]ss comprised
[tw]o boats built in
[the] Netherlands.

[...] tubes in the two
[Dutch] boats were fitted
[with] liners to enable
[inte]rnational standard
[21in] (533mm) torpe-
[doe]s to be launched,
[and] from 1939
[onw]ards only such [tor]pedoes were embarked. The main gun was located at the foot of the forward [fac]e of the bridge tower behind a large gunshield, an arrangement which [enjo]yed a brief vogue in the late 1930s.

Both boats had unusual careers. First-of-class *Orzel* was operating in [the] Baltic on 15 September 1939 when she was forced to put into the [Lith]uanian port of Talinn, where, to everyone's surprise, the authorities [inte]rned both the boat and her crew. They escaped three days later and [man]aged to reach Scotland, where *Orzel* came under the operational [con]trol of Britain's Royal Navy. Unfortunately, this boat and her brave crew [we]re lost, cause unknown, on a North Sea patrol in June 1940. Second-of-[clas]s *Sep* was still undergoing builder's trials when her captain and crew [seiz]ed control and sailed her to Gdynia. Once war broke out and Polish [def]eat was inevitable she was sailed to Sweden where she was interned [for] the duration of hostilities. She was returned to Poland in October 1945 [and] served on until 1970.

B-class

Type: coastal patrol.
Total built: 6.
Completed: 1926-30.
Displacement: surfaced 420 tons; submerged 545 tons.
Dimensions: length 167ft 4in (51.0m); beam 17ft 6in (5.3m); draught 11ft (3.5m).
Propulsion: 2 x Sulzer diesels, 2 x 450bhp; 2 x electric motors, 2 x 350shp; shafts.
Performance: surface – 14.8kt; submerged – 11kt; maximum operating di depth 164ft (50m).
Weapons: 4 x 18.0in (456mm) TT (bow – 2, stern – 2), 1 x 3in (76mm) gun.
Complement: 23.

History: Like its Nordic neighbours Denmark and Sweden, Norway maintai a small flotilla of submarines, which were constructed in its own ya although design was sometimes put out to contract. In the case of the B-cl the design was prepared by the Electric Boat Co. of Groton, Connecticut, U in 1915, but due to World War I (in which Norway was neutral) construc could not be started for several years and the first-of-class was not launc until August 1922, followed by three more in 1923 to 1924. After that there a five year gap until the last two boats were launched. Construction took p at the Royal Norwegian Navy's Marinens Hovdewerft (= admiralty yard Horten. The boats were very conventional, but were one of the last design mount 18in (457mm) torpedo tubes, with two forward and two aft.

Series I-class

Type: medium-range patrol.
Total built: 6.
Completed: 1929-30.
Displacement: surfaced 933 tons; submerged 1,354 tons.
Dimensions: length 249ft 4in (76.0m); beam 21ft 4in (6.5m); draught 12ft (3.8m).
Propulsion: 2 x diesels, 2 x 1,300bhp; 2 x electric motors, 2 x 800shp; shafts.
Performance: surface – 14kt; submerged – 9kt; range surfaced 7,000nm at submerged 105nm at 4kt; maximum operating diving depth 246ft (75m).
Weapons: 8 x 21in (533mm) TT (bow – 6, stern – 2) 14 x torpedoes; 1 x (102mm) gun; 1 x 45mm gun; 1 x 0.30in MG; 8 x mines.
Complement: 53.

History: The six boats of the D-class were the first attempt following Bolshevik Revolution to rebuild the Soviet submarine fleet, the design be based on that of the Bars-class of 1915-16 (qv). The class was originally ca the D-class and the boats were given individual names, that of the first-of-c being *Dekabrist*; but they were later simply numbered from *D-1* to *D-6*. O *D-1* commenced sea-trials in 1930 it was found that there were m problems, some due to shortcomings in the basic design, others to the shod standards in Soviet industry. There was a lack of stability, particular tendency to list when surfacing, which was eventually cured, but there w much more dangerous tendency for the quick-dive tank to flood suddenl depth. The design and construction of the battery tank also left a lot to

**ove: B-3, launched on 25 January 1924, was scuttled in May 1940
'en the Germans invaded Norway.**

All six boats were still in service when the Germans invaded Norway in
-0. *B-1* escaped to England, where it served as a target boat for ASW training
il stricken in 1944, while *B-3* was scuttled. The other four were captured by
 Germans: the fate of *B-2* and *B-4* is not known, but *B-5* and *B-6* were
nmissioned into the German Navy as *UC-1* and *UC-2*, but served for only a
rt while before being stricken and broken up.

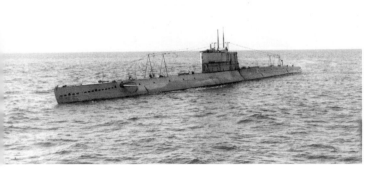

ove: Soviet Series I-class submarine Yakobinec (D-6).

ired, and installation, maintenance and removal of the electric storage cells
e always very difficult processes. The boats were refitted on several
sions, the last in 1940 and were subject to many modifications.
    The first loss was *D-1*, which disappeared without trace while on a training
rcise in November 1940; no cause was ever established but it may have
n due to the flooding problem mentioned earlier. *D-3* was mined (July 1942),
 was sunk by German surface warships (December 1943) and *D-6* was
aged at sea in an air attack, but returned to port only to be destroyed by
bers in dry dock. The two remaining boats were stricken in the 1950s.

Series III/V/Vbis/Vbis2/ X/Xbis-class

SOVIET UNIO

Type: coastal patrol.

Series	III	V	Vbis/Vbis^2	X/Xbis
Total built	4	19	21	53
Completed	1931-32	1933-34	1935	1936-37
Displacement surfaced submerged	578 tons 704 tons	589 tons 708 tons	607 tons 749 tons	590 tons 708 tons
Dimensions length beam draught	187ft 0in (57.0m) 20ft 4in (6.2m) 12ft 5in (3.8m)	191ft 11in (58.5m) 20ft 4in (6.2m) 14ft 1in (4.3m)	192ft 9in (58.8m) 20ft 4in (6.2m) 14ft 1in (4.3m)	192ft 9in (58.8 20ft 4in (6.2m) 14ft 1in (4.3m)
Propulsion main engines power electric motors power battery shafts	2 x diesels 2 x 685bhp 2 2 x 400shp 2 x 56 cells two	2 x diesels 2 x 800bhp 2 2 x 400shp 2 x 56 cells two	2 x diesels 2 x 685bhp 2 2 x 400shp 2 x 56 cells two	2 x diesels 2 x 800bhp 2 2 x 400shp 2 x 56 cells two
Performance speed: surface submerged range: surfaced submerged maximum diving depth	12.5kt 8.5kt 3,250nm/8kt 110nm/2kt 295ft (90m)	14kt 8kt 6,700nm/8kt 100nm/2kt 295ft (90m)	14kt 8kt 6,700nm/8kt 100nm/2kt 295ft (90m)	15kt 8.7kt 6,140nm/7k 122nm/2kt 295ft (90m)
Weapons TT location torpedoes guns	6 x 21in (533mm) bow – 4, stern – 2 10 1 x 45mm 2 x 0.3in MG	6 x 21in (533mm) bow – 4, stern – 2 10 2 x 45mm 1 x 0.3in MG	6 x 21in (533mm) bow – 4,stern – 2 10 2 x 45mm AA –	6 x 21in (533n bow – 4 stern 10 2 x 45mm A 1 x 0.3in M
Complement	35	40	40	40

History: The Schulka-class of medium submarines was built in very la
numbers and was the subject of steady development through three m
types – Series III, Series V (three sub-types) and Series X (two sub-types).
was the first original submarine design produced in the USSR and remaine
constant production, incorporating a steady stream of improvements, f
1929 to 1948. At the time of its entry into service in the mid-1930s the Se
V was only marginally smaller than the contemporary German Type V

ove: **Kambala** *(Shch-203) of the Series Vbis.*

ough the Soviet boat's performance and capabilities were far less.

First to appear was the Series III, three of which were approved as part of First Five Year Plan, but with a fourth paid for by popular subscription. They e double-hull boats with saddle tanks covering some two-thirds of the ssure hull, which was sub-divided into six watertight compartments. Power s provided by two 8-cylinder, 685bhp Soviet-made diesels, giving a kimum surface speed of 13kt; endurance was 20 days. Thus, they had poor je, low endurance and to add to all this were particularly noisy.

Many of the shortcomings of the first four boats were addressed in the ch more numerous Series V, which had a longer hull, sub-divided into seven ipartments, and more powerful engines, while rearrangement and ension of the bunkers increased fuel capacity from 25 to 50 tons. There e two minor variations in this group, the Series Vbis and Vbis2 (originally to e been designated the Series VIII) which had a slightly longer hull, but rted to the earlier, less powerful engines. The Series X was generally lar to the earlier boats, but with more powerful engines, while some at least a sloping forward edge to the bridge tower. By this time endurance had bled to 40 days and the Series X boats were no longer coastal boats, but an ocean-going capability. In the Series Xbis the major improvements were cerned with enabling production to be both easier and quicker.

The construction programme was complicated and reflects the difficulties ted by the vast geographical spread of the USSR. Thus, boats for the Black Fleet were built in the 61-Kommunar and Marti Yards in Nikolayev in the ea, and those for the Baltic Fleet by the Marti, Ordzhonikidze and Zhdanov s in Leningrad. The Marti and Ordzhonikidze yards also fabricated parts ch were then shipped to the Far East for assembly by the Dalzavod yard and ice with the Pacific Fleet.

t appears that the numbering system was originally intended to be based e yards; for example, the Dalzavod yard built *Shch-101* to *-112* (Series V), *1-113* to *-121* (Series Vbis), *Shch-122* to *-125* (Series Vbis2), *Shch-126* to (Series X) and *Shch-135* to *-138* (Series Xbis). However, the apparent logic e sequence was marred when *Shch-131* to *-134*, and *Shch-139* to *-141* e built at other yards. Further complications were caused by renumbering. All the boats served in the Great Patriotic War and some were quite essful. *Shch-307* sank the German *U-144* in the Baltic (9 August 1941) e *Shch-211* sank the German tanker *Peles* in the Black Sea (15 August). Thirty-three boats were lost during the war and the remainder served on the 1950s except for 11 Series Xbis which survived into the 1960s.

Series VI/XII-class

Type: coastal patrol.

Series	VI/VIbis	XII/XIIbis
Total built	VI - 30, VIbis - 20	XII - 4; XIIbis - 45
Completed	1933-37	1938-43
Displacement surfaced submerged	160 tons 200 tons	206 tons 218 tons
Dimensions length beam draught	124ft 0in (37.8m) 10ft 3in (3.1m) 8ft 6in (2.6m)	146ft 0in (44.5m) 10ft 10in (3.3m) 10ft 1in (3.1m)
Propulsion main engines power electric motors power shafts	1 x diesel 1 x 685bhp 1 x PG60 motor 1 x 240shp one	1 x diesel 1 x 800bhp 1 1 x 400shp one

History: The original Series VI was a response to a naval staff requiren
for a small submarine for employment in defending harbours and
coastline. The official Russian type designation was *maliye lodki*, us
abbreviated to *malodki* (= small submarine) and the actual design was ba
on that of the AG-class (qv) which had been very successful
in the Imperial Russian Navy. The Series VI boats were built
at the Gorky Shipyard on the Volga river and then transported
by rail on specially constructed railcars to the Black Sea
where they ran trials. They were then replaced on the railcars
and transported to Vladivostock for service with the Pacific
Fleet. They were single-hull boats and were the first Soviet
boats to use welding, but this was confined to the bridge
tower and casing. One of the major design constraints was
that the dry weight of the boats could not exceed 120 tons,
since this was the maximum capacity of the railcars.

The original Series VI boats had a number of
shortcomings, mainly their very limited armament – just two
torpedoes – restricted range (1,600nm at 8.5kt on the
surface and 55nm at 3.5kt submerged), and a poorly
designed hull. The latter was partially overcome in the Series
VIbis which had a much better hull, and the 20 boats were
built by more exeprience shipyards at Leningrad and
Nikolayev.

The other problems had not been resolved and this led to
the Series XII which was longer, with a stronger hull, more
powerful engines and two reload torpedoes. The outcome
was a far more satisfactory boat, with much greater range, a
deeper operating depth and much improved internal

...formance		
...eed: surface	13kt	14kt
...ﬞmerged	6kt	8kt
...ge: surfaced	1,600nm/8.3kt	3,440nm/9kt
...ﬞmerged	55nm/2.5kt	107nm/3kt
...ximum		
...ng depth	200ft (60m)	246ft (75m)
...apons		
	2 x 21in (533mm)	2 x 21in (533mm)
...ation	bow	bow
...ﬞedoes	2	4
...s	1 x 45mm AA	1 x 45mm AA
...mplement	16	20

...ipment. Only four were built since construction then switched to the ...es XIIbis, which had a better designed bridge tower and increased fuel ...kerage. A total of 45 were completed between 1937 and 1941. One ...es XII and one Series XIIbis were converted to take a Special Purpose ...enerating Power Unit (ie, an air-independent propulsion system); this is ...cribed in the Quebec-class entry in the AIP section.

...There were no war losses among the Series VI boats, but losses in the ...er groups were: Series VIbis – 8, Series XII – 2; Series XIIbis – 26. The ...ivors served on into the 1950s and were then scrapped, except for a ...ll number which were passed to friendly navies: Bulgaria – three Series ...s; China – one Series VI, one Series XIIbis, North Korea – one Series ...s. A further development was the larger Series XV built between 1940 ...1947.

...w: M-35, a coastal submarine of Series XIIbis.

Series IX/IXbis/XVI-class SOVIET UN

Type: coastal patrol.

Series	IX	IXbis/XVI
Total built	3	IXbis - 39; XVIbis - 6
Completed	1936	1937-40
Displacement		
surfaced	840 tons	856 tons
submerged	1,070tons	1,090 tons
Dimensions		
length	255ft 1in (77.8m)	255ft 1in (44.5m)
beam	21ft 0in (6.4m)	21ft 0in (6.4m)
draught	13t 3in (4.0m)	13ft 4in (4.1m)
Propulsion		
main engines	2 x diesel	2 x diesel
power	2 x 2,000bhp	2 x 2,000bhp
electric motors	2	2
power	2 x 550shp	2 x 550shp
shafts	two	two
Performance		
speed: surface	19.5kt	18.9kt
submerged	9kt	8.8kt
range: surfaced	9,800nm/10kt	9,800nm/10kt
submerged	148nm/3kt	148nm/3kt
maximum		
diving depth	328ft (100m)	328ft (100m)
Weapons		
TT	6 x 21in (533mm)	6 x 21in (533mm)
location	bow – 4; stern – 2	bow – 4; stern – 2
torpedoes	12	12
guns	1 x 3.9in (100mm)	1 x 3.9in (100mm)
	1 x 45mm AA	1 x 45mm AA
		1 x 0.3in MG
Complement	46	45

History: The Soviet Navy was not satisfied with the design of the Series VI (Pravda-class) and requested *Ingenieurskantoor voor Scheepsbouw* (I.v.S.), the German submarine design office located in the Hague, to produce a design for a medium-displacement, ocean-going submarine. The result was the Series IX, an excellent design which was produced at the same time that I.v.S. was working on the *Gür* for the Turkish Navy and the Type IA for the German Navy; the three bear marked resemblances to each other, as well as to the German

*ove: **S-102**, Stalinetz-class, returns to her Arctic base.*

e VII, which was developed later. The Series IX was a single-hull with a
dle tank and an armament of six torpedo tubes and a deck gun located at
foot of the forward edge of the bridge tower, behind a large gunshield. It
s slightly larger than the *Gür* and Type IA, with a more powerful propulsion
tem. Soviet designers then refined the design, resulting in the Series IXbis,
 of the major changes being to move the gun (whose shield not only caused
siderable hydrodynamic drag but also made the gun very difficult to work)
ward to an open mount, which then also enabled the shape of the bridge
er to be refined. The design was improved yet further with the Series XVI,
ch was constructed of tougher steel, with an all-welded hull, and the deck
 was moved to a new position abaft the tower. These boats were also
wn as the S-class, some sources claiming that this stood for *srednaya* (=
dium), others that it meant *Stalinetz*, after the dictator who took a great
rest in naval matters.

The original Series IX comprised just three boats, all built at the
zhonikidze Yard under German supervision. This was followed by an order
44 Series IXbis, which included four paid for by public subscription, although
 of these boats were not completed due to the German invasion. The Series
, which were idnetical in all major respects to the Series IXbis, were
pleted in 1947-49.

The Series IX boats fought in all theaters and proved themselves to be the
t all-round boats in the Soviet Navy. All three Series IX were lost in the war;
 was blown up to prevent its capture, one was mined and one was sunk.
the 39 Series IXbis completed, 13 were lost in the war to variety of causes;
surviviving boats served on into the 1950s-60s, but four were transferred to
na in 1955. The six Series XVI were built after the war and all served into the
0s, when they were scrapped; none was transferred to foreign navies.

*ow: **Series IX** was designed by German-run bureau I.v.S.*

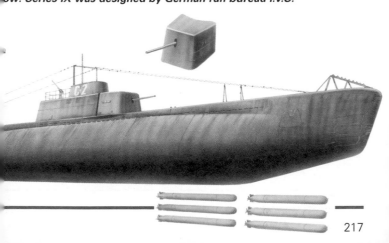

Series XIV

Type: ocean-going patrol.
Total built: 11.
Completed: 1940-42.
Displacement: surfaced 1,498 tons; submerged 2,095 tons.
Dimensions: length 320ft 4in (97.7m); beam 24ft 3in (7.4m); draught 14ft ¹
(4.5m).
Propulsion: 2 x diesel, 2 x 4,200bhp; 2 x electric motors, 2 x 1,200shp; bat
4 x 60 cells; two shafts.
Performance: surface – 21kt; submerged – 10kt; range surfaced 14,000nn
9kt, submerged 160nm at 3kt; maximum operating diving depth 263ft (80n
Weapons: 10 x 21in (533mm) TT (bow – 6, stern – 2, rotating mount – 2), 2
torpedoes; 2 x 3.9in (100mm) guns, 2 x 45mm cannon; 20 x mines.
Complement: 60.

History: Despite the failure of the Series IV (Pravda-class) the Soviet naval l
command persisted with its goal of a "big navy", one element of which w
large, ocean-going *kreyser* (= cruiser). The next step was the Series XI
totally new, double-hulled design, with a range of some 14,000nm at 9kt ar
submerged displacement of 2,095 tons, which was considerably larger than
submarine operated by the British Royal Navy and in the same league as
German Type XB and U.S. Gato-class. The armament was particularly he
comprising 10 torpedo tubes (six in the bow, two in the stern and two c
rotating mount in the after casing) with a total of no fewer than 24 torpede
There were also two 3.9in (100mm) guns, one at each end of the bridge to

C/D-classes

Type: ocean-going patrol.

Class	C	D
Total built	6	3
Completed	1928-30	1947-54 (see notes)
Displacement surfaced submerged	916 tons 1,290 tons	1,065 tons 1,480 tons
Dimensions length beam draught	247ft 0in (75.3m) 20ft 10in (6.3m) 13ft 6in (4.1m)	275ft 6in (84.0m) 21ft 9in (6.6m) 13ft 2in (4.0m)
Propulsion main engines power electric motors power shafts	2 x Vickers diesels 2 x 1,000bhp 2 2 x 375shp two	2 x Sulzer diesels 2 x 2,500bhp 2 2 x 675shp two

ove: Series XIV boat returns to port after a war-time patrol.

two 45mm AA guns in single mounts. In addition, while not minelayers as
h, the boats had internal chutes and a mine-room carrying 20 mines.
Eleven boats were completed between 1940 and 1942, leaving one
mplete hull on the slips. There was a post-war plan to complete this boat,
this did not come to fruition and the boat was scrapped, still incomplete, in
ut 1949. During the war six boats operated in the Arctic, but plans to
sfer the remaining five from the Baltic were thwarted by the German
sion. Five were lost in the war and the remainder served on until the mid-
0s, when they were scrapped.

rformance		
ed: surface	16kt	20.5kt
merged	8.5kt	9.5kt
ge: surfaced	6,800nm/10kt	9.000nm/12kt
merged	125nm/4.5kt	
ximum		
ing depth	262ft (80m)	300ft (90m)
apons		
	6 x 21in (533mm)	6 x 21in (533mm)
ation	bow – 4, stern – 2	bow – 4, stern – 2
pedoes	10	..
s	1 x 75mm AA	1 x 4.7in (120mm)
		4 x 37mm AA
mplement	40	60

tory: The C-class was an Electric Boat Co. design built under licence in
in, and was, in essence, a development of the B-class (qv), the main change
g an increase from four to six torpedo tubes and the adoption of the
rnational standard 21in (533mm) torpedo tubes. A total of six were built,
g launched between 1927 and 1929.
The D-class was an entirely new design, intended for long-range oceanic
ols. The torpedo armament of six tubes was not particularly heavy for the
and role of the submarines, although the 4.7in (120mm) gun was of larger
re than usual. A combination of the Spanish Civil War and World War II

meant that construction was particularly protracted: *D-1* was laid down in 19
launched in 1944 and completed in 1947, while *D-2*, laid down in 1934
launched in 1944, but did not join the fleet until 1951. *D-3* was not even
down until 1945, and was completed in 1952.

The C-class all became involved in the Spanish Civil War, in the cou
of which four were lost, two of them in December 1936, *C-3* being sunk
an Italian submarine (21 December), while *C-5* simply disappeared, ca
and date unknown. The other two were lost as a result of air attacks:
was so badly damaged that she had to be scuttled (20 October 1937), w
C-1 was sunk by bombs and although recovered was never repaired.
other two, *C-2* and *C-4*, survived because they spent most of the con
undergoing refits in France and were handed over to the victori
Nationalists in March 1939; *C-4* was lost in a peacetime accident (J
1946) and *C-2* was stricken in 1952.

Because of their long construction time, the D-class boats w
essentially out-of-date before they were first commissioned and
realtively short service lives. *D-1* was stricken in the late 1960s and
other two followed in 1971.

*Right: The C-class was a Holland-type Electric Boat Co. design built in
Spain. This is C-2, which, while under refit in France, was surrendered
the Nationalists in 1939 during the Spanish Civil War, and was stricken
in 1952.*

Draken/Sjölejonet/
U-1-classes

SWE

Type: coastal patrol.

History: Sweden continued its policy, established in the early years of the
century, of maintaining domestic submarine design and construction capabilities
ordering successive classes to be built in small numbers. Thus, three Bävern-c

Classes	Draken	Sjölejonet U-1	
Total built	3	9	9
Completed	1927-31	1937-42	1942-45
Displacement surfaced submerged	667 tons 850 tons	580 tons 760 tons	367 tons 450 tons
Dimensions length beam draught	216ft 10in (66.1m) 21ft 0in (6.4m) 10ft 10in (3.3m)	210ft 8in (64.2m) 21ft 0in (6.4m) 11ft 2in (3.4m)	162ft 9in (49.6m) 15ft 5in (4.7m) 12ft 6in (3.8m)

Propulsion			
Main engines	2 x Götawerken	2 x M.A.N.	1 x M.A.N.
power	2 x 960bhp	2 x 1,050bhp	1 x 1,350bhp
Electric motors	2	2	2
power	2 x 500shp	2 x 500shp	2 x 500shp
Shafts	two	two	two
Performance			
Speed: surface	13.8kt	16.2kt	13.8kt
submerged	8.3kt	10kt	7.5kt
Weapons			
Torpedo tubes	4 x 21in (533mm)	6 x 21in (533mm)	4 x 21in (533mm)
	bow – 3, stern – 1	bow – 3, stern – 1, rotating mount – 2	bow – 3, stern – 1
Guns	1 x 4.1in (105mm)	2 x 40mm Bofors	1 x 20mm AA
	1 x 25mm AA	–	–
Complement	35	38	26

[Björ]k submarines were built in the early 1920s, followed by a single Valen-class minelayer, which led to the Draken-class, launched at the Karlskrona Navy Yard between 1926 and 1930. These were double-hulled boats, armed with four torpedo [tube]s, three in the bows and one, internally mounted, in the stern.

Next came the Delfinen-class minelayers and then, with the probability of a [Eur]opean war clearly evident, by far the largest group of patrol submarines yet [built] for the Sweish Navy: the nine-strong Sjölejonet-class. These were slightly smaller than the the Draken-class but with a heavier armament, comprising three bow and one stern tubes, all internally mounted, and two external tubes in a rotating mount located on the upper casing abaft the bridge tower. They all served for some 18-23 years, and were stricken between 1959 and 1964.

For some years the size of the patrol submarines had been steadily increasing, so that the Sjölejonet-class were 210ft 8in (64.2m) long and displaced 760 tons, but this trend was reversed by the next group, known simply as the U-1-class, which was only 162ft 9in (49.6m) long and displaced 367 tons. These were commissioned between June 1943 and early 1945 and helped in the task of maintaining Sweden's neutrality. Armament was four torpedo tubes, with three in ther bows and one mounted externally in a fixed mount at the stern. The propulsion system was an unusual combination of a single diesel engine and two electric motors. *U-1* and *U-2* were stricken in 1960 followed by *U-3* in 1964 but the remaining six boats were taken in hand between 1960 and 1964 and converted to ASW submarines.

Right: **Sjölejonet, one of nine built between 1936 and 1941.**

Barracuda-class

UNITED STA

Type: fleet.
Total built: 3.
Completed: 1924-26.
Displacement: surfaced 2,000 tons; submerged 2,620 tons.
Dimensions: length 334ft 6in (102.0m); beam 27ft 7in (8.4m); draught 2in (4.6m).
Propulsion: 2 x Busch-Sulzer diesels, 2 x 2,250bhp; 2 x M.A.N. aux engines, 2 x 1,000bhp; 2 x Elliott electric motors, 2 x 1,200shp; batter 60 Exide cells; two shafts.
Performance: surface – 18.7kt; submerged – 9kt; range surfaced 6,00 at 11kt, submerged 10hr at 5kt; maximum operating diving depth 2 (61m).
Weapons: 6 x 21in (533mm) TT (bow – 4, stern – 2); 12 x torpedoes; 1 (127mm) gun.
Complement: 88.

History: The three-strong Barracuda-class was part of a group of known as the "V-boats": Barracuda-class *V-1, V-2, V-3*; Argonaut-(minelayer) *V-4*; Narwhal-class *V-5, V-6*; Dolphin-class *V-7*; and Cach class *V-8, V-9*. (The boats were known by these numbers until 1931, v all submarines were given names, but this did not interfere with thei numbers in the overall U.S. Navy system: thus, *V-1* was also SS-163.)

The Barracuda-class was the first to be built after World War I anc boats were large by contemporary standards, their size being dictate the need to be capable of 20kt surface speed to meet the perceived

ve: Nameship **Barracuda** *(SS-163), which was broken up in 1945.*

ány navies in the 1920s for a "fleet submarine". But, as with all the
rs, the Barracuda-class failed to meet this goal, in this case by a margin
st over 1kt. Armament was not heavy for the size of the boat: six
edo tubes, all in the bows, with a 5in (127mm) gun, as built, although
was replaced by a 3in (76mm) gun in 1928.

The Barracuda-class was not a real success and all three boats were put
reserve in the late 1930s. They were reactivated for training, and at one
there was a plan to convert them into transports, but this never came
uition. All three were stricken in March 1945.

Narwhal-class

Type: fleet.
Total built: 2.
Completed: 1930.
Displacement: surfaced 2,730 tons; submerged 3,900 tons.
Dimensions: length 371ft 0in (112.1m); beam 33ft 3in (10.1m); draught 11in (5.24.6m).
Propulsion: 2 x M.A.N. main diesels, 2 x 2,350bhp; 2 x M.A.N. auxi engines; 2 x 450bhp; 2 x Westinghouse electric motors, 2 x 800shp; batte x 120 Exide cells; two shafts.
Performance: surface – 17.4kt; submerged – 8kt; range surfaced 18,000nr 10kt, submerged 10hr at 5kt; maximum operating diving depth 300ft (91m
Weapons: 6 x 21in (533mm) TT (bow – 4, stern – 2); 40 x torpedoes; 2 x (152mm) gun.
Complement: 89.

History: These two boats were essentially the same as the *Argonaut* Special-Role, Minelayer section) but with the minelaying facilities deleted the space used to provide an extremely heavy armament of 40 torpedoes, six in the tubes, 20 reloads carried internally, and a further 14 external storage containers inset under the gun deck. Gun armament comprised two (152mm) guns and the rounds were so heavy that special access trunks power hoists were required to bring them up from the magazines.

Like the Barracuda-class, these were not a great success. They were large (they were several feet longer than today's Los Angeles-class SS

Dolphin-class

Type: patrol.
Total built: 1.
Completed: 1932.
Displacement: surfaced 1,618 tons; submerged 2,240 tons.
Dimensions: length 319ft 3in (97.3m); beam 27ft 11in (8.5m); draught 13f (4,0m).
Propulsion: 2 x M.A.N. main diesels, 2 x 1,750bhp; 2 x M.A.N. aux engines; 2 x 450bhp; 2 x Electro-Dynamic electric motors, 2 x 875shp; ba 2 x 120 Exide cells; two shafts.
Performance: surface – 17kt, submerged – 8kt; range surfaced 16,000nr 7kt, submerged 10hr at 5kt; maximum operating diving depth 250ft (76m)
Weapons: 6 x 21in (533mm) TT (bow – 4, stern – 2), 18 x torpedoes; 1 x (102mm) gun.
Complement: 63.

History: By the standards of the day the Barracuda- and Narwhal-classes v huge and this led to a reassessment of the requirement. The most I operational scenario appeared to be that U.S. Navy submarines would hav operate on their own at some 3,000nm from their base on patrols lasting u 90 days, which made the range, torpedo battery, reliability and crew condi the most valuable attributes, while high surface speed was of le significance. Sheer size was also of reduced importance, both because would improve handling and also, at a time of financial stringency, it w reduce both building and running costs. The first outcome of this new p was a 2,215-ton boat initially designated *V-7*, but later named *Dolphin* (SS-

ht: **Nautilus;** *note
ge size, 6in (152mm)*
.

ch made them
cult to manoeuvre,
ecially when sub-
ged, while the size
ibined with their
ensive flat decks and
large gun platform
le them slow to dive.
sheer size also made it
to detect them, both
he surface and when
merged. Their design
ed on the surface was
17kt, but they were unable to make more than 14kt in practice.

Nautilus was modified in early 1941 to take a large stock of aviation fuel for
elling seaplanes, but when war came it was found that this had little
rational relevance. Both ships were refitted in 1941-42, being modernised
given new main engines as well as a further four external torpedo tubes.
se measures were meant to make them more effective patrol submarines,
when they returned to the fleet they were actually used as transports,
ily for personnel, their large size enabling them to accommodate 120 troops
short periods. They took part in the landings on Makin Island in 1942 and on
u Atoll in 1943. Both boats were scrapped in 1946.

ve: **Dolphin, first of the medium-sized, long-range boats.**

e design phase, *Dolphin* was termed a "cruiser submarine" but in size,
it and general appearance she was, in effect, the first of the fleet type that
ld lead to the outstanding Gato/Balao-classes; indeed, *Dolphin*'s
surements are virtually identical to those of the later boats. *Dolphin* was
ed with six torpedo tubes, four in the bow and two in the stern, and, as
carried a total of 18 torpedoes, all internally, but external stowage for a
er three was added in 1933. The single 4in (102mm) gun was located on
after deck and was served through a door in the bridge tower, rather than
ig a separate access trunk.

Dolphin was a front-line submarine throughout the 1930s and carried out
e wartime patrols. During the second she developed a serious oil leak
h led to her being referred to as a "death-trap" and after one further patrol
vas relegated to training duties. She was scrapped in 1946.

Cachalot-class

Type: patrol.
Total built: 2.
Completed: 1933-34.
Displacement: surfaced 1,120 tons; submerged 1,650 tons.
Dimensions: length 271ft 1in (82.9m); beam 24ft 9in (7.5m); draught 14ft 0in (4.3
Propulsion: 2 x M.A.N. main diesels, 2 x 1,535bhp; 2 x M.A.N. auxiliary engine
x 450bhp; 2 x Westinghouse electric motors, 2 x 800shp; battery 2 x 120 E
cells; two shafts.
Performance: surface – 17kt, submerged – 8kt; range surfaced 11,000nm at
submerged 10hr at 5kt; maximum operating diving depth 250ft (76m).
Weapons: 6 x 21in (533mm) TT (bow – 4, stern – 2); 16 x torpedoes; 1 x
(102mm) gun.
Complement: 45.

History: The Cachalot-class was the last in the "V-boat" series, and there we
number of separate influences all pressing for a smaller design. There was a
group calling for smaller designs for tactical and budgetary reasons, while
recently concluded London Naval Conference had imposed a limit on
submarine tonnage, so that smaller boats would mean greater overall numbers.
outcome was a double-hulled design that was smaller than any of the other V-b
and which was heavily influenced by the German *U-135*. The boat also included
new M.A.N. engines, procured direct from Germany, which offered greater p
for considerably less space. Another measure was to reduce the main gun t
(76mm) caliber, which caused some derision in the Submarine Force which

Porpoise/Shark/Perch-classe

Type: fleet.

History: These were the first "all-electric" submarines, in which the shafts
turned only by the electric motors, which could either be powered by the batt
or the diesel-generators; ie, there was no direct drive from the main engines t
propellers. Such a system offered several advantages, but in particular it got
from the vibration problems associated with direct drive from the diesels to
shafts, and it also broke the hold of M.A.N. licenses. Thus, there were four W

Class	Porpoise	Shark	Perch
Total built	2	2	6
Completed	1935	1936	1936-37
Displacement surfaced submerged	1,316 tons 1,934 tons	1,316 tons 1,968 tons	1,330 tons 1,997 tons
Dimensions length beam draught	301ft (91.8m) 24ft 11in (7.6m) 14ft 1in (4.3m)	298ft 1n (90.8m) 25ft 1in (7.6m) 15ft 1in (4.6m)	300ft 7in (91.6 25ft 1in (7.7m 15ft 2in (4.6m

...ht: Cuttlefish, first submarine built by ...ctric Boat since 1924.

...e used to 6in (152mm) and 5in (127mm) guns. ...gnificant event, unrelated to the design, was ... decision to allocate construction of one of ...se two boats, *Cuttlefish* (SS-171), to the ...ctric Boat Company at Groton, Connecticut. ...s company had not built any submarines for ... U.S. Navy since *S-47* (SS-158), which was ...ched in 1924, and the company's most ...ent work had been the four R-class (qv) built ...Peru. The company was allowed to develop its ...n ideas for the interior layout of their boat, ...ch resulted in some major advances, ...ecially where crew comfort was involved. ...ther innovation was the installation of the first ...edo Data Computer (TDC), a mechanically operated analogue computer, which ...ved to be a major advance over all previous U.S. systems, and far ahead of ...hing in any foreign navy at the time.

Once again, the overall result was not particularly satisfactory. The boats proved ...cult to maintain, while the M.A.N. engines suffered from such excessive and ...rable vibration that they had to be replaced by General Motors engines of a type ...ch was not actually optimised for submarine installation, but proved, ...ertheless, to be a great improvement. When war came both boats carried out ...e operational patrols and were then transferred to training duties. They were ...ken and scrapped immediately after the end of the war.

...pulsion			
...n engines	4 x Winton	4 x Winton	4 x Winton
...ver	4 x 1,300bhp	4 x 1,300bhp	4 x 1,300bhp
...ctric motors	4 x Elliott	4 x Elliott	8 x General Electric
...ver	4 x 1,075shp	4 x 1,075shp	8 x 538shp
...tery	2 x 120 Exide	2 x 120 Exide	2 x 120 cells
...fts	two	two	two
...formance			
...ed: surface	18kt	18kt	18.8kt
...merged	8kt	8kt	8kt
...ge: surfaced	11,000nm/10kt	11,000nm/10kt	11,000nm/10kt
...merged	10hr/5kt	10hr/5kt	10hr/5kt
...ximum			
...ng depth	250ft (76m)	250ft (76m)	250ft (76m)
...apons			
	6 x 21in (533mm)	6 x 21in (533mm)	6 x 21in (533mm)
...tion	bow – 4, stern – 2	bow – 4, stern – 2	bow – 4, stern – 2
...edoes	16	16	16
...s	1 x 3in (76mm)	1 x 3in (76mm)	1 x 3in (76mm)
	2 x 0.5in MG	2 x 0.5in MG	2 x 0.5in MG
	4 x 0.3in MG	4 x 0.3in MG	4 x 0.3in MG
...mplement	50	50	50

diesels, all of which could be brought on line for maximum speed or, for cruis
three could power the motors while the fourth recharged the cells, and they
had sufficient electrical power to drive the air-conditioning system that was insta
in U.S. submarines for the first time. Even the U.S.-sourced diesels had proble
however, and the first type fitted suffered repeated breakdowns and had to
replaced by a lower-powered model.

As built, torpedo armament was the standard four bow tubes and two in
stern, with a total of 16 torpedoes. The officers of the Submarine Force deemed
to be insufficient in combat and most boats were fitted with an additional two
tubes early in the war; these were externally mounted, bringing the bow salv
to six and total carried to 18.

The Porpoise- and Shark-classes were Navy Department designs, but finar
by the 1933 National Recovery Act, with the first two being built by Portsm

Salmon/Sargo/Seadragon/
Tambor-classes

UNITED STA

Type: fleet.

History: These four very similar classes represent the final development of the
Navy's fleet submarine to peacetime standards. The Salmon-class marked
addition of two more torpedo tubes aft, which necessitated an enlargement c
hull, and the bridge tower was a different design. A new type of "composite d

Class	Salmon	Sargo/Seadragon	Tambor
Total built	6	10	12
Completed	1938	1939-40	1940-41
Displacement surfaced submerged	1,449 tons 2,210 tons	1,450 tons 2,350 tons	1,475 tons 2,370 tons
Dimensions length beam draught	308ft 0in (93.9m) 26ft 2in (8.0m) 15ft 7in (4.8m)	310ft 6n (94.6m) 27ft 1in (8.3m) 16ft 8in (5.1m)	307ft 3in (93.6 27ft 3in (8.3m 15ft 0in (4.1m

vy Yard and having riveted hulls. The second pair was built by the Electric Boat
mpany and, while having the same measurements and armament, had many
ferences, one of the most important being that they were the first U.S.
bmarines with all-welded hulls. (Note that despite their names starting with "S"
ey were P-class boats.) The Perch-class were virtually repeat Sharks.

All 10 boats served in the war. The two Porpoise-class boats were relegated to
ining duties in 1942 and survived, following which they became dockisde trainers
til being broken up in 1957. Of the Shark-class, *Shark* (SS-174) was lost in
bruary 1942, cause unknown, while *Tarpon* (SS-175) sank while under tow to the
eakers in August 1957. Of the Perch-class, three were war losses and three
rvived to be broken up, one in 1947, the other two in 1957.

low: **Porpoise, (SS-172), first of the 10-strong P-class.**

opulsion			
ain engines	4 x H.O.R.*	4 x H.O.R.*	4 x General Motors
wer	2 x 1,535bhp	4 x 1,535bhp	4 x 1,535bhp
ectric motors	4 x Elliott	4 x General Electric	4 x General Electric
wer	4 x 667shp	4 x 685shp	4 x 1,375shp
ttery	2 x 126 Gould	2 x 126 Exide	2 x 126 Exide
afts	two	two	two
rformance			
eed: surface	17kt	20kt	20.8kt
bmerged	8.75kt	8.75kt	8.75kt
nge: surfaced	11,000nm/10kt	11,000nm/10kt	11,000nm/10kt
bmerged	48hr/2kt	48hr/2kt	48hr/2kt
aximum			
ving depth	250ft (76m)	250ft (76m)	250ft (76m)
eapons			
	8 x 21in (533mm)	8 x 21in (533mm)	10 x 21in (533mm)
cation	bow – 4, stern – 4	bow – 4, stern – 4	bow – 6, stern – 4
rpedoes	20	20	24
ns	1 x 3in (76mm)	1 x 3in (76mm)	1 x 3in (76mm)
	2 x 0.5in MG	2 x 0.5in MG	2 x 0.5in MG
	2 x 0.3in MG	2 x 0.3in MG	
mplement	55	55	60

ooven, Owens, Rentschler

was introduced in which one diesel engine and two electric motors were connec[t]
to each shaft, while two more diesel engines were used to recharge the batteri[es]
an arrangement which proved to be physically cramped, but worked well in w[ar?]
Three boats were built in Navy yards and were powered by a new model of Gene[ral]
Motors diesels which proved very satisfactory, but the three built by Electric B[oat]
were powered by Hooven, Owens, Rentschler (H.O.R.) engines, which prov[ed]
troublesome and had to be replaced by General Motors engines during warti[me]
refits. The Sargo-class was very similar, except for certain internal rearrangeme[nt]
and a hull lengthened by 2 ft 6in (0.8m) to improve crew conditions. Also introdu[ced]
was a new type of high-capacity cell (Exide VLA47B) which remained in use [for]
many years and was always known as the "Sargo battery". The Seadragon-cla[ss]
(four boats) was virtually identical to the Sargo-class except that, in a last min[ute]
change, propulsion was once again all-electric. The Tambor-class consisted of [12]
boats (although the last six had names beginning with the letter "G") in which [the]
forward torpedo battery was increased to six tubes and the total torpedoes carr[ied]
to 24, but these were otherwise identical to those of the earlier groups.

These were the latest boats in commission at the time of the Japanese att[ack]
on Pearl Harbor and all fought a very hard war. *Stingray* (SS-186) carried out [?]
combat patrols, the highest number by any U.S. submarine in World War [II.]
Nameship of its class *Salmon* (SS-182) survived one of the heaviest depthcha[rge]
attacks on record and was forced so deep that the pressure hull wrinkled arou[nd]
some of the frames; she and her crew survived but the damage was so severe [that]
she never went on another operation. Four boats were stricken and broken-up [in]
1946, while *Seal* (SS-183) survived until 1956. *Skipjack* (SS-184) achieved [the]
dubious distinction of being sunk as a target twice, first at Bikini (July 1946), but s[he]
was then raised and sunk as an aircraft target on 11 August 1948.

Of the Sargo-class, *Squalus* (SS-192) was lost on sea trials due to the failure [of]

Gato/Balao/Tench-classes   UNITED STAT[ES]

Type: fleet submarine.

History: At the time of the Japanese attack on Pearl Harbor on 7 Decem[ber]
1941 there was just one Gato-class boat in commission: *Drum* (SS-228). By [the]
war's end almost four years later 221 Gatos and their very closely related Bal[ao]
and Tench-classes had been built in a great feat of engineering and producti[on]
and the boats' crews had played a major role in bringing Japan to defeat. [The]
Gatos were the outcome of the steady development which could be trac[ed]
back in a direct line to the *Dolphin* (SS-169) of 1932. These three classes w[ere]
always referred to as "fleet" boats but they were never meant to operate w[ith]
the main battlefleet as the name implied; instead they conducted very lo[ng-]
range, independent missions in the western Pacific, their high surface spe[ed]
being used to get them rapidly to their patrol areas and back again.

The design was essentially the same as that of the Tambor-class, the o[nly]
change of any significance being that an extra watertight bulkhead was insta[lled]
to sub-divide the somewhat large engine room; this required the hull to [be]
lengthened by 5ft (1.5m). The hull was of all-welded construction and t[his,]
combined with increased strengthening, enabled the new boats to be clea[red]
to operate at 300ft (91m). Armament and general performance remained [the]
same as the Tambor-class. As soon as war was declared the design was fro[zen]
for mass-production and 77 were completed, of which 20 were lost in comb[at.]

The Gato-class was followed into production by the Balao-class, which w[as]
virtually identical except that the hull was made from high tensile rather th[an]
the earlier mild steel, which increased operational diving depth to 400ft (122[m).]
The total number of orders placed was 256, but there were many cancellati[ons.]

e main induction valve, and 26 men were lost; the boat was then raised, refitted, named *Sailfish* (also SS-192) and put into service. There were two war losses: *ulpin*, (SS-191) was sunk by Japanese destroyers (19 November 1943), with 48 n rescued to become prisoners-of-war, of whom just 12 survived to be released August 1945. The other war loss was *Swordfish* (SS-193) which was lost with all ds in January 1945. The remainder were stricken after the war.

The Seadragon-class boat *Sealion* (SS-195) was in refit at Cavite in the ilippines when the Japanese attacked, and was so badly damaged in an air attack t she had to be scuttled (10 December 1941). *Seawolf* (SS-197) was sunk by U.S. stroyer-escort (30 October 1944) and the other two were scrapped in 1948. ven of the 12 Tambor-class were lost in the war; the others were either expended targets or stricken between 1948 and 1960. The Tambor-class lost seven of its mber, more than 50 per cent, but one of those that survived, *Tautog* (SS-199), not y shot down a Japanese aircraft during the attack on Pearl Harbor, but then went to achieve the highest score in terms of ships sunk – 26 – of any U.S. submarine.

low: **Tuna *(SS-203)* of the Tambor-class.**

ove: **Tinosa *(SS-283)* returns wearing many "kill" flags.**

Class	Gato	Balao	Tench
Total built	77	119	25
Completed	1941-43	1943-45**	1944-45**
Displacement surfaced submerged	1,526 tons 2,410 tons	1,525 tons 2,415 tons	1,570 tons 2,415 tons
Dimensions length beam draught	311ft 9in (95.0m) 27ft 3in (8.3m) 15ft 3in (4.7m)	311ft 9in (95.0m) 27ft 3in (8.3m) 15ft 3in (4.7m)	311ft 8in (95.0n 27ft 3in (8.3m) 15ft 0in (4.1m)
Propulsion main engines* power electric motors* power battery* shafts	4 x General Motors 2 x 1,535bhp 4 x General Electric 4 x 1,375shp 2 x 126 Exide cells two	4 x General Motors 4 x 1,535bhp 4 x General Electric 4 x 1,375shp 2 x 126 Exide two	4 x Fairbanks, Mor 4 x 1, 600bhp 2 x General Elect' 2 x 2,700shp 2 x 126 Gould ce two
Performance speed: surface submerged range: surfaced submerged maximum diving depth	20.25kt 8.75kt 11,000nm/10kt 48hr/2kt 300ft (91m)	20.25kt 8.75kt 11,000nm/10kt 48hr/2kt 400ft (122m)	20.25kt 8.75kt 11,000nm/10kt 48hr/2kt 400ft (122m)
Weapons TT location torpedoes guns	10 x 21in (533mm) bow – 6, stern – 4 24 1 x 3in (76mm) 2 x 0.5in MG 2 x 0.3in MG	10 x 21in (533mm) bow – 4, stern – 4 24 1 x 3in (76mm) 2 x 0.5in MG 2 x 0.3in MG	10 x 21in (533mn bow – 6, stern – 28 1 x 3in (76mm) 2 x 0.5in MG
Complement	81 (wartime)		

* Various different makes of diesel, electric motors and batteries were installed.

** A few more were completed after the war; see next section.

and only 119 were actually completed. There were nine war losses, the l
number being due to the fact that the Balaos entered service late in the wa

Externally, the Tench-class was virtually indistinguishable from the Ba
class, but there were many internal differences. Combat experience resulte
a major rearrangement of the ballast and fuel tanks to make them l
vulnerable to damage, while further rearrangements of living and storage sp
forward resulted in a further four torpedoes being shipped.

Although these are generally recorded as · three separate classes,
differences, apart from the stronger steel introduced in the Balao-class, w
minimal, and, in any case, many changes were retrofitted into older boats
they entered refit. As in other navies, gun armament varied widely betw
boats and local commanders and commanding officers often added or remo

ve: Gato-class **Perch** *(SS-313), here seen post-war.*

pons according to their perceived requirements. The original Gatos, for mple, were built with a platform suitable for a 5.5in (140mm) gun, but were ally completed with the standard 3in (76mm) gun. However, Rear-Admiral kwood, the Commander Submarines Pacific (COMSUBPAC), soon ensured as many 4in (102mm) and 5in (127mm) guns were mounted as he could is hands on.

A few Gatos operated in the Atlantic for a short period in 1943, dur
which one was lost and another sank a U-boat, but that apart they spent th
entire war in the Pacific, where they bore the lion's share of the submarine
against the Japanese. They were capable of very long patrols and their m
task was to carry out offensive action in enemy sea lanes, although they w
also used to lay mines, run supplies to Philippine guerrillas, reconnoitre land
beaches, pick up downed U.S. aircrew, and even carry out sh
bombardments. Their primary targets were enemy merchant ships, the high
tonnage sunk being by *Flasher* (SS-249) with 100,231grt, although *Barb* (
220), *Rasher* (SS-269) and *Silversides* (SS-236) were close behind with c
90,000grt each.

When the war ended there were large numbers of these boats in serv
with more under construction. Further orders were immediately cancelled
Gatos, Balaos and Tenches proved not only to have long lives but also to be v
adaptable, providing the U.S. Navy with its main body of submarines well
the 1960s, while some remained in service with foreign navies right up to
end of the 20th century (see Guppy-class).

Below: **Gato *(SS-212),* as she appeared in August 1942.**

ove: Mingo *(SS-261) after post-war transfer to Japan.*

Diesel-Electric Patrol Submarines 1947-2002

During the 1950s it appeared that the days of the diesel-electric submar were numbered and that all future boats in the major navies would nuclear-powered; indeed, some of the smaller European navies, such as Royal Netherlands Navy, also seriously considered nuclear propulsi However, matters have not worked out that way and at the start of the 2 century there are large and growing numbers of diesel-electric submarine service around the world, with the number of navies operating such bo gradually increasing, although the production capability clearly exceeds present requirements by a considerable margin. Even the advent of non-nuc air-independent propulsion systems has not seriously affected the posit since for the foreseeable future such systems will be in addition to and replacements for diesel-electric propulsion.

The influence of even a very small number of such boats has b demonstrated on numerous occasions as they have exerted strategic operational effects out of all proportion to their numbers. Thus, just Argentine submarine was at sea in the 1982 Falklands War, but it cau extreme concern in the British task force, which had no choice but to deplo sizable ASW force to keep it away from its two vital aircraft carriers. Simil the three Russian Kilo-class boats purchased by Iran have changed the n strategic equation in the Gulf, and the three Swedish Sjöormen-class bo purchased by Singapore have had a similar impact in South-East Asian wate

The position today is that among the designers and builders of submar for export, the position of Germany is almost unassailable and in ev international competition the German entry is the one to beat.

China

As it has done throughout its history, China has taken a very long-term view has slowly built up a large diesel-electric submarine fleet, together with appropriate design and construction capabilities. Its diesel-electric subma designs have been developed from Russian-supplied boats, and it has achie a few export orders, notably four to Egypt in the 1980s. It continues to buil

designs in small numbers and has also recently purchased four Kilo-class
ts from Russia.

nce

nany's main competitor as an exporter is France, which still designs and
ds diesel-electric boats, even though the French Navy itself does not intend
uy any more. Currently, three Agosta 90s are building for Pakistan and two
rpénes for Chile, while France is also actively competing for other orders,
ecially from Malaysia and Saudi Arabia.

many

present influence of German designers cannot be underestimated. There
five different versions of the Type 209 on offer, with 53 in service around
world with 13 navies. Other German submarines in service are two TR-
)s in Argentina, three Dolfin-class in Israel and six Ula-class in Norway, and
e are firm orders for four Type 212 for Germany and two for Italy, with a
er three Type 214 on order for Greece. One reason for the German
antage is a readiness to help potential customers establish their own
narine-building facilities, with particular success having been achieved in
ey.

at Britain

last diesel-electric boat to be completed was HMS *Unicorn* in 1993,
ugh refitting the four Upholders for delivery to Canada brought some more
to the yard. It appears unlikely, however, that the UK will build any further
el-electric boats, concentrating instead on SSNs for the Royal Navy.

was once among the great designers and builders of submarines. The last

w: Soviet Tango-class is inspected by a NATO helicopter.

Italian-designed submarine was completed in 1995. In the 1990s Italcar offered to sell two reconditioned Toti-class boats to the United Arab Emir (UAE), which would have been followed by an order for new builds, but it not taken up. At home, the Italian Navy spent a long time considering indigenous design for its next class, but has now ordered two Gerr designed Type 212As, with an option on two more, although these will be in Italy.

Japan
The JMSDF has one of the largest and certainly the most modern diesel-ele fleets in the world. It has followed a careful policy of construction by two y which have built a succession of evolutionary designs, with new boats b commissioned at a rate of one per year. This has ensured an up-to-date f coupled with a steady and predictable flow of work in the shipyards, and probably fortunate for the submarine-exporting countries that Japan industry is prevented by law from exporting warlike material.

North Korea
The North Koreans have built small numbers of Romeos and have designed and built their own coastal submarines, all for employment ir decades-old confrontation with South Korea.

Netherlands
The most recent Dutch-built submarine to be completed was the final Wa class boat in 1993, but the Dutch company RDM has been very active in t to obtain foreign orders. In 1995 RDM bought the two recently re Zwaardvis-class boats from the Dutch Navy and has attempted to sell a re version to Egypt, Malaysia and a number of other customers. It also has a design, the Moray-class, which has also been offered to Egypt and Mala but again with no takers, so far. The most likely customer for the Moray-is Egypt, but with the boats actually being built by Ingalls in the United St which would not only enable the deal to be paid for by U.S. offs procurement funds but would also help Ingalls to reacquire a diesel-ele building expertise.

Russia
Russia still operates a small number of Kilos and has exported to several coun including 10 to India and four to China. It is also trying to secure an order from S Korea for two refitted Russian Navy boats, together with two new constru boats, but without success, so far. Russian designer Rubin has also offered a design, the Amur, for export, but it has not yet attracted any orders.

Spain
The Spanish yard IZAR is currently assembling two French-designed Scorp class boats for Chile which, the company hopes, will lead to a contract Daphne-replacement for the Spanish Navy.

Sweden
Like Japan, but on a much smaller scale, Sweden produces a steady strea its own designs for the Royal Swedish Navy and this domestic requiremer continue. For many years the Swedish policy of neutrality precluded exp but this was relaxed to enable Kockums to achieve a major success wit Collins-class for Australia, although the project has since hit snags. Swede also sold four elderly submarines to Singapore which gives it a pos advantage for a future order when these need to be replaced. Sweden is the leader in the Nordic project for a new submarine for the Danish, Norw and Swedish navies.

...an

...arly 2001, the United States promised Taiwan a large package of naval ...pment, including eight new diesel-electric submarines for delivery starting ...010. This is an extremely large contract which has excited considerable ...national interest, primarily because the USA, as described below, has no ...gn or manufacturing base for diesel-electric boats. The proposal has also ...sed extreme indignation from Beijing which is bringing very strong ...sure on any country considering involvement in the deal, as it did with the ...erlands over the Hai Lung-class order, and both Germany and the ...erlands were very quick in disassociating themselves from the deal.

...ed States

...world's greatest naval power, the United States has had an all-nuclear ...marine fleet since the 1980s, which has meant that it is unable to supply ...el-electric boats to allies. There can be no doubt that the technical and ...strial might of the USA could design and build a new class of diesel-electric ...narine if it wished to do so, but such a project would be extremely ...nsive. However, the prospect of an order for eight boats for Taiwan could ...e spur that encourages a return to this field.

...ding Facilities

...n negotiating a submarine purchase, some countries have insisted that the ...act must include assistance in establishing a domestic submarine ...truction facility; such countries have included Argentina, Australia, Brazil, ..., Turkey, Greece, South Korea and Pakistan. This involves very ...iderable work in establishing the industrial base, and in transferring ...nical know-how in both submarine technology and advanced industrial ...niques. This inevitably causes additional expense and usually results in ...r delays in the programme. In most cases the initial order is met, but the ...ems arise when new work must be obtained to keep the yard and workers ...oyed and the indigenous navy has no requirement for further boats for at ...a decade.

...w: German export Type 209 submarine for India.

Collins-class

Type: patrol.
Total built: 6.
Completed: 1996-2001.
Displacement: surfaced 3,051 tons; submerged 3,353 tons.
Dimensions: length 253ft 10in (77.4m); beam 25ft 7in (7.8m); draught 23f
(7.0m).
Propulsion: 3 x Garden-Island Hedemora B210 diesel generator sets,
2,000bhp; 1 x Jeumont-Schneider electric motor, 1 x 7,000shp; 1 x emerg
propulsor, 100shp; one shaft.
Performance: surface – 10.5kt; submerged – 21kt; range surfaced 11,50
at 10kt, submerged 480nm at 4kt.
Weapons: 6 x 21in (533mm) TT (bow); 23 x Harpoon SSM/Mk 48 torpedo
Complement: 42.

History: The Royal Australian Navy (RAN) operated a small numbe
submarines for many years, always British-built, but the six Oberon-class
acquired in the 1970s proved to be the last of that particular line. Planning
successor began in the early 1980s, the basic assumptions being that it v
be a totally new design, tailored to meet RAN operational requirements,
most importantly, would be built in Australian yards using as many Aust
materials and components as possible. A hard-fought international compe
then took place which was eventually won by the Australian Subm
Corporation, a consortium composed (at that time) of Swedish subm
designers and builders, Kockums; the partially government-owned Aust
Industrial Development Co (AIDC); and two Australian companies, Wo
International Ltd. and CBI Constructors Pty. The contract was placed on 18
1987 for what was then the largest and most complex defence project
undertaken in Australia.

Kockums has designed and built a series of submarines for the
Swedish Navy, of which the largest is the current Gotland-class (qv), v
displacement of 1,494 tons and length of 198ft 9in (60.6m). The Collins-cla
however, not only a totally new design but is also considerably larger, displ
3,353 tons and with a length of 253ft 10in (77.4m). It is armed with six
(533mm) torpedo tubes for which it carries 23 weapons, a mix of M
torpedoes and UGM-84C Harpoon missiles. It is also fitted w
comprehensive range of the latest sensors and electronic equipment, an
entire system is controlled by a purpose-built fire-control system. Propuls
by means of three Australian-built Hedemora diesel-generators and a s
water-cooled 5,250kW electric motor driving a seven-bladed skew
propeller. From the second boat onwards the hull is totally covered in ane
tiles.

The project has encountered problems, not only with the minor
systems as is inevitable in any new project, but also with a number of
systems and components, the most important being the combat dire
system. As a result, a great deal of remedial work has had to be do
considerable extra cost and with consequent delays to the boats' entr
service, all of which has led to the project becoming embroiled in contro
There have been numerous reviews, all trying to establish what went w
why, and how to put it right, one of the most important being
McIntosh/Prescott Report to the Australian Minister for Defence dated 20
1999. All the problems are being addressed and progressively solved, incl
the most challenging of them all, software integration, and the Collins-clas
undoubtedly become one of the most successful diesel-electric submari
the first two decades of the 21st century, but it has been a salutary, expe

...ove: Collins-class Farncomb (S-72) *prior to her launch in December ...5. Four of the six boats are based at HMAS Stirling in Western ...stralia, and the other two at HMAS Platypus.*

...often painful experience.

...In the early stages of the project the RAN had an option on two more boats ...it was planned not only that these would be fitted with an air-independent ...pulsion (AIP) system but also that the first six boats would then be ...fitted with the same AIP system. A number of AIP systems were ...mined, but in view of the problems experienced with the design the option ...ulls #7 and #8 has been cancelled, and plans for AIP postponed indefinitely.

...ow: Collins – biggest industrial project in Australian history.

Ming-class

Type: patrol.
Total built: 19.
Completed: 1975-onward.
Displacement: surfaced 1,584 tons; submerged 2,113 tons.
Dimensions: length 249ft 3in (76.0m); beam 24ft 10in (7.6m); draught 16f' (5.1m).
Propulsion: 2 x Type 6E390ZC diesels, 2 x 2,600bhp; 2 x electric motors, 1,750shp; two shafts.
Performance: surface – 15kt, schnorkel – 10kt, submerged – 18kt; ra schnorkel 8,000nm at 8kt, submerged 330nm at 4kt; maximum operating di depth 984ft (300m).
Weapons: 8 x 21in (533mm) TT (bow – 6, stern – 2), 16 x torpedoes.
Complement: 55.

History: After it came into existence in 1949 the submarine arm of the Peo, Liberation Army Navy (PLAN) depended initially upon boats supplied from Soviet Union, but a construction facility was established and copies of Sc boats were then built under licence. Large numbers of Romeo-class boats v built as the PLAN's Project 033, but production eventually switched to Project 035, known in the West as the Ming-class, with the first being launc in 1975.Production has continued at a slow rate since and at least 17 are in service.

The Ming is based on the Romeo design but has a fuller hull, which is 0in (0.6m) shorter but 3ft 0in (0.9m) broader in the beam. Armament is e

Delfinen-class

Type: coastal.
Total built: 4.
Completed: 1960-64.
Displacement: surfaced 595 tons; submerged 643 tons.
Dimensions: length 177ft 2in (54.0m); beam 15ft 5in (4.7m); draught 13f' (4.0m).
Propulsion: 2 x Burmeister & Wain diesels, 2 x 600bhp; 2 x Brown-Bc electric motors, 2 x 600shp; two shafts.
Performance: surface – 15kt; submerged – 15kt; range surfaced 4,000n 8kt; maximum operating diving depth 300ft (91m).
Weapons: 4 x 21in (533mm) TT (bow), 8 x torpedoes.
Complement: 33.

History: The Delfinen-class were the first submarines to be designed and in Denmark after World War II. They were contemporary with the Fr Arethuse-class (qv) and similar in operational concept and size, although Danish boats have twin propellers as opposed to the French boat's one. On the four boats was paid for by U.S. Offshore Funds. Although the Danes maintained a submarine construction capability, the Delfinen-class was the to be designed by the Royal Copenhagen Dockyard and the next class, Narvhalen-class, was a German design, built under licence. There considerable hesitation about ordering a replacement for the Delfinen-class eventually the Danes opted for purchasing a number of surplus Kobben-c boats from Norway and the Delfinens were stricken in 1983 (one), 1984 and 1989 (two). Under present plans Denmark intends to remain part of

ve: Ming-class, a Chinese improved-Romeo design.

edo tubes, of which two are in the stern, making this one of the very few
dern submarines with stern tubes. A total of 16 torpedoes are carried, with
ads only for the bow tubes. The Ming is fitted with Chinese-designed
els, which are a little more powerful than those installed in the Romeos.
Ming has been offered for export, but as of 2002 no foreign navy had taken
he offer.

ve: Springgaren, of the Danish Delfinen-class.

g consortium with Sweden and Norway to develop a common future
marine for all three navies.

La Créole-class

Type: patrol.
Total built: 5.
Completed: 1949-54.
Displacement: surfaced 970 tons; submerged 1,250 tons.
Dimensions: length 241ft 0in (73.5m); beam 21ft 0in (6.5m); draught 14f
(4.2m).
Propulsion: 2 x Sulzer diesels, 2 x 1,500bhp; 2 x electric motors, 2 x 700
two shafts.
Performance: surface – 15.5kt, submerged 9.3kt; range surfaced 8,800n
10kt; maximum operating diving depth 330ft (100m).
Weapons: 10 x 21.7in (550mm) TT (bow – 4, amidships – 4, stern – 2); 1 x 3
(88mm) gun (first three only), 1 x 20mm AA.
Complement: 62.

History: When the French signed the Armistice in 1940 there were five
built Aurore-class submarines lying in various French shipyards and one
Créole, which had been towed semi-complete to England. After the wa
Créole, still incomplete, was towed back to France and together with two o
sisters, L'Africaine and L'Astrée, was completed, entering service in 1949.
design was modernised to a certain extent, with a larger bridge tower a
surface armament of a single German 88mm gun (naval version) forward a
twin 20mm mounting aft. The number of torpedo tubes was also incre
from 9 to 10, with 4 in the bows, 2 in the stern and 4 external tubes, 2 forw
and 2 aft. Another two boats, L'Artémis and L'Andromede, were given a r

Narval-class

Type: patrol.
Total built: 6.
Completed: 1957-60.
Displacement: surfaced 1,635 tons; submerged 1,910 tons.
Dimensions: length 257ft 0in (78.4m); beam 26ft 0in (7.8m); draught 17f
(5.2m).
Propulsion: 2 x Schneider diesels, 2 x 2,200bhp; 2 x electric motors,
2,500shp; two shafts.
Performance: surface – 16kt, submerged – 18kt; range surfaced 15,000n
8kt; maximum operating diving depth 656ft (200m).
Weapons: 8 x 21.7in (550mm) TT (bow – 6, stern [external] – 2),
torpedoes.
Complement: 63.

History: In 1947 the French Navy issued its first post-war operat
requirement for a submarine, whose capabilities were to include a subme
speed in excess of 16kt and a snorkelling range of 15,000nm. France had b
allocated one of the German Type XXIs – U-2518 – which had b
commissioned into the Marine Nationale as the Roland Morillot, and this h
heavy influence on the design of the new boat, with the Narval-class be
many similarities to the Type XXI. The French boats were, however, sli
larger, had marginally better performance, and, being free of wartime short
and bombing attacks which had plagued the German programme, were r
better built. They were armed with eight torpedo tubes of the unique Fr
21.7in (550mm) calibre, with six tubes in the bow and two, externallymou

ve: **La Créole, *unfinished in 1940, was completed in 1949.***

stantial conversion with a large, streamlined fin and a schnorkel, similar to
in the U.S. Guppies (qv), while *L'Artémis* was also given the first of a new
of fire control equipment. *La Créole* was given a schnorkel in a subsequent
All were stricken and scrapped in the 1960s.

ve: **Narval, *a design that was based on the German Type XXI.***

e stern; there were six reloads for the bow tubes, none for the stern..
six boats were built, *Narval, Marsouin, Dauphin, Requin, Espadon* and
se, with the last two being completed in 1960. As built, Schneider two-
e, seven-cylinder diesels were installed, but these were not totally
factory and were replaced by three SEMT-Pielstick 12-cylinder diesels in
ife refits which took place between 1965 and 1970. The six boats served
the French Navy's Atlantic Squadron until the mid-1980s, when all but one
stricken and scrapped. The exception was *Dauphin*, which was used to
the bow section for the new Améthyste-class SSNs, the new structure
asing its length by 9ft 2in (2.8m); with this installed she continued in
ce until 1992 when she, too, was scrapped.

Arethuse-class

Type: attack *(sous-marins de chasse)*.
Total built: 4.
Completed: 1958-60.
Displacement: surfaced 869 tons; submerged 1,043 tons.
Dimensions: length 163ft 0in (49.7m); beam 19ft 0in (5.8m); draught 13ft 0in (4.0
Propulsion: 2 x SEMT-Pielstick diesels, 2 x 530bhp; 1 x electric m
1,300shp; one shaft.
Performance: surface – 12.5kt, submerged – 16kt.
Weapons: 4 x 21.7in (550mm) TT (bow), 8 x torpedoes.
Complement: 39.

History: The Arethuse-class were designed to meet an operational requirem
for a *sous-marin de chasse*, a concept known in other navies as an "atta
"ASW" or "hunter-killer" submarine (see also U.S. Navy Barracuda-class).
were intended for service in the Mediterranean, where their mission wa
prevent hostile submarines from attacking the considerable traffic expecte
wartime between France's (then) North African colonies and Metropo
France, particularly troop convoys. They were required to be particularly
and were, therefore, fitted with electric drive and one propeller, in which
single electric motor was driven either by the battery when submerged
the twin diesel-generator sets when on the surface; ie, the diesels were
coupled to the shaft. All four boats – Arethuse, Argonaute, Amazone and A
– spent their entire operational careers in the Mediterranean. They
stricken between 1979 and 1982.

Daphné-class

Type: patrol.
Total built: 25.
Completed: 1964-70.
Displacement: surfaced 869 tons; submerged 1,043 tons.
Dimensions: length 190ft 0in (57.8m); beam 22ft 0in (6.8m); draught 17f
(5.3m).
Propulsion: 2 x SEMT-Pielstick diesel-generator sets, 2 x 650bhp; 2 x ele
motors, 2 x 800shp; two shafts.
Performance: surface – 13.5kt, submerged – 16kt; range surfaced 4,500n
5kt.
Weapons: 12 x 21.7in (550mm) TT (bow – 4, stern – 4, external – 4),
torpedoes.
Complement: 45.

History: Following World War II the French Navy had some 14 different
of submarine in service, ranging in size from ocean-going to midgets, son
them 20 years old. It was, therefore, very necessary both to modernise a
standardise, and for the medium-sized boat they selected a new design, v
was essentially a scaled-up version of the Arethuse-class. The new Dap
class was the result of careful attention being paid to silent operation, wit
hull shape subjected to extensive tank testing and all mooring equipment r
retractable. Microphones were fitted around the hull which enabled
members inside to monitor ambient noise levels and to regulate spee
manoeuvre accordingly. Armament was 12 21.7in (550mm) torpedo tu
eight of them in the bows in two vertical rows of four, internally mounted

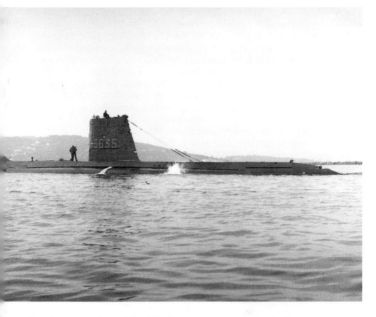

ve: Arethuse, designed for Mediterranean attack missions.

*ve: Pakistan's Daphné-class Ghazi, built in France, bought from
tugal in December 1975*

out reloads. The remaining four tubes were aft, all externally mounted in
casing, with two launching directly over the stern and two mounted further
ard and launching at an angle of about 30 degrees.
The Daphné-class was an immediate success and 11 entered service with
French Navy between 1964 and 1970. A further 10 were built in France for

sale to foreign navies – South Africa (3); Pakistan (3); and Portugal (4) – while
were built in Spain with French technical help. Pakistan subsequently increased
fleet to four by purchasing one of the Daphnés from Portugal. One of th
Pakistani boats, *Hangor*, sank the Indian Navy frigate, *Khukri*, during the 1971 w

The class suffered a series of disasters in French service, starting with
inexplicable disappearance of *Minerve* in the Mediterranean in 1968. This
followed by the equally mysterious disappearance of *Eurydice* in 1970. Th
tragic losses were nearly followed by a third in 1971 when *Flore*'s schno
sprang a leak but an alert captain reacted promptly and saved his b
Modifications were quickly implemented and there were no more incide
equally, there were no further overseas sales.

All the navies involved carried out mid-life updates to their boats.
French boats were stricken in between 1988 and 1998, while the Spanish bo

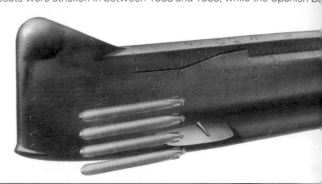

Agosta (S-70/A-90B)-class   FRAN

Type: attack.
Total built: 10.
Completed: 1977-2005.
Displacement: surfaced 1,510 tons; submerged 1,760 tons.
Dimensions: length 221ft 9in (67.6m); beam 22ft 4in (6.8m); draught 17ft
(5.4m).
Propulsion: 2 x SEMT-Pielstick diesel-generator sets, 2 x 850kW; 1 x electric m
3,500kW; 1 x creep motor, 23hp; battery 320 cells; one shaft.
Performance: surface – 12.5kt, schnorkel – 10.5kt, submerged – 20.5kt; ra
schnorkel 8,500nm at 9kt, submerged 280nm at 3kt; maximum operating d
depth 984ft (300m).
Weapons: 4 x 21.7in (550mm) TT (bow), 20 x SM-39 Exocet/torpedoes.
Complement: 54.
Specifications are for Agosta S-70, as built.

History: The Agosta-class (S-70) is an ocean-going design, which was authoris
the French Navy's 1970-75 programme, with the four boats for the French
entering service in 1977 (two) and 1978 (two). This was followed by two e
orders. The Spanish order was for four, which were built under licence by B
(now IZAR) at Cartagena and entered service in 1983 (two), 1985 (one) and
(one). The other order was for two for South Africa to be built in France,
construction was well in hand in 1977 when the order had to be cancelled bec
of the United Nations arms embargo. Work continued at a slower pace for a
but Pakistan then took up the order in November 1978 and the boats en
service in 1979 and 1980.

remain in service until at least 2003. The others will remain in service with Pakistani, Portuguese and South African navies for a few years after that, aning that the Daphné design will have been in service for at least 40 years, mean record for a submarine.

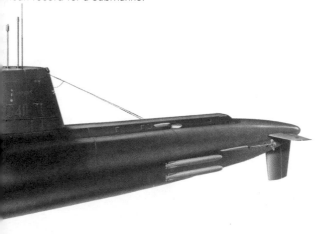

ove: The Daphné-class was sold to three foreign navies.

ht: Two Agosta-
ss, last diesel-
ctric boats for the
nch Navy.

The French then tinued marketing the gn for some years but out success until 1994 n a further contract signed with Pakistan hree boats designated sta A-90B and known akistan as the Khalid-s. The A-90B has ally identical measure-ts to the S-70, but the is fabricated from S-80 steel (equivalent e U.S. HY-100), published figures giving an operating depth of 1,050ft (320m), ough it is probably rather more. The A-90B also has entirely new internal pment, including an integrated weapon/fire control system and greater mation, which enable the crew to be reduced from 54 to 36. The first boat was entirely in France and delivered in September 1999, while sections for the nd were fabricated in France and sent to Pakistan for assembly, fitting out and pletion in 2002/03. The third boat is to be built entirely in Pakistan for an nated completion in 2006, but is to a modified design, incorporating the French-gned air-independent propulsion system MESMA.

Hai-class (ex-Type XXIII)   GERMA

Type: coastal.
Total built: 2.
Completed: 1957.
Displacement: surfaced 234 tons; submerged 275 tons.
Dimensions: length 118ft 6n (36.1m); beam 9ft 9in (3.0m); draught 12ft (3.7m).
Propulsion: 1 x Mercedes-Benz diesel, 635bhp; 1 x electric motor, 580sh x "creep" motor, 35shp; battery 62 cells; one shaft.
Performance: surface – 9.7kt, submerged – 12.5kt; range surfaced 1,350nr 9k, submerged 285nm at 6kt.
Weapons: 2 x 21in (533mm) TT (bow), 2 x torpedoes.
Complement: 17.

Type 201/205-classes   GERMA

Type: short-range patrol.

Type	201	205
Total built	3	10
Completed	1962	1962-69
Displacement surfaced submerged	395 tons 433 tons	419 tons 455 tons
Dimensions length beam draught	142ft 9in (43.5m) 15ft 0in (4.6m) 13ft 0in (4.0m)	144ft 5in (44.0m) 15ft 0in (4.6m) 13ft 0in (4.0m)
Propulsion diesel generators power electric motors power shafts	2 x Mercedes-Benz 2 x 600bhp 1 1 x 1,500shp one	

story: These two boats were built ~~ring World War II as Type XXIII and~~ ~~nmissioned in 1945 as *U-2365* and~~ *2367,* but both were sunk prior to ~~German surrender, the former in a~~ ~~mb attack (8 May 1945) and the~~ ~~er after a collision (5 May 1945).~~ ~~new Federal German Navy, the *ndesmarine,*~~ was formed in 1955 ~~in 1956~~ these two boats were ~~sed~~ and completely rebuilt as *Hai* ~~N-20)~~ and *Hecht* (UW-21). The ~~ginal M.W.M. diesel was replaced~~ ~~a modern Mercedes-Benz unit and~~ ~~ew, larger bridge tower was fitted.~~ ~~pulsion was totally electric, with~~ ~~diesels being used only to~~ ~~harge the battery, and all propulsion~~ ~~ng by the electric motor. They were~~ ~~ployed as training boats for the new~~ ~~y submarine crews. *Hai* foundered~~ ~~he North Sea (14 September 1966)~~ ~~*Hecht* was scrapped in 1969.~~

t: Two Type XXIIIs were raised in the 1950s.

ove right: The newly rebuilt Hai leaves the dock.

rformance	
~~ee~~d: surface	10kt
~~o~~merged	17.5kt
~~ge~~: schnorkel	3,950nm/4kt
~~o~~merged	228nm/4kt
~~xi~~mum	
~~in~~g depth	492ft (150m)
eapons	
~~ation~~	8 x 21in (533mm)
~~oe~~does	bow
	8
mplement	21

tory: The Type 201 was designed by the German submarine design bureau ~~e~~*nieurkontor L beck* (IKL) as West Germany's first post-war class for ~~ol~~oyment primarily in the Baltic. It was decided that the hull should be ~~c~~structed of austenitic (non-magnetic) steel and the order for 12 was placed ~~l~~arch 1959, with the first, *U-1* (S-180), launched in October 1961, followed ~~U~~-2 and *U-3* in early 1962. Unfortunately, the project hit a major problem as ~~t~~anspired that the water of the Baltic had a highly corrosive effect on the ~~ic~~ular type of non-magnetic steel then in use; the effect was so rapid and ~~s~~evere that *U-1* and *U-2* had to be taken out of commission within months. ~~was also completed but was loaned to Norway as a training boat, since~~ ~~vegian~~ waters had no effect on the steel.

Construction of the next five boats, *U-4* to *U-8*, was already well in hand had to be allowed to continue, but their exteriors were completely covered thin film of tin, which meant that severe constraints had to be placed on t operational performance. Meanwhile, construction of the remaining boats, to *U-12*, was postponed until a totally new, non-corrosive, non-magnetic steel had been developed and they were then completed to the same design but with the new hull. Finally, *U-1* and *U-2* were returned to the yard, where their old hulls were removed and replaced by the new material. *U-3* was never rebuilt.

After all this, there were some minor differences between the boats; *U-11* and *U-12* had different rudders from the rest, while there were four different varieties of bridge. *U-4* to *U-8* spent their entire service from 1963 to the mid-1970s with the training organisation, after which they were scrapped. The remainder served on into the 1990s, except for *U-11* and *U-12* which were still in service in 2002 having been extensively modified as the Type 205A and 205B, respectively. *U-11* will be stricken in 2003 but *U-12* will remain in service until 2006.

There was also a Type 202, a very small (137 tons submerged displacement) coastal submarine. Two were completed in 1966, but after extensive trials it was decided that they were far too small and

Type 206-class and Gal-class

Type: patrol.
Total built: 18.
Completed: 1972-74.
Displacement: surfaced 456 tons; submerged 500 tons.
Dimensions: length 159ft 6in (48.6m); beam 15ft 0in (4.6m); draught 14ft (4.3m).
Propulsion: 2 x Mercedes-Benz diesel generators, 2 x 600bhp; 1 x electric m 1,500shp; batteries 3 x 92 cells; one shaft.
Performance: surface – 10kt, submerged – 17.5kt; range surfaced 3,950nm at submerged 200nm at 5kt; maximum operating diving depth 492ft (150m).
Weapons: 8 x 21in (533mm) TT (bow), 16 x torpedoes.
Complement: 21.
Specifications are for Type 206, as built.

History: Designed, like all post-war German submarines, by the IKL design bur the order for the first 12 (*U-13* to *U-24*) Type 206 was placed in 1969, followe the order for *U-25* to *U-30* in 1970. The boats were launched between 1971 1974, with production being shared between Rheinstahl-Nordeseewerke, En (10), and Howaldtswerke, Kiel (8). The design was little changed from the 201/205, except that there was a new rounded bow housing the sonar do

*Right: **U-30**, fitted with a strap-on mine "girdle".*

type was not put into production. The two completed boats were scrapped the early 1970s.

low: **U-1** *after conversion to test an air-independent system.*

Improvements include better manoeuverability, greater silencing, and the ability launch wire-guided torpedoes. They can carry up to 24 mines internally in lieu torpedoes, but can be fitted with a strap-on mine "girdle" carrying a total of mines without reducing the number of torpedoes. Twelve boats were upgraded Type 206A standard, which included updated electronics, new periscopes improved crew accommodation.

Five of the six unconverted Type 206 boats were to have been sold to Indone and matters proceeded to the point where, while still in German waters, they w manned by Indonesian crews and flying the Indonesian flag, but the sale was t cancelled and the boats handed back to the Germans in 1998. All six Type 2 were then scrapped. Disposal of the Type 206As started with one in 2002, and continue with one in 2004 and two in 2005, but the details for the remainder h yet to be announced.

Three of a modified version of the Type 206 were built for the Israeli Navy the Gal-class, although, for political reasons, the boats had to be built by the British shipyard, Vickers, Barrow. The most obvious external difference was the larger sail which was intended to accommodate an anti-helicopter missile system, although this was never actually installed. They were regularly updated, with Sub-Harpoon being installed in 1983, making them by far the smallest

Type 207-class (Kobben-class)

GERMANY (NORW.

Type: coastal patrol.
Total built: 15.
Completed: 1964-67.
Displacement: surfaced 370 tons; submerged 530 tons.
Dimensions: length 149 ft 0in (45.4m); beam 15ft 0in (4.6m); draught 14ft (4.3m).
Propulsion: 2 x Maybach diesel generators, 2 x 600bhp; 1 x electric mo 1,200shp; batteries 3 x 92 cells; one shaft.
Performance: surface – 10kt, submerged – 17kt; range schnorkel 5,000nn 8kt, submerged 141nm at 6kt; maximum operating diving depth 623ft (190 **Weapons:** 8 x 21`in (533mm) TT (bow), 8 x torpedoes.
Complement: 18.
Specifications for Type 207, as built

History: After World War II the Royal Norwegian Navy used five British U- cl boats, supplemented in 1950 by three German Type VIICs and one Type X supplied from stocks held by the British. When it was decided to obtain m modern boats, the Norwegians turned to Germany and in 1959 ordered boats from Nordeseewerke, Emden, with half the funding provided by United States. The design was based on that of the German Type 207, but v a strengthened hull to allow deeper diving in the waters off the Norweg coasts. One boat, *Svenner* (S-309), was 3ft 3in (1m) longer than the oth

marines to carry this weapon. Updated sensors and fire control equipment were
ed in 1994/95, but they were all stricken in 1999. At one stage a sale to Ecuador
s under serious consideration, but fell through.

ove: U-16, an early Type 206.

*ove: **Kobben**, one of the Type 207s built for Norway.*

ce it is used for officer training and mounts a second periscope.
 Six boats were modernised in 1989-91, being lengthened by 6ft 7in (2m),
en new MTU diesel engines, and fitted with new electronics and a
dernised fire control system. In 2002 four of these remained in service, but
 likely to be progressively retired, with the last going in 2006. Of the
nodernised boats, one was transferred to the U.S. Navy in 1991, four were
cken and scrapped and four were transferred to Denmark between 1989
 1991. (Only three were purchased by Denmark, but one was lost on tow
ing delivery, and was replaced by the Norwegians.)

Type 209-class

Type (Example)	Type 209/1100 (Greece)	Type 209/1200 (S. Korea)	Type 209/1300 (Venezuela)	Type 209/1400 (Turkey)	Type 209/1500 (India)
Displacement surfaced submerged	1,100 tons 1,207 tons	1,100 tons 1,285 tons	1,265 tons 1,295 tons	1,464 tons 1,586 tons	1,660 tons 1,850 tons
Dimensions length beam draught	177ft 6in (54.1m) 20ft 3in (6.2m) 19ft 5in (5.9m)	184ft 0in (56.1m) 20ft 4in (6.2m) 17ft 11in (5.5m)	200ft 10in (61.2m) 20ft 8in (6.3m) 18ft 0in (5.5m)	203ft 5in (62.0m) 20ft 4in (6.2m) 18ft 0in (5.5m)	211ft 3in (64.4m) 21ft 3in (6.5m) 19ft 8in (6.0m)
Propulsion diesels power electric motors power battery shafts	4 x M.T.U. 4 x 550bhp 1 x Siemens 5,000shp 4 x 120 cells one	4 x M.T.U. 4 x 800bhp 1 x Siemens 5,000shp 4 x 120 cells one	4 x M.T.U. 4 x 600bhp 1 x Siemens 4,600shp 4 x 120 cells one	4 x M.T.U. 4 x 800bhp 1 x Siemens 5,000shp 4 x 120 cells one	4 x M.T.U. 4 x 800bhp 2 x Siemens 4,600shp 4 x 132 cells one
Performance speed: surface submerged range: schnorkel submerged maximum diving depth	11.5kt 22kt 8,600nm/4kt 230nm/8kt 820ft (250m)	10kt 22kt 6,000nm/8kt 230nm/8kt 820ft (250m)	11kt 21.5kt 8,200nm/8kt 400nm/4kt 820ft (250m)	11kt 21.5kt 8,200nm/8kt 400nm/4kt 1,050ft (320m)	11kt 22kt 13,000nm/1 8,000nm/8 853ft (260
Weapons TT location torpedoes/ missiles	8 bow 14	8 bow 14	8 bow 14	8 bow 14	8 bow 14
Complement	31	34	32	30	40

History: The German Type 209 is one of the most important diesel-elec submarines in the world. Fifty-one are in service with 13 navies construction has taken place in Germany and in five other countries ur licence: Argentina, Brazil, India, South Korea and Turkey. In 2002, firm or were in place for a further 12 and others are in the pipeline. The Type 209 came onto the market in the mid-1960s, at a time when several smaller na wanted to purchase submarines for the first time, while many exis operators were starting to look for replacements for their second-hand U.S. British World War II submarines, both because they were getting old because they required high levels of crewing: 86 men for a Guppy III, example. At the time only a few new Western submarine designs w

ilable, and all were large, expensive to buy and to operate, and designed for
d War operations, with few concessions to export requirements. Export
marines were available from the USSR, but no Western and few Latin
erican or Asian customers wanted to deal with the Soviets while the Cold
r lasted. Thus, the Type 209 provided a good solution: a powerful weapons
tem at a reasonable price, and with almost a century of German submarine
erience behind it; above all, it was designed specifically for export, but
vely backed, especially where training was concerned, by the
ndesmarine.

The Type 209 is a single-hull design with two main ballast tanks, and
vard and after trim tanks. Forward and after ends are free-flooding, as is the
.. There is an electric drive system, with four M.T.U. diesels and four A.E.G.
erators. The original engine was the MTU 493-V12, but recent boats and
ts are using the MTU 396-V8, which has lower specific fuel consumption,
uced noise levels and greater time between overhauls. Most versions have
r 120-cell batteries delivering 11,500 ampere-hours and weighing some 257
s, driving a single A.E.G. electric motor, the exception being the Indian Type
/1500 which has four 132-cell batteries and two motors. Earlier Type 209s
a five-bladed propeller, but the latest versions have a large-diameter, seven-
led, skew-back propeller whose slow rate of revolution allied to the low
peller load results in a highly efficient propulsion system. The hull is
structed of HY 80 steel, but could be constructed of non-magnetic steel if a
tomer wished, although this would be a very expensive option and no nation
yet requested it. Cruising range is some 400nm between two snorting
ods, based on a speed of 4 kt and 80 per cent battery discharge, and the
l cruising range is more than 12,000nm at 4kt submerged. Provisions are
ied for 50-day patrols.

Two air-independent propulsion (AIP) options are now on offer, both of
ch would require a plug-in section some 19ft 8in (6m) long to be inserted
nediately abaft the sail. The systems use either fuel cells or closed-cycle
sels, both with liquid oxygen for the reaction process.

There are five basic models, the Types 209/1100, /1200, /1300, /1400 and
00, the second figure denoting the submerged displacement. In essence,

ow: Atilay, Type 209/1400 for Turkey.

TYPE 209 - ORDERS/DELIVERIES

Type	Country	Orders		Entered	In Servi
		Number	Total	Service	2002
209/1100	Greece	4	4	1971-72	4
209/1200	Argentina*	2		1974	1
	Colombia	2		1975	2
	Greece	4		1979-80	4
	Korea, South**	9		1993-?	8
	Peru	6		1974-83	6
	Turkey	6	29	1976-90	6
209/1300	Ecuador	2		1977-78	2
	Indonesia	2		1981	2
	Venezuela	2	6	1976-77	2
209/1400	Brazil	5		1989- 2003	4
	Chile	2		1984	2
	South Africa	3		2005-07	0
	Turkey	8	18	1994-2006	4
209/1500	India	6	6	1986-2005	4
	TOTAL		63		51

* 1 stricken in 1997.

** Last one may not be completed.

the extra size is obtained by stretching the pressure hull to enable extra fue
additional sensors to be carried, or, in the case of the Indian Type 1500, a Ga
rescue sphere, the only such system installed in any Western submarine.

Argentina

Argentina ordered two Type 209/1200s in 1968, which were built in
sections by Howaldtswerke (HDW) at Kiel, Germany, and shipped to Argen
for assembly in Buenos Aires at the Rio Santiago Navy Yard. On the outbr

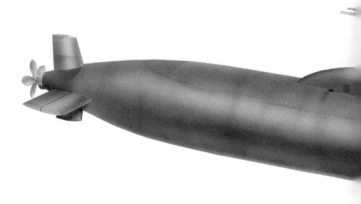

Above: **San Luis,** *a Type 209/1200 of the Argentine Navy.*

the Falklands (Malvinas) War in 1982 both immediately went to sea to ınter the British task force, although *Salta* returned due to a mechanical blem and then remained in harbour for the rest of the conflict. *San Luis* ried out two attacks, launching torpedoes on both occasions, but scored no s; the reason for the failure of the torpedoes has never been established, at st in public. Despite the lack of actual hits, the campaign by *San Luis* caused British task force a serious problem and remains an excellent example of influence that can be exercised by even one quiet submarine. *Salta* derwent a mid-life modernisation 1988-95 and was fitted with new engines, apons and electrical systems. *San Luis* was stricken in 1997.

zil

 order for Type 209/1400 Mod. 3 boats (Tupi-class), signed in 1984, was zil's first ever order from a German shipyard. The original plan was to chase six boats, of which one would be built in Germany and the remaining in Brazil. Following lengthy delays the total to be built in Brazil was reduced three in 1992 and the last of these (and fourth in total) was completed in 9. An order for another boat was, however, reinstated in 1994 and this boat, ına (S-34), will be completed in 2003. This will be to a greatly improved ign, being 2ft 9in (0.85m) longer and fitted with new diesels, a different ctric motor and more modern command-and-control, electronic and sensor ıipment. All Brazilian Type 209/1400s carry eight reload torpedoes for their es, for a total of 16, whereas all other Type 209s can accommodate only six ads. A plan to build a Brazilian-designed diesel-electric successor to the i-class was cancelled in 1993 and work is now proceeding on a nuclear-vered design.

le

 Chilean Navy ordered two Type 209/1400s in 1980, which were delivered 984. These submarines are of standard IKL design except that both have sail and associated masts raised by 19.7in (50cm) to cope with the high ves encountered off the Chilean coast. While many other Type 209 users return their submarines to Germany for refitting by HKW, the Chilean Navy uses its own ASMAR navy yard, at Talcahuano, and both these boats have undergone 10-month refits there, *Thompson* completing in late 1990 and *Simpson* in 1991. At one stage the Chilean Navy planned to buy two more Type 209s but this was cancelled, following which serious consideration was given to the purchase of the four

redundant British Upholder-class submarines (qv), but this came to nought.
order was placed in 1997 for two French-designed Scorpéne-class boats, v
one being built by DCN, Cherbourg, the other by IZAR, Cartagena (form
Bazan), for delivery in 2004/2005.

Colombia
The two Colombian Type 209/1200s were ordered in 1971 and delivered
1975, and are virtually identical to the Greek Glavkos-class. Both were refit
by HDW, Kiel, in 1990-91, which included a complete replacement of the m
batteries. The Colombian Navy has a requirement for two more submarines
has shown an interest in more new Type 209s as well as the two Type 17
(qv) offered for sale by Argentina, but funding has never been available.

Ecuador
Ecuador ordered two Type 209/1300s in 1974, which were delivered
1977/78. Both underwent major refits at HDW in Germany in 1983-84 an
local refit in 1993-94. The Chilean ASMAR yard has made a bid to carry out t
next refit, but this has yet to be accepted.

Greece
The Hellenic Navy was the first customer for the Type 209; the initial or
for four Type 209/1100s was placed in the mid-1960s and they w
delivered in 1971-72. They underwent a major modernisation in the 199
bringing them up to the same standard as the German Navy's Type 2(
and extending their lives well beyond the nominal 30-year point, which v
reached in 2001-2002. The Hellenic Navy took delivery of a further four T
209/1200s in 1979-80, a lengthened version of the Type 209/1100 v
additional fuel bunkerage. The modernisation of the Type 209/1100s hav
been completed, the Type 209/1200s are now undergoing the sa
process. The Hellenic Navy has ordered three of the new Type 214
delivery from 2009 onwards.

India
The Indian contract was signed in December 1981 and covered
construction in Germany of two Type 209/1500 submarines; the supply
`packages' for the building of two more boats at Mazagon, Bombay; train
specialists for the design and construction of the Mazagon pair; logi
services during the trials and early part of the commissions;
consultation services in Bombay. The two German-built boats were
down in 1982 and arrived in India in 1987. The third boat was laid dow
Mazagon in June 1984, but work was delayed by assembly problems
to faulty welding, a problem by no means unique to the Mazagon yarc
plan to build two more was cancelled on several occasions, but finally gi
the go-ahead in 1999, with delivery scheduled for 2004/05. The T
209/1500 is the largest variant of the German design and one unus
feature is the IKL-designed, integrated escape sphere, which can carry
full crew of 40 men. The sphere sits just forward of the sail, has an oxy(
supply for eight hours, and can withstand pressures at least as great
those that can be withstood by the submarine's pressure hull.

Indonesia
These two submarines were ordered in 1977 and delivered in 1981. T
underwent major refits at HDW during 1986-89, a process the Indonesian N
considered to take too long and to be too expensive. As a result the next re
in the mid/late 1990s were carried out in Indonesia. Indonesia has been seel
more submarines for years, one possibility being two more Type 209s, w
the Netherlands is known to have offered the two redundant Zwaardvis-c
submarines.

Republic of Korea (RoK)
The ROK ordered three Type 209/1200 boats in late 1987, the first being b
at Kiel and handed over in October 1992 and the other two assembled
Daewoofrom material packages transported from Germany; these v

nmissioned in 1994-95. A second batch of three was ordered in October
39 and a third batch, also of three, in January 1994. The first batch of Korean
e 209/1200 are very similar to those built for the Turkish Navy, with a heavy
pendence on Atlas Elektronik sensors and STN torpedoes, but there has
n a progressively greater Korean content in each boat as it is built.

ru

Peruvian boats were ordered in pairs: SS 35 and SS 36 in 1973; SS 31 and
32 in 1976; and SS 33 and SS 34 in 1977. All have undergone a mid-life
dernisation refit.

key

Turkish Navy operated a sizeable force of ex-U.S. Navy World War II
marines for some years and then decided in the late 1960s to purchase
dern submarines and selected the Type 209/1200, not least because HDW
e ready to help establish a shipyard in Turkey. The first three of the first
er were built at HDW, Kiel, with Turkish technicians and artificers under
ning, and the boats were delivered in 1975-78. The next three were then
t at Gölcük Navy Yard with technical help form HDW, these boats being
vered rather more slowly, with one each in 1981, 1985 and 1990. These will
be modernised in the current decade. The initial order was for 12 Type
/1200s but was stopped at six because the Turkish Navy decided to build
of the larger Type 209/1400. The order for first two was signed in November
7 and the option on a further pair was taken up in 1993, all built at the
cük Navy Yard with assistance from HDW. However, the total order is now
eight. These boats, the Preveze-class, are 8ft 6in (2.6m) longer than the
ier class, have more advanced electronics, and can launch both Sub-
poon missiles and Tigerfish Mk 24 Mod 2 torpedoes, giving them
siderably more hitting power.

ezuela

Venezuelan Navy originally planned to procure four submarines, but
ncial considerations limited this to two, which were delivered in 1976/77.
h were refitted at HDW, Kiel, in the early 1980s and again in the early 1990s.
latter slightly lengthening the hull to accommodate a new sonar
e, raising the forward casing and installing new engines, fire-control, sonar
attack periscopes.

ow: **Nanggala,** *Type 209/1300 of the Indonesian Navy.*

Type 210 (Ula-class)

Type: patrol.
Total built: 6.
Completed: 1989-92.
Displacement: surfaced 1,040 tons; submerged 1,150 tons.
Dimensions: length 193ft 7in (59.0m); beam 17ft 8in (5.4m); draught 15ft
(4.6m).
Propulsion: 2 x M.T.U. diesels, 2 x 1,260bhp; 1 x Siemens electric m(
6,000shp; one shaft.
Performance: surface – 11kt, submerged – 23kt; range schnorkel 5,000nr
8kt; maximum operating diving depth 820ft (250m).
Weapons: 8 x 21in (533mm) TT (bow), 14 x torpedoes.
Complement: 20.

History: When it was decided to replace half the Kobben-class the result
the most expensive project ever undertaken by the Royal Norwegian N
(RNorN). Designated the Ula-class (known in Germany as the Type 210)
contract for six boats was signed on 30 September 1982; there was an op
for two more, but this was not taken up. The first hull was manufacture
Germany, while the remainder were made by Kvaerner Brug in Norway
then transported to Kiel, Germany. The equipment was truly internatic
American navigation system (Rockwell-Collins); British radar (Kelvin Hu(
Type 1007) and EW suite (Racal Sea Lion); French conformal arrays (Thom
Sintra); German sonar (STN Atlas DBQS-21F), torpedoes (AEG DM 2A3 Se
Italian periscopes (Riva-Calzoni); and Norwegian fire-control system (N

Dolfin-class
(IKL Type 800)

Type: patrol.
Total built: 3.
Completed: 1999-2000.
Displacement: surfaced 1,565 tons; submerged 1,720 tons.
Dimensions: length 187ft 8in (57.3m); beam 24ft 3in (7.4m); draught 20f
(6.2m).
Propulsion: 3 x M.T.U. diesels, 3 x 800bhp; 3 x generator sets, 3 x 313kW
Siemens motors, 2,850shp; battery 2 x 216 cells; one shaft.
Performance: surface – 11kt, submerged – 20kt; range surfaced 14,000n
4kt, schnorkel 8,000nm at 8kt, submerged 420nm at 8kt; maximum opera
diving depth 1,150ft (350m).
Weapons: 10 x 21in (533mm) TT (bow), 16 x torpedoes/Sub-Harpoon/T
(see notes).
Complement: 30.

History: The Israeli Navy sought additional submarines for many years a
mid-1988 Ingalls Shipbuilding in the USA became prime contractor for two
designed submarines; sections were to be fabricated in Germany and
shipped to the United States for assembly, fitting out and trials. The b
would have used a U.S. command system and be funded by the
Government under the FMS (Federal Military Sales) programme, but the pr
was cancelled in November 1990 due to pressures on U.S. defence funds

ve: Ula, nameship of a class of six Norwegian Type 210s.

varsteknologie).

The programme seems to have suffered more than its fair share of ▪lems. *Ula* (S-300) was hit by its own practice torpedo on trials; *Uredd* (S- hit a jetty while coming alongside and in a separate incident had a fire in ▪control room; and *Uthaug* (S-304) collided with an uncharted rock while ▪nerged, and ran aground later the same day while returning to port on the ▪ce.

The RNorN plans to purchase four submarines of a new design to replace ▪emaining four Type 207s, possibly in the 2010-2015 time frame. To this end ▪s joined with Denmark and Sweden in the Nordic submarine project.

ve: The Dolfin-class was built in Germany for Israel.

▪act was resurrected following the April 1991 Gulf War, but this time with ▪nan Government funding for two submarines with an option on a third. That ▪n was taken up in 1994, but this time with funding shared equally between ▪nany and Israel. The first hull was launched in April 1996, followed by the ▪nd in 1997 and the third in 1998. The Dolphin-class is generally similar to ▪German Type 212 in design but with the forward hydroplanes atop the ▪ard hull rather than on the sail, as in other modern German-designed ▪narines. Another specifically Israeli feature is the incorporation of a 'wet ▪dry' compartment for special forces swimmers. These boats will be used ▪terdiction, surveillance and special forces' operations.

Type TR-1700

Type: ocean-going patrol.
Total built: 2.
Completed: 1984-85.
Displacement: surfaced 2,116 tons; submerged 2,264 tons.
Dimensions: length 216ft 6in (66.0m); beam 23ft 11in (7.3m); draught 21f
(6.5m).
Propulsion: 4 x M.T.U. diesels, 2 x 1,680bhp; 4 x alternator sets, 4 x 1.1
1 x electric motor, 8,970shp; one shaft.
Performance: surface – 15kt, schnorkel – 15kt, submerged – 25kt; ra
surfaced 12,000nm at 8kt, submerged 4,650nm at 6kt; maximum opera
diving depth 984ft (300m).
Weapons: 6 x 21in (533mm) TT (bow), 22 x torpedoes.
Complement: 26.

History: These two boats remain the largest submarines built in Germany s
the end of World War II and are the fastest known diesel-electric submarin
the world, with a burst speed of 26kt. The original contract, signed in Nover
1977, was for six submarines: two TR-1400s and four of the larger TR-17
but the order for the two TR-1400s was subsequently changed to two m
TR-1700s. The first two boats were built at Emden, Germany, and delive
on time, but the remaining four were to be built in Argentina by Astilleros
Domecq Garcia in Buenos Aires, and this element of the contract hit
endless problems, and by early 1996 *Santa Fé* (S-43) was 52 per cent
complete, *Santiago del Estero* (S-44) just 30 per cent complete, and no
work had been done on either for at least 12 months. Both hulls were
offered for sale and at one point a plan was considered whereby they
would be sent to Thyssen Nordseewerke for completion and resale to a
third party (possibly Taiwan), which would have rid the Argentine Navy of
a financial and public relations embarrassment and also cleared the
yard for privatisation. The third hull had been laid down, but that
was about all and nothing had been done on the fourth. In the
event all plans came to nought and not one of the four Argentine-
built boats was ever completed, the parts being used instead to
keep the two German-built boats going.

*Below: Designed and built by Thyssen, only two TR-
1700s were built, both for Argentina.*

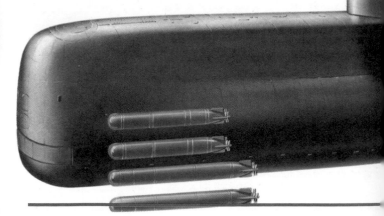

Above: Santa Cruz *departs for Argentina in December 1984.*

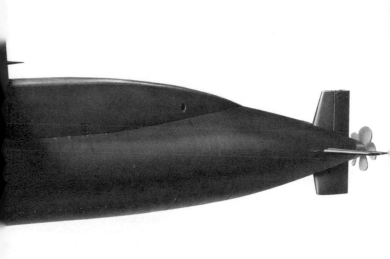

T-class Conversion/ Streamline

Type: ocean-going patrol.
Total converted: 8.
Converted: 1949-56.
Displacement: surfaced 1,535 tons; submerged 1,734 tons.
Dimensions: length 293ft 6in (89.5m); beam 26ft 7in (8.1m); draught 16ft (4.9m).
Propulsion: 2 x Admiralty Standard Range supercharged diesels, 4 x 700bhp Laurence Scott electric motors, 4 x 1,500shp; battery 4 x 112 cells; two shafts
Performance: surface – 14kt, schnorkel – 9.4kt, submerged – 15.4kt; maxim operating diving depth 350ft (107m).
Weapons: 6 x 21in (533mm) TT (bow), 12 x torpedoes.
Complement: 68.
Specifications are for Tabard group, as converted.

History: In the late 1940s, the British Royal Navy, as with the U.S. Navy, decide modernise a number of its World War II boats in order to provide some mo operational boats quickly. They were also needed to provide fast-moving target its surface ASW warships. Eight of the all-welded T-class boats were selected their pressure hulls were cut in two and a plug inserted, which varied in le between 12ft (3.7m) in three, 14ft (4.3m) in one and 20ft (6.1m) in the remair The original diesels were retained, but the plug enabled an extra pair of ele

A-class Conversion

Type: ocean-going patrol.
Total converted: 14.
Converted: 1955-60.
Displacement: surfaced 1,443 tons; submerged 1,620 tons.
Dimensions: length 279ft 90in (85.3m); beam 22ft 3in (6.8m); draught 18f (5.5m).
Propulsion: 4 x Admiralty Standard Range supercharged diesels, 4 x 1,075 2 x electric motors, 2 x 625shp; two shafts.
Performance: surface – 19kt, schnorkel – 11kt, submerged – 15kt; ra surfaced 11,000nm at 11kt, submerged 114nm at 3kt; maximum opera diving depth 500ft (152m).
Weapons: 6 x 21in (533mm) TT (bow – 4, stern – 2), 16 x torpedoes; 1 x (102mm) gun (see notes).
Complement: 63.

History: The A-class boats were built specifically for the World War II Pa campaign but were completed too late to see war service. As a result, British Royal Navy found itself in the late 1940s with 16 virtually submarines on its hands. They were well-built, but according to pre-Type standards of propulsion and streamlining. The early boats were not compl with schnorkels; this new device was fitted in boats from *Alliance*, the boat, onwards, and retrofitted in the others during their first refit, but r more improvements were clearly needed, although pressure of events shortage of funds kept these boats in service in their original state for s years. Following the success of the T-class conversion, however, the A-

...ht: Tireless, T-class ...tial modernisation ...h new sail.

...ors to be installed ...ether with a fourth battery ...12 cells, and propulsion ... changed from direct to ...el-electric drive. The ...iralty-pattern diesels ...e provided with a ...ercharger and a schnorkel ...installed.

Externally, the gun was ...oved, the bow and stern were reshaped, and all external pro-tuberances were ...er removed or made retractable. A large streamlined sail was installed, which ...rporated the bridge in two (*Tabard* and *Trump*) while in others there was a small ...ge constructed low in front of the fin. Armament was reduced to six tubes, all ...he bow, with 12 torpedoes carried (mines could be carried as an alternative). ...er equipment was updated or replaced. The result was a thoroughly serviceable ...t with its underwater speed actually doubled. Two were transferred to Israel in ...4-65, but one was lost on its delivery voyage and was replaced by a third boat ...968. The remaining British boats were stricken and broken up in the early 1970s.

As with the U.S. Navy's Fleet Schnorkels, five riveted T-class boats were given ...rtial modernisation, which consisted of removing the gun and some external ...gs and installing a higher, more streamlined sail and a schnorkel.

...ht: Amphion, *one ...4 A-class given a ...rough rebuild ...5-60.*

...e taken in hand and ...were thoroughly ...lernised between ...5 and 1960 (the only ...ts not converted ...e *Affray*, lost on 16 ...1951, and *Aurochs* ...ch in 1964 was found ...e in a bad state of ...ir and not worth ...verting). The work ...not involve length- ...g the pressure hull, ...were the propulsion ...hinery and batteries changed, but the hull was reshaped fore and aft, and ...external fittings streamlined, made retractable or removed. A fully ...amlined sail was fitted, at 26ft 6in (8.0m) the highest installed in any RN ...marine to date. The external torpedo tubes were removed, but the ...nting for the 4in (102mm) gun was left in place so that the gun could be ...nted, if required. This proved to be a perceptive measure, since there were ...mber of British campaigns, particularly in Asia, where the weapon came in ...useful for challenging small vessels. The various measures had a good but ...dramatic effect: the submerged speed increased by some 2kt.

Porpoise/
Oberon-classes

Type: ocean-going patrol.
Total built: 22.
Completed: 1958-67.
Displacement: surfaced 1,975 tons; submerged 2,303 tons.
Dimensions: length 290ft 3in (88.5m); beam 26ft 6in (8.1m); draught 18f
(5.6m).
Propulsion: 2 x Admiralty Standard Range diesels, 2 x 1,840bhp; 2 x En
Electric electric motors, 2 x 3,000shp; battery 448 cells; two shafts.
Performance: surface – 12kt, submerged – 17kt; range surfaced 9,000n
12kt, schnorkel 11,000nm at 8kt; maximum operating diving depth 6
(200m).
Weapons: 8 x 21in (533mm) TT (bow – 6, stern – 2), 18 x torpedoes.
Complement: 71.
Specifications for Porpoise-class, as built.

History: The first British submarines to be designed after World War II were
hydrogen-peroxide-powered experimental submarines, *Explorer* and *Exca*
(qv), but the first operational diesel-electric boats were the Porpoise-c
Orders for eight boats were placed in 1951, although the first-of-class was
actually laid down until 1955 and was not completed until 1958. The de
incorporated the lessons learnt from the war, plus those derived from det
examination of the captured German boats, such as the Type XXI, as we
post-war experience with the T-class conversions and observation of U.S. M

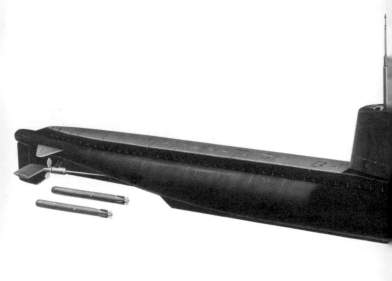

...ve: Oberon-class SSK in Australian service.

...rammes. The hull was of a very clean design and this, coupled with the ...powerful batteries, gave a submerged speed of 17kt and also ensured that ...travelling at slow speed they were very quiet. They were stricken ...een 1977 and 1990, not because they had reached the end of their service ...but due to RN financial and manpower cuts.

...After the eight Porpoise-class came the Oberon-class, whose dimensions,

...w: Oberons were the most successful second generation SSKs in ...navy and the last British submarines to be exported.

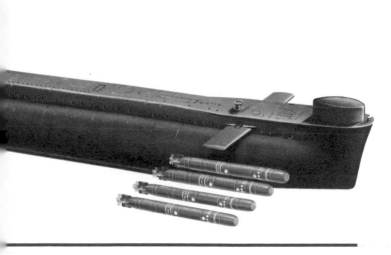

displacement and propulsive machinery were identical to that in
Porpoise-class, but there were important developments in weaponry, s
and construction. The all-welded pressure-hull was the same as on
Porpoise-class, but fabricated from a higher quality steel which incre
the diving depth to a reported 1,000ft (305m). The superstructure
made of steel only in the first-of-class; in the second boat, *Orpheus*, it
made of aluminium, while in the remainder it was made of glass-reinfo
plastic (GRP), the first time such a material had been used in a large s
in a RN warship. The sonar outfit was also considerably improved and
class was able to launch Mk 24 homing torpedoes.

A grand total of 27 Oberons were built, with 13 being delivered to
RN in 1960-67. One of those building for the RN was bought on the st
by the Royal Canadian Navy (RCN) and a replacement boat was then ac
to the RN's order. A total of 14 were exported: Australia – six (Oxley-c
1968-78); Brazil – three (Humaita-class, 1973-78); Canada – three (Oji
class, 1965-68); Chile – two (Hyatt-class, 1976).

The RN boats were upgraded several times during their service,
boats from the class took part in both the Falklands (1982) and Gulf (1
Wars, as well as playing a very energetic role in Cold War operations.
RN cut its SSK force in 1991, as a result of which these Oberons wer
of service early. Five were scrapped in 1991-92, while a number v
bought by UK-based civil companies in order to refit them and sell t
abroad; in the event no sales were achieved.

Right: Sealion, *a Porpoise-class SSK.*

Upholder/
Victoria-class   GREAT BRITAIN (CAN/

Type: attack.
Total built: 4.
Completed: 1990-93.
Displacement: surfaced 2,185 tons; submerged 2,400 tons.
Dimensions: length 230ft 7in (70.3m); beam 24ft 11in (7.6m); draught 18
(5.5m).
Propulsion: 2 x Paxman Valenta diesel generators, 2 x 2,035bhp;
alternators; 1 x electric motor, 5,400shp; battery 2 x 240 cells; one shaft.
Performance: surface – 12kt, schnorkel – 919kt, submerged – 20kt; r
schnorkel 8,000nm at 8kt, submerged 270nm at 3kt; maximum operating d
depth over 820ft (250m).
Weapons: 6 x 21in (533mm) TT (bow), 18 x torpedoes.
Complement: 44.

History: The Upholder-class was originally conceived as a hunter-killer fc
British Royal Navy, their Cold War mission being to lie in wait for S
submarines seeking to pass through the Greenland-Iceland-UK gaps.
were intended to be replacements for the Porpoise/Oberon-classes, the la
which had been launched in 1967, but they were commissioned just a
Cold War came to an end. The British government quickly concluded tha
RN could no longer afford to maintain fleets of both nuclear and conventi
powered submarines, and so the four Upholder-class were taken out of se

ve: **Victoria,** *first of four British Upholders sold to Canada.*

despite the large amount of money expended first on designing and building these four boats and then on resolving various problems once they were in service. They were then offered for sale to various countries, including Australia, Chile and South Africa, while Taiwan made an unsolicited bid which was rejected under pressure from China. No purchaser could be found until 1998 when they were acquired by Canada on an eight-year lease, at the end of which they will be purchased for a nominal £1 sterling.

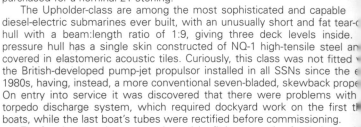

The Upholder-class are among the most sophisticated and capable diesel-electric submarines ever built, with an unusually short and fat tear-drop hull with a beam:length ratio of 1:9, giving three deck levels inside. pressure hull has a single skin constructed of NQ-1 high-tensile steel an covered in elastomeric acoustic tiles. Curiously, this class was not fitted the British-developed pump-jet propulsor installed in all SSNs since the e 1980s, having, instead, a more conventional seven-bladed, skewback prope On entry into service it was discovered that there were problems with torpedo discharge system, which required dockyard work on the first t boats, while the last boat's tubes were rectified before commissioning.

The four boats underwent a substantial refit in preparation for their transfe Canada, and the first boat, renamed HMCS *Victoria*, was delivered in May 200

Enrico Toti-class

IT

Type: coastal hunter/killer.
Total built: 4.
Completed: 1968-69.
Displacement: surfaced 535 tons; submerged 591 tons.
Dimensions: length 151ft 6in (46.2m); beam 15ft 5in (4.7m); draught 13f (4.0m).
Propulsion: 2 x diesels, 2 x 1,100bhp; 1 x electric motor, 2,200shp; one s
Performance: surface – 9.7kt, submerged – 14kt; range surfaced 3,000n 5kt; maximum operating diving depth 680ft (300m).
Weapons: 4 x 21in (533mm) TT (bow), 8 x torpedoes.
Complement: 26.

History: The Italian Navy's post-war submarine fleet initially consisted bewildering array of pre-war and wartime designs, most of which were in condition. Many were scrapped in 1947 and the remainder were lost in 194 a result of the Peace Treaty, except for two passed to the USSR and two w remained in Italian hands disguised as "battery chargers". The bar submarines expired in 1952 and the two "battery chargers" were returne commission as operational boats. The Italian Navy also acquired a numbe boats from the U.S. Navy: Guppy IB – 2; Guppy II – 2; Fleet Schnorkel – 3; Tang-class – 2. Although these were all sound designs they were somew large for Mediterranean operations, and were also very manpower intensi

The first new-build boats were the Toti-class, for which the operat requirement changed several times, with the design recast accordingly, u was finally settled upon as a coastal hunter/killer for employment under N

...ve: The Upholder-class was built to block the GIUK gap.

...t: The Italian
...y's Toti-class was
...igned to be fast
agile.

...mand in the central
...iterranean and
...atic. As a result,
...size was kept to a
...mum and long
...e was not a
...irement. The Totis
...e small and highly
...oeuvrable, with a
..."rdrop" hull, diesel-
...tric drive, and a
...e propeller. Like
...r hunter-killers of
...ime, they mounted
...ctive sonar in a large
...e on the bows and
...ssive sonar aft. The
...gn was offered for
...rt but never won
...orders. The four
...s joined the fleet in
...-69 and were
...ten in 1991-93.

Nazario Sauro-class

Type: ocean-going patrol.

Class	Sauro	Pelosi	Longobardo
Total built	4	2	2
Completed	1980-82	1988-89	1993-95
Displacement surfaced submerged	1,4565 tons 1,641 tons	1,476 tons 1,662 tons	1,653 tons 1,826 tons
Dimensions length beam draught	209ft 7in (63.9m) 22ft 5in (6.8m) 18ft 9in (5.7m)	211ft 2in (64.4m) 22ft 5in (6.8m) 18ft 7in (5.7m)	217ft 8in (66.4 22ft 5in (6.8m) 19ft 8in (6.0m)
Propulsion diesel power electric motors power battery shafts	3 x GMT 3 x 1,070bhp 1 x Marelli 1 x 3,650shp 2 x 148 cells one	3 x GMT 3 x 1,070bhp 1 x Marelli 1 x 3,650shp 2 x 148 cells one	3 x GMT 3 x 1,070bhp 1 x ABBI 1 x 4,270shp 2 x 148 cells one
Performance speed: surface submerged range: surfaced schnorkel submerged maximum diving depth	12kt 20kt 7,000nm/8kt 2,500nm/12kt 250nm/4kt 984ft (300m)	11kt 19kt 6,150nm/11kt 2,500nm/12kt 250nm/4kt 984ft (300m)	12kt 20kt 7,000nm/8kt 2,500nm/124k 250nm/4kt 984ft (300m)
Weapons TT location torpedoes	6 x 21in (533mm) bow 12	6 x 21in (533mm) bow 12	6 x 21in (533r bow 12
Complement	49	50	50

History: The Nazario Sauro-class of four submarines was built by Italcan Monfalcone yard, the only Italian post-war submarine builder. The hull, ma HY-80 steel, is tear-drop shaped with cruciform after control surfaces a seven-bladed propeller. The forward hydroplanes are mounted American on the fin. There are six torpedo tubes and a total of 12 torpedoes, v seems a little inadequate for such a large boat intended for 45-day patrols French Agosta-class, for example, of equivalent size, carried a total of 20 Italian boats were given a mid-life update from 1990 inwards which inc new cells, improved habitability and a new fire control system.

At one time it was proposed to replace the Sauros by a totally new d

ove: Sauro-class submarine, Carlo Fecia di Cossato.

ɔ the title of "Submarine for the 90s" (S90) but this fell through and an
roved version of the Sauro was built instead. Completed in 1988-89, the
boats of the Salvatore Pelosi-class were slightly longer and fitted to launch
-Harpoon, but otherwise were a little advance on the Sauros. Faced with a
d to keep the yard occupied and with the S90 design still not finalised, two
e boats were built, completing in 1993 and 1995, respectively. The Primo
gobardo-class was again marginally longer, giving an increase in fuel
xerage, but otherwise showed no real advance.

The four Sauro-class boats continue in service, but one is used almost
ly for trials. The two Pelosi-class boats underwent a mid-life refit in 2000-
ɬ and the Longobardo-class will be refitted in due course. The replacement
ll these boats will not be the Italian S90, as originally planned, but will be a
ce-built version of the German Type 212, the first of which is due in service
ɔ05.

w: Nazario Sauro, *first of a class of eight SSKs.*

Oyashio-class

Type: patrol.
Total built: 1.
Completed: 1960.
Displacement: surfaced 1,139 tons; submerged 1,420 tons.
Dimensions: length 258ft 6in (78.8m); beam 22ft 11in (7.0m); draught 15f￼
(4.6m).
Propulsion: 2 x diesels, 2 x 1,350bhp; 2 x electric motors, 2 x 2,980shp; bat￼
4 x 120 cells; two shafts.
Performance: surface – 13kt, submerged – 19kt; range surfaced 10,000n￼
10kt.
Weapons: 4 x 21in (533mm) TT (bow).
Complement: 65.

History: Following the end of World War II all Japanese submarines ￼
destroyed, the great majority by scuttling, but a few by scrapping. The ￼
submarine to serve in the newly created Japanese Maritime Self-Defense F￼
(JMSDF) was a U.S. Navy Gato-class boat, formerly USS *Mingo* (SS-2￼
renamed *Kuroshio* (SS-510), which was transferred in 1955 under the ￼
Mutual Defense Aid Pact (MDAP). She did not have any form of modernis￼
prior to transfer (ie, not a Guppy boat) and was used almost entirely as a tra￼
boat until stricken in 1966.

The first submarine to be built for the JMSDF was *Oyashio* (SS-511) ￼
was laid down in 1957, launched in 1959 and commissioned in 1960. She ￼
a "long/narrow" hull, similar to many boats being built at that time, and alth￼

Hayashio/Natsushio-classes

Hayashio
Type: coastal hunter/killer.
Total built: 2.
Completed: 1962.
Displacement: surfaced 650 tons; submerged 800 tons.
Dimensions: length 193ft 6in (59.0m); beam 13ft 6in (4.3m).
Propulsion: 2 x diesels, 2 x 675bhp; 2 x electric motors, 2 x 850shp; two sh￼
Performance: surface – 12kt, submerged – 15kt.
Weapons: 3 x 21in (533mm) TT (bow). 6 x torpedoes.
Complement: 43.

Natsushio
Type: coastal hunter/killer.
Total built: 2.
Completed: 1963-64.
Displacement: surfaced 690 tons; submerged 850 tons.
Dimensions: length 200ft 1in (61.0m); beam 21ft 2in (6.5m); draught 13￼
(4.1m).
Propulsion: 2 x diesels, 2 x 675bhp; 2 x electric motors, 2 x 850shp; two sh￼
Performance: surface – 12kt, submerged – 15kt.
Weapons: 6 x 21in (533mm) TT (bow). 12 x torpedoes.
Complement: 43.

History: These two closely related classes appeared in the early 1960￼
were modelled on the U.S. Navy's Barracuda-class (qv), thus starting a Col￼

ove: **Oyashio**, *first post-war Japanese-built submarine.*

viously incorporating the latest equipment she bore a more than passing semblance to the Japanese World War II ST-class (qv). For example, lengths are ST – 259ft (78.9m), *Oyashio* – 258ft (78.6m), while submerged splacements were ST – 1,450 tons and *Oyashio* – 1,420 tons. The physical semblance was also very strong, with an uncluttered exterior and upper sing, a tall sail, and a vertically deployed schnorkel. *Oyashio* served as a front-e boat for some years and was then transferred to a training role in 1975 and rapped in 1976.

ove: **Hayashio**, *as completed, at sea in the 1960s.*

nd in which Japanese naval developments reflected U.S. advances. These nter/killers were intended to sit off a maritime choke point and acquire Soviet gets using the powerful bow-mounted sonar, whereupon they would attack. oan's first post-war submarine, *Oyushio* (SS-511) (qv), had a traditional long, rrow hull, but these two classes had a shorter hull in which the beam was sportionally greater, starting a gradual Japanese evolution towards the Jbacore hull." Another change was that in Japanese submarines up to the d of World War II the crew's living conditions had received a very low priority, t beginning with this class matters started to improve and air-conditioning as introduced. Attention was also paid to manoeuvrability and joystick-control as used for the first time. The two Hayashio-class boats were stricken in 79, but the one year younger Natsushio-class went the previous year.

Uzushio/Yushiuo/ Harushio-classes

Type: ocean-going patrol.

Class	Uzushio	Yuushio	Harushio
Total built	7	10	7
Completed	1971-78	1980-89	1990-97
Displacement surfaced submerged	1,850 tons 3,600 tons	2,200 tons 2,450 tons	2,450 tons 2,750 tons
Dimensions length beam draught	236ft 3in (72.0m) 32ft 6in (9.9m) 24ft 7in (7.5m)	250ft 0in (76.2m) 32ft 6in (9.9m) 24ft 7in (7.5m)	253ft 11in (77.4 32ft 10in (10.0m 25ft 4in (7.7m)
Propulsion diesel power electric motors power Battery shafts	2 x Kawasaki/MAN 2 x 1,800bhp 2 2 x 3,600shp n.k. one	2 x Mitsubishi-M.A.N. 2 x 1,700bhp 2 x Fuji 2 x 3,600sgp 2 x 480 Nihon cells one	2 x Kawasaki 2 x 1,700bhp 2 2 x 3,600shp 2 x 480 Yuasa ce one
Performance speed: surface submerged maximum diving depth	12kt 20kt 656ft (200m)	13kt 20kt 1,300ft (400m)	12kt 20kt –
Weapons TT location torpedoes	6 x 21in (533mm) amidships 20	6 x 21in (533mm) amidships 20	6 x 21in (533mm amidships 20
Complement	80	77	75

History: JMSDF policy has been one of steady progress, with a series classes, none of which has been a revolutionary advance on its predecess but resulting in a series of what have been among the very best diesel-elect submarines of their era. All have featured an Alabcore-type hull and forwa hydroplanes mounted midway up a large sail, and until the current Oyash class had a very large sonar array in the bow, which displaced the six torpe tubes to the midships position, as in U.S. Navy SSNs. The tubes are used launch Japanese-designed torpedoes (Type 72, Type 80 or Type 89) and fre the Yuushio-class onwards, UGM-84 Sub-Harpoon; all classes are fitted with tubes and carry a total of 20 torpedoes/missiles. Production has been shar equally between two Kobe-based shipyards, Mitsubishi and Kawasaki, w

**ove: Isoshio*, third of the JMSDF's Uzushio-class.*

ats being commissioned at a rate of one per year, almost invariably in the
onth of March.

The seven-strong Uzushio-class (SS-566 to SS-572) were the first JMSDF
ats to have Albacore-style tear-drop hulls and were generally similar to, but
ghtly larger than, the U.S. Navy's Barbel-class. The hull was constructed of
-63 steel which gave a maximum operating depth of 660ft (200m) and the
at was fitted with an automatic steering system. The first two boats were
icken in 1987-88, but the other five were converted to auxiliary and training
omarines (ATSS) between 1989 and 1993 as the Harushio-class boats came
o service. These, too, were then stricken at a yearly rate from 1992 onwards.

Next came 10 Yuushio-class (SS-573 to SS-582), which were slightly larger,
ich better equipped and made of NS-80 steel, giving a deeper diving
bability. They mounted a Japanese ZQQ-4 or -5 sonar in the bows, modified
rsions of the U.S. Navy's AN/BQS-4 sonar and certain boats were fitted to
e Sub-Harpoon. After the ZQR-1 towed array had been trialled in *Nadashio*
S- 577) it was fitted in all the remainder. First-of-class *Yuushio* (SS-573)
came a training boat in 1996, followed by the remaining boats at a rate of one
r year as the Oyashio-class came into service.

Third in this group came the Harushio-class (SS-583 to SS-589), completed
tween 1990 and 1997 as replacements for the Uzushio-class.. They have
proved noise reduction and all have been fitted with the ZQR-1 towed array
iilc building. The pressure hull is built of NS-110 steel, allowing a further
crease in operating depth. Last-of-class *Asashio* (SS-589) incorporated a
mber of changes, including increased automation which allowed a reduction
crew numbers and was the first Japanese boat to be built with anechoic tiles.

**low: Yushio *shows the classic
ear-drop" hull.*

Oyashio-class

Type: ocean-going patrol.
Total built: 10.
Completed: 1996-2005.
Displacement: surfaced 2,750 tons; submerged 3,600 tons.
Dimensions: length 268ft 0in (81.7m); beam 33ft 9in (10.3m); draught 24ft 3in (7.4
Propulsion: 2 x Kawasaki diesels, 2 x 1,700bhp; 2 x electric motors, 7,750s
one shaft.
Performance: surface – 12kt, submerged – 20kt; maximum operating div
depth at least 1,300ft (400m).
Weapons: 6 x 21in (533mm) TT (bow), 20 x torpedoes/missiles.
Complement: 69.

History: The latest Oyashio-class breaks with the 30-year custom
progressive enhancements to a basic design by introducing a totally n
design, with a new shape of pressure hull, which is made of a new and ev
stronger steel (but of undisclosed specifications) and is coated in anechoic ti
There is a rather higher upper casing than in previous classes, possibly to cre
storage space for the towed array, aft of the sail. The torpedo tubes have be
restored to their traditional position in the bows and are mounted high in the

---

Sang-O-class

Type: coastal/special forces.
Total built: 22.
Completed: ca. 1980-?
Displacement: surfaced 275 tons; submerged 360 tons.
Dimensions: length 111ft 7in (34.0m); beam 12ft 6in (3.8m); draught 10ft
(3.2m).
Propulsion: 1 x diesel generator set, 300bhp (est), electric motor, 200shp (e
one shaft.
Performance: surface – 7.2kt, submerged – 4kt; range surfaced 1,500r
schnorkel 2,700nm/8kt; maximum operating depth 492ft (150m).
Weapons: 4 x 21in (533mm) TT (bow), 4 x torpedoes.
Complement: 14.
Specifications for torpedo-armed version; see notes for special forces versi

History: The North Korean Navy obtained four Whiskey-class submarines fr
the Soviet Union in the 1960s and then received a number of Chinese-b
Whiskeys and Romeos in the 1970s. Several submarine building facilities w
then established at Mayang Do in North Korea and some 18 Romeos w
completed between 1976 and 1996. North Korea has only one enemy – Sol
Korea – and has long pursued a policy of infiltrating special forces into
southern neighbour's territory, and one method has been by submarine
number of M100-D mini-subs (also known as the Una-class) were bought fr
Yugoslavia in the 1980s and the North Koreans developed this design int
rather more effective vessel, known in the West as the "Yugo-class", a
some 40 were built at one of their own shipyards. The next stage was to des
a completely new type, based on experience gained with the Romeo- and Yu
classes; this has been designated by U.S. Intelligence agencies as the Sang
(= shark) class, and 22 have been built. There are two versions. One is torpe
armed, with four bow-mounted 21in (533mm) tubes and no reloads, while
other is a swimmer delivery vehicle with a lock-out chamber a

ove: Latest JMSDF SSK **Oyashio** *at sea.*

n a chin-mounted sonar array below. The sail is of a different shape and is
her back along the hull, indicating that the control room is now further aft
n in previous classes. First-of-class *Oyashio* (SS-590) cost $US534,000,000
1993 prices. These are undoubtedly among the very finest diesel-electric
marines in existence.

ove: Sang-O **grounded off South Korean coast in 1996.**

ommodation for up to 15 special forces troops in the torpedo space. This
cial forces version can also carry 16 mines.

In a spectacular failure, one of these boats ran aground on the South Korean
st on 17 September 1996. There had been 26 aboard and all appear to have
ashore. The South Koreans quickly captured one man and found the bodies
1 others who had committed suicide, but it took them over six weeks to
l with the remainder, killing 13 of them – just one man escaped. The North
eans insisted that it had been a training mission and that the boat had
ered an engine fault which resulted in it drifting on to the southern shore, a
y which nobody believed.

Dolfijn-class

Type: ocean-going patrol.
Total built: 4.
Completed: 1960-66.
Displacement: surfaced 1,494 tons; submerged 1,826 tons.
Dimensions: length 260ft 10in (79.5m); beam 25ft 7in (7.8m); draught 15ft (4.8m).
Propulsion: 2 x M.A.N. diesels, 2 x 1,250bhp; 2 x Smit electric motors, 2,100shp; battery 2 x 168 Chloride cells; two shafts.
Performance: surface – 14.5kt, submerged – 17kt; maximum operating div depth 985ft (300m).
Weapons: 8 x 21in (533mm) TT (bow – 4, stern – 4), 22 x torpedoes.
Complement: 67.
Specifications are for Dolfijn-class, as built.

History: These four boats were built to a unique design by M. F. Gunning which three separate but interconnected pressure hulls were enclosed wi an outer hull. The uppermost (and largest) hull contained the control centre, torpedo tubes (four at each end), storage spaces and the crew accommodat Below were two parallel hulls, slightly shorter and of smaller diameter, e containing one complete power train, consisting of machinery, batteries stores. The advantage of this arrangement was that it combined great stren with compactness, and made the best possible use of the steel then availa

s was, however, somewhat offset by the cramped conditions in the lower
ls, with machinery maintenance at sea being particularly difficult.

These Dutch boats had an exceptional diving depth for their day and were
y highly regarded by other NATO navies, although the high cost of
nstruction and the availability of higher-strength steels meant that the design
s not repeated. However, Gunning's basic concept of multiple hulls,
veloped in the 1940s, seems to have reappeared in the Soviet Typhoon-class
BNs in the 1970s (qv).

The first two boats, *Dolfijn* and *Zeehond*, were laid down in 1954 and
mpleted in 1960-61, but laying down the second pair was delayed by several
ars while consideration was given as to whether to install nuclear power-
nts. In the end this was not done and *Potvis* and *Tonijn* were laid down in
52 and completed in 1965-66, and differed from the first two in being shorter
.3m) and having Swedish Varta cells.

All four boats served as part of the Netherlands' contribution to NATO for
ny years. Three boats were stricken at the end of their operational lives:
lfijn – 1985, *Tonijn* – 1991 and *Potvis* – 1992. *Zeehond* was to have been
ired in 1987, but her life was extended for three years due to a fire in *Walrus*
), after which she was purchased by her builders, RDM, and used as a test-
d for a new AIP system.

low: Dutch submarine **Dolfijn** *had three pressure hulls.*

Zwaardvis/
Hai Lung-classes

Zvaardvis
Type: ocean-going patrol.
Total built: 2.
Completed: 1972.
Displacement: surfaced 2,408 tons; submerged 2,640 tons.
Dimensions: length 219ft 0in (66.9m); beam 28ft 0in (8.4m); draught 23ft (7.1m).
Propulsion: 3 x Werkspoor diesels, 3 x 1,400bhp; 1 x Holec electric mo
5,100shp; battery 2 x 196 cells; one shaft.
Performance: surface – 13kt, submerged – 20kt; range schnorkel 10,000nm
9kt; maximum operating diving depth 722ft (220m).
Weapons: 6 x 21in (533mm) TT (bow), 20 torpedoes.
Complement: 67.

Hai Lung
Type: ocean-going patrol
Total built: 2.
Completed: 1987-88.
Displacement: surfaced 2,376 tons; submerged 2,660 tons.
Dimensions: length 219ft 7in (66.9m); beam 27ft 7in (8.4m); draught 22ft 0in (6.7
Propulsion: 3 x Bronswerk/Stork-Werkspoor diesels, 3 x 1,350bhp; 1 x Ho

---

Walrus-class

Type: ocean-going patrol.
Total built: 4.
Completed: 1990-94.
Displacement: surfaced 2,465 tons; submerged 2,800 tons.
Dimensions: length 222ft 1in (67.7m); beam 27ft 6in (8.4m); draught 22ft 1 (7.0m).
Propulsion: 3 x SEMT-Pielstick diesels, 3 x 2,300bhp; 1 x Holec electric mo
5,430shp; battery 3 x 140 cells; one shaft.
Performance: surface – 13kt, submerged – 21kt; range schnorkel 10,000nm
9kt; maximum operating diving depth 984ft (300m).
Weapons: 4 x 21in (533mm) TT (bow), 20 torpedoes.
Complement: 52.
Specifications for first pair, as built.

History: This is, in effect, an improved version of the Zwaardvis-class, w
similar dimensions and general appearance, the only noticeable exter
difference being the use of X-configured stern hydroplanes. The pressure
is built from Marel steel, giving a 50 per cent increase in operating depth o
the Zwaardvis. The first two, *Walrus* and *Zeeleeuw*, were ordered in 1978-
but the project did not get off to a good start. First, construction w
delayed by a decision to replace the planned diesels by different and m
powerful models, which required the hull to be lengthened. Then, wh
Walrus was conducting builder's trials in August 1986 she was so sever
damaged by fire that she had to be taken back into dock and complet
rebuilt, being relaunched in September 1989. Meanwhile, a second p

*ht: Hai
..g, one of
..exported
Taiwan, to
fury of
..nmunist
..na.*

..ctric motor, 5,100shp; battery 2 x 196 cells; one shaft.
..formance: surface – 12kt, submerged – 20kt; range schnorkel 10,000nm at
maximum operating diving depth 787ft (240m).
..apons: 6 x 21in (533mm) TT (bow), 20 torpedoes.
..nplement: 79.

..tory: The design of the Zwaardvis-class was closely based on that of the
.. Navy's Barbel-class (qv), the last diesel-electric boats to be built for the
..ted States. The Dutch boats were laid down in 1966 and completed in 1972,
..are of single-hull construction with three main internal divisions. Forward
..the sonars, torpedo tubes and torpedo-handling room and aft are the
..chinery spaces, housing three diesel-generator sets, mounted on a false
..k, a large Holec electric motor and the single shaft. In the centre is the
..trol centre, with the crew accommodation below, and the batteries below
.. Virtually all equipment is of Dutch design and manufacture. Two were
..olied to the Republic of China in 1987/88 as the Hai Lung-class.

*ht: The
..ch
..rus-class
..videly
..sidered to
..one of the
..st SSK
..igns of
..20th
..tury.*

..fijn and *Bruinvis*) were ordered in 1984-85 and completed in 1993-94,
..plans to order a fifth and sixth were cancelled by the Dutch Parliament
..988.
..These boats enjoy a high reputation for efficiency and effectiveness and are
..ng the finest diesel-electric boats yet built. They have a particularly
..prehensive outfit of sensors and are fitted to launch Sub-Harpoon, although
..nissiles have been purchased. Assuming they have a 30-year life they will
..ue for replacement in the 2020s, but there is no talk, as yet, of a project for
..ccessor.

Whiskey-class

Type: ocean-going patrol.
Total built: 236.
Completed: 1951-58.
Displacement: surfaced 1,080 tons; submerged 1,350 tons.
Dimensions: length 249ft 3in (76.0m); beam 21ft 3in (6.5m); draught 16ft (4.9m).
Propulsion: 2 x Type 37D diesels, 2 x 2,000bhp; 2 x electric motors, 1,350shp; 2 x creep motors, 2 x 50shp; two shafts.
Performance: surface – 18.5kt, schnorkel – 7kt, submerged – 13.1kt; ra surfaced 8,500nm at 10kt, submerged 335nm at 2kt; maximum opera diving depth 560ft (170mm).
Weapons: 6 x 21in (533mm) TT (bow – 4, stern – 2), 12 x torpedoes; 2 x 25 AA (1 x 2).
Complement: 54.
Specifications for Whiskey I, as built.

History: In 1943 the Soviet Naval Staff issued a requirement for a submarine to replace the widely-used S- and Shch-classes (qqv), which resu in Project 608, essentially a modernised version of the S-class with var modifications resulting from wartime experience, together with a sonar w was reverse-engineered from a set supplied by their British ally. Ther September 1944, the Soviet Navy recovered *U-250*, a German Type VIIC w had been sunk in the Gulf of Finland several weeks previously, and deta examination showed that Soviet designs had slipped well behind those of enemy (the salvage team also recovered an Enigma machine, a Zaunk torpedo and many secret documents – no mean haul). Project 608 immediately cancelled so that the design could be reworked to incorporate lessons of the Type VIIC. Later the design was altered yet again to inc some of the lessons of the Type XXIs captured at the end of the war. outcome was a larger design, finalised in 1948 as Project 613, which w become known to NATO as the Whiskey-class, but was by no means the XXI-clone as often suggested in the West.

The first-of-class was launched in 1951 and by the time production er

958 four yards had produced a total of 215 for the Soviet Navy (Baltic – 19, x'iy – 113, Komsomolsk – 11, and Nikolayev – 72) and a further 21 were embled in China from parts supplied by the Soviet Union. A total of 39 rational boats were transferred from the Soviet Navy to foreign navies ania – 4; Bulgaria – 2; China – 5; Egypt – 7; Indonesia – 12; North Korea – 4; nd – 5). These were followed by four non-operational boats: battery ging hulks (to Cuba – 1, Syria – 1) and for cannibalisation (to Indonesia – 2). The Whiskey was a double-hulled boat with twin propellers, each shaft ng its own diesel engine, electric motor and creep motor, and for the first in a Soviet submarine all these were mounted on shock absorbers. ament comprised six torpedo tubes, four in the bow and two in the stern an outfit of 12 torpedoes. The five major variants identified by Western il intelligence concerned the guns. Whiskey I was the original version with gle 25mm AA mount on a platform before the bridge tower, while Whiskey d an additional twin 57mm mounted at deck level immediately abaft the er, the only version to mount this particular weapon. Whiskey III had no gun ament but retained the platforms and Whiskey IV had the forward 25mm but no 57mm; it was also the first to be fitted with a schnorkel. The final ion, Whiskey V, was streamlined and had no guns at all, the platforms being oved; a total of 60 boats were upgraded to this standard in mid-life ernisation refits, but the programme was ended when more modern new-d submarines began to join the fleet. The Soviet Navy's Whiskey fleet began un down in the 1970s, with unmodernized boats being scrapped, and by 2 only 60 remained, reducing to 18 in 1992 and the last were scrapped the wing year.

There were a number of conversions. One boat was converted to serve as issile test platform – Whiskey Single-Cylinder – and was followed by six ational boats armed with two SS-N-3 – Whiskey Twin-Cylinder (qv) – and a er six with four missiles – Whiskey Long Bin (qv). Four were converted as r pickets – Whiskey Canvas Bag – while other boats were employed on s which required little modification, such as two for fishery research.

w: The Whiskeys were sturdy and reliable work-horses.

Romeo-class
(Project 633)

Type: ocean-going patrol.
Total built: 112.
Completed: 1958-95.
Displacement: surfaced 1,330 tons; submerged 1,700 tons.
Dimensions: length 252ft 8in (77.0m); beam 22ft 0in (6.7m); draught 16ft 1in (4.
Propulsion: 2 x diesels, 2 x 2,000bhp; 2 x electric motors, 2 x 1,350shp
creep motors, 2 x 50shp; battery 2 x 112 cells; two shafts.
Performance: surface – 15.5kt, submerged – 13kt; range surfaced 16,000n
10kt, schnorkel 7,000nm at 5kt; maximum operating diving depth 984ft (300m
Weapons: 8 x 21in (533mm) TT (bow – 6, stern – 2), 14 x torpedoes.
Complement: 56.

History: The Soviet Navy's requirement for a new class of submarine
issued in the early 1950s and designated Project 633 (NATO = Romeo-clas
was to be an improved version of the Project 613 (Whiskey-class), powere
the Kreislauf AIP system (see Quebec-class), but when that system pre
impracticable the design was modified for normal diesel-electric drive. It v
double-hull design, divided into seven internal compartments, and altho
deck fittings for a gun were included no such weapon was ever mounted
important change from the Whiskey-class was the addition of two r
torpedo tubes in the bows. The new sonar outfit was a major advance on
installed in Project 613, paralelling that being installed on the new Project
(Foxtrot class) ocean-going submarines and offering greatly improved ta
acquisition and localisation capabilities. Derived from the World War II Ger
GHG/Balkon system and installed in a bow "onion", the MG-10 Feni
system offered a reasonable submarine detection capability. Directly above
was the MG-200 Arktika-M active scanning sonar that supplied target da
the new Leningrad fire-control system. A sonar intercept system was inst
in the sail structure. Finally, a small underwater telephone was installed or
of the MG-200 set to give the bow "rhino-horn" characteristic of this class

The early 1950s were a period of great ambition in the Soviet Navy ar
one point it was planned to build no fewer than 560 Romeos, but in
President Kruschev issued orders that the production of all non-nu
submarines should cease. The Soviet Naval Staff fought this decision, arg
that nuclear submarines were very expensive and, in any case, diesel-ele
boats were much better in littoral waters. However, the Project 641 (Fox
class) was already on the drawing boards and there was clear duplic
between the two, so it was decided to end production of the Romeo in 1
with the 21st unit. With hindsight this appears to have been the wrong
decision, since the Romeo was a quieter and generally more
effective design, but the decision could not be reversed. A total
of 15 of these were transferred to friendly navies and
those that remained in the Soviet Navy were used
mainly for research or as auxiliaries. All had
been stricken by 1987.

Meanwhile, it was decided to help
China establish its own submarine building
capability and since there was no longer a
Soviet requirement the production
drawings and tooling were transferred to
the PRC, where the type was built in large

ve: A Chinese-built copy of the Soviet Romeo-class design.

bers. The PRC seems to have concentrated its efforts on simply producing
ieos in large numbers; there have been minor upgrades in equipment but
significant improvements to the design, except for the Ming-class (qv).
)t, however, modernised its four Chinese-built Romeos from 1992
ards, with many U.S. systems being installed and the boats being given the
y to launch Sub-Harpoon. The North Koreans also built 12 Romeos, of
:h they have lost two.

n summary, a total of 112 Romeos were built: Russia – 21 (entered service
)58-62); China – 72 (in service 1960-84); North Korea – 19 (in service 1973-
The Soviet Navy transferred a number from its own stocks: Algeria – 2;
aria – 4; Egypt – 6; Syria – 3. China built eight specifically for export: Egypt
North Korea – 4. North Korea built 12, of which two were lost in 1985. By
? some 84 remained in service: Bulgaria – 1; China – 64 (many in reserve);
:h Korea – 19.

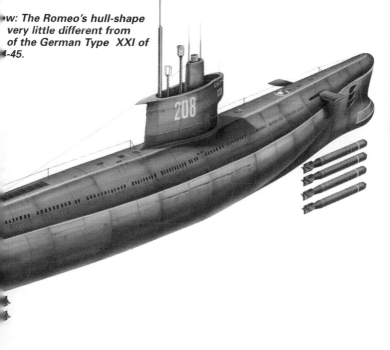

*w: The Romeo's hull-shape
very little different from
of the German Type XXI of
I-45.*

Zulu-class (Project 611)

RUS

Type: ocean-going patrol.
Total built: 26.
Completed: 1958-95.
Displacement: surfaced 1,900 tons; submerged 2,350 tons.
Dimensions: length 295ft 3in (90.0m); beam 24ft 7in (7.5m); draught 19f (6.0m).
Propulsion: 3 x diesels, 3 x 2,000bhp; 3 x electric motors, 3 x 1,750shp; ba 4 x 112 cells; three shafts.
Performance: surface – 18kt, submerged 16kt; range schnorkel 9,500n 8kt; submerged 480nm at 4kt; maximum operating diving depth 655ft (20 **Weapons:** 10 x 21in (533mm) TT (bow – 6, stern – 4), 22 x torpedoes; 57mm guns (1 x 2); 2 x 25mm AA.
Complement: 70.
Specifications for Zulu I, as built.

History: Project 611 (NATO = Zulu) was the lineal successor to the pre-w class (qv) and was also the large displacement design prepared in parall that of Project 613 (Whiskey-class). Design work started in 1943, but it qu became clear that the original specifications would result in a boat that obsolete before it entered service, so the requirement was altered three ti in 1944, 1946 and, finally, in 1947, with the actual design being finalized and the first-of-class launched in 1952.

The boat was of conventional double-hull construction, but had an unu machinery arrangement, with three shafts, each driven by a 2,000bhp dies a 1,750shp electric motor. The three-shaft arrangement had some theore advantages, principally in that when running on the surface the two engines could be used to propel the submarine while the centre engine used to recharge the batteries. In addition, when the boat was submerge extra propeller, in combination with the large 448-cell battery, could be either to raise maximum speed or to extend the range. However, the proved unrealisable because the three propellers and their shafts ca considerable vibration when running at specific speeds, the noticeable fl giving rise to very real fears of structural failure, which resulted in o banning the use of particular revolutions to prevent the harmonics. Indepen

ve: A Soviet Navy Zulu IV-class diesel-electric boat.

is it also transpired that there were inherent weaknesses in the hull, which
ented the Zulus from descending below about 164ft (50m). As a result,
very limited construction occurred, ending with the 26th unit and a major
·sign took place, leading to the Foxtrot-class (qv).

As built, the Zulus had two 57mm and two 25mm guns, but these were
ived starting in 1956, while schnorkels, which had not initially been fitted, were
lled. NATO identified four different versions of the basic class: Zulu I, as in the
ifications above, while Zulu II, III and IV had no deck guns, but did have a
orkel and differed from each other in minor details only. However, one Zulu
converted as a missile test-bed, and five were subsequently converted to
me the first operational SSBs (see Zulu V). In view of the restrictions placed on
, Zulus saw little operational service and most were used for trials and
rimental work. Most were scrapped in the early 1980s.

w: The Zulu was designed in parallel to the Whiskey.

Foxtrot-class (Project 641)

Type: ocean-going patrol.
Total built: 62.
Completed: 1961-83.
Displacement: surfaced 1,957 tons; submerged 2,484 tons.
Dimensions: length 299ft 6in (91.3m); beam 24ft 7in (7.5m); draught 19f¹
(6.0m).
Propulsion: 3 x 2D-42 diesels, 3 x 2,000bhp; 3 x electric motors, 3 x 1,750
battery 4 x 112 cells; three shafts.
Performance: surface – 16.6kt, submerged – 15.9kt; range surfaced 20,00
at 8kt, submerged 380nm at 2kt; maximum operating diving depth 8
(250m).
Weapons: 10 x 21in (533mm) TT (bow – 6, stern – 4), 22 x torpedoes.
Complement: 75.

History: The problems with Project 611 (Zulu-class) (see previous entry) ca
the Soviet naval staff to issue an urgent new requirement for a replacen
which would fulfil the mission set for that project but without the crip
problems. The result was the Project 641 (NATO = Foxtrot-class) which
essentially a major redesign of the Zulu-class. The Foxtrots had a double
with the pressure hull having especially heavy framing to overcome the e
problems. The power-train was a virtual repeat of that for the Zulu-c
retaining the triple-shaft arrangement, but with a greatly revised stern v
combined a new profile with much stronger framing in an effort fo overc
the vibration problems. Surface power was originally provided by three 2
diesels (each 2,000bhp) but these were replaced in later
production versions by three Type 40-D diesels (each 1,740bhp),
this version being designated Project 641K; performance was
little affected by the reduction in horsepower. Although these
measures largely overcame the hull vibration problems, the
triple propellers still suffered from acoustic interference,
enabling NATO submarines to detect them with ease.

This new class never had gun mounts and a schnorkel was

Above: Foxtrot; note the three sonars – one is in the forward edge o
sail, one atop the bows and the third is a long array around the bow

ve: An export Foxtrot, operated by the Cuban Navy.

alled from the start. The Foxtrot introduced a new generation of sensors, uding a large passive sonar array (Feniks; NATO = Trout Cheek) in the upper which was covered by a prominent silver dielectric cover. A prominent e atop the bow casing housed the Herkules (NATO = Piker Jaw) active ar, and some boats had a further small cylindrical dome atop this housing an rwater telephone system. As usually happened with the Soviet Navy the nal grandiose plans for some 160 were reduced to 60, which were built veen 1958 and 1984. Production in the later years was for export: Cuba – 3 9084), India – 8 (1968- 75), and Libya – 6 (1976-83). In addition, two were olied to Poland in 1987/88 from Soviet Navy stocks.

Several missile-armed versions of the Foxtrot were planned but never e to fruition. One of these, however, the Project 641A armed with four SS-Shaddock missiles, eventually led to the Project 651 (NATO = Juliett-class) , whose hull, in turn, was used as the basis for the Project 641BUKI (NATO ngo-class) attack submarine (qv). The Foxtrots gave excellent service to the Soviet Navy and in their heyday were to be found in every ocean in the world. They were stricken from the 1980s onwards.

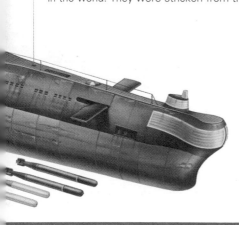

Tango-class
(Project 641BUKI)

Type: ocean-going ASW .
Total built: 18.
Completed: 1972-81.
Displacement: surfaced 2,700 tons; submerged 3,556 tons.
Dimensions: length 295ft 11in (90.2m); beam 20ft 2in (8.6m); draught 18f
(5.7m).
Propulsion: 3 x Type 2D-42 diesels, 3 x 1,825bhp; 3 x PG-102 electric mo
3 x 1,750shp; 2 x creep motors, 2 x 140shp; battery 4 x 112 cells; three sh
Performance: surface – 13kt, submerged – 16kt; range surfaced 20,000n
11kt, schnorkel 14,000nm at 7kt, submerged 450nm at 2.5kt; maxir
operating diving depth 984ft (300m).
Weapons: 6 x 21in (533mm) TT (bow), 24 x torpedoes/SS-N-15 missiles.
Complement: 75.

History: As described in the previous entry, a planned version of the Fox
class, Project 614A, led to the Juliett-class missile submarine (qv). How
Juliett-class production was ended early, as a result of which there we
number of surplus hulls. Thus, when an urgent requirement arose f
specialised ASW submarine it was decided to combine these hulls with no
Foxtrot-class components to produce a new type, designated Project 641I
(NATO = Tango-class), the number indicating that it was seen as a variatic
of the Foxtrot design, while the suffix "I" indicates a high priority design. Th
first-of-class *B- 380* was delivered on 20 May 1973 and appeared at the Ju
1973 Sebastopol naval review in the Black Sea, although for many years th
only known operational deployments were with the Northern Fleet; howeve
some boats later deployed in the Baltic. The Tangos were among the fir
Soviet boats to be coated with anechoic tiles and, like many such boats in
navies, were frequently to be seen with missing tiles.

*Below: The Tango-class caused much alarm in the West as the
purpose for a new "long-thin" diesel-electric boat was unclear.
It was later learnt that the mission was "bastion defence"
protecting Soviet SSBNs from attack by U.S. forces.*

ve: A Tango beats its way into a head sea, its patrol ended.

The Tangos were conceived to meet a requirement for "bastion defence"; rotecting Soviet SSBNs, particularly the Delta-class, from U.S. and British s. The crew had a higher proportion of officers than is common – 17 ers compared to 8 in a Foxtrot – which suggests that the systems were iderably more complex than usual. There was an unusual rise in the hull ʋard of the sail, suggesting a need for greater volume forward for the weapons and their reloading system. No Tangos were exported and the first three boats were stricken in 1995, followed by a further two in 1996, and the remainder have become progressively unserviceable through lack of maintenance and shortage of manpower. As of 2002, nine remained, but all were in reserve. The Tango's main claim to fame is that it is the largest diesel-electric patrol boat ever to enter service.

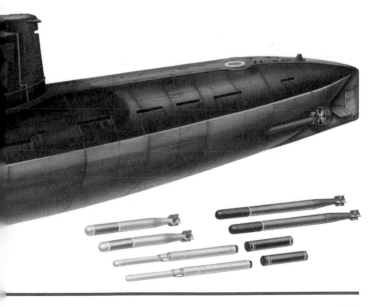

Kilo-class

Type: ocean-going patrol.

Class	Kilo (Project 877)	Improved Kilo (Project ⬚
Total built	12	9
Completed	1980	1987-88
Displacement surfaced submerged	2,325 tons 3,076 tons	2,350 tons 2,126 tons
Dimensions length beam draught	238ft 2in (72.6m) 32ft 6in (9.9m) 21ft 7in (6.6m)	242ft 1in (73.8m) 32ft 6in (9.9m) 21ft 7in (6.6m)
Propulsion diesel power electric motors power creep motors power battery shafts	2 x Type 4-2D 2 x 1,825bhp 1 5,900shp 2 x MT-186 2 x 204shp 2 x 120 cells one	2 x Type 4-2AA-42M 2 x 1,825bhp 1 5,500shp 2 x MT-186 2 x 204shp 2 x 120 cells one
Performance speed: surface submerged range: schnorkel submerged maximum diving depth	10kt 17kt 6,000nm/7kt 400nm/3kt 984ft (300m)	12kt 20kt 7,500nm/7kt 400nm/3kt 984ft (300m)
Weapons TT location torpedoes SAM	6 x 21in (533mm) bow 18 x torpedoes/SS-N-16 1 x Fasta-4	6 x 21in (533mm) bow 18 x torpedoes/SS-N 1 x Fasta-4
Complement	53	52

History: The first Type 877, launched in 1980, was built specifically for trials b
Soviet Navy, resulting in many modifications and improvements, which were
incorporated into the second and subsequent boats. The overall design is relat
short and fat, with a single main propeller, but retains the traditional Russian do
hull, which not only enhances survivability but also provides valuable space ou
the pressure-hull for equipment such as steering gear and high-pressure air bo
All Type 877 variants have a common pressure-hull 169ft 11in (51.8m) long a
common outer hull 238ft 2in (72.6m) long, with the large, well-shaped bow g
good hydrodynamic and acoustic performance, as well as being the optimum s

ve: Indian Navy Sindhuratna*, an export Kilo-class SSK.*

he sonar; it also enables six torpedo tubes to be installed. There were five ions, the first being the sole prototype (Type 877). Next came Type 877M, ch incorporated the lessons learnt from testing the prototype; 14 were built for Russian Navy. The export variant of this model was the Type 877EM, which was lied to: Algeria (2), China (2), India (9), Poland (1) and Romania (1). The Type MK was the -M model with a much improved command system, which was lied to the Russian Navy (7), while the Type 877EMK was the export version, hich the Russian Navy had two (for training foreign crews), and three went to (1992-97).

The improved Type 636 appeared in the mid-1980s, one of the primary rences being greater noise reduction, which included mounting the electric or on a flexibly mounted raft; halving the shaft speed (from 500 to 250 rpm); signing many auxiliary systems; revising the bow profile to reduce flow noise further; and removing all noise-producing equipment from the forward partment. Much greater use was made of automation and new, more powerful more fuel-efficient diesel engines were also installed, together with more erful electric motors. The exterior of the hull is totally coated in anechoic tiles e from rubber with a classified additive. Eight have been built so far, six for the sian Navy and two for the Chinese Navy.

The Types 877 and 636 share two unusual features. First, they have two small, iary propellers, each driven by a 75kW electric motor, which are housed in two (4m) long tunnels in the stern casing, both of which have hydraulically operated ance and exit doors. These propel the submarine at some 3kt in a "get-you-e" role, but are also used for mooring and when traversing restricted erways. The other unusual feature is a portable SAM launcher. An automatic system would have been too heavy, so a manually operated launcher is used a well in the sail between the snorkel and the radio antenna masts. The SAM consists of two men: a launcher operator and a loader who extracts new ds from the missile container.

w: Kilo was the first
iet diesel-electric design
ave an "Albacore" tear-
o hull.

Hajen-class

Type: Baltic patrol.
Total built: 6.
Completed: 1957-60.
Displacement: surfaced 720 tons; submerged 900 tons.
Dimensions: length 216ft 6in (66.0m); beam 16ft 8in (5.1m); draught 16f
(5.0m).
Propulsion: 2 x Pielstick diesels, 2 x 830bhp; 2 x ASEA electric motors;
shafts.
Performance: surface – 16kt, submerged – 20kt.
Weapons: 4 x 21in (533mm) TT (bow), 8 x torpedoes.
Complement: 44.

History: These were Sweden's first post-World War II submarines and v
built after a 10-year gap following the completion of the last of the U-1-cla
1944, the main reason for this gap being the German Type XXI. The F
Swedish Navy knew that its submarine designs had been outdated at a st
by the German Type XXI and XXIII, but since their country had been neutr
the war it was not privy to the design information available to the victor
Allies. However, by a fortunate stroke of fate, a German crew had scuttle
3503, a Type XXI boat, off the entrance to Gøteborg on 8 May 1945, follo
which they had surrendered and been interned. The Swedish Navy recov
the hulk in 1946 and subjected it to the most detailed examination be
scrapping it. The Swedes took their time in studying the lessons, as a resu
which the first of the new Hajen-class was not laid down until 1953.

Draken-class

Type: Baltic patrol.
Total built: 6.
Completed: 1961-62.
Displacement: surfaced 835 tons; submerged 950 tons.
Dimensions: length 226ft 6in (69.3m); beam 16ft 9in (5.3m); draught 17f
(5.3m).
Propulsion: 2 x Pielstick diesels, 2 x 800bhp; 2 x ASEA electric motors,
840kW; one shaft.
Performance: surface – 17kt, submerged – 22kt.
Weapons: 4 x 21in (533mm) TT (bow), 12 x torpedoes.
Complement: 36.

History: The second post-World War II class for the Royal Swedish Navy.
Draken-class was essentially an improved version of the Hajen-class. It reta
the long, thin hull and careful streamlining of the German Type XXI, the n
difference being the replacement of the small, fast-rotating twin propeller
a single, much slower-revving design. This not only gave higher speed, but
considerably reduced the submarine's acoustic signature.

The normal practice for the RSwedN at this time was to build one
class of six boats every decade, with each class serving for 20 years
receiving a major modernisation at approximately the 10-year point. There
however, an interruption in this very logical process, caused partly by the
rapid developments in both submarine and anti-submarine technology from
1950s onwards and also by the ever-escalating cost of defence equipm
Thus, it would have been normal practice for the entire Draken-class to s

ove: **Bavern** *emerges from its solid rock shelter.*

Although somewhat smaller than the Type XXI, these 720-ton vessels were
largest built so far for the RSwedN and their long, smooth hull and careful
amlining, especially of the fin, and high battery power resulted in a very
ctive design. They had twin, fast-rotating propellers, giving a maximum
lerwater speed of 16kt, although they were somewhat noisy by later
idards. They were armed with four torpedo tubes, all in the bow, and were
first Swedish submarines for some 40 years not to have any guns. They
e designed for fast diving and were the first Swedish submarines to be
:d with schnorkels. All six boats were stricken in 1980.

ove: **Draken-class** Nordkaparen *amidst the Baltic ice.*

to approximately 1980, but this did not happen. All six boats were
Jernised in 1970-71, but only *Draken* and *Gripen* were stricken in 1981 in
ordance with previous practice, when they were replaced by the three-
ng Näcken-class. The other four, however – *Vargen, Delfinen, Nordkaparen*
Springaren – were given a major rebuild in 1981-83 and then served on until
king in 1988 (thus serving for some 26 years), when they were replaced by
four-strong Västergotland-class. At one stage in the mid-1980s two of the
Jilt-Draken class were offered to the Royal Malaysian Navy for the initial
ning of a submarine arm prior to an order for new-build boats, but the plan
through.

Sjöormen (A-11)-class

Type: Baltic patrol.
Total built: 5.
Completed: 1968-69.
Displacement: surfaced 1,125 tons; submerged 1,400 tons.
Dimensions: length 165ft 7in (50.5m); beam 20ft 0in (6.1m); draught 19ft (5.1m).
Propulsion: 2 x Hedemora-Pielstick diesels, 2 x 525bhp; 1 x ASEA ele motor, 1,500 hp; one shaft.
Performance: surface – 12kt, submerged – 20kt; maximum operating di depth 492ft (150m).
Weapons: 4 x 21in (533mm) TT (bow), 8 x torpedoes; 2 x (400mm) TT (bow x torpedoes.
Complement: 23.

History: The Sjöormen-class was designed in the early 1960s, with five be entering service between 1967 and 1969, where they replaced the Abbo (rebuilt U-1)- class. This was the first of a succession of Swedish design break away from conventional practice, its principal novelty being a "tear-dr hull, although it would be incorrect to describe it as an "Albacore-hull" sinc is quite different in shape to that revolutionary U.S. submarine. The Sjöorm control surfaces were also of a totally new layout for Swedish submarines, X-planes aft and sail-mounted forward hydroplanes. Finally, the design introduced the unique Swedish torpedo layout, with a row of four 21in (533r tubes above and the two shorter 15.7in (400mm) tubes below, with reload

Näcken (A14)-class

Type: Baltic patrol.
Total built: 3.
Completed: 1980-81.
Displacement: surfaced 1,050 tons; submerged 1,145 tons.
Dimensions: length 162ft 5in (49.5m); beam 18ft 8in (5.7m); draught 18ft (5.5m).
Propulsion: 1 x M.T.U diesel, 2,100bhp; 1 x Jeumont-Schneider electric mc 1,150kW; one shaft
Performance: surface – 20kt, submerged – 25kt; maximum operating di depth 984ft (300m).
Weapons: 6 x 21in (533mm) TT (bow), 8 x torpedoes; 2 x 15.7in (400mm (bow) 4 x torpedoes.
Complement: 19.

History: As usual in Sweden, laying down the first of the next submarine c followed closely on completion of the previous class and in this case Näcken design followed on from the last of the Sjöormen-class a replacement for three of the six-strong Draken-class. The first-of-class Nä was laid down in November 1972 and the three boats entered servic 1980/81. Following construction of the Sjöormen-class the RSwedN examined the design using computer analysis and arrived at a rather diffe result with a longer, parallel-sided hull with a high beam-to-length ratio, a very angular sail located further aft. There is a large bow-mounted sonar anc main accommodation space is abaft the control room with machinery spa right aft. Unlike most other submarines, there is just one combined search

ght: The design of the
Sormen-class began to show a
finite Swedish style.

right: The design of the Sjöormen-class began to show a definite Swedish style.

tubes positioned on an automated
ding rack immediately behind. The
l in this class is set far forward on
e hull, indicating that the control-
om is also far forward.

All five boats were modernised in
84-85, among the main changes
ing the installation of a new
mbat data/fire-control system, and
new sonar suite. *Sjölejonet* and
Sjöhunden then received a "mid-life"
date in 1992-94, which included
another new sonar suite, and the
me electronic system as that
talled in the Näcken-class during
eir latest refits. This extended the
erational lives of these two boats into the late 1990s.

All five boats have been sold to the Singapore Navy. *Sjöhunden* was
nsferred in 1995 to serve as a training boat, and was followed by *Sjöormen*,
Sjölejonet and *Sjölhästen* which were fully refurbished as operational boats
fore being transferred in 1999-2001. The fifth boat, *Sjöbjornen*, was retained
Swedish waters and is serving as a source of spares.

Above: Näcken, seen here after lengthening as an AIP test-bed.

ack periscope. Arma-ment is very heavy for the size of the hull, with six 21in
3mm) tubes and eight torpedoes, with a further two 15.7in (450mm) tubes
d four torpedoes below.

Näcken was converted into a hybrid-powered submarine in 1987-88, being
gthened by 19ft 8in (6.0m) so that two Stirling closed-cycle engines, two
X (liquid oxygen) tanks and the necessary control systems could be installed.
e Stirling engines are used for submerged patrols at low speed, with low use
battery power. LOX provides the combustible air and the exhaust products
solve in water.

Västergotland (A17)-class SWED

Type: Baltic patrol.
Total built: 4.
Completed: 1987-90.
Displacement: surfaced 1,070 tons; submerged 1,143 tons.
Dimensions: length 159ft 2in (48.5m); beam 20ft 0in (6.1m); draught 18ft (5.6m).
Propulsion: 2 x Hedemora diesels, 2 x 1,300bhp; 2 x Jeumont-Schnei generator sets, 2 x 760kW; 1 x ASEA electric motor, 1,800shp; one shaft.
Performance: surface – 11kt, submerged – 20kt; maximum operating div depth 984ft (300m).
Weapons: 6 x 21in (533mm) TT (bow), 12 x torpedoes; 3 x 15.7in (400mm) 6 x torpedoes.
Complement: 20.

History: The design contract for the replacement of the last three of Draken-class was awarded to Kockums in April 1978 and the construct contract in December 1981. As had now become the practice, the bow a stern sections were built by Karlskronavarvet and then shipped to Malmö wh Kockums built the centre section and was responsible for final assembly a trials. The four Västergotland-class boats are of single-hull design, wit computer-controlled indexed (ie, X-configured) rudder/after hydroplane. The comprises two compartments separated by a watertight bulkhead, and there an escape chamber for the crew situated aft of the sail, which is designec mate with the RSwedN's URF-class rescue submersible. The hull is covered with a coating of anechoic tiles. There are nine bow torpedo tubes, six 21in (533mm) and three 15.7in (400mm), together with one reload per tube, one of the heaviest batteries ever installed in a submarine of this relatively small size. At one stage the RSwedN considered installing four vert launch tubes in the sail for RBS-17 anti-ship missiles (a version of the Saab R 15 surface-skimmer), but this did not take place, mainly because the miss were not considered to be cost-effective in the context of submarine operati in the Baltic. Another proposal was to retrofit these submarines with Ster engines, but this, too, has been dropped..

Two of these boats, *Södermanland* and *Östergötland*, are currently be rebuilt and given a 32ft 10in (10m) extension to enable them to accommoc two Sterling Mk 3 closed-cycle engines and the associated tanks and contr and will return to service in 2004. At that point the other two bo

Guppy I-class
Conversions UNITED STA

Type: ocean-going patrol.
Total converted: 2.
Completed: 1947.
Displacement: surfaced 1,900 tons; submerged 2,400 tons.
Dimensions: length 307ft 6in (93.7m); beam 27ft 4in (8.3m).
Propulsion: 4 x main diesel generators, 4 x 1,350bhp; 2 x electric motors, 1,370shp; battery 4 x 126 cell; two shafts.
Performance: surface – 17.8kt, submerged – 18.2kt; range surfaced 11,000 at 8kt; maximum operating diving depth 400ft (122m).

ght: Västergotland, *seen ere at "launch", shows e typically Swedish hull ntours.*

stergotland and *Hälsingland,* ll be stricken, leaving the SwedN with an entirely erling-powered sub-marine et. (The latest Götland-ss is described in the AIP ction.)

ove. This class has a heavy bow battery six 21in (533mm) and three 15.7in (400mm) torpedo tubes.

eapons: 10 x 21in (533mm) TT (bow – 6, stern – 4), 28 x torpedoes.
mplement: 79.
ecifications for Guppy I, as converted.

tory: At the end of World War II the U.S. Navy possessed a huge fleet of marines, almost all of them war-built Gato-, Balao- and Tench-classes. Pre-r boats were immediately scrapped, together with a number of the older tos, while most boats still under construction were broken up on the ways, rt from four, on which work was suspended against possible future use.

Some boats were converted for specialised roles such as radar pickets, hunt
killers, amphibious transports, oilers and missile launchers, while others we
used in various types of research, but most were given a GUPPY (Great
Underwater Propulsion Program) upgrade, which included streamlining the h
and superstructure, removing unnecessary protuberances, increasing batte
power and fitting a schnorkel. These measures resulted in greater range, mu
increased underwater speeds and increased tactical effectiveness. There we
six Guppy conversions, plus the fleet schnorkel.

Guppy I.
Two boats were converted in 1945-47 to provide high-speed underwa
targets for U.S. ASW forces to train against, with external streamlinir
particularly of the sail, and extra batteries; this enabled them to achieve ju
under 18kt submerged, a 100 per cent increase in speed. They also had sor
internal reorganisation and, where necessary, equipment was updated, b
they were not fitted with a schnorkel. The specifications for the two boa
concerned are given above. Both were later converted for a second time,
this occasion to Guppy II.

Guppy IA.
The Guppy II programme (see next entry) proved rather expensive, so a le
elaborate conversion was evolved, designated Guppy IA. This still includ
streamlining and a schnorkel, but did not include a fourth 126-cell batte
instead of which the boats were given three batteries of a new type of cell; t
was known as the "Sargo II battery". The internal rearrangement was also le
elaborate than in the Guppy II conversion. This Guppy IA conversion w
applied to 10 Balao- and Tench-class boats and took place in 1951-52.

Guppy IB.
If Guppy IA was an austere version of Guppy II, then Guppy IB was an auste

Guppy II-class
Conversions

Type: ocean-going patrol.
Total converted: 24.
Completed: 1949-51.
Displacement: surfaced 2,040 tons; submerged 2,400 tons.
Dimensions: length 307ft 0in (93.6m); beam 27ft 4in (8.3m).
Propulsion: 3 x main generator diesels, 3 x 1,350bhp; 2 x electric moto
2 x 1,370shp; battery 4 x 126 cell; two shafts.
Performance: surface – 18kt, submerged – 16kt; range surfaced 11,000
at 8kt; maximum operating diving depth 400ft (122m).
Weapons: 10 x 21in (533mm) TT (bow – 6, stern – 4), 28 x torpedoes.
Complement: 85.
Specifications for Guppy II, as converted.

History: Learning from the Guppy I programme, the U.S. Navy embark
on an even more ambitious conversion in which 24 boats were conver
to Guppy II standard in 1948-51. This involved 17 serving Balao- and Ten
class boats, five unfinished hulls on which work had been suspended at
end of the war, and the two Guppy Is. The work involved similar additic
batteries and the streamlining of the sail and hull as in Guppy I, but diffe
in including a schnorkel. By this time the boats, large as they were, h
become overcrowded and considerable internal reorganisation w
required to fit everything in.

rsion of Guppy IA. This conversion was devised for four boats transferred
road in the early 1950s, two to the Netherlands and two to Italy.

low: Guppy IB; Italian da Vinci, *ex-USS* Dace (SS-247).

ove: Thornback (SS-418), *a Guppy IIA conversion.*

ppy IIA.
urther 16 Balao and Tench boats were converted to a generally similar
ndard to the Guppy II, but with less drastic internal reorganisation. Both
ppy IIs and IIAs were badly overcrowded and after several years' service

one engine and one generator were removed. This reduced performance, but this was more than offset by the gains in space and ease of maintenance.

Guppy III-class Conversions

Type: ocean-going patrol.
Total converted: 9.
Completed: 1959-63.
Displacement: surfaced 1,975 tons; submerged 2,870 tons.
Dimensions: length 322ft 0in (98.1m); beam 27ft 4in (8.3m).
Propulsion: 4 x main generator diesels, 4 x 1,350bhp; 2 x electric moto 2 x 1,370shp; battery 4 x 126 cells; two shafts.
Performance: surface – 17kt, submerged – 14kt; range surfaced 11,000 at 8kt; maximum operating diving depth 400ft (122m).
Weapons: 10 x 21in (533mm) TT (bow – 6, stern – 4), 28 x torpedoes.
Complement: 95.
Specifications for Guppy III, as converted.

History: Nine Guppy IIs were given an even more drastic conversion in 19 62 as part of the Fleet Rehabilitation And Modernization (FRAM) program the need in this particular case being to maintain the effectiveness of submarine fleet until sufficient SSNs were in service. The greatest sir element of the work involved cutting the pressure-hull in two at a point wh the forward battery compartment joined the control room and inserting a (4.6m) "plug" to provide much-needed additional volume for the crew, the e growing amount of electronic equipment, and extra torpedoes. The sail v extended and inside it the conning tower was also lengthened to accommoc

low: Brazilian Guanabara, *a Balao-class Guppy II.*

ove: Guppy III Cobbler *(SS-344); note sonar domes.*

itional equipment. Externally, these conversions were instantly recognisable
the three large fins covering the hydrophones of the PUFFS passive sound-
ging equipment, and by the very high sail.

Originally it was intended that all the Guppy IIs would have be
brought up to this standard, but financial constraints compelled a reduct
to just nine. The work was completed between 1959 and 1963 but
boats remained in service for only a few years and most were transfer
to foreign navies in 1973: Brazil – 2; Greece – 1; Italy – 2; Turkey – 2.

Fleet Schnorkel Conversions

UNITED STAT

Type: ocean-going patrol.
Total converted: 19.
Completed: 1947-52.
Displacement: surfaced 2,040 tons; submerged 2,400 tons.
Dimensions: length 312ft 0in (95.1m); beam 27ft 4in (8.3m).
Propulsion: 4 x main diesel generators, 4 x 1,350bhp; 2 x electric motors,
1,370shp; battery 4 x 126 cell; two shafts.
Performance: surface – 17.8kt, submerged – 18.2kt; range surfaced 11,000
at 8kt; maximum operating diving depth 400ft (122m).
Weapons: 10 x 21in (533mm) TT (bow – 6, stern – 4), 28 x torpedoes.
Complement: 83.

History: Even the "austere" Guppy IA and IIA conversions proved
expensive to be applied to the entire fleet of the U.S. Navy's diesel-elec
boats, so an even more limited programme was instituted, the main purpos
which was to install the schnorkel in as many boats as possible. Two differ
types of schnorkel had been developed during the war by the Germans
Japanese, and had entered service on a number of their submarines from e
1944 onwards. A much improved version was developed by the U.S. Navy a
matter of urgency in the immediate post war years. The first fleet boat to
fitted being USS *Irex* (SS-482) in 1947. In essence this conversion sim
involved a higher, semi-streamlined sail containing the periscopes and
schnorkel mast, while no effort was made to remove the guns or ot
protuberances on the upper casing. Following successful testing, the schno
was approved for service and was installed in all Guppy boats from the Gu
II onwards.

t of these Guppy IIIs to retire from active service with the U.S. Navy was
S *Tiru* (SS-416), which was also the last of the Gato-/Balao-/Tench-classes
iich had served the Navy so well.

ow: Greek Guppy III, Katsonis, *with sonar domes removed.*

ove: Sabalo *(SS-302); "Fleet Schnorkel" limited conversion.*

The "fleet schnorkel" was a very limited conversion, carried out in the
rse of routine refits and involved the installation of a schnorkel together with
ne streamlining, the removal of guns, and, in some later cases, the
allation of a GRP sail. By no means all the boats classified as "fleet
norkels" were identical and there were a variety of sail profiles and upper
ing work. Internally, apart from the ducting and controls associated with the
norkel, very few alterations were made. All were converted in 1951-52 and
r the following 20 years considerable differences developed between them.
ne remained as they had been when they left the yards in the 1950s but
ers were given the very tall streamlined GRP sail of the Guppy III, while
e (*Piper, Sterlet* and *Sea Owl*) retained the original sail but were given very
e bow sonar domes. All had been stricken from the U.S. Navy by 1970, and
ne were then transferred to foreign navies. Some other boats which were
sferred to foreign navies in the 1950s were given the equivalent of a fleet
norkel refit prior to being handed over.

Barracuda-class

Type: hunter/killer.
Total built: 3.
Completed: 1951-52.
Displacement: surfaced 765 tons; submerged 1,160 tons.
Dimensions: length 196ft 1in (59.8m); beam 24ft 7in (7.5m); draught 14ft (4.4m).
Propulsion: 2 x General motors diesels, 2 x 525bhp; 2 x General Mo electric motors; two shafts.
Performance: surface – 13kt, submerged – 8.5kt.
Weapons: 4 x 21in (533mm) TT (bow – 2, stern – 2).
Complement: 37.

History: An operational concept was developed in the late 1940s for a m produced hunter/killer submarine (also known as an "SSK"), which w position itself off enemy bases or in maritime choke-points just before a started and then ambush enemy submarines as they sailed for their stations. The operational requirement for the submarine to fulfil such a miss stressed quietness; a long-range, passive sonar; low cost; and ease manufacture in large numbers. High speed and deep diving capabilities w not required and thus the "thin-skinned" Gatos were particularly suitable, a total of seven of these were converted to the SSK role in 1951-53. A purp built design was also developed, being known originally as the K-class and l as the Barracuda-class.

The Barracudas were smaller than contemporary U.S. Navy submar

Tang/Darter-class

Type: attack.
Total built: 7.
Completed: 1951-56.
Displacement: surfaced 1,560 tons; submerged 2,260 tons.
Dimensions: length 269ft 2in (82.0m); beam 27ft 2in (8.3m); draught 17ft (5.2m).
Propulsion: 3 x Fairbanks-Morse Type 3 diesels, 3 x 1,500bhp; 2 x ele motors, 2 x 1,800shp; two shafts (see notes).
Performance: surface – 15.5kt; submerged – 18.3kt.
Weapons: 8 x 21in (553mm) TT (bow – 6, stern – 2).
Complement: 83.
Specifications are for Tang-class, as built.

History: The Tang-class was the U.S. Navy's first post-war, totally new at submarine design and thus equivalent to the Soviet Whiskey- and the Br Porpoise-classes (qqv). Like those other two classes the design assimilated lessons of the war and took account of the examination of captured Type boats. They thus had a long, thin and carefully streamlined hull, and high po batteries. To reduce the size of the submarine a totally new design of di engine was selected; made by General Motors. The new design was, howe a failure, proving to be mechanically unreliable and very difficult to maintain, on several occasions Tang-class boats had to be towed across the Atlantic repairs in the United States. The problem was so severe that a major and expensive programme had to be set in train to replace these trouble engines with a lightweight Fairbanks-Morse model; this required the hull t

ɔve: Barracuda *(SST-3), here seen as a training boat.*

n a massive dome in the bows for the BQR-4 sonar. They served in this role
· until 1959 when the mission was recognised as impracticable; the bow
ar was removed from all three, whereupon two were reclassified as attack
marines, while the third became a training boat.

These boats are an example of how even the highly logical U.S. Navy
ignation system occasionally becomes muddled. The boats were originally
given names but numbers with a "K" prefix: *K-1* (SSK-1), *K-2* (SSK-2) and *K-*
SK-3). Then, in December 1955, two of them were given names and hull
bers in the usual "SS-" series; thus, *K-2* (SSK-2) became *Bass* (SS-551) and
(SSK-3) became *Bonita* (SS-552). The former *K-1* (SSK-1), however, retained
original number until July 1959 when it became *Barracuda* (SST-3) (SST =
ing submarine), but although it was reclassified yet again as an attack
marine in 1972 it was never given a hull number in the full U.S. Navy series.
s and *Bonita* were scrapped in 1967 but *Barracuda* survived until 1974.

ɔve: USS *Darter (SS-576), a lengthened version of the Tang.*

thened by 9ft (2.7m) and even then only three engines could be installed.
last two boats, *Gudgeon* (SS-567) and *Harder* (SS-568) were lengthened
re-engined while still under construction, but the other four *Tang* (SS-563),
ger (SS-564), *Wahoo* (SS-565) and *Trout* (SS-566) had to be returned to the
der's yards for a major reconstruction in the late 1950s. In a further rebuild
e late 1960s the boats were again lengthened, this time by 18ft (5.5m) to
ble them to accommodate the PUFFS sonar system and to provide more
n for the crew. These boats were instantly recognisable by the
acteristic three fin-shaped domes on the upper casing.

Darter (SS-576) was essentially a repeat of the lengthened/re-engined
sion of the Tang-class, with improved control systems. Only one was built.

Abtao-class

Type: patrol.
Total built: 4.
Completed: 1954-57.
Displacement: surfaced 825 tons; submerged 1,400 tons.
Dimensions: length 243ft 0in (74.1m); beam 22ft 0in (6.7m); draught 14ft (4.3m).
Propulsion: 2 x General Motors diesels, 2 x 1,200bhp; 2 x electric motors, 1,200shp; two shafts.
Performance: surface – 16kt, submerged – 10kt; range surfaced 5,000nm at 1
Weapons: 6 x 21in (533mm) TT (bow – 4, stern – 2); 1 x 5in (127mm) gun.
Complement: 40.

History: This class had three claims to fame. The first was that they were only submarines in the world to retain a deck-gun to the very last year of 20th century, some 40 years longer than any other navy; second, they w direct descendants of one of the most unpopular classes ever to have ser in the U.S. Navy; and, third, they were the last submarines to be built in a Un States shipyard for an export customer. In the late 1940s the Peruvian N sought new submarines which were smaller than the surplus "f submarines" then becoming available, but would incorporate recent advan such as streamlining and extra battery power.

The Electric Boat Company based the design on the Mackerel-class, tw which had been built for the U.S. Navy in the late 1930s as a smaller and m economical alternative to the "fleet submarines". *Mackerel* (SS-204) and *M*

Barbel-class

Type: patrol.
Total built: 3.
Completed: 1959.
Displacement: surfaced 2,146 tons; submerged 2,894 tons.
Dimensions: length 219ft 2in (66.8m); beam 29ft 0in (8.8m); draught 20ft (6.3m).
Propulsion: 3 x Fairbanks-Morse diesels, 3 x 1,600bhp; 1 x Westingho electric motor, 3,150shp; one shaft.
Performance: surface – 15kt, submerged – 21kt.
Weapons: 6 x 21in (533mm) TT (bow).
Complement: 83.

History: These were the last three diesel-electric submarines to be built for U.S. Navy, all three being launched in 1958 and completed in 1959. Their de was derived from the lessons learnt with *Albacore* (AGSS-569), w demonstrated the many advantages of the short, fat hull, technically know a "body-of-revolution" but popularly described as a "tear-drop" shape, and showed the superiority of the single- over the double-propeller propul system. The latter arrangement made it impossible to mount torpedo tu firing astern. The Barbel design was based on that of the Albacore and as the boats had bow diving planes, although this was changed during service to sail-mounted planes. Unlike other U.S. Navy submarines of period they were not fitted with the PUFFS sonar system, possibly because three fin-shaped domes would have caused too much hydrodynamic drag.

Bonefish (SS-582) suffered a serious fire at sea on 24 March 1988, resu

t: Tiburon, re-
ed Abtao *in 1957,*
of four boats built
e USA for Peru.

205) proved too
ll and of little value
were deeply dis-
d within the Sub-
ne Force, as a
lt of which they
e relegated to training tasks until the war's end, when they were quickly
oped. Despite this unpromising background, the basic design proved
ible and the hull and sail were streamlined as requested. To the
iiderable surprise of the Electric Boat Company, however, the Peruvians
insisted on a gun, and a 127mm (5in) "wet mount" was duly fitted on the
casing.

The four submarines were regularly upgraded during their service, with
r refits at Electric Boat in 1965 for two boats and in 1968 for the other two.
work included replacing the original stepped sail by a tall type modelled on
of the Guppy III and removing the deck gun on two of the boats. In 1981
batteries were shipped and the engineering and electrical systems
ernised. and Eledone sonar fitted. *Angamos* (S-43) was stricken in 1990,
wed by *Iquique* (S 44) in 1993, but the remaining pair (which happened to
ie two retaining the gun) served on until 1999, when both were scrapped. The
s were originally named *Tiburon, Atun, Lobo* and *Merlin*, but these were
ged during their service to *Abtao, Angamos, Dos de Mayo* and *Iquique*.

ve: **Barbel was the U.S .Navy's last diesel-electric boat class.**

ree fatalities and causing so much damage that she was stricken and
)ped. The other two, *Barbel* (SS-580) and *Blueback* (SS-581), lasted only
years longer, being stricken in 1990, the last of a very long line of diesel-
ric submarines that had served the U.S. Navy so well over a period of 80
.

Air-Independent Propulsion (AIP) Submarines

Since the very earliest submarines, designers have tried to find a system submerged propulsion which is independent of the atmosphere. Init this power was provided by the crew themselves, either using their arm turn a crank or their legs to operate a treadle, but such human power clearly inadequate, even in the CSS *Hunley* which employed eight bra crewmen. One of the earliest mechanical systems was invented by Englishman, George Garrett, who attempted to harness the power of la steam so that one propulsion plant sufficed for both surface and subme propulsion; it was ingenious and the world's first air-independent propu (AIP) system, but was never made to work properly. Other 19th cen designers used compressed-air or electricity from accumulators, both of w were clean and economical, but were very short-ranged and required a re to harbour for recharging; they were, therefore, only suitable for boats invo in harbour or coastal defence.

For many years, the combination of a battery for submerged power and inte combustion engines – kerosene, gasoline or diesel – for surface power recharging the battery reigned supreme. In the late 1930s, however, enginee Russia and Germany started to examine the use of closed-cycle engine submerged propulsion. The German Professor Walter was particularly a producing a host of designs based on the use of hydrogen-peroxide, but alth numerous prototypes were produced none of his designs ever saw opera service. Nevertheless, after World War II the American, British and Soviet n examined his ideas very closely, but hydrogen-peroxide proved difficult to use

advent of nuclear propulsion proved a far more cost-effective and much less ǝerous alternative for the larger navies.

For several more decades the smaller navies were forced to rely on diesel-tric propulsion, but the subject of "air-independent propulsion" began to be ⟩xamined from the 1970s onwards, particularly in Germany, France, Sweden the USSR. At first it was thought that an AIP system could be found which ⅼld totally replace the electric-storage battery for submerged propulsion, but proved impossible and all present AIP plants provide a relatively low-power ⟩e capability, but a battery is still needed for high- speed operations.

The known current AIP programmes involve various nations and a number fferent technologies. Fuel-cell projects are being pursued by Germany and for their Type 212 submarines, while Russia is working on a different type ⅰel-cell for installation in both new and existing boats. The Stirling system ⟩inues to be developed, with Japan also showing a close interest. A group ⟩ritish, Dutch and German firms are cooperating in the development of the ⟩tre closed-circuit diesel (CCD) system, while France and Spain are ⟩erating on the MESMA system. Finally, Canada is also known to have an project. So, for the next few years, the fuel-cell and the Stirling engine will ⅼe main systems and both appear to be equally promising, but AIP is an where rapid technological development, possibly even major ⅼthroughs, can be expected.

⟩w: Germany's "Ex-U1," one of many AIP test-beds.

Drzewiecki Man-powered Submarines

Type: air-independent human power.

History: Although these would today be classified as "minisubs", Drzewiecki submersibles are significant as one of the few successful powered designs. A Pole, Stefan Drzewiecki (1844-1942), was one of t extraordinary men who turn their minds to a bewildering variety of area: early invention was a distance-measuring device for Parisian horse-drawn t another an automatic plotter which marked a ship's track on a chart, whil later became involved in aeronautics and a specialist in propeller design. In during the Russo-Turkish War he turned his mind to submarines and desi a craft – Drzewiecki No 1 – which had a crew of just one man, who sat un small conning-tower and was assisted by a periscope and other innovation; powered the boat using his feet to operate a treadle which drove the s propeller. The towed mines were to be attached to the target ship by operator who remained in his craft. Trials were successful but the war e and the Russian Navy lost interest, although the army ordered an impr version, the Type II, and then placed a production order for 50 of improved Type III. Two Type IIIs were converted to electrical propulsi

Hunley

Type: air-independent human power.
Total built: 1.
Completed: 1863.
Displacement: not known.
Dimensions: length 39ft 6in (12.0m); beam 3ft 10in (1.2m); height of hu 3in (1.3m).
Propulsion: 8-man; manual; one shaft.
Performance (estimated): surface – ca 3-5kt; submerged – 2-3kt.
Weapons: 1 x spar torpedo.
Complement: 9.

History: Named after its designer/builder, the Confederate submarine *Hunley* carried out the first successful underwater attack in history when it USS *Housatonic* (17 February 1864). The hull was fabricated from a s boiler with a very sharp bow, and entry was by two watertight hatches forward also serving as the conning tower for the captain. Amidships, a ve tube extended some 4ft (1.2m) above the hull to serve as a primitive schn when travelling awash, with a stop-cock that could be shut prior to diving. T were ballast tanks at each end of the boat with sea-cocks open to the out the tanks were filled by opening the cocks and emptied by means of a mar operated pump; depth was assessed by means of a simple mercury tube. The craft was steered by the captain, using levers to control the midships diving-planes and a wheel to control the rudder. The inside was painted white and lighting was by means of one or more candles. There was a single shrouded propeller attached to a long

ss	Type I	Type II	Type III
mpleted	1877	1879	1878-81
mber in class	1	1	50
placement	n.k.	ca 2.5 tons	ca 2.5 tons
ensions gth m ught	15ft (4.5m) 5ft (1.5m) 5ft (1.5m)	20ft (6.1m) 5ft (1.5m) 3ft 6in (1.0m)	20ft (6.1m) 5ft (1.5m) 3ft 6in (1.0m)
pulsion	1 x shaft treadle	2 x shaft treadle	1 x shaft treadle
formance	ca 1.5kt	2kt	2-3kt
apons	2 mines	2 mines	2 mines
mplement	1	4	4

4 and another to gasoline-propulsion in 1905.

k, which was turned by the crew of eight men.

The weapon was a "spar torpedo", with a fused copper cylinder containing b (65kg) of explosive mounted at the end of a 17ft (5.2m) long iron tube nted some 4in (10cm) above the foot of the bow. The concept was that the marine would approach at such a speed that barbs would be lodged in the et's wooden hull, whereupon the charge was detonated by a lanyard ated by the captain. A 4,000lb (1,814kg) cast-iron keel was fitted, which red that the craft remained upright and which could be released from the e in an emergency.

The *Hunley* sank three times during training, with the loss of 23 men, each due to water lapping over the forward hatch, whose cover was open while ing awash. She was raised and recommissioned on each occasion. Vast unts of money were offered to her fourth crew for the attack on *satonic*. But it appears that she was too close to the explosion and was ged down by her victim. She has now been raised.

w: Hunley *was powered by eight men turning a crank.*

Nordenfelt-class SWEDEN/UNITED KINGD

Type: air-independent steam-power.
Total built: Nordenfelt I – 1; Nordenfelt II – 2.
Completed: Nordenfelt I – 1885; Nordenfelt II – 1886-87.
Displacement: surfaced 100 tons; submerged 160 tons.
Dimensions: length 100ft 0in (30.5m); beam 12ft 2in (3.7m).
Propulsion: Lamm steam-compound engine, 250ihp; one steam accumu
for underwater propulsion; one shaft.
Performance: surface – 8kt; submerged – 4.5kt, 14nm/4kt; maxir
operational depth 50ft (15m).
Weapons: 2 x 14in (356mm) external TT (bow) (2 torpedoes); 2 x Norde
MGs
Complement: 7.
Specifications are for Nordenfelt II, as built.

History: Later steam-powered submarines used steam for surface propu
only and relied on a battery for underwater propulsion, but it was first usec
singular manner. These three submarines were the result of cooper
between the Swedish armaments manufacturer, Thorsten Nordenfelt, ar
eccentric British clergyman, Reverend George Garrett, who had b
responsible for *Resurgam*, a steam-powered experimental submarine.
first boat, *Nordenfelt I*, was built in Sweden in 1885 and sold to Greece, v
the two slightly larger *Nordenfelt IIs* were built in England and sold to Turk
1886.

The power system was ingenious. The boats were powered on the su
by a steam engine, using steam from a boiler in the normal way, but with s
steam being fed into a special accumulator tank, where it passed throu
heat-exchanger, heating the water in that tank before being pumped back
the boiler. On submerging, the super-heated water in the accumulator wa:
back into the main boiler, where it flashed into steam and drove the over
pistons. The system worked after a fashion but had drawbacks, not lea

Le Plongeur FRA

Type: air-independent compressed-air power.
Total built: 1.
Completed: 1863
Displacement: surfaced 420 tons; submerged 435 tons.
Dimensions: length 146ft 0in (44.5m); beam 19ft 8in (6.0m); draught 9f
(2.8m).
Propulsion: 4-cylinder compressed-air engine, 80hp; one shaft.
Performance (estimated): surface – 4.1kt, 7.5nm/2.4kt; submerged – ca
5.7nm/3.8kt.
Weapons: 1 x spar torpedo.
Complement: 13.

History: This was by far the largest and one of the most imaginative
century submarine designs, and the first to find an alternative to manpowe
submerged propulsion. *Plongeur*, designed by Captain Bourgois of the Fr
Navy in cooperation with engineer Charles Brun, was powered by an er
driven by compressed-air. The air was carried in 23 containers, with a
capacity of 4,520cu ft (128m³) at 171psi (12kg/cm²), which had to be recha
in port. This enabled the 85hp engine to propel the submarine at some 4kt,

ve: Nordenfelt's boats were powered by latent steam.

ch was that steam had to be raised three days prior to sailing in order to heat
accumulator effectively.

The boats operated by a system of positive buoyancy to ensure that they
rned to the surface. To submerge, water was allowed into the main ballast
until the boat was just under the surface when two vertical propellers on
craft's bottom were engaged to drive the boat downwards. The propellers
to be constantly driven to maintain depth, but to surface, particularly if
ething had gone wrong, the propellers were stopped and the boat
matically returned to the surface.

None of the three boats became operational. They were allowed to rust
y, although during World War I the Germans found the rusting hulks of the
denfelt IIs in a shed in Constantinople (Istanbul) and attempted to make
n usable. A further design, *Nordenfelt IV*, was built, also in England. This
much larger, displacing 245 tons, and had a more powerful propulsion
em, but still using the latent steam principle. It was bought by the Russian
y but sank off the Danish coast on its delivery voyage.

he surface and when submerged, but range was very low.

Unfortunately, the one insoluble problem in the design was stability, the
come of a combination of her long, flat hull-shape and an intricate
tem of internal piping which was intended to maintain balance by
ving water from one end of the boat to the other. This system reacted
vly and then tended to over-compensate, resulting in a series of
erwater lurches, which was extremely un-nerving for the crew. Various
edies, such as enlarged after hydroplanes and a vertical propeller, were
d but without success.

Among the successful ideas was the first use of compressed-air to drive
er out of the ballast tanks, which had previously been done by pumps, an
later adopted by every submarine designer in the world. Another unusual
was the ship's boat which sat, upside down, in a recess on the hull, and
held in place with bolts, but with an air overpressure to prevent water
age through the bolt-holes. The weapon was a spar torpedo and, as always
this weapon, the problem was to make it powerful enough to damage the
et but without damaging the attacking boat. *Plongeur* was a fascinating
gn, particularly for 1863, and had great potential, but was dropped by the
ch Navy because of its stability problems.

Aleksandrowski

Type: air-independent compressed-air power.
Total built: 1.
Completed: 1865.
Displacement: 355 tons.
Dimensions: length 110ft 0in (33.5m); beam 13ft (4.0m); draught 12ft (3.8
Propulsion: 2 x compressed-air engines; two shafts.
Performance (estimated): surface – 1.5kt; maximum operational depth 30ft (
Weapons: 2 x mines.
Complement: 22.

Pochtovy

Type: air-independent diesel/compressed-oxygen.
Total built: 1.
Completed: 1908.
Displacement: surfaced 134 tons; submerged 146 tons.
Dimensions: length 113ft 0in (34.4m); beam 10ft (3.0m); draught 9ft 3in (2.8
Propulsion: 2 x gasoline engines, 260hp; two shafts.
Performance (estimated): surface – 10.5kt; submerged – 6.2kt.
Weapons: 4 x Drzewiecki torpedo drop-collars.
Complement: 22.

History: This was a fascinating design, another product of the remarkable b
of Stefan Drzewiecki. His main aim was to power the submarine by a si
internal-combustion engine for both surfaced and submerged propulsion,
a supply of compressed-oxygen held in 45 air bottles (350ft^3/9.91m^3)
pressure of 2,500psi (0.2kg/m^2), which was fed to the engine when submer
Exhaust gases were ejected under pressure from a perforated pipe loc
under the keel. Unfortunately, Drzewiecki was unable to find a suitable d
and had to use two gasoline engines instead. The system seems to h
worked reasonably well, giving a submerged range on one engine of 28 n
(44.8km). The main disadvantages, which appear to have been consid
insuperable, were the very heavy condensation when submerged, and the
prominent bubble-wake on the surface, which gave away the submari
position without the need for any acoustic devices. As a result, the idea
dropped, although as with the French *Plongeur* (qv) further development
very interesting idea might well have paid considerable dividends.

Drzewiecki was a Polish scientist and one of those men whose inter
covered an immense range of topics. Thus, he made considerable contribut
in fields such as aeronautics, gliding, ship and submarine design, and the th
and manufacture of propellers for both ships and aircraft. Although he did
pursue his idea of feeding compressed-air to an internal combustion eng
this basic concept is used in several of today's AIP submarines.

Right: **Pochtovy, a 1908 attempt at a true AIP submarine, which invol
feeding compressed oxygen to a gasoline engine; with more work an
money the idea might have been made to be practicable.**

tory: I. F. Alexandrowski was the second submarine designer to try to use
npressed- air, his design being ordered in 1863 and completed in 1865. The
t was quite sophisticated for the period, with a chamber in the bow which
ers could enter and leave underwater, and a sail. The submarine stored
)cu ft (6.2m³) of air at a pressure of 1,500psi (0.11kg/m³) which was sufficient
an operating radius of 2.5nm. She appears not to have lived up to
ectations and was then used for diving trials, attaining 60ft (18m) without
arent difficulty, but was later crushed at 100ft (30m).

Gymnôte/Gustave Zédé/ Morse-classes

FRAN

Type: air-independent all-electrical power.

Class	Gynmôte	Gustave Zédé	Morse
Completed	1888	1893	1899-1901
Total built	1	1	3
Displacement: surfaced submerged	30 tons 31 tons	266 tons 272 tons	143 tons 149 tons
Dimensions: length beam draught	58ft 5in (17.8m) 5ft 11in (1.8m) 5ft 6in (1.7m)	159ft 1in (48.5m) 10ft 6in (3.2m) 10ft 79in (3.2m)	119ft 9in (36.5 9ft (2.7m) 9ft 3in (2.8m)

History: These three designs represent the French attempt to produce effective all-electric submarine, which seemed to hold considerable promis the 1890s. The first, *Gymnôte*, designed by Gustave Zédé, was a very sr single-hulled craft, with one electric motor powered by a battery of 204 c As built, it was difficult to control, but the addition of three hydroplanes per cured this and it proved a most successful design, making some 2,000 d during its 10-year operational life. Next came *Gustave Zédé* (originally nar *Sirène*, but renamed after the early death of *Gymnôte*'s designer), which much larger and constructed of bronze, but also suffered from cor problems, which were cured in the same way, with hydroplanes. This boat also a success and recorded over 2,500 dives. Finally came the Morse-cl which was intended to combine the best points of both *Gymnôte* and *Gus Zédé*. The second and third boats of this class (*Algerien* and *Français*) v

opulsion:			
ttery	204 cells	720 cells	n.k.
ctric motor	1 (33.4shp)	1 (208shp)	1 (284shp)
aft	one	one	one
rformance:			
rface	7.3kt, 65nm/5kt	9.2kt, 220nm/6kt	7.3kt, 90nm/4kt
bmerged	4.3kt, 25nm/4kt	6.5kt, 105nm/5kt	5.5kt
eapons:	2x14in (356mm)	1 x 17.7in (450mm)	
rpedoes	2	3	
mplement	5	19	13

cifications for Morse-class are for first-of-class, as built.

htly larger, with a submerged displacement of 160 tons and with the ament of three 17.7in (450mm) torpedoes rearranged into one bow tube two externally mounted Drzewiecki drop-collars.

Another class of all-electric boats was built: the three-strong Farfadet- ss, displacing 202 tons and powered by a single electric motor. Launched in)1-03, they had short lives, two being stricken in 1906, one in 1907 and the in 1913.

All these boats performed well but the all-electric concept suffered an erent disadvantage, in that the boat always had to return to port to recharge battery, which was operationally unsound. All had been scrapped by)8-09.

ow: Gustav Zédé, one of several all-electric drive designs.

Isaac Peral

Type: air-independent all-electrical power.
Total built: 1.
Completed: 1890.
Displacement: surfaced 77 tons; submerged 85 tons.
Dimensions: length 72ft 2in (22.0m); beam 9ft 5in (2.9m); draught 9ft (2.8m).
Propulsion: 2 x electric motors, 2 x 30HP; two shafts.
Performance (estimated): surface – 7.8kt, 400nm/3kt; submerged – 3kt.
Weapons: 1 x 14in (356mm) TT (bow) (3 torpedoes).
Complement: 10.

History: Although the original Spanish submarine, *Ictineo*, was launched 1859 and underwent trials in 1860-61, the *Peral* is generally acknowledged be the first successful design. It was the idea of a serving naval officer electrical specialist, Lt. Isaac Peral (1851-95), and was commissioned in 18 The boat was extremely well streamlined and was powered by two elec motors, driving one propeller each, with vertical movement controlled by ba tanks and two small propellers, one under the bow, the other under the st The boat was fitted with a small conning-tower and a periscope, and probably the first to use chemicals to re-oxygenate the crew's air supply w submerged. Armament comprised a single tube in the bow, with th Schwarzkopf torpedoes carried. The submarine was powered by two elec motors driven by a battery of 613 cells. The boat performed very success and earned its designer a jewelled sword from the Queen of Spain, but Pe

Type XVIIB

Type: air-independent Walter system power.
Total built: 3.
Completed: 1944-45.
Displacement: surfaced 307 tons; submerged 332 tons.
Dimensions: length 136ft 2in (41.5m); beam 10ft 10in (3.3m); draught 14ft (4.3m).
Propulsion: 1 x Deutz diesel, 210hp; 1 x Walter turbine, 2,500hp; 1 x elec motor, 77shp; one shaft.
Performance: surface – 8.5kt, 3,000nm/8kt; submerged – 21.5kt, 150nm/2
Weapons: 2 x 21in (533mm short) TT (bow) (4 torpedoes).
Complement: 19.

History: Professor Helmut Walter was a gifted engineer and inver who,although few of his submarine designs were built and none beca operational, nevertheless played an important role in Germany's U-b development in World War II. His concepts covered both the design of submarine and their propulsion and the key to his ideas was the use hydrogen-peroxide (H_2O_2), which was stored in external plastic bags, with normal pressure of sea-water being used to force the fuel into the boat, wh it served as the oxidant in a closed-cycle diesel operation. His first boat, four-man *V-80*, had a submerged speed of 26.5kt and this was followed by much larger *V-300* and then four boats using the Walter principles but desig by B+V (*U-792/-793*) and Germania (*U-794/-795*). These had all b experimental, but in January 1943 an order was placed for 24 Type XVIIs w were intended to be fully operational, split into 12 Type XVIIBs built by B+V

ove: **Isaac Peral** *had all-electric power, using 613 cells.*

so many inventors, appears to have made enemies and eventually resigned
m the navy, dying a disappointed man in 1895. Fortunately, his submarine
vives and is on public display in Cartagena, Spain. Although never used in
mbat, this was a very impressive design and its designer deserved a better
e.

A Portuguese-designed, all-electric submarine was launched in 1892.
med *Plongeur,* it underwent some tests and survived until 1910, but does not
em to have aroused much enthusiasm in the Portuguese Navy.

ove: **Walter's** U-1407 *used hydrogen-peroxide propulsion.*

Type XVIIGs by Germania. The order was later cut-back to six Type XVIIBs of
ich only three were actually Completed: *U-1405* – December 1944, *U-1406*
ebruary 1945, and *U -1407* – March 1945. All were scuttled on 5 May 1945,
were raised by the Allies, following which *U-1406* went to the USA and *U-*
07 to the UK, where it was commissioned as HMS *Meteorite*. The U.S.
y's sole use of hydrogen-peroxide was in the X-1, whose design was based
that of the British wartime X-craft, but with a Walter-type propulsion system.
e suffered a major internal explosion in February 1958, but was rebuilt with
sel engines and then served until 1973. Walter was undoubtedly a brilliant
n, but his designs tended to bring too many novel ideas together, resulting
rotracted development programmes.

Explorer-class

Type: air-independent Walter system power.
Total built: 2.
Completed: 1956-58.
Displacement: surfaced 980 tons; submerged 1,076 tons.
Dimensions: length 225ft 0in (68.7m); beam 15ft 8in (4.8m); draught 18ft (5.5m).
Propulsion: 1 x Vickers hydrogen-peroxide turbine, 15,000bhp; 1 x elec motor, 400shp; two shafts.
Performance: surface – 27kt; submerged – 18kt.
Complement: 41-49.

History: Having raised *U-1407,* the Royal Navy took it to the UK where it v commissioned as HMS *Meteorite* and subjected to extended trials. They a took Professor Walter and key members of his team to England where he sp several years at Vickers, Barrow. It was believed that the Russians w continuing work on hydrogen-peroxide (true) and this, combined with the ne for high-speed targets for ASW forces, led to the development of these t unarmed boats. The hydrogen-peroxide was stored in internal open-top plastic tanks, and proved very difficult to work with, since, if it came into con with any dirt, dust or metal there would be an immediate and violent react producing vast amounts of steam which could cause the submarine to b apart. (Indeed, a small leak of hydrogen-peroxide in a torpedo aboard the S-cl submarine, HMS *Sidon,* in 1955 caused an explosion, not involving warheads, which resulted in 12 deaths. The Royal Navy then ceased all work

Type 212/Type 214

Type: air-independent fuel-cell power.
Total on order: Type 212 – 6; Type 214 – 3.
Completed: Type 212 – due 2003-2006; Type 214 – due 2009-2012.
Displacement: surfaced 1,450 tons; submerged 1,840 tons.
Dimensions: length 184ft 8in (56.3m); beam 22ft 4in (6.8m); draught 23ft (7.0m).
Propulsion: 1 x MTU 8V183 SE83 diesel, 1,040kW; 1 x Siemens Perma motor, 2.8mW (3,821hp); 9 x Siemens Polymer Electrolytic Membrane cells; one shaft.
Performance: surface – 12kt, 8,000nm/8kt; submerged – batteries 20kt, cells 8kt, 420nm/8kt.
Complement: 27.
Specifications are for Type 212 (Germany) as being built.

History: German submarine companies have developed a new AIP syst using fuel cells, which was successfully trialed in *ex-U-1* in 1988-89. Follow completion of the Type 206 (qv) programme in the mid-1970s, there was a l gap in submarine construction for the German Navy until 1998 when w started on the first Type 212. This is very much larger than the Type 206 – v a submerged displacement of 1,850 tons compared to 520 tons – but the m important difference is the propulsion system, which has three elements: a di engine for surface propulsion and charging the battery; the lead-acid battery high-speed underwater propulsion; and the fuel cell for underwater cruise.

The pressure hull is constructed of austenitic (non-magnetic) steel and a safety factor of two between the maximum operating depth and calcula

ove: HMS **Explorer,** *known to her crew as "Exploder".*

:h a dangerous substance.) The sailors' attitude to these two boats is nmed up in their nicknames – *Exploder* and *Excrutiator* – and there were no rets when the boats were scrapped and the use of hydrogen-peroxide in marine propulsion systems consigned to history, except in certain types of ssian torpedoes.

lapse. The pressure hull is a hybrid shape with large diameter forward and aller diameter after sections, connected by a short, conical section. The fuel l plant is housed in the conical section, with the liquid oxygen (LOX) and Irogen storage tanks grouped around the after hull, inside the free-flooding er casing. *Ex-U-1* had 16 fuel cells using liquid electrolyte, each generating :W of power, but the Type 212's production system consists of nine PEM ymer electrolyte membrane) fuel cells, using solid polymer technology, :h providing some 30-50kW power. This enables the boat to cruise merged for 420nm at 8kt, and much further at lower speeds, while it can in 20kt submerged, using its silver hydride battery.

Unlike all earlier German submarines, the Type 212 has two innovations in er to achieve greater manoeuvrability: the forward hydroplanes have been ved from the lower bows to the sail, and the after control surfaces are an " configuration. A further innovation is that after long use of "swim-out" edo launches, the Type 212 uses a hydraulic water-ram system, which is med to give low-noise discharge, even of heavyweight torpedoes, an ence of swell or bubbles, high discharge velocity, and no restrictions on marine operation up to 12 knots. Mines can be carried internally in place of edoes (three ground or two anchored mines per tube) but there is also a cially developed mine "girdle" carrying 24 mines; this reduces speed and urance, but enables a full load of torpedoes to be carried and it can be soned at any time.

Even before the first boat has been launched two foreign orders have been ted: two by Italy for two Type 212As (with an option on two more), while the ek Navy has ordered three of an improved version, the Type 214. This has a 213ft (65m) hull and a displacement of 1,700 tons, with diving depth ncreased to 1,300ft (400m). There will be eight torpedo tubes, of which four will also be able to launch guided missiles, such as UGM-84 Sub-Harpoon. Overall mission endurance is 84 days, with up to 14 days at a time being spent submerged.

Right: When dived Germany's Type 212 will be powered by fuel cells giving a 14-day submerged endurance at a speed of about 4 knots.

Quebec-class (Project 615)   RUS

Type: air-independent Kreislauf system power.
Total built: 30.
Completed: 1955-58.
Displacement: surfaced 460 tons; submerged 540 tons.
Dimensions: length 183ft 9in (56.0m); beam 16ft 5in (5.1m); draught 12ft (3.8m).
Propulsion: Kreislauf system; 1 x Type 32D diesel, 900bhp; 2 x Type M-diesels, each 700bhp; 1 x creep electric motor, 100shp; three shafts.
Performance: surface – 18kt, 2,750nm at cruising speed; submerged – 16
Weapons: 4 x 21in (533mm) TT (bow) (8 x torpedoes); 2 x 25mm AA.
Complement: 30.

History: In the 1930s the Soviet Navy built the M-class "coastal defe submarines" which needed high submerged speed, but not the exten endurance of ocean-going boats. Two of these were powered by experime closed-cycle systems, the first of which used liquid-oxygen (LOX) as oxidant, with the exhaust passing overboard. In the next version the exh was passed through a cooler filled with lime to leach-out the carbon dioxide then enriched with oxygen (from the LOX) before returning it to the eng Work was suspended during World War II, but afterwards developm restarted and the propulsion system was installed in the Project 615 (NAT Quebec) submarines, of which 30 were completed in the 1950s. The Wes Allies had examined Professor Walter's closed-cycles systems in the post-years and the first assumption by NATO was that the Quebecs were powe by a development of the Walter system, but this was incorrect (the Soviets

ld one Walter boat, Project 617, NATO = Whale, but it suffered an
plosion and was scrapped). The Russian system did not use the scarce
d expensive but energy-rich hydrogen-peroxide of the Walter system.
vertheless, even LOX has severe operational limitations and can be
red for only a limited period, so in the mid-1950s a further development
oject 637) appeared in which the exhaust was passed through a
er/enricher consisting of granules containing both a carbon dioxide (CO_2)
orbent and bonded oxygen; this combined the process of leaching-out
CO_2 and adding oxygen. One Quebec-class boat was fitted with this
tem in 1959, but the success of nuclear propulsion made the
gramme redundant and it was ended in 1960.

The Kreislauf system installed in the majority of the Quebec-class was very
gerous, the boats being known to their crews as "cigarette lighters", and
nerous boats suffered accidents, usually involving fires.

ow: Quebec-class used the Kreislauf propulsion system.

Gotland (Type A-19)-class SWED

Type: air-independent Stirling system power.
Total built: 3.
Completed: 1996-97.
Displacement: surfaced 1,384 tons; submerged 1,494 tons.
Dimensions: length 196ft 11in (60.6m); beam 20ft 4in (6.1m); draught 18ft (5.6m).
Propulsion: 2 x Hedemora V12A/15-Ub diesels, 2 x 1,300bhp; 1 x ASEA elec motor, 1,800shp; 2 x Stirling V4-275R Mk II engines, 2 x 75kW; one shaft.
Performance: surface – 11kt; submerged – battery 20kt, AIP 5kt.
Weapons: 4 x 21in (533mm) TT (bow) (12 x torpedoes); 2 x 15.7in (400mm) (4 torpedoes); 22 x mines in external belt (optional).
Complement: 23.

History: The research contract for a new class to replace the Sjöormen-cla (qv) in the mid-1990s was awarded to Kockums in 1986. The operatic requirement included stealthy signature, high shock tolerance, long submerg endurance, and substantial weapons load. The outcome was a design wh was essentially a progressive development of the Västergotland-class, but v the addition of a section containing two Stirling engines, which had alrea been trialed in the Modified Näcken. The production order was placed in Ma

90 and all three boats entered service in September 1999. Plans for a further
o have been cancelled.

The Kockums V4-275R Mk2 engine has four 275cc cylinders in a V layout,
erates at a constant 2,000rpm and uses the Sterling principle to convert heat
o mechanical work through a thermodynamic process. The engine uses
ndard diesel fuel from the boat's normal fuel tanks and liquid oxygen (LOX),
ich is stored in cryogenic tanks in the lower level of the AIP section (ie,
:hin the pressure hull). These are combined in a ratio of 4 parts diesel fuel to
)art LOX and are burnt inside a circular combustion unit, with the resultant
at being passed through a heat exchanger to the working gas (helium) which
)ands over each piston when heated and contracts below each piston when
)led, thus driving the piston up and down, and rotating the crankshaft. The
naust gas passes through a cooler which reduces its temperature from
)deg C to about 25deg C and then through an absorber, where it is mixed
:h seawater, cooling it even further; it is then expelled, without bubbling, into
e surrounding seawater.

The next Swedish submarine project is the Viking-class, a joint project with
rway and Denmark, which will start to enter service in about 2010.

low: Sweden's Gotland-class uses the Stirling engine.

Steam-powered Submarines

By the late 19th century steam technology was well understood and for so
years submarine designers tried to harness it for use in submarines. T
first such system was in many ways the most imaginative, since it endeavou
to use steam for submerged as well as surface propulsion, thus providing a tr
air-independent capability, but this Nordenfelt-Garrett system, while used
three different designs, never worked properly.

Some designers then turned to using steam to provide sufficient power
high speed on the surface, combined with charging the batteries for submerg
use. Steam, however, suffered from two major drawbacks. First, it took a l
time to raise sufficient steam, both when leaving harbour and after surfacing
sea, and it also took time to damp-down the plant prior to submerging; Frer
steam-powered submarines, for example, were reckoned to take 15 minutes
submerge. One way around this was used in the British K-class, which had
additional diesel engine to propel the submarine, albeit at a relatively s
speed, while the steam system was being started or stopped.

Secondly, the steam plant required many more penetrations through

essure hull for funnels, intakes, and vents, each of which was a source of tential disaster, the danger being enhanced because all were only a short stance above the waterline. One K-class captain made a personal pection to see that every opening was closed prior to diving, which rtainly ensured his men's safety but would scarcely have been practicable action.

By the early 1930s the last K-boat had been retired and the era of steam propulsion appeared over. However, there was a brief resurgence of interest in late 1940s when the U.S. Navy, which had never used steam propulsion fore, investigated the use of a pressure-fired boiler for a steam turbine to oduce very high surface speeds for radar picket submarines, but the plan was opped. Then, however, came the final triumph of steam, since in nuclear propulsion it is steam that is the agent which carries the power from the nuclear nt to the turbines.

low: K-class – most notorious of steam-powered submarines.

Narval/Sirène

Total built: Narval 1; Sirène 4.
Completed: Narval – 1899; Sirène – 1901.
Displacement: surfaced 157 tons; submerged 213 tons.
Dimensions: length 106ft 7in (32.5m); beam 12t 10in (3.9m); draught 8ft (2.5m).
Propulsion: triple-expansion steam engine, one boiler, 250ihp; one elec motor, 100shp; one shaft.
Performance: surface – 9.8kt, 600nm/8kt; submerged – 6kt; range 55nm/3.
Weapons: 4 x 17.7in (450mm) Drzewiecki drop-collars (4 torpedoes).
Complement: 13.
Specifications are for Saran-class (see text), as built.

History: *Narval* was among the first steam-electric submarines and won 1896 design competition for a boat with ranges of 100nm on the surface 10nm submerged. Operationally, the design was a submersible torpedo-b which spent most of its time on the surface, but which could submerge wr necessary. The oil-fired tubular boilers drove a triple-expansion steam engine surface propulsion and battery charging, although it took 20 minutes (la reduced to 12) to blow-off steam before diving. Other innovations were double-hull design with the ballast tanks between the hulls, a pattern follov by many successors to this day.

The Saran-class was the production version, slightly shorter, with an 11 increase in displacement and marginally more powerful engine. Major effe were made to reduce the diving time, but it still took 6-9 minutes, although

---

Pluviôse/Archimède-classes

Total built: Pluviôse – 18; Archimède – 1.
Completed: Pluviôse – 1908-11; Archimède – 1909.
Displacement: surfaced 398 tons; submerged 550 tons.
Dimensions: length 167ft 4in (51.1m); beam 16ft 4in (4.9m); draught 16ft (3.0m).
Propulsion: reciprocating steam engine, two boilers, 700ihp; two elec motors, 450shp; two shafts.
Performance: surface – 12kt, 1,500nm/9kt; submerged – 8kt, 50nm/5kt.
Weapons: 1 x 4 x 17.7in (450mm) TT (bow); 2 x Drzewiecki drop-collars torpedoes), 4 x cradles (4 torpedoes).
Complement: 24.
Specifications are for Pluviôse-class, as built.

History: Built to a design by the famous French naval architect, Laubeuf, th were numerically the largest class of steam-powered submarines ever b They were powered by reciprocating steam engines and, while they took t to blow off steam, lower the funnel and seal the vents, they were g seaboats and served throughout World War I. Six were lost: three san collisions with merchant ships, one collided with a battleship, and two w destroyed by Austro-Hungarian surface warships.

Archimède was an improved version of the Pluviôse-class, somew longer (197ft/60.5m overall) and with considerably more powerful machine 1,700ihp compared to 700ihp. The design was considered a great success the boat sank four enemy transports during the war. It was stricken in 191

The steam propulsion system was found adequate in the Mediterran

ove: French **Narval***, one of the first steam-electric boats.*

s not too serious a disadvantage in the early 20th century. Although the
ice of steam seems perverse by modern standards, it should be
embered that at the time these boats were being built the alternative for
face propulsion and battery-charging was either gasoline engines, which
e very dangerous, or kerosene engines which were smelly and emitted a
se cloud of white smoke. *Narval* was stricken in 1909, but the four Saran-
s boats all survived World War I, to be stricken in 1919.

in French coastal waters, but some of this class were sent into the North
during the war, where their low freeboard was a disadvantage, while the
nel and its associated watertight valve system were always vulnerable.

ow: No fewer than 18 of the **Pluviôse***-class were built.*

Gustave Zédé/
Dupuy de Lôme

Total built: Gustave Zédé – 1 (see notes); Dupuy de Lôme – 2.
Completed: Gustave Zédé - 1913; Dupuy de Lôme - 1915-16.
Displacement: surfaced 833 tons; submerged 1,287 tons.
Dimensions: length 246ft 1in (75.0m); beam 21ft 0in (6.4m); draught 11ft
(3.6m).
Propulsion: Delaunay-Belleville 3-cylinder reciprocating steam engines
two du Temple boilers, 3,500ihp; two electric motors, 1,640shp; two shafts
Performance: surface – 17kt, 2,350nm/10kt; submerged – 11kt, 120nm/5k
Weapons: 6 x 17.7in (450mm) TT (bow – 2; inboard 4) (8 torpedoes);
external cradles (2 torpedoes).
Complement: 43..
Specifications are for Dupuy de Lôme, as built.

History: Although separate classes, the specifications and histories of th
two groups of two boats each are so similar are treated together. *Gustave Z*
was the lead-ship of a two-ship class, but while she was powered by a ste
unit, the other boat, *Néréide*, was powered by Schneider-Carels diesels (
diesel-electric section). *Gustave Zédé* was powered by Delaunay-Belleville u
identical to those in the Dupuy de Lôme-class, as shown above; the latter c
was marginally longer, 246ft (75.0m) compared to 242ft 9in (74.0m), and h
slightly greater displacement, 1,287 tons versus 1,098 tons, but t

Swordfish

Total built: 1.
Completed: 1916.
Displacement: surfaced 932 tons; submerged 1,105 tons.
Dimensions: length 231ft 4in (70.5m); beam 22ft 11in (7.0m); draught
11in (4.5m).
Propulsion: Parsons geared impulse reaction steam turbines, one Yar
boiler, 4,000ihp; 2 x electric motors, 1,400shp; 2 batteries, each of 64 c
two shafts.
Performance: surface – 18kt, 3,000nm at 8.5kt; submerged – 10kt.
Weapons: 2 x 21in (533mm) TT (bow) (2 x torpedoes); 4 x 18in (457mm
(beam) (8 x torpedoes); 2 x 3in (76mm) guns.
Complement: 42.

History: One of the requirements set by the Admiralty's Subma
Committee in 1912 was for an "overseas" submarine with a 1,000-
displacement and a surface speed of 20kt. The Italian designer Ces
Laurenti submitted a bid, which was initially rejected in favour of *Nau*
(qv) but was later accepted, and an order was placed with Scott fc
modified version. The power required for such a high speed could
produced only by steam propulsion and *Swordfish* became the Royal Na
first steam-powered submarine, being powered by Parsons gea
turbines, although even with these an absolute maximum of 18kt wa
that could be achieved. The funnel was raised and lowered electrically
was the watertight cover, an operation which took about 1.5 minu
although blowing-off steam took considerably longer. As with all ste

aments were identical. After World War I, however, all three were fitted
diesels removed from surrendered German U-boats, and in the same refit
arged bunkers were installed together with new bridges and ventilation
tems. Guns were also mounted, usually one 75mm gun.

The official performance figures for both classes include a submerged
ed of 11kt and radius of 120nm at 5kt for the Dupuy de Lôme-class and
ntly more for the Gustave Zédé-class, both of which are difficult to believe.

ow: **Sané *(de Lôme-class), as completed in 1916.***

vered submarines there was considerable heat and condensation below,
ulting in frequent short-circuits at the main switchboard and several
ries. The boat was also unstable when surfacing and submerging, rolling
uch an extent as to alarm the crew. Various Italian features, particularly
regard to safety, impressed the British, but overall the design was a
re and after lengthy trials she was converted into a surface patrol boat,
vhich she also failed to excel.

ow: **Swordfish*, the first British steam-powered submarine.***

K/K-26-classes

GREAT BRIT

Total built: K – 17; K26-class – 1.
Completed: K – 1917-18 ; K-26 class – 1923.
Displacement: surfaced 1,980 tons; submerged 2,566 tons.
Dimensions: length 339ft 0in (103.4m); beam 26ft 7in (8.1m); draught 17ft 0in (5.
Propulsion: Brown-Curtis or Parsons geared steam turbines, two Yar
boilers, 10,500bhp; 1 x "E-class" auxiliary diesel, 800bhp; 4 x electric mot
1,440shp, two shafts.
Performance: surface – 24kt, 3,000nm/13.5kt; submerged – 9kt, 13.5nm/
maximum operational depth 200ft (61m).
Weapons: 10 x 18in (457mm) TT (bow – 4; beam – 4; revolving mount – 2)
torpedoes); 2 x 4in (102mm) guns; 1 x 3in (76mm) AA.
Complement: 59.
Specifications are for K-class, as built.

History: The Royal Navy remained committed to a high surface speed, i
increased to 24kt. This could be achieved only with eight of the latest di
engines, which was clearly impracticable; so a further attempt was mad
steam-propulsion, the outcome being the notorious K-class. By the standar
the day, they were large and very complicated boats and were offic
described as double-hulled although, in fact, the outer hull was abreast
upper half of the pressure hull only, and did not totally envelope it. As origi
built, the K-class had a long low bow (similar to the Nautilus-class), wi
narrow superstructure from the enclosed bridge (the first in the Royal Navy
to include the funnels. It was originally intended to mount 21in (533
torpedo tubes but only 18in (457mm) tubes were available and were u
instead, with four in the bow, four in the beam and two in a rotating moun
the superstructure, intended for use in night surface operations. There w
single 4in (102mm) mount fore and aft and a 3in (76mm) mount on
superstructure.

The steam units worked well but became excessively hot and humid, w
the funnels, watertight hatches and vents could be closed in 30 sec
although small obstructions could prevent the latter closing, thus endange
the boat and its crew. Normal diving time was about 5 minutes, although
boat achieved 3 minutes 25 seconds. A major feature was the auxiliary die
which was used for a quick get-away while steam was being raised, either f
port or after surfacing, which took about 20 minutes. Most boats could exc

Below: K-3 in original condition with low bow.

ove: **K-26** *had many modifications, including a raised bow.*

t on the surface but endurance submerged was very poor – 30nm at 4kt and
m at 1.5kt.
  Problems were quickly found once the first boats entered service. The bow
pe resulted in a very "wet" boat, so a new bulbous "swan" bow was
ed, which required another deck-level on the bridge to see over the top. The
vard 4in (102mm) gun and the revolving torpedo mount in the
erstructure proved unusable and were removed. There was some talk of
unting a single 5.5in (140mm) gun but as far as is known this never
pened, although some boats were fitted with depth-charge throwers in
8. In addition, extra fans were fitted in the boiler room to reduce
perature and humidity.
  A total of 17 K-class boats was completed, of which 13 survived World War
be sold between 1921-26. *K-1* was lost in a collision with *K-4* off the Danish
st (November 1917) and *K-5* foundered in the Bay of Biscay (January 1921),
le *K-13* sank during builder's trials but was raised and returned to service as
2, being sold in 1926. The most infamous event in the K-class history,
ever, was the ironically named "Battle of May Island" (31 January 1918)
en nine K-class boats put to sea from Rosyth, Scotland, in company with a
nber of battlecruisers, at night and at a speed of 20kt. During this operation
4's helm jammed, initiating a complicated series of collisions that resulted in
sinking of two K-class boats, severe damage to three more and the loss of
r 100 lives – and all without any enemy involvement whatsoever.
  In an effort to overcome all the shortcomings a modified class was
gned, of which only *K-26* was actually completed. The hull was longer
ft/107m) and displacement increased to 2,530 tons. All three 4in (102mm)
s were mounted on the superstructure, which was lengthened and raised
(0.9m) compared with the earlier boats. Torpedo armament was
ngthened by installing six 21in (533mm) tubes in the bow (12 torpedoes),
ough the four 18in (457mm) beam tubes (eight torpedoes) were retained,
were removed in 1929. The machinery was the same, resulting in a slightly
ver maximum speed, while a rearrangement of the tanks made diving very
ch quicker. The improved design was considered superior in every way and
were ordered in 1918, although only *K-26* was ever completed. She entered
ice in 1923 and was scrapped in 1931.

Nuclear-powered Attack Submarines (SSNs)

From the very first, submariners dreamt of a vessel that would be comple free of the surface for long periods, but they were frustrated by tl factors. Electric storage batteries consumed no oxygen, but could hold or strictly limited charge before they had to be replenished. Such recharging c only be done by diesel engines, which needed oxygen to work, and this m that the boat had to surface, thus becoming vulnerable to enemy action. Tl these batteries could not produce enough power both to propel the vessel to sustain life for a protracted period. Nuclear power, however, changed all and its potential for use in submarines was seen from about 1942 onwards

The first American nuclear-powered submarine (SSN) was completed in 1 after an almost unparalleled development effort, giving the USA an estimated years' lead over the Soviet Union. Later in the Cold War the Soviet Union over the United States in numbers of SSNs and by the 1980s was approaching United States in terms of quality as well – perhaps being even ahead in some ar But the end of the Cold War and the collapse of the Soviet Union, both polit and financially, has left the United States Navy pre-eminent.

The main stream of development has been large, multi-purpose bc powered by pressurised-water nuclear reactors, but there have been nume attempts to find different or more effective solutions. Both the Americans the former Soviet Union tried liquid metal-cooled reactors, which hold out promise of considerably greater efficiency and power for a given weight early U.S. attempt was *Seawolf* (SSN-575) but this was abandoned after

years and the reactor replaced by a conventional pressurised-water
tem. The Soviets tested their system in the remarkable Alfa-class SSNs, but
proved highly complicated to operate, the type achieving the unusual
inction of requiring an all-officer crew.

In the early years of the 21st century the U.S. Navy is equipped almost
lusively with Los Angeles-class SSNs, with just two of the older Sturgeons
and two out of three Seawolf (SSN-21)-class in service and a third
roaching completion, while work on the first four Virginia-class has already
ted. Together these form the largest and most capable attack submarine
:e in the world. In contrast, the Russian Navy is now but a shadow of its
ner self. In its heyday, the Soviet Navy operated a large, well-equipped and
ective force of attack submarines, and in the 1970s and '80s their SSNs were
world leaders. But that is no more and today they probably have fewer than
SSNs even nominally in service. Many of those are in a sad state of disrepair,
there is no certainty that a successor class will ever reach production.

Among the second rank navies the British operate a small and efficient SSN
lla, as do the French. Both have a successor class under development. The
y other navy with SSNs in service is China's PLA-N, and its force will
loubtedly increase in both quantity and quality. India is known to have an
N under development and Brazil is known to aspire to such status.

ow: British Swiftsure-class SSN, HMS Splendid.

Han-class

Total built: 5.
Completed: 1970-90.
Displacement: surfaced 4,500 tons; submerged 5,000 tons.
Dimensions: length 295ft 4in (90.0m); beam 29ft 6in (9.0m); draught 24ft (7.4m).
Propulsion: 1 x pressurised-water nuclear reactor, 48mW; 2 x steam turbir 12,000shp; one shaft.
Performance: surface – 25kt; submerged – 30kt; maximum operating de 984ft (300m).
Weapons: 6 x 21in (533mm) TT (bow).
Complement: 75.
Specifications for #401, as built.

History: This was a most important project, being not only China's first indiger submarine design, but also her first nuclear-powered submarine. The Chinese N (PLA-N) had acquired Soviet diesel-electric submarines in the late 1940s and sta to produce Soviet designs under license in the 1950s, but despite being s beginners the high command quickly understood the importance of nuc propulsion. As a result, a national programme was started in the mid-1950s, w led to the first SSN being laid down in 1968 and launched in 1971, although it not become fully operational until the early 1980s, due to problems with propulsion system. Construction then continued slowly with the second hull b launched in 1977, but both then underwent a lengthy refit/reconstruction in 1980s. Meanwhile, three more were launched (in 1983, 1987 and 1! respectively) which were 26ft 3in (8.0m) longer than the first two and incorpor; additional weapons and equipment.

This was not only the PLA-N's first nuclear-propelled submarine design, was also the first with a shorter, fatter "Albacore" hull and single propelle

Below: The Han-class was a sophisticated design for its era.

ove: Han-class SSN of the Chinese PLA-Navy.

ce of the traditional long, thin, twin-propeller design. The Han is certainly not
opy of any other design, but it is of classic SSN layout, with an Albacore-type
and diving planes mounted high on the forward-mounted sail. All five were
t at Huladao, entering service in 1974 (#401), 1980 (#402), 1984 (#403),
38 (#404) and 1991 (#405); all serve in the North Sea Fleet.

In one well-publicised incident a Han-class boat tracked the USS *Kitty Hawk*
rier battle-group in the Yellow Sea for several days in October 1994. A U.S.
vy S-3 Viking patrol aircraft detected the submarine when it was some
)nm from the carrier and heading in the direction of the carrier at periscope
oth. The submarine came within 20nm of *Kiitty Hawk* before turning away
it seems clear that its commander meant to be seen so as to make it clear
t there was a new challenge to U.S. naval supremacy in the area. A
cessor class (Project 093) is being designed with assistance from the Rubin
sign Bureau of St. Petersburg, Russia.

Rubis/Amethyste-classes (SNA-72)

FRAN

Total built: Rubis 4; Amethyste 2.
Completed: Rubis 1983-88; Amethyste 1992-93.
Displacement: surfaced (Rubis) 2,388 tons, (Amethyste) 2,410 to submerged (both) 2,670 tons.
Dimensions: length (Rubis) 236ft 6in (72.1m), (Amethyste) 241ft 6in (73.6 beam (both) 24ft 10in (7.6m); draught (both) 21ft 0in (6.4m).
Propulsion: 1 x CAS 48 pressurised-water nuclear reactor, 48mW; 2 x tu alternator sets, each 3,950kW; 1 x electric motor, 9500shp; 1 x SE Pielstick/Jeumont Schneider 8PA4V185SM diesel-electric auxiliary eng 450kW; 1 x battery-driven emergency motor; one shaft.
Performance: submerged – 25kt; operational diving depth 984ft (300m).
Weapons: 4 x 21in (533mm) TT (bow); 14 x missiles/torpedoes.
Complement: 66 (two crews).

History: In France, President De Gaulle exerted such strong pressure on French Navy to produce a nuclear deterrent capability that all efforts w concentrated on development of ballistic missiles and the submarines to ca them, and the development of nuclear-propelled attack submarines deliberately postponed. Thus, it was not until 1974 that an SSN developm programme was started, with the first of the Rubis-class being laid dow December 1976 and launched in 1979; it then underwent extensive trials did not join the fleet until 1983.

As built, the Rubis-class were the smallest SSNs in any navy, their hull des armament, sonar and fire control systems being closely based on those of Augusta-class diesel-electric submarines (qv). However, the design proved to

*Below: The original Rubis-class
proved to be somewhat noisy,
leading to the more refined and
quieter Amethyste-class.*

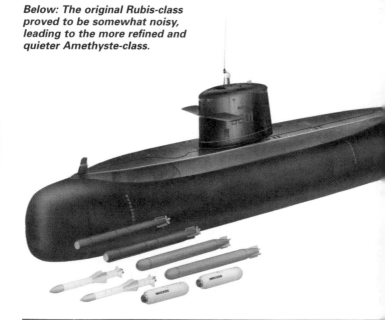

...ove: French Amethyste-class SSN.

...prisingly noisy, which led to the *Amethyste* programme (<u>AME</u>lioration <u>T</u>actique ...drodynamique <u>S</u>ilence <u>T</u>ransmission <u>E</u>coute), which was introduced into the fifth ...class (coincidentally also called *Amethyste*) and the sixth, *Perle,* while building. ... *Amethyste* programme also involved changes to sonar and other ASW ...ipment to match the change in role from anti-ship to anti-submarine.

   Amethyste and *Perle* are longer than the earlier boats – 241.5ft (73.6m) as opposed to 236.5ft (72.1m) – and have a revised bow form, a new sonar, a towed sonar array, a more streamlined superstructure, and improved electronics. Once the new build standard had proved itself, the first four boats were rebuilt between 1989 and 1995, with a new bow section which increased their length to that of *Amethyste*. *Saphir* recommissioned in July 1991, *Rubis* in February 1993, *Casabianca* in June 1994 and *Emeraude* in late 1995. All six boats are based at Toulon but frequently deploy to the Atlantic and, unusually among SSNs, they are operated with two ...ws. Normal endurance is limited to 45 days by the stock of food that can be ...ried, although this can be extended to 60 days if operationally necessary.

   Rubis collided with a tanker on 17 July 1993 and had to undergo extensive ...airs. *Emeraude* suffered a serious steam leak on 30 March 1994 while ...merged, which caused 10 deaths among the crew, including that of the ...mmanding officer. The casualities were in the compartment containing the ... turbo-alternators and were not associated with the nuclear plant.

   The next class of French SSN is to be known as the Barracuda-class and, ...ording to current information, will have a displacement of 4,500 tons. Six ...ts are scheduled to be built, with the Rubis-class being stricken one-for-one ...the new boats enter service between 2010 and 2020.

Dreadnought-class

Total built: 1.
Completed: 1963.
Displacement: surfaced 3,000 tons; submerged 4,000 tons.
Dimensions: length 265ft 9in (81.0m); beam 32ft 3in (9.8m); draught 26ft (7.9m).
Propulsion: 1 x Rolls-Royce/Westinghouse S5W pressurised-water nuc reactor, 2 x geared steam turbines, 15,000shp; diesel-electric auxil propulsion; one shaft.
Performance: surface – 15kt; submerged – 28kt.
Weapons: 6 x 21in (533mm) TT (bow); 24 x torpedoes.
Complement: 88.

History: Britain initiated the study of the possibility of nuclear propulsion submarines in 1946, although for several years it was considered that Walter system might provide a viable and less expensive alternative (Explorer-class). It was soon realised that systems based on hydrogen pero> were too dangerous and in 1953 a naval section was established at the Ato Warfare Research Establishment (AWRE), Harwell, which initiated studie cooperation with the Admiralty, Vickers-Armstrong, Rolls-Royce and Fos Wheeler. The outcome was a land-based prototype submarine reactor, bui the nuclear research establishment at Dounreay in Scotland; work starte spring 1958 and it went critical in 1965.

Design of this British propulsion system was based on that of the U Navy's Westinghouse S5W pressurised water-cooled reactor, but it was

Valiant-class

Total built: 5.
Completed: 1966-71.
Displacement: surfaced 4,000 tons; submerged 4,900 tons.
Dimensions: length 285ft 0in (86.9m); beam 33ft 3in (10.1m); draught 27ft (8.2m).
Propulsion: 1 x Rolls-Royce PWR.1 pressurised-water nuclear reactor, gea steam-turbine, 15,000shp; 1 x diesel-electric propulsion system; 1 x 112 battery; one shaft.
Performance: surfaced – 20kt; submerged – 28kt.
Weapons: 6 x 21in (533mm) TT (bow); 26 x torpedoes.
Complement: 103.

History: The Valiants were the first class of entirely British SSNs, the first b being ordered in August 1960 and completed in June 1966, followed by second, *Warspite*, completed in 1967. There was then a three-year gap be the last three, *Churchill, Conqueror* and *Courageous*, were completed in 1971, and these are sometimes listed as a separate class, although differences were no more than progressive modifications to be expected in lengthy production run and they are shown here as one class. The design v generally similar to that of *Dreadnought*, but the hull was 19ft (5.8m) lon mainly in order to accommodate the slightly larger Rolls-Royce PWR.1 nuc reactor. The crew was also larger – 103 compared to 88.

In 1967 *Valiant* travelled 10,000 miles (16,100km) submerged fr Singapore to the UK in 28 days. *Conqueror* is the only SSN in any navy to h sunk an enemy warship in combat, having launched two Mk VIII torped

ove: **Dreadnought, *the Royal Navy's first SSN.***

ady in time for HMS *Dreadnought*. So, in order to get a British SSN to sea
quickly as possible, a complete S5W was bought from the USA and
stalled in *Dreadnought*, which was launched in October 1960 and
mmissioned in April 1963. The bow section of this boat, containing the
pe 2001 sonar, was of entirely British design and was much blunter than
ntemporary U.S. designs.

    Dreadnought was a fully operational attack submarine. She was laid up
1983, the nuclear reactor was dismantled and the core removed; she was
en placed in storage, where she remains.

ainst the Argentinian
uiser *General Belgrano* on
May 1982 during the
klands War.

    Starting in 1988 the
actors began to show
ns of age and it was
cided not to modernise
ese boats, as had been
eviously planned. They
re accordingly decom-
ssioned between 1990
d 1992 and their reactors
cored.

ght: **Valiant-class SSN**
ds a torpedo. One of
s class, Conqueror, *is*
e only SSN to sink an
emy ship in combat.

Swiftsure-class

Total built: 6.
Completed: 1973-81.
Displacement: surfaced 4,400 tons; submerged 4,900 tons.
Dimensions: length 272ft 0in (82.9m); beam 32ft 4in (9.8m); draught 27ft (8.2m).
Propulsion: 1 x Rolls-Royce PWR.1 pressurised-water nuclear reactor, 2 x GE Alsthom geared steam-turbines, 15,000shp; Paxman auxiliary diesel, 4,000b 1 x 112-cell battery; one shaft.
Performance: surface – 20kt; submerged – 30kt.
Weapons: 5 x 21in (533mm) TT (bow); 21 x torpedoes, 4 x Sub-Harpoon Tomahawk SLCM.
Complement: 116.

History: The third class of British SSNs was the six-strong Swiftsure-class, the f of which joined the fleet in April 1973. The hull was 13ft (4m) shorter than Valiants with a flat outer casing giving a completely different appearance to tha the humped-back of the earlier SSN classes. This new, shorter, fatter shape evidence of the greater internal volume of the pressure hull, giving more equipm space and better living conditions. The diving planes are set very much lower a are not visible when the boats are on the surface. There are five torpedo tubes a 25 weapons are carried, usually, 21 torpedoes and four missiles.

These boats introduced a number of significant improvements o previous British submarines. One of these was a conformal covering anechoic tiles on the hull and sail, which was intended to pro-vide a dramatic

---

Trafalgar-class

Total built: 7.
Completed: 1983-91.
Displacement: surfaced 4,740 tons; submerged 5,208 tons.
Dimensions: length 280ft 2in (85.4m); beam 32ft 2in (9.8m); draught 27ft (8.3m).
Propulsion: 1 x Rolls-Royce PWR.1 pressurised-water nuclear reactor, t GEC steam turbines, 11.2mW (15,000bhp); two Paxman diesel alternato 2.1mW (2,800hp); one shaft, pump-jet propulsor.
Performance: submerged – 32kt.; maximum diving depth in excess of 98 (300m).
Endurance: 85 days.
Weapons: 5 x 21in (533mm) TT (bow); 25 x torpedoes, Sub-Harpoon Tomahawk SLCM.
Complement: 130.

History: Seven Trafalgar-class boats were completed between 1983 and 19 making this the largest class of SSNs built for the Royal Navy. All w constructed by VSEL at Barrow-in-Furness and they replaced the orig *Dreadnought* and the Valiant-class. The design was essentially an "improv Swiftsure" but with refinements to ensure that it was both faster and m quieter, as well as having greater endurance. One of the quietening measu is that both the pressure hull and all outer surfaces are covered with confor anechoic noise reduction tiles using new adhesives which reduces the num of tiles lost on a voyage.

The Trafalgar-class have the same beam as the Swiftsure-class, but are

ht: Superb, of the iftsure-class. UK Ns do not have l-mounted droplanes.

:tion in the acoustic nature. These were the first boats to fitted with a pump- propulsor – in ence a truncated ical shroud sur- nding the propeller des – a major sign feature which now been pted by many er navies.

Swiftsure was undergoing a long refit in the early 1990s when a major blem with the reactor was discovered; as a result, she was retired in 1992. e remainder were all refitted in the 1990s, which included being modified launch Tomahawk cruise missiles. A number have suffered from blems with their nuclear reactors, mainly cracking, which have required ly extensive repairs, thus reducing operational availability. Retirement es are: *Splendid* – 2003; *Sovereign* – 2005; *Spartan* – 2006; *Superb* –)7; and *Sceptre* – 2008.

ove: Trafalgar-class SSN, Tireless.

1in (2.5m) longer, and are built of NQ-1 steel, which is equivalent to the U
Navy's HY80. There are three decks divided into four pressure-ti
compartments, with escape hatches fore and aft. The forward hydroplanes
retractable and the sail is strengthened for under-ce operations.

The Royal Navy had been engaged in debate for some time about the r

November-class
(Project 627A)

RUS

Total built: 14.
Completed: 1959-63.
Displacement: surfaced 4,500 tons; submerged 5,300 tons.
Dimensions: length 363ft 11in (110.0m); beam 29ft 6in (9.0m); draught 25ft
(7.7m).
Propulsion: 2 x VI-A pressurised-water nuclear reactors, each 70mW;
2 x turbines, each 17,500shp; 2 x creep electric motors , each 450shp;
shafts.
Performance: surface – 15kt; submerged – 30kt; maximum operational di
depth 984ft (300m).
Weapons: 8 x 21in (533mm) TT (bow); 24 torpedoes.
Complement: 80.

History: These large and generally conservatively designed boats were the
Soviet submarines to have nuclear propulsion. All were built at Severodv
between 1959 and 1963. To a certain degree the technology was based
information gained through espionage from the United States in 1955, altho
it would seem that, at that time, the Soviet designers failed to appreciate

neration submarine to replace the Swiftsure-class. Initially, there was going be an entirely new design, the "SSN-20" (also known as the "W-class"), ich, among other features, would have been powered by a modified version the PWR-2 used in the Vanguard-class SSBNs. By 1990, however, it had come clear that unit cost (not including R&D) would be of the order of £400 lion and this, coupled with the rapidly reducing defence budget led to the ject being cancelled in 1991. It was then decided to go for a less ambitious sign, which was originally known as the "Batch 2 Trafalgar-class" (frequently reviated to "B2TC"), which implies that the submarines will be straight velopments of the original Trafalgars (which, by inference, have now come "Batch 1 Trafalgars"). The name has, however, been changed to Astute-class, of which three are currently under construction with neduled in-service dates of 2005, 2007 and 2008, with a further three to ordered shortly.

The new SSN will be powered by a derivative of the PWR.2 which powers the Vanguard-class SSBNs, and it will incorporate all the weapon systems, sensor and command-and-control improvements going into the Trafalgar-class. The Astute-class will also have fully reelable towed arrays rather than the clip-on type currently used.

Left: Trafalgars can launch a wide array of weapons, and in addition to the torpedoes, mines and Sub-Harpoon seen here, can now launch Tomahawk land-attack cruise-missiles.

ove: The November-class were the first Soviet SSNs.

antages of the "teardrop" hull, which had been under test in the United tes since 1953 (see Albacore-class). Accordingly, the November-class had classic long, conventional hull with two propellers. There were two arate power-trains, both of which were required for maximum speed, but ough cross connections one turbine could power both shafts in the cruise ime. The nuclear reactors were the VI-A and were identical to those used in

Above: A November-class SSN in distress in October 1970.

the contemporary SSBNs and SSGNs, hence the NATO designation HEN (H—
Echo-November). By 1963 a total of 14 had been built, the production
continuing despite the fact that the design had been overtaken by |

Victor I/II/III-classes
RUS:

History: The first Victor was laid down in 1965 and entered service in 1⊆
following which the class was built at the Admiralty Yard, Leningrad, at a
of two per year until 1974, when it was succeeded on the ways by the Vict
class. The Victor was the first Soviet submarine with a "body-of-revoluti
hull, similar to, but by no means based on, the U.S. Navy's Albacore hull-fo
It was also the first Soviet SSN to have its two nuclear reactors positioned s

Class	Victor I	Victor II	Victor III
Project	671	671RT	671RTM
Total built	15	7	26
Completed	1967- 76	1972-1978	1977-1991
Displacement surfaced submerged	4,300 tons 5,100 tons	4,500 tons 5,700 tons	4,900 tons 6,000 tons
Dimensions length beam draught	311ft 8in (95.0m) 32ft 10in (10,0m) 23ft 0in (7.0m)	334ft 6in (102m) 32ft 10in (10.0m) 23ft 0in (7.0m)	341ft 2in (104n 32ft 10in (10.0⎯ 23ft 0in (7.0m)

hnology, illustrating the inflexibility of Soviet construction programmes, allied
heir preference for long production runs.

Four of the class suffered from reactor accidents and one, *K-8*, sank in the
antic off Cape Finisterre in April 1970 after a reactor-related fire; all the crew
e saved. The surviving boats were stricken between 1989 and 1991.

pulsion		
ctor	2 x VM-4P nuclear	
am-turbines	two sets	
wer	30,000shp	
afts	one	
ep motor	two (2 x 505shp)	
Ltery	2 x 112 cells (8,000 amp/hour)	
rformance		
omerged	30kt	28kt
ximum		
erating depth	1,312ft (400m)	
durance	80 days	
eapons		
es	6 x 21in (533mm)	2 x 21in (533mm), 2 x torpedoes
oedoes	18 x torpedoes	4 x 25in (650mm), 12 x SS-N-16
mplement:	94	

side, which not only reduced the length, but also provided an excess of
ver, which came in very useful later in the development of the longer-hulled
or II and III. Armament consisted of six 21in (533mm) torpedo tubes,
itioned in two horizontal rows, with two in the top row, four in the lower, but

Above: Successor to the November, a Victor-class SSN at sea.

Right: Victor I was highly effective at the time it appeared.

the two outer tubes in the bottom row were outside the pressure hull and t
non-reloadable. The main shaft ended in a five-bladed propeller, and there w
also two more auxiliary propulsion units for "creep" movement. One Vict
was damaged beyond repair during refit in 1985 and the remainder w
stricken between 1993 and 1996.

The Victor II was redesigned and lengthened in order to accommodate
SS-N-16 system. These missiles were launched from 25.6in (650mm) tuk
which replaced the four internally mounted and reloadable tubes. The
externally mounted, non-reloadable 21in tubes remained, being used for ei
conventional torpedoes or the ultra high-speed *Shkval* missile. Seven Victo
were built and all were stricken between the early 1990s and 1997.

*Below: The Victors were the first Soviet SSNs
with "body-of-revolution" hull. Note also the
large pod on the rudder which housed a trailing-
wire sonar and its winch.*

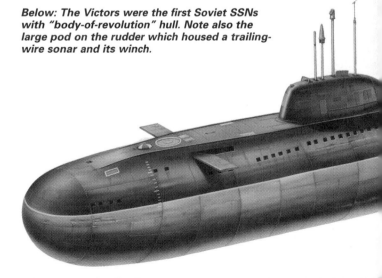

Finally came the Victor III, which was essentially a longer and tidied version of Victor II with a more comprehensive sensor fit and impro silencing; a total of 26 units were built. The Victor III was 43ft (13.2m) lor than Victor II, but the most visible difference was a large streamlined mounted atop the stern fin, which housed a towed sonar array dispenser. Wi environment sensors were also mounted at the front of the fin and on forward casing as in the Akula II and Sierra classes (qqv). Increme improvements were made to the design and the last nine of the class w even quieter than the others. One of the class had a trials installation for SS 21 SLCM mounted on the forward casing and was sometimes referred to

Alfa-class (Project 705)

RUS

Total built: 7.
Completed: 1972-83.
Displacement: surfaced 2,800 tons; submerged 3,680 tons.
Dimensions: length 267ft 1in (81.4m); beam 31ft 2in (9.5m); draught 23ft (7.0m).
Propulsion: 2 x liquid-metal cooled nuclear reactors, 45,000shp; one shaft.
Performance: submerge – 43-45kt; maximum operating depth 2,300ft (700)
Weapons: 6 x 21in (533mm) TT (bow); 18 x torpedoes/SS-N-15 missiles.
Complement: 31 (all officers).

History: The Alfa-class was remarkable for its time in three respects. First v its very high speed which was due to its very powerful, liquid-metal coc nuclear reactors. Second, was its deep diving depth, which was made poss by the exceptional strength of its titanium hull. Finally, there was its very sr crew of 31 men, the result of an exceptional degree of automation, althou uniquely, they were all officers. The first boat was completed in 1971 underwent three years' trials before being broken up in 1974, possibly beca the liquid metal coolant was inadvertently allowed to solidify. The remaining boats, all of which took much longer than usual to build, entered ser between 1979 and 1983.

The relatively short overall length (267ft/81m compared to 312ft/95m f Victor I), combined with the high submerged speed of some 45kt, indica very sophisticated hydrodynamic design and the use of laminar f techniques. The hull was constructed of titanium, a material which comb lightness with great strength and resulted in the great diving de

Victor IV (Type 671 RTMK). Early Victor IIIs had a seven-bladed propeller, but ne Victor IIs and most Victor IIIs had an unusual propeller, which consisted wo, tandem, four-blade, co-rotating units mounted at 22.5 degrees to each er on the same shaft. It is assumed that this offered some acoustic antage, although it was not repeated on any other Russian submarines, and s replaced by a seven-bladed type in the surviving Victor IIIs in the late)0s. A total of 26 Victor IIIs were built, but by 2002 only eight remained in vice.

ow: Victor III; the pod caused great interest in the West.

ove: Alfa-class, powered by liquid-metal nuclear reactors.

-60ft/750m crush depth), but this metal is very difficult to work and even the at Russian metallurgical expertise did not allow production of more than a of these submarines.

The lead-bismuth liquid-metal reactors provided exceptional power density, ng these boats an underwater speed well in excess of 40kt. This was onstrated when one ran under a NATO convoy during an exercise in the th Atlantic; it was a deliberate demonstration of its performance, and one ch caused consternation in Western naval circles. The Alfa generated siderable noise at such a speed, which enabled surface warships to track its gress with great precision, but it also showed them that in war they would have no means of counteracting it. This led to urgent NATO programme[s] develop much deeper diving and faster torpedoes, resulting in the Bri[tish] Spearfish and the U.S. Navy's Mk48 ADCAP and Mk50.

One boat was scrapped in 1988 and another four were defuelled [and] scrapped in 1992/93. The remaining boat had an accident in 1982 which le[d to] a very lengthy rebuild in which she was fitted with an experimental type[of] pressurised-water reactor. After a period of trials, she, too, was scrapped in [the] mid-1990s.

Below: The Alfa's exceptional performance – it once went under a NA[TO] convoy at over 40 knots – led to vast expenditure in Western navies t[o] developing submarines and torpedoes that could catch it.

Sierra I/II-class
(Project 945)

RUS[SIA]

History: The Sierra-class was built in parallel to the Akula-class (qv), with [two] Sierra Is completed in 1984 and 1987, followed by two Sierra IIs in 1990 [and] 1993. A fifth boat (Project 945B, which would probably have received the N[ATO]

Class	Sierra I	Sierra II
Project	945	945A
Total built	2	2
Completed	1987	1990-93
Displacement surfaced submerged	6,300 tons 8,300 tons	6,470 tons 8,500 tons
Dimensions length beam draught	351 ft 0in (107.0m) 54ft 2in (16.5m) 28ft 11in (8.8m)	362ft 6in (110.5m) 54ft 2in (16.5m) 30ft 9in (9.4m)

pulsion		
ctor	1 x OK-650A pressurised-water	1 x OK-650B pressurised-water
⸱o-alternators	two	two
⸱ver	190mW	190mW
fts	one	one
⸱ep motor	two (2 x 750shp)	two (2 x 750shp)
formance		
⸱face	12kt	12kt
⸱merged	33.6kt	33.6kt
⸱ximum		
⸱rating depth	1,804ft (550m)	1,970ft (600m)
durance	90 days	100 days
apons		
⸱es	4 x 25.6in (650mm) 4 x 21in (533mm)	8 x 25.6in (650mm)
⸱pedoes	40 x torpedoes/SS-N-16 missiles	40 x torpedoes/SS-N-16 missiles
mplement	59	61

gnation Sierra III) was cancelled during construction in 1992 and scrapped.
The original Sierra I was slightly smaller than the Akula and its primary

mission was to attack U.S. and other NATO naval task groups, with a secon
mission against coastal targets. Its performance and capabilities were gene
comparable with the U.S. Navy's earlier Los Angeles-class SSNs, althoug
internal quietening systems and a coating of anechoic tiles, designated "Clu
Guard" by NATO, were reported to give it a superior acoustic performanc
huge torpedo room gave it a capacity of no fewer than 40 torpedoes
missiles for its eight torpedo tubes, four 21in (533mm) and four 25.6in (650r
tubes. Like the Alfa-class it had a titanium hull. Two were built, followed by
two Sierra IIs some years later.

Below: The Sierra shows its weapons and sensors.

Akula-class

Class	Akula I	Improved Akula I	Akula II
Project No	971	971U	971A
Total built (see text)	6	3	1
Completed	1984-90	1992-95	1996-2000
Displacement surfaced submerged	8,140 tons 10,700 tons		9,830 tons 12,390 tons
Dimensions length beam draught	361ft 11in (110.3m) 44ft 7in (13.6m) 31ft 9in (9.7m)		375ft 0in (114. 44ft 7in (13.6 31ft 9in (9.7n
Propulsion reactor/ power shafts	1 x IK-650B pressurised-water nuclear reactor, 190m 1 x GT3A turbine, 35mW 2 x auxiliary diesels, each 750bhp one		

ve: Four Sierras were built; the Akula design was better.

formance			
face	10kt		
merged	35kt		
ximum			
rating depth	1,970ft (600m)		
durance	80 days		
apons			
es internal	4 x 26.4in (650mm)	4 x 26.4in (650mm)	4 x 26.4in (650mm)
	4 x 21in (533mm)	4 x 21in (533mm)	4 x 21in (533mm)
es external	–	6 x 21in (533mm)	6 x 21in (533mm)
nplement	73		

ory: The Akula-class was divided into three groups: Akula (Project 971) – 7
s; Improved Akula I (Project 917U) – 4 boats; Akula II (Project 971A) – 2
s. The Akula-class (Project 971), designed by the St. Petersburg-based
akhit Design Bureau, was the follow-on to the Victor III-class, and the largest
ever built for the Soviet Navy. It was built in parallel to the Sierra-class (qv)
was constructed from low-magnetic steel rather than the much more
nsive and difficult to work titanium. One of the most notable visual
ires of the Akula class is the long fin, which is carefully faired into the hull,
reas in most other SSN designs the fin/hull junction is a stark 90 degrees.
was almost certainly a product of the long-standing Russian study into
tic life-forms such as whales, sharks and porpoises, and is almost certainly

intended to cut down hydrodynamic swirl – and thus noise. All Akulas also h
a large pod on the vertical stern fin for the Skat 3 thin-line, towed sonar a
and a rescue pod for the crew in the sail.

Earlier Russian submarines were notorious for their noise signatures,
the Akula-class changed that and the design was continually improved v
reduced noise levels, boundary-layer suppression and active noise cancella
in the later groups. One of the major reasons for the 3.7 m (12.14 ft) longer
in the Akula II is to enable it to accommodate yet further noise reduc
measures.

Below: An Akula I with its assembly of weapons.

Nautilus-class

UNITED STA

Total built: 1.
Completed: 1954.
Displacement: surfaced 3,674 tons; submerged 4,092 tons.
Dimensions: length 323ft 0in (98.5m); beam 27ft 0in (8.2m); draught 22f
(6.7m).
Propulsion: 1 x S2W pressurised-water nuclear reactor, ca. 15,000shp;
shafts.
Performance: surfaced – 18kt; submerged – 23kt; maximum operational di
depth 400ft (122m).
Weapons: 6 x 21in (533mm) TT (bow).
Complement: 111.

History: From the earliest days in the U.S. nuclear programme it had b
realised that, apart from its use for the most powerful explosions
known, nuclear reactions could be controlled and thus used as a sourc
power. One particularly advantageous application would be in submar
and as soon as World War II ended a naval research and development te
assembled at the Oak Ridge nuclear research centre, led by Captain Hy
G. Rickover, U.S. Navy, an outspoken but hitherto little known elect
engineer.

Rickover forced the pace and eventually contracts were placed with
Electric Boat Company for the first SSN and with Westinghouse for the
powerplant. This led to an operational reactor, the Submarine Thermal Rea
Mark II, which under the designation S2W was installed in the hull of *Nau
during her 27-month construction period. USS *Nautilus* (SSN-571)

ove: Akula is now the Russian Navy's only SSN class.

The original Akula has four 26.4in (650mm) and four 21in (533mm) torpedo
es, but Improved Akula Is and the Akula IIs both a further six 21in tubes mounted
he forward casing and outside the pressure hull, which adds to the firepower,
makes them impossible to reload at sea. In addition, in all three types the 26.4in
es can be fitted with liners to enable them to launch 21in torpedoes.

One of the distinguishing features of the Akula II is the number of prominent
-acoustic sensors on the leading edge of the sail and on the forward casing,
ch are similar to devices tested on a Hotel II in the early 1980s.

The first Akula I ran trials for several years and was then stricken, so that only
of this first group actually entered service. Five Improved Akula Is were laid
n but it appears that, at most, only three were completed and the other two,
ially complete, are being leased to India in 2002-07.

ve: Nautilus, the world's first nuclear-propelled submarine.

ched on 21 January 1954 and on 17 January 1955 was able to send her
oric signal: "Underway on nuclear power."

Nautilus was designed with what was at that time a conventional long,
amlined hull, not dissimilar to that of the German Type XXI. Her great power
e her through the water at a speed of about 23kt, but she then began to

experience the control problems inherent in such a design.

Despite her revolutionary power-plant, *Nautilus* was always considere
be an operational attack boat and was a great success. Within three month
her first run on nuclear power she made a 1,381nm (2,558km) underwa
voyage from New London to San Juan, Puerto Rico, in 90 hours at an aver
speed of some 16kt. By August 1958 there was sufficient confidence in
nuclear plant for her to make the first-ever Polar transit, starting from F
Harbor, Hawaii, and finishing at Portland, England. She steamed 62,56:
(115,865km) on her first nuclear core, 91,324nm (169,132km) on her sec
and some 150,000nm (277,800km) on the third. After a very successful ca
she was withdrawn from active service in 1980 and is now at a museun
Groton, Connecticut.

Right: USS **Nautilus** *married the*
great power of nuclear propulsion to
the out-dated traditional and
inherently slow long/thin hull. It was
the Albacore "teardrop" design that
resolved the problem.

Seawolf (SSN-575)-class UNITED STA

Total built: 1.
Completed: 1955.
Displacement: surfaced 3,741 tons; submerged 4,287 tons.
Dimensions: length 337ft 6in (102.9m); beam 27ft 8in (8.4m); draught 22f
(6.7m).
Propulsion: 1 x S2G liquid sodium-cooled nuclear reactor, ca.15,000shp;
shafts.
Performance: submerged – 20kt.
Weapons: 6 x 21in (533mm) TT (bow).
Complement: 105.
Specifications are for Seawolf (SSN-575), as built.

History: *Seawolf* (SSN-575) was authorised, designed and built in parallel
Nautilus (qv) in order to provide valid comparisons between the latter's pressur
water and nuclear reactor and a different type of reactor using liquid sodium. L
a molten metal (with a graphite moderator) was considered a promising altern
because it offered a ten-fold increase in temperature in the reactor, which w
lead to a much more efficient transfer of heat to the steam in the secondary ci
However, it suffered from a general problem in that the sodium had te
maintained in a molten state at all times; it also was considered less reliable
the pressurised-water alternative and suffered at least one leak. Apart from
power-plant, *Seawolf* was a very conventional design, similar but not identic
Nautilus, with a long, thin hull, twin propellers and a stepped fin similar to r
Guppy submarines. Unilke *Nautilus*, she had a distinct rise in the bow wit
externally mounted sonar dome.

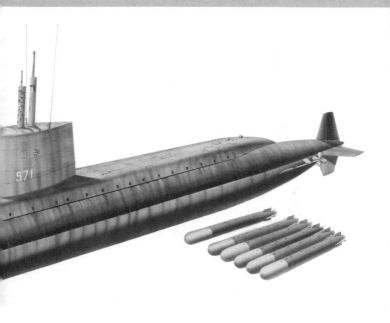

ve: **Seawolf** *(SSN-575) had a liquid sodium reactor.*

Seawolf was used on trials for two years but was then rebuilt with an S2Wa
surised-water nuclear reactor. In 1969 four externally mounted thrusters
e added (two forward, two aft), indicating a new role requiring very precise
tioning, which may have been related to intelligence-gathering activities.
;, despite the lack of success of her original powerplant, she had a long and
ul career and was eventually decommissioned in 1987. (It should be noted
the Soviet Navy later tried liquid-metal reactors in its Alfa-class (qv)).

Skate-class

Total built: 4.
Completed: 1957-59.
Displacement: surfaced 2,550 tons; submerged 2,848 tons.
Dimensions: length 267ft 8in (81.6m); beam 25ft 0in (7.6m); draught 20ft (6.3m).
Propulsion: 1 x pressurised-water nuclear reactor, S3W (*Skate, Sargo*), S (*Swordfish, Seadragon*), ca. 6,600shp; two shafts.
Performance: submerged – 20kt.
Weapons: 8 x 21in (533mm) TT (bow – 6; stern – 2).
Complement: 84.

History: Following the design of *Nautilus* and *Seawolf*, the U.S. Navy turne
its first series production SSN, the Skate-class. This was a considerably sm
design, very similar in size to the contemporary U.S. Navy Tang-class di
electric submarines. The only smaller operational SSNs have been the Fre
Navy's Rubis-class (qv). One surprising feature of the design was the rever
to stern torpedo tubes, which was practicable only because of the t
propeller design.

Despite their size, the four Skate-class boats served for many years
established a number of "firsts" including the first ever surfacing at the North
by USS *Skate* (SSN-578) on 17 March 1959. All underwent a number of refits
refuellings, and were eventually decommissioned between 1984 and 1989.

Right: **Skate** *and* **Seadragon** *at the North Pole, August 1962.*

Skipjack-class

Total built: 6.
Completed: 1959-61.
Displacement: surfaced 3,070 tons; submerged 3,500 tons.
Dimensions: length 251ft 9in (76.8m); beam 31ft 8in (9.7m); draught 25f (7.7m).
Propulsion: 1 x S5W pressurised-water nuclear reactor, ca. 15,000shp; shaft.
Performance: submerged – ca. 30kt.
Weapons: 6 x 21in (533mm) TT (bow); 24 x torpedoes.
Complement: 85.

History: The six Skipjack-class boats benefited from a number of n
advances in submarine technology. First, they adopted the "tear-drop" hull
single propeller which had been proven by USS *Albacore* (AGSS-569)
second, they introduced the new S5W nuclear reactor; and, third, they adop
for the first time in a major U.S. operational submarine, a single-hull design.
result was a great success and for the first time the U.S. Navy possess
submarine capable of travelling for long periods at the same speed (perh
even faster) as a surface task group, thus finally realising the dream of
"fleet submarine". Their maximum submerged speed of 30+kt was
exceeded until the advent of the Los Angeles-class some 20 years later, v
the manouevrability remains unparalleled. The single propeller meant that s
torpedo tubes were no longer practicable.

A further demonstration of the success of the design was that it prov
fairly simple process to adapt a number of Skipjacks already under constru

Above: Snook (SSN-621) enters Rio de Janeiro harbour.

and add a totally new missile section to produce the equally successful George Washington-class SSBNs (qv).

One of this Skipjack-class of boats, *Scorpion* (SSN589), was lost. She underwent an extended overhaul from October 1967 to February 1968 and then operated in the Mediterranean until early May, when she set out to return to the USA. Her last position report was from a point some 50nm south of the Azores and after

Below: The Skipjack-class was the first to adopt the "teardrop" hull – compare with Nautilus *on page 365.*

Thresher (Permit)-class UNITED STATE

Total built: 14.
Completed: 1961-67.
Displacement: surfaced 3,750 tons; submerged 4,311 tons.
Dimensions: length 278ft 6in (84.9m); beam 31ft 8in (9.7m); draught 25ft (7.7m).
Propulsion: 1 x S5W pressurised-water nuclear reactor, ca. 15,000shp; ₁ shaft.
Performance: surfaced – 20kt; submerged – 27kt; maximum operating de 1,300ft (396m).
Weapons: 4 x 21in (533mm) TT (amidships); torpedoes, SubRoc, plus S Harpoon missiles in some.
Complement: 94.

History: The first four of the Thresher-class were originally ordered as SSC to carry the Regulus II cruise missile, but when that weapon was cancelle 1958 they were re-ordered and re-designed as SSNs. They were initially kno as the Thresher-class, but when the nameship of the class was lost (
below), they were renamed the Permit-class. This accident also caused design to be re-examined and the last three were delayed in constructio incorporate the lessons learned. The principal ASW weapon system v SubRoc, conrtrolled by the BQQ-2 sonar system. Four torpedo tubes w mounted amidships, two on each beam, and angled outwards.

Jack (SSN-605) of this class had a modified hull, 296ft 9in (90.5m) long, was fitted with contra-rotating propellers, with one shaft inside the other turning in the opposite direction. This was one of the U.S. Navy's numer

days of no further transmissions she was declared overdue. After a huge
arch the hulk of the submarine was found at the end of October; it was lying
a depth of some 10,000ft (3,050m) about 400nm SW of the Azores, in three
ajor pieces: the forward part including the control room; the after part
:luding the engineroom; and the sail. No explanation for the tragedy, which
st the lives of all 99 men aboard, has ever been found. The surviving
ipjacks were decommissioned between 1986 and 1990.

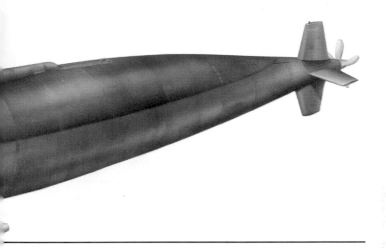

ove: Thresher-class **Haddock** *(SSN-621) in Subic Bay*

attempts to find a really quiet propulsion system and although apparer reasonably successful it was not repeated.

Thresher (SSN-593) was lost on 10 April 1963, while undergoing pc overhaul trials off the United States' East Coast. It was the first SSN loss in a navy and took the lives of 129 people; 112 Navy and 17 civilians. The remain boats in the class had successsful service careers and were withdrawn fro service between 1989 and 1996.

Right: Permit *(SSN-594)*. Note the subtle change in hull shape compared to the Skipjack-class (pp 368-9) and much higher position of the forward hydroplanes on the sail.

Sturgeon-class

Total built: 36.
Completed: 1967-75.
Displacement: surfaced 4,250 tons; submerged 4,780 tons.
Dimensions: length 292ft 0in (89.0m); beam 31ft 8in (9.7m); draught 28ft 1 (8.8m).
Propulsion: 1 x S5W pressurised-water nuclear reactor, 2 x steam turbin 15,000shp; one shaft.
Performance: surface – 15kt; submerged – 28kt.
Weapons: 4 x 21in (533mm) TT (amidships); torpedoes, Harpoon, Tomaha SLCM.
Complement: 136.
Specifications for SSN-637 to SSN-687, as built.

History: The 36 Sturgeon-class SSNs were slightly enlarged and impro versions of the Permit-class, with an elongated teardrop hull, torpedo tubes amidships and the bow taken up with the various components of the confor sonar system. Sturgeons could be distinguished visually from Permits by th taller fin (the top was 20ft 6in/6.3m above the hull), which accommodated m masts of various types and was suitable for under-ice operations. The div planes were set further down than in the Permit-class, and rotated to vertical for ice penetration.

Several problems were experienced between the builders and the l Navy over this class: *Pogy* (SSN-647) was reallocated to another yard completion, while *Guitarro* (SSN-655) was delayed for more than two ye after sinking in 35ft (10.7m) of water while fitting-out, an incident describec

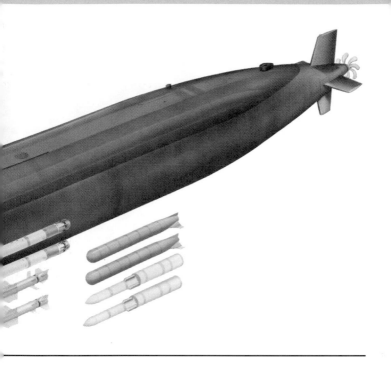

ove: **Pintado** *(SSN-672) with Deep-Sea Rescue Vehicle.*

Congressional committee as "totally avoidable".

The last 10 units in the class, SSN-678 to SSN-687, were built some 10ft (3.1m) longer, giving an overall length of 302ft 0in (92.1m), and placement increased to 4,460 tons surfaced and 4,960 tons submerged. wever, this was not to accommodate extra equipment but to improve bitability, and to provide extra volume for future developments.

Right: Sturgeon-class Richard B Russell *(SSN-687).*

Numerous conversions were made, including four to take one DDS each use by SEALs, and at least four were modified to accept a Deep-Sea Resc Vehicle (DSRV), if required. *Silversides* (SSN-679) was fitted with an extens abaft the sail, the purpose of which has never been revealed. The most radi modification was given to *Parche* (SSN-683) between 1987 and 1991, when s was given a 100ft (30.5m) extension forward of the sail, together with a lar hump on the foredeck. Her official mission is "research and development" a this is understood to include intelligence gathering activities, such as recover debris from the ocean floor (including from foreign missile tests) using grapple. The only two Sturgeons still in service in 2002 are one of the D conversions, *L. Mendel Rivers* (SSN-686), and *Parche*. The latter is due to decommissioned in 2003.

Tullibee/Lipscomb/ Narwhal-classes

UNITED STAT

Class	Tullibee	Narwhal	Glenard P Lipscon
Hull No	SSN-597	SSN-671	SSN-685
Total built	1	1	1
Completed	1960	1969	1974
Displacement surfaced submerged	2,316 tons 2,670 tons	5,284 tons 5,830 tons	5,800 tons 6,480 tons
Dimensions length beam draught	272ft 10in (83.2m) 23ft 4in (7.1m) 21ft 0in (6.4m)	314ft 11in (96m) 37ft 9in (11.5m) 25ft 11in (7.9m)	365ft 0in (111.3 31ft 9in (9.7m) 31ft 0in (9.5m)
Propulsion reactor power shafts	1 x S2C PWR ca. 2,500 shp one	1 x S5G PWR ca 17,000shp one	1 x S5Wa PWR one

rformance			
rface	15kt	25kt	18kt
omerged	15-18kt	30kt	25kt
eapons			
es - 21in	4	4	4
3mm)	amidships	amidships	amidships
	torpedoes	torpedoes/SUBROC	torpedoes/SUBROC
mplement	56	120	120

tory: These three "one-offs" were not related to each other, but are treated e together. *Tullibee* (SSN-597), one of the smallest SSNs ever built, was the l stage in the U.S. Navy's search for a hunter-killer (SSK) (see Barracuda- ss). These were intended to wait outside Soviet ports or in narrow straits and bush enemy submarines as they left on patrol; this required detection by g-range sonar and then sinking by high-speed, homing torpedoes. *Tullibee* placed only 2,640 tons submerged, its small size meaning that, although she s very manoeuvrable, she was also very slow, with a submerged speed of : 15kt, while the lack of space meant that newer, more sophisticated and s almost inevitably larger, equipment and electronics could not be commodated. She was the first to be fitted with BQQ-2 sonar, whose formal array took up most of the space in the bow, thus displacing the pedo tubes to an amidships position, a practice followed in all psequent U.S. Navy SSNs. She was also fitted with the PUFFS system, h its characteristic "shark's fin" sonar domes. Propulsion used the

specially developed S2C reactor, whose size constraints meant that it had o
a comparatively low power output, and turbo-electric drive in order to elimin
the self-generated noise made by reduction gearing in earlier SSNs. Despite
disadvantages and unique design, *Tullibee* served for some 28 years, splitt
her time between home waters, where she carried out training and AS
development work, and four operational deployments to the Mediterrane
She was decommissioned in 1988 and scrapped in 1989, and was the L
Navy's last attempt to produce a small ASW submarine.

Narwhal (SSN-671) was an experimental SSN, built in 1967-69 to test
ultra-quiet S5G natural-circulation reactor, which had no pumps, making
boat the quietest in any navy at that time. This system proved a success a
was adtoped for the S8G reactor in the Ohio-class SSBNs (qv). The hull des
was based on that of the Sturgeon-class, but somewhat larger, while
sensors, weapons and equipment were the same, thus making for va
comparisons. *Narwhal* was always regarded as a fully operational attack bc
She was modifed to conduct "special operations" which included operatin
remotely operated vehicle (ROV). A large "hump" was installed aft, wh
according to some reports housed the ROV, although it was also claimed tha
housed the reel for a new type of towed sonar array. After many years' serv
Narwhal was decommissioned 1999.

The third boat, USS *Glenard P. Lipscomb* (SSN-685), was the U.S. Nav
second attempt to find a staisfactory Turbo-Electric Drive (TED) the first hav
been the *Tullibee* (see above). *Lipscomb* was generally similar to the Sturge
class, but somewhat larger, the major difference being the TED. The machin
was larger and heavier and power output was considerably lower than in
Sturgeons, with the result that speed was lower. *Lipscomb* was a fully comb
capable submarine and served for many years, but the more traditional pump
systems were adopted for the Los Angeles-class. *Lipscomb* v
decommissioned in 1990 and stricken in 1997.

ove and below: Tullibee *(SSN-597) was one of the smallest and (being derpowered) slowest SSNs ever, having been designed specifically for ASW mission; note the three "sharks fin" PUFFS sonar domes.*

Los Angeles-class

Class	Los Angeles-class				Improved Los Angeles-cla	
Hull No	SSN 688-699	SSN 700-714	SSN 715-718	SSN 719-725, +750	SSN 751-770	SSN 771-77
Total built	12	15	4	8	20	3
Completed	1976-81	1981-83	1983-85	1985-89	1988-95	1995-9
Displacement surfaced submerged	6,080 tons 6,927 tons	6,130 tons 6,977 tons	6,165 tons 7,012 tons	6,255 tons 7,102 tons	6,300 tons 7,147 tons	6,330 t 7,177 t
Dimensions length beam draught	360ft 0in (109.7m) 33ft 0in (10.1m) 32ft 0in (9.8m)					
Propulsion reactor power shafts	1 x S6G pressurised-water nuclear reactor ca 30,000shp one					
Performance submerged maximum op depth	ca 33kt 1,480ft (450m)					
Endurance	90 days					
Weapons 21in (533mm) TT Vert launch tubes Load Torpedoes/ missiles Tomahawk Mine capable	4 – 22 – no	4 – 22 – no	4 – 22 – no	4 12 22- 12 no	4 12 22* 12 yes**	4 12 22* 12 yes
Complement	141					

* May also include further Tomahawks, but at expense of torpedoes.

** From SS-756 onwards.

History: This was one of the most expensive of all the defence programm undertaken during the Cold War, and, with 62 units, is the largest class of SS ever built; indeed, since 1945 only the Soviet diesel-electric Whiskeys Foxtrots were built in larger quantities. Hull numbers ran continuously f SSN-688, completed in November 1976, to SSN-733, completed in Septem 1996 – a 20-year production run unprecedented in submarine history. Th

*ove: **Santa Fe** (SSN-763) of the SSN-688 Improved-class.*

s, however, a gap in the numerical sequence since numbers #726 to #749 re allocated to Ohio-class SSBNs. The overall cost of the programme would almost impossible to calculate, but the building costs of a single boat (in en-year" U.S. dollars) were: 1976 – $221million; 1979 – $326million; 1981 –)6million; and 1990 – $900million. (However, it should be noted that the new ginia-class will cost an estimated $2billion each and SSN-23 over $3billion.)

The Los Angeles-class boats were much larger than any previous U.S. Navy √, primarily in order to accommodate the larger and much more powerful 3 nuclear reactor, which was needed to raise the maximum speed. Officially maximum underwater speed was stated to be "20+ knots" but it is widely epted that the boats were actually capable of some 32kt, making them the t class to exceed the speed of the Skipjacks, built in the late 1950s. It was ginally intended to construct them of HY-100 steel but this proved too icult with the technology that then existed and in the event HY-80 was used, ept that the pressure hulls of SSN-753 and -754 were partially fabricated m HY100 to test the construction processes for the Seawolf-class. The ire bow area of these new boats was taken up by the dome for the BQQ-5 ar system, while a towed array was carried in a sheath on the outside of , a neater and more hydrodynamically efficient arrangement than the large ds on Soviet SSNs. The torpedo tubes were located amidships and used to nch the SubRoc ASW weapon, as well as the Mk48 and Mk48ADCAP iventional torpedoes. Weapons load was later increased to include Sub- poon and Tomahawk missiles. Despite the increase in size, however, they considered quite cramped, with a number of crewmen having to use eping bags. All the boats have a Fairbanks-Morse 38D8Q diesel-generator I batteries for emergency propulsion.

Naturally, in a programme involving so many boats produced over such a g period, there have been changes, but the class can be divided into three ad groups, plus one boat converted for special purposes. The first group isisted of 32 boats (SSN-688 to SSN-718) which, apart from changes of ail, were identical. When the Tomahawk SLCM was introduced, the apons were stored in the torpedo room and launched from the torpedo

tubes. The next eight boats (SSN-719 to SSN-725 and SSBN-750) incorpora
a major change in the weapons arrangements. When Tomahawks were carr
internally it could only be at the expense of torpedoes, so it was decided t
from SSN-719 onwards 12 Tomahawks would be carried in vertical launch tul
positioned between the sonar dome and the pressure hull in space that h
previously been occupied by ballast tanks. These boats also had a longer-
core for their nuclear reactors.

More changes were made in the third group (23 hulls, SSN-751 - SSN-7;
which is referred to as the "Improved Los Angeles" or "688I"class (l
Improved). The most important of these changes was that they were m
"Arctic capable" by installing a strengthened sail and by relocating the div
planes from the sail to the bows. In addition, quietening was greatly improv
the sonar suite was enhanced and two anhedral stern fins were added, a;
the Seawolf-class. Some of the later units in this group also have shrou

mp-jet propulsors. All these have the 12 vertical tubes for Tomahawk, but m SSN-756 onwards they also have a mine-laying capability. The fourth up comprises just one boat – USS *Memphis* (SSN-691) – which was mpleted as a standard SSN in 1977, but in 1981 was reroled as a dedicated uls boat and has since carried out a large number of trials. It retains its combat pability and is therefore still designated SSN, although its actual employment uld be bettter indicated by an auxiliary (AGSSN) designation.

During their Cold War service Los Angeles-class boats carried out missions all oceans of the world, the great majority of them of a clandestine nature. eir activities usually came to light only through mishaps, such as collisions th Soviet submarines, two known occurrences affecting *Augusta* (SSN-710) the Atlantic (October 1986) and *Baton Rouge* (SSN-689) in the Barents Sea

low: The launch of Miami *(SSN-755), 12 November 1988.*

(February 1992). Two came to prominence when they launched Tomaha[
Land-Attack Missiles (TLAM) against Iraq in the Gulf War, *Louisville* (SSN-7[
launching eight and *Pittsburgh* (SSN-720) four. Closer to home, *San Juan* (SS
751) collided with *Kentucky* (SSBN-737) off Long Island in March 1998.

During the production run of the Los Angeles-class many plans
alternatives were considered, one example being in the early 1980s wh
Congress forced the Navy to examine designs for a small, cheaper SSN, b
none of these ever came to anything. Later, when it became clear just h
expensive the successor Seawolf- and Virginia-classes would be, it w
proposed that production of the 688I should continue instead, but this, t
came to nought because there was no potential for system growth left in wl
had become a 25-year-old design.

All Los Angeles-class boats were built for a 30-year life, althou
experience suggests that, with proper refits, recores of the reactor a
modernisation, they could actually be expected to last for up to 50 yea
However, a mixture of factors, including the end of the Cold War, the result
requirement to reduce operating costs and manning requirements, and a des
to avoid the costs of recoring during refits, have resulted in a reduction in t
fleet. The U.S. Navy started to retire ships of the original Los-Angeles class
the mid-1990s, the past retirements and future forecast up to 2008 being: 1S
– 2; 1996 – 1; 1997 – 3; 1998 – 3; 1999 – 2; 2000 – 1; 2001 – 3; 2005 – 1; 2C
– 1; 2007 – 1; 2008 – 1. Thus, by 2008, some 19 boats will have been retire
all of them of the original SSN-688 to SSN-750 group, leaving 34 in commiss
(11 SSN-688; 23 SSN-688I). A number of those which the Navy intends to ke
have been modified to carry one Dry Deck Shelter (DDS) plus a detachment
SEALs: SSN-688, SSN-690, SSN-700, SSN-701 and SSN-715.

Below: Los Angeles *(SSN-688)*. The artwork does not give a true impression of the great size of this boat which is 360ft (110m) long and some 33ft (10m) in diameter.

ove: USS Phoenix *(SSN-702) in the Atlantic, May 1982.*

ove: Birmingham *(SSN-695) surfaces dramatically.*

Seawolf (SSN-21)-class   UNITED STA

Total built: 3.
Completed: 1997-2004.
Displacement: surfaced 7,467 tons; submerged 9,137 tons.
Dimensions: length 353ft 0in (107.6m); beam 42ft 0in (12.8m); draught 36ft (11.0m).
Propulsion: 1 x S6W pressurised-water nuclear reactor, 200mW; one pump propulsor, 45,500shp.
Performance: submerged – 35+kt; maximum operating depth 1,970ft (600m).
Weapons: 8 x 26.5in (673mm) TT (amidships); ca. 50 Mk 48ADCAP torpedoe Tomahawk SLCM, or up to 100 mines.
Complement: 133.
Specifications for SSN-21, as built.

History: The Seawolf-class, the most advanced submarines currently at sea, ha troubled inception. The project for a Los Angeles-class successor started in 1980s but there was constant discussion about the requirement and the costs, then, when these had been resolved, there was a serious dispute over which v – Newport News or Electric Boat – should build it. Then, during construction of first-of-class, there were delays due to welding difficulties and these were follow by problems with the covers for the flank sonar arrays. At a less important le traditionalists were upset by the numbers allocated – SSN-21,~SSN -22, SSN-2 which are totally out of sequence in the U.S. Navy's excellent and well-establis hull-numbering system, apparently having arisen out of the project title "SSN for 21st Century" which was abbreviated to "SSN-21." The name of the third b *Jimmy Carter* (SSN-23), was also considered inappropriate by many, even tho the ex-president was a former nuclear-qualified officer in the submarine service

The Seawolf-class hull is of generally the same shape as that of the Angeles-class and is entirely covered in anechoic tiles. The sail is spec strengthened for under-ice operations and incorpoates a large fillet at the forw end, designed to improve the waterflow over the structure. A shrouded propu

ove: **Seawolf *(SSN-21) prior to launch.***

aces the customary propeller, and there are six fins: the customary cruciform, one at 135 degrees and one at 225 degrees.

The first two boats of the Seawolf-class are 7ft 0in (2.13m) shorter than the Los eles class, but with a greater diameter to give a considerable increase in internal me. Nevertheless, even this proved insufficient and the third boat, *Jimmy Carter* N-23), will incorporate a 27ft (8.23m) plug abaft the sail to enable her to carry a 50-strong Special Operations Forces detachment and their equipment. There will also be facilities for operating and controlling a variety of remotely operated vehicles (ROVs). This boat will not now be delivered until June 2004, some 2 years 3 months behind the original schedule and will cost, for this one boat, $US3.2billion.

The Seawolf-class is armed with eight 26in (660mm) torpedo tubes and carries a total of approximately 50 weapons, the actual mix of Tomahawk cruise missiles, Harpoon anti-ship missiles and Mk48ADCAP torpedoes depending upon the operational situation, although the normal load-out of Tomahawks is 12. Mines can also be carried on a basis of two mines replacing each torpedo.

It was originally planned to build 12 SSN-23 class boats and a figure of 29 was under consideration at one time. In the event, only three are actually being built and these will be followed by the Virginia-class, of which 30 are currently planned, with the first due for delivery in 2004. Even well before the first-of-class was completed work had started on its successor, currently dubbed "SSXN", which is scheduled to start joining the fleet in the 2020s.

Left: SSN-21 submerged. Note the triple flank-array sonars, forward hydroplanes and midships position of torpedo tubes.

Cruise Missile Carriers

The Germans were the first to examine the possibility of launching roc[ ]powered missiles from submarines, when some short-range army rock[ ]were launched from *U-551* in 1942. Although both surface and submer[ ]launches were successful the idea was not pursued, but in 1943 *Kriegsmarine* produced a plan to launch the pulsejet-powered, winged V-1 f[ ]U-boats, with New York as the principal target, but the missile was a *Luftw[ ]project and they flatly refused to cooperate. The concept was picked[ ]immediately after the war by both the Soviet and United States navies.

The U.S. Navy used a Japanese-designed aircraft shelter, which was[ ]right size to accommodate a V-1 missile, mounted on the after deck [ ]modified fleet submarine. Known as the "Loon" system, this was insta[ ]aboard two submarines and was tested from 1947-53. Most launches w[ ]successful but it was overtaken by the American-developed Regu[ ]programme, which became operational aboard converted fleet submarines, [ ]two purpose-built Grayback-class diesel-electric SSGs and the sole nucl[ ]powered Halibut-class SSGN. But only a few years later the Regulus sys[ ]was halted due to the success of the Polaris programme and the U.S. Navy t[ ]concentrated on the SSBN/SLBM combination.

The Americans saw Loon and Regulus as land-attack missiles, but [ ]Soviet Navy was much more interested in anti-ship missiles to counter [ ]threat from U.S. carrier groups operating close to the Soviet littoral. Follow[ ]tests with the German V-1, Soviet designers developed the SS-N-3 (Shadd[ ]cruise missile and produced some very inelegant Whiskey-class conversion[ ]get them to sea. This was followed by a succession of increasingly effec[ ]

clear-powered cruise missile carriers, the Echo-class (and its diesel-electric ck-up, the Juliett-class), Charlie-class, the one-off Papa-class and, finally, the y powerful Oscar-class. There was also the Yankee Notch, in which the viet Navy made use of four surplus SSBNs to produce four vessels carrying d-attack missiles. In the 1990s the Russian Navy had plans for a successor ise missile submarine, the Severodvinsk-class, but construction of the first been suspended and in view of the financial situation it seems highly probable that it will ever be completed.

The only other navy to develop a dedicated cruise missile carrier is the nese Navy, which produced the one-off Wuhan-class diesel-electric vered boat in the 1980s. This has, however, remained a prototype and no her boats of this type have been built.

Having rejected the SLCM in the 1960s, the U.S. Navy later returned to it in the '0s, but this time it was to be launched out of a standard torpedo tube, where missile became part of the standard load-out of Los Angeles-class SSNs. This uced the number of torpedoes that could be carried, so external vertical launch es for the SLCMs were developed, which were fitted in the later Los Angeles-s. A recently announced future project, however, is a return to the specialised se missile carrier, with a projected conversion of four surplus Ohio-class SSBNs carry a battery of 154 Tomahawk land-attack missiles, together with facilities for 5-strong SEAL force. This would be an extremely powerful warship posing a very ng threat to any country within the Tomahawk's 1,400nm range.

ow: Grayback (SSG-574), an early cruise missile carrier.

Wuhan-class (Project 033G) CHI

Total built: 1.
Converted: 1987.
Displacement: surfaced 1,650 tons; submerged 2,100 tons.
Dimensions: length 251ft 3in (76.6m); beam 24ft 11in (7.6m); draught 17ft (5.3m).
Propulsion: 2 x Type 1Z38 diesels, 2 x 2,400bhp; 2 x electric motors, 1,350shp; 2 x "creep" motors, 2 x 100shp; two shafts.
Performance: surface – 15kt, 14,000nm at 9kt; submerged – 10kt; range 330 at 4kt.
Weapons: 8 x 21in (533mm) TT (bow – 6, stern – 2) (14 torpedoes); 6 x C-cruise-missiles.
Complement: 58.

History: The Wuhan SSG was a converted Romeo (qv), rebuilt as a "proo concept" boat for a surface-launched cruise missile platform, with the launch tu for the six C-801 missiles built into the raised casing abreast the sail. An additi mast for a Snoop Tray radar antenna was mounted between the two periscope provide target data. This was essentially a Chinese version of the concept emplo by the Soviet Navy in the Juliett-class SSGs and, like the Juliett, this Chir submarine had to surface in order to acquire the target and then fire the miss This would undoubtedly have rendered the submarine vulnerable to detection attack by a sophisticated enemy, but against most Asian navies, particularly th lacking any form of seaborne air surveillance, it could have proved effective. submarine was stationed with the North Sea Fleet and may still be there altho

Whiskey-class Conversions RUS

Class	Whiskey Single-cylinder	Whiskey Twin-cylinder	Whiskey Long-
Project No	613Kh	644	665
Converted	1956	1958-60	1960-63
Number Converted:	1	6	6
Displacement: surfaced submerged	1,050 tons 1,340 tons	1,070 tons 1,360 tons	1,200 tons 1,500 tons
Dimensions: length beam draught	249ft 4in (76.0m) 20ft 8in (6.3m) 16ft 5in (5.0m)	249ft 4in (76.0m) 20ft 8in (6.3m) 16ft 5in (5.0m)	274ft 11in (83.8 20ft 8in (6.3m) 16ft 5in (5.06m
Propulsion	2 x Type 37-D diesels, 4,000bhp 2 x electric motors, 2,700shp 2 x creep motors, 100shp two shafts		

ove: Chinese Wuhan-class cruise-missile carrier.

questionable whether it would be used in a conflict.

The missile was the Mach 0.9 C-801 Ying Ji (Eagle Strike) for which there
e six launchers, three each side of the sail. This was a rocket- propelled
sile with a rocket booster, and on launch it climbed to about 164ft (50m)
descended to 65-100ft (20-30m) until its radar seeker acquired the target.
en descended further to a height of some 16-23ft (5-7m), from which point
sed the nose-mounted, monopulse radar seeker for the terminal approach
se.

It was proposed at one time to produce a similarly converted version of the
g-class (qv) but this has not been proceeded with.

rformance:			
face			
eed	18.3kt,	18.3kt,	13.5kt
ge	8,580nm/10kt	8,580nm/10kt	n/k
omerged			
eed	13.1kt	13.1kt	8kt
ge	335nm/2kt	335nm/2kt	n/k
ximum			
erational depth	656ft (200m)	656ft (200m)	656ft (200m)
eapons			
pedo tubes	8 x 21in (533mm) (bow – 4; stern – 2)		
pedoes	12 torpedoes/22 mines		
ise missiles	1 x SS-N-3	2 x SS-N-3	4 x SS-N-3
mplement	53	56	60

tory: The Whiskey-class (qv) design proved to be very suitable for
difications and a number were used as launchers for the Chelomey P-5
se missile, known to NATO as the SS-N-3 "Shaddock". The first boat to be
verted was a trials unit which carried one missile in a simple elevating tube
top of the casing abaft the sail. The aft-facing tube normally rested on the
k, but prior to launch it was raised to about 40 degrees and the two heavy
-caps were raised by electric motors. The turbojet-powered SS-N-3 flew at
ut 470kt (later increased to over 600kt) and was armed with a 200kT

warhead. Successful trials with the single missile version led to a service version with two launchers (Whiskey Twin-cylinder), which were also abaft the sail, but mounted each side of the casing. Again, the tubes faced aft, with large blast deflectors at the forward end. The whole installation was crude and created a great deal of underwater noise, which made them easy for Western submarines to detect. One of these boats sank with all hands in January 1961, but was found in 1969 and raised the following year.

Next came a much more substantial rebuild in which the hull was lengthened by 25ft 7in (7.8m) and the four launch cylinders were fixed and facing forward, with two on each side of a greatly enlarged sail. This was the Soviet Navy's Project 665, which was known to NATO as "Whiskey Long-bin". Six were completed but they did not remain long in service.

Right: An early SSG, Whiskey Long Bin carried four SS-N-3.

Juliett-class (Project 651) RUS

Total built: 16.
Completed: 1960-68..
Displacement: surfaced 3,000 tons; submerged 3,750 tons.
Dimensions: length 295ft 3in (90.0m); beam 32ft 10in (10.0m); draught 23ft (7.0m).
Propulsion: 3 x Type 37-D diesels, 7,000bhp; 3 x electric motors, 5,000shp; two shafts.
Performance: surface – 16.0kt, 9,000nm/7kt; submerged – 17.0kt, 300nm/2.8kt; maximum operational depth 1,300ft (396m).
Weapons: 6 x 21in (533mm) TT (bow) (16 torpedoes); 4 x 16in (406mm) TT (aft) (12 torpedoes); 4 x SS-N-3B cruise missiles.
Complement: 78.

History: The conventionally powered Juliett was the non-nuclear equivalent to the Echo-class (qv), but carried only half the number (ie, four) of SS-N-3 missiles. These were mounted in forward-facing bins which were raised for launch. Defects in the design included the large cavities of the thrust-deflectors at the after end of each tube, which were open to the sea at all times and created considerable noise.

The Julietts had three main engines; the two

er engines powered the propellers, while the centreline engine powered
enerator, which could either drive the two propellers in a low speed
de, or charge the battery. There were unconfirmed reports that towards

ow: Juliett: missiles raised, radar open, ready for launch.

the end of their lives some Julietts were given an air-independent propulsion (AIP) plant. Most boats had Punch Bowl satellite targeting system and all had the Front Door/Front Piece missile guidance radar in the forward edge of the sail. They also carried a full sonar and torpedo outfit, the latter consisting of six 21in (533mm) tubes forward and four 16in (406mm) tubes aft. These 16in torpedoes were specifically intended for use against attacking ASW escorts.

A total of 16 were built, and these were originally deployed with half in the Black Sea fleet and half in the Northern Fleet. However, the surviving Northern Fleet boats were transferred to the Baltic in the 1980s, indicating a change from a strategic to a theatre-level role against targets in Western Europe. All were scrapped between 1989 and 1994.

Echo-class
(Projects 659/675)

RUS

Total built: Echo I – 5; Echo II – 29.
Completed: Echo I – 1961-62; Echo II – 1962-67.
Displacement: surfaced 5,000 tons; submerged 6,000 tons.
Dimensions: length 377ft 4in (115.0m); beam 29ft 6in (9.0m); draught 24ft (7.5m).
Propulsion: 1 x HEN nuclear reactor, 24,000shp; two shafts.
Performance: surface – 20kt; submerged – 23kt.
Weapons: 6 x 21in (533mm) TT (bow) (12 torpedoes); 2 x 16in (406mm) TT (8 torpedoes); 8 x SS-N-3a cruise missiles.
Complement: 90.
Specifications for Echo II, as built.

History: The Echo I (Project 659) armed with six SS-N-3 missiles was inten
for the strategic attack role and lacked the necessary sensors for an anti-
role. Five were built and all were later converted to the attack (SSN) role,
survivors being scrapped in the early 1990s.

The Echo II (Project 675) had the same weapons systems as the Echo I
was some 13ft (4.0m) longer and with a 500-ton greater submer
displacement. This enabled it to incorporate an additional pair of launchers
well as the sensors necessary for anti-ship missions. This class were the So
Navy's primary anti-carrier submarines in the 1960s and 1970s. The miss
which could be launched only while the submarine was on the surface, w

ove: Juliett with front tubes raised, SS-N-3B just launched.

ove: Echo II, back in port after a reactor problem in 1989.

mounted in pairs on top of the pressure hull and elevated prior to laun
Guidance was by means of the Front Door radar, whose antenna was moun
in the forward end of the sail on a base which rotated through 180 degrees
total of 14 were converted to take SS-N-12 missiles and some were a
adapted to take the Punch Bowl satellite targeting system. All surviving bo
were disposed of in the early 1990s.

Both Echo I and II had the HEN nuclear propulsion system (which was a
fitted in the Hotel- and November-classes) and suffered a number of accide

Charlie-class
(Projects 670/670M)

Total built: Charlie I – 11; Charlie II – 6.
Completed: Charlie I – 1968-73; Charlie II – 1973-80.
Displacement: surfaced 4,300 tons; submerged 5,100 tons.
Dimensions: length 340ft 0in (103.6m); beam 32ft 10in (10.0m); draught 2
3in (8.0m).
Propulsion: 1 x VM-4-1 pressurised-water nuclear reactor; 18,800shp;
shaft.
Performance: surface – 15kt; submerged – 20kt; maximum operational de
1,300ft (400m).
Weapons: 4 x 21in (533mm) TT (bow) (12 torpedoes); 2 x 16in (406mm)
(bow) (4 torpedoes); 8 x SS-N-9 cruise missiles.
Complement: 98.
Specifications for Charlie II, as built.

History: The shortcomings of the Echo II class were readily apparent to
Soviet Navy and the next class of SSGN – the Charlie-class – largely recti
them. They had the same hull form and machinery as the Victor I-class SS
and a similar high speed. The major advance over earlier Soviet SSGNs was
the missiles were mounted in launch tubes which were fully faired into the b
casing and there were no deep thrust deflector wells, making them m
quieter, although still not as quiet as contemporary Western submarines.

Charlie I was armed with eight SS-N-7 anti-ship cruise missile,

hough none was actually lost. Two Echo Is suffered underwater fires, while Echo IIs had nuclear-related accidents. In addition, four were involved in llisions: two with U.S. submarines, one with a Soviet research ship, and one th an unknown object while submerged. The final problem was a leak in the clear primary reactor circuit in 1989 which was so serious that it resulted in submarines equipped with the HEN reactor being withdrawn from service.

low: Echo II was powered by the dangerous HEN reactor.

ght: One Charlie-class GN was lent to India the 1980s.

derwater-launched ver-n of the SS-N-2 Styx ssile used by numerous sses of Soviet surface rships, which was veloped in a rush due to failure of the *Amethyst* ssile which was being veloped for the Papa-ss SSGN (qv). The arlie II was armed with SS-N-9 (Siren), which d a much superior formance.

A unique event in the Charlie history is that one was lent to the Indian Navy, o named it INS *Chakra*. The Indians wished to learn how to operate a clear-powered submarine, but this was frustrated by the reported Soviet usal to allow the Indian crew into either the missile control room or the clear reactor compartment. As a result, the Indians refused to renew the se when it ended in 1991.

One Charlie I sank in the Pacific in 1983, was raised, sank again in port and s then raised for a second time, but was thereafter used as a training vessel. ost Charlie Is and IIs were stricken in the early 1990s, but one Charlie II nains in service in 2002.

Papa-class (Project 661)

Total built: 1.
Completed: 1969.
Displacement: submerged 5,197 tons.
Dimensions: length 350ft 9in (106.9m); beam 372ft 9in (11.5m); draught 2 3in (8.0m).
Propulsion: 2 x pressurised-water nuclear reactor; 80,000shp; 2 x 153- batteries; two shafts.
Performance: surface – 16kt; submerged – 42kt; maximum operational de 1,300ft (400m).
Weapons: 4 x 21in (533mm) TT (bow) (12 torpedoes); 10 x SS-N-9 cru missiles.
Complement: 82.

History: The single Papa-class SSGN, *K-162,* established the world underwa speed record of 44.7kt (51.5mph/83km/h) in 1970-71, an incred achievement. As far as is known, the record still stands. Design work starter 1959 for an SSGN with a titanium hull, deep operating depth and high spe armed with the *Amethyst* missile. Design and construction proved to lengthy, partly because of delays in the supply of titanium, but also because submarine incorporated so many new systems. The forward end consister two cylinders in a vertical figure-8 installation, with the missile tubes alongs the upper cylinder and fully encased within the outer casing, as in the Char class.

The Papa was one of the few nuclear-powered submarines to have t

---

Yankee Notch-class (Project 667AT)

Total built: 3.
Converted: 1984-88.
Displacement: surfaced 9,250 tons; submerged 11,500 tons.
Dimensions: length 464ft 2in (141.5m); beam 38ft 1in (11.6m); draught 26ft (8.1m).
Propulsion: 2 x VM-4 pressurised-water nuclear reactors, 155mW; two GT- 635; 38.2mW (50,000hp); two shafts.
Performance: surface – 12kt; submerged – 26kt; maximum operational de 1,050ft (320m).
Weapons: 6 x 21in (533mm) TT (bow) (18 torpedoes); 8 x 21in (533m (amidships) TT for cruise missiles; 32 x SS-N-21 (Sampson) cruise- missiles
Complement: 120.

History: The "Yankee Notch" was a conversion applied to three surp Yankee-class SSBNs in the mid-1980s to produce a dedicated cruise mis carrier for the SS-N-21 (Sampson) land-attack cruise missile. This was Russian equivalent of the U.S. Tomahawk. It was launched from a 2 (533mm) torpedo tube and flew at a speed of Mach 0.7 and a height of so 650ft (200m) to a range of 1,620nm (3,000km).

The conversion resulted in an increase in length of 39.4ft (12m) as a res of the "notch waisted" central section, despite the removal of the balli missile section. The new section housed four 21in tubes amidships on ea

ove: One Papa-class was built; it carried SS-N-9 missiles.

dependent nuclear propulsion systems, each generating some 40,000shp, d each driving its own propeller. The design speed was 38kt but 42kt was hieved on trials, and, as mentioned above, 44.7kt was eventually achieved. wever, there was considerable buffeting above about 35kt, which in tracted runs led to damage in the upper casing and would have generated ise which would have been detected many miles away. Only one was built d this was retired in 1991, but is apparently still in reserve in 2002.

ght: Three nkee-class BNs were nverted to nkee Notch GNs; they rried 32 x S-N-21 ampson) uise issiles.

am, with an internal magazine holding an additional 24 SS-N-21s, but it is lieved that this magazine could accommodate additional torpedoes or mines tead of missiles. Further elements of the modification included the placement of the two 16in (406mm) torpedo tubes by a further pair of 21in es and the lengthening of the sail, probably to accommodate a new type of mmunications buoy.

The Yankee Notch conversions reached the end of their lives because, like the U.S. Navy's Tomahawk, the SS-N-21 had only nuclear warheads and us had to be withdrawn as a result of the various nuclear weapons reduction aties. Two submarines were retired in 1996 and the other in 1997.

Oscar-class (Project 949)

Total built: Oscar I – 1980-82; Oscar II – 1986-97.
Completed: Oscar I – 2; Oscar II – 11.
Displacement: surfaced 14,700 tons; submerged 19,400 tons.
Dimensions: length 505ft 3in (154.0m); beam 59ft 8in (18.2m); draught 30ft
(9.2m).
Propulsion: 2 x OK-650B pressurised-water nuclear reactors, 2 x 190mW; tv
OK-9 steam turbines, 98,000shp; two shafts.
Performance: surface – 15kt; submerged – 31kt; maximum operational dep
2,000ft (600m).
Weapons: 4 x 21in (533mm) TT (bow); 4 x 25.6in (650mm) TT (bow); total of
SS-N-16 missiles or torpedoes; 24 x SS-N-19 (Stallion) cruise missiles.
Complement: 107.
Specifications are for Oscar II, as built.

History: The Oscar I was introduced in 1980 and represented a major advan
on the Echo II, having 24 "over-the-horizon" submerged-launch SS-N-
missiles in a hull which, at the time, made it the third largest submarine in t
world. Only two were built and these were followed by the even larger Osc
II with a 36ft (11m) increase in hull length and 4,000-ton increase in submerg
displacement. These huge submarines are designated *Atomniy Podvoc
Kresery I Ranga* (nuclear-powered submarine cruisers of the first rank) and we
intended to play a major role in the battle against U.S. carrier battle groups. T
choice of the word "cruiser" is interesting and indicates a role which includ
a major commitment to surface action.

The missile tubes are in two banks of 12 running down each side of a
outside the 27.9ft (8.5m) diameter pressure hull, which results in a gap of sor
9.8ft (3m) between the outer and inner hulls, and in a very large beam. The g
between the hulls is filled with rubber, which results in excellent anti-torpe
protection and good sound reduction. The SS-N-19 missile tubes are inclined
40 degrees, with one hatch covering each pair and the targeting data was to
provided by radar satellite downlink to the Punch Bowl antenna.

The reason for the longer Oscar II is not clear, but may have been either t
result of some shortcoming in the first-of-class (which could not be correctec
time to change hull number two) or may have been the result of a plan (ne
realised) to install SS-N-24 missiles in due course. All but the first Oscar I ha

Below: Oscar-class, armed with 24 SS-N-19 cruise missiles.

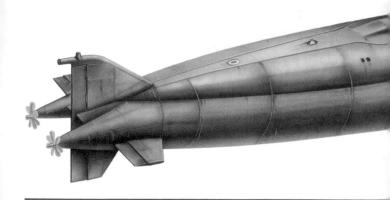

ove: Oscar-class SSGN; note the missile bins.

...e atop the rudder fin used to dispense a thin-line towed sonar array.

The two Oscar Is were based in the Northern Fleet but became non-...erational in 1995 and were stricken in 1996/97, while the 11 Oscar IIs ...ere divided between the Pacific Fleet (7) and the Northern Fleet (4). On ... August 2000, however, *Kursk* sank while on exercise with surface units ...the Barents Sea. All 118 aboard died in the tragedy, whose cause has yet ... be determined.

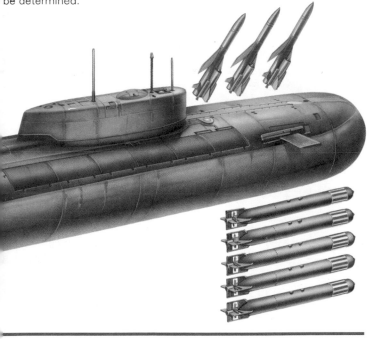

Fleet Submarine Cruise Missile Conversions

Total built: Loon – 2; Regulus – 2.
Converted: Loon – 1948; Regulus – 1952-55.
Displacement: surfaced 1,525 tons; submerged 2,130 tons.
Dimensions: length 312ft 0in (95.1m); beam 27ft 4in (8.3m).
Propulsion: 4 x Fairbanks-Morse 10-cylinder 2-stroke diesel engines, 2 1,600bhp; 2 x General Electric electric motors, 2,740shp; battery 2x 126-c Exide cells; two shafts.
Performance: surface – 14kt; submerged – 9kt.
Weapons: 6 x 21in (533mm) TT (bow); 2 x Regulus I cruise missiles.
Complement: 85.
Specifications are for SSG-317 (Regulus I), as converted.

History: During World War II the Germans conceived the idea of submari launched cruise missiles (SLCM), but failed to pursue it, and it was left to U.S. Navy to bring the idea to reality. The first missile to be used was a U made copy of the German pulsejet-powered, winged V-1 missile and this w successfully launched from a ramp on the afterdeck of *Cusk* (SS-348) on February 1947. *Cusk* and *Carbonaro* (SS-337) were then fitted with a cylindri hangar and launching ramp for a development of Loon, which could be given flight course corrections from modified submarines. The Loon program ended in 1953, to be replaced by Regulus I, which was similar in concept Loon but larger and considerably more sophisticated.

ove: **Tunny** *(SSG-282), Gato-class converted to SSG.*

Tunny (SSG-282) followed by *Barbero* (SSG-17) were converted to carry the w missile, the work including a snorkel, missile launch ramp, hangar for two ssiles, and control, guidance and servicing facilities. *Tusk* received a new eamlined sail during conversion, but *Barbero* did not receive hers until later. make way for the new equipment, the stern torpedo tubes and various other uipment were removed, including one main engine in *Tunny* and two in *rbero*.

The Regulus programme was a success and the missile was also deployed oard *Grayback* (SSG-574) (qv) and *Halibut* (SSGN-587) (qqv), but the ogramme was halted in 1964, with the success of the Polaris system.

low: **Carbonero** *(SS-337) converted to trial Loon missile.*

Grayback-class

Total built: 2.
Completed: 1958.
Displacement: surfaced 2,540 tons; submerged 3,515 tons.
Dimensions: length 322ft 4in (98.3m); beam 30ft 0in (9.1m); draught 17ft (5.3m).
Propulsion: 3 x Fairbanks-Morse 10-cylinder 2-stroke diesel engines, 3 1,500bhp; 2 x Elliott electric motors, 2 x 2,800shp; two shafts.
Performance: surface – 20kt; submerged – 12kt.
Weapons: 8 x 21in (533mm) TT (bow —6; stern – 2); 4 x Regulus I or II cru missiles.
Complement: 84.
Specifications are for SSG-574 (Regulus II), as built.

History: These two submarines were originally intended to be sister-ships the attack submarine *Darter* (qv), but were converted to SSGs dur construction by inserting a plug and adding a large, ungainly bow structu housing two cylindrical hangars. This increased their length, *Grayback* by 5 (15.3m) and *Growler* by 54ft (16.5m). Each missile cylinder was 70ft (21.3 long and 11ft (3.4m) high and contained two Regulus I or II missiles. The could be launched only from the surface. As soon as the upper casing was cl of the water the watertight doors were opened, following which a missile w extracted rearwards onto a launching ramp sited in the well between the rais bow and the sail. Once the missile was secure the ramp was turned to beam for launch. Not surprisingly, this was a time-consuming process.

Halibut-class

Total built: 1.
Completed: 1960.
Displacement: surfaced 3,846 tons; submerged 4,895 tons.
Dimensions: length 360ft 0in (106.7m); beam 29ft 6in (9.0m); draught 20ft (65.3m).
Propulsion: 1 x Westinghouse S3W nuclear reactor, 6,600shp (approx); t shafts.
Performance: surface – 15kt; submerged – 15.5kt.
Weapons: 6 x 21in (533mm) TT (bow – 4; stern – 2); 5 x Regulus I or Regulus II cruise missiles.
Complement: 111.

History: The single nuclear-powered Halibut-class SSGN was the last boat be built for the Regulus missile. She was laid down as the third in conventionally-powered Grayback-class (qv), albeit with a larger miss compartment faired into the foredeck, but was redesigned to take nucl power. She was fitted with a Westinghouse S3W nuclear plant, similar to t in the Skate-class SSNs and also driving two shafts. She carried either f Regulus I or two Regulus II missiles, which were brought up a ramp to launched from a rotating launcher, and she launched numerous training miss in the years 1961-65.

On the termination of the Regulus programme in 1965 the miss equipment was removed, a ducted bow-thruster (for precise manoeuvring) w installed and *Halibut* was reroled as a research submarine, although she w given an SSN designation. There is, however, good reason to believe that s

ove: **Grayback *(SSG-574)* with Regulus I on launcher.**

Each submarine conducted nine deterrent patrols armed with Regulus I
ssiles before the Regulus programme was halted in 1964. *Grayback* was then
roled as an amphibious transport (LPSS), for which she was lengthened by
ft 8in (3.5m) and the missile containers converted into Swimmer Delivery
hicle (SDV) hangars. The conversion included raising the sail and the
stallation of the PUFFS sonar system with its characteristic three fins on the
per casing. Due to the expense involved, *Growler* was not converted. Both
omarines were stricken in 1984.

ove: **The SSGN, Halibut, *carried five Regulus I missiles.***

s actually engaged in intelligence-gathering and it is reported that it was a
omersible launched from *Halibut* that found the sunken Soviet Golf-class
omarine in the Pacific; she may also have been employed in recovering
oended Soviet missile warheads. She was decommissioned in 1976 and later
apped. A further three improved SSGNs were cancelled in 1965 and
ordered as Permit-class SSNs.

401

Ballistic Missile Carriers

In the early 1950s it appeared that strategic warfare – by which was meant
ability of the USA and the Soviet Union to conduct direct attacks on e*
other's homelands – belonged to long-range bombers and land-bas
intercontinental ballistic missiles (ICBMs). However, both systems suffe
form a fundamental disadvantage, since both the airfields and the missile si
were clearly known and could be targeted in a pre-emptive strike. T
introduction of submarine-launched ballistic missiles (SLBMs), particularly wh
the submarine was nuclear-powered (SSBN), totally changed all that since
launch platform was inherently stealthy and, while a potential enemy might
able to locate one or two at a time, the chances of being able to locate 1C
more were extremely remote. These odds became even greater as the rar
of the missiles increased, thus enabling submarines to launch their miss
from areas dominated by their own ASW forces.

The idea of launching ballistic missiles from the sea originated in 1942 v
a German named Lafferenz, who suggested that a V-2 rocket should be plac
inside a submersible barge which would then be towed across the Atlantic
a U-boat. Once in position, both would surface, and the barge would be flooc
to bring it upright; the missile would be then be fuelled and launched agai
New York. Somewhat surprisingly, this suggestion was given a low priority
the Germans. After the war both the United States and the Soviet Un
examined the barge concept and the latter actually produced some prototyp
but the tests resulted in premature explosions and that particular idea v
abandoned. These studies did, however, lead both navies to realise
strategic potential of a submarine armed with ballistic missiles and the So*
Navy forged ahead to become the first to produce a workable solution, the Z
V, a converted diesel-electric submarine. This carried two liquid-fuelled miss
in vertical tubes extending from the keel to the top of the sail. This early syst
required the submarine to be on the surface, where the missile was raised
an elevator until clear of the tube, a slow procedure which had obvic
operational limitations, but it was a start. The Soviet Navy then progres*
rapidly through in-tube launches to submerged launches, with accompany
improvements in range, payload and accuracy.

In the early 1950s the U.S. Navy, in collaboration with the U.S. Arr
started development of a navalised Jupiter ICBM, the plan being to mount th
of these 60ft (18.3m) liquid-fuelled missiles in a 10,000-ton, nuclear-powe
submarine. Fortunately, the development of solid fuel and miniaturis
components offered greater potential, and when a project team led by Adrr
W. F. Raborn was formed in the early 1950s it decided from the start to opt
missiles with solid propellants which would be ejected from a vertical tu
while the submarine was submerged. The resulting Polaris project, howe*
involved much more than this, including lightweight ablative RVs, iner
guidance and miniaturised nuclear warheads. For the submarine, new syste
of navigation, noise reduction, deployments and launch procedures w
required. Despite its complexity, the whole project came together without
serious hitches and Polaris became operational in November 19
Improvement programmes led to Polaris A-2 and A-3, then Poseidon, follov
by Trident I and the current Trident II. What is so impressive, however, is t
Admiral Raborn and his team of naval officers and scientists got the concep*
exactly right in the 1950s that today's Ohio/Trident combination is insta
recognisable as a lineal descendant of the original Polaris/Washington of
years ago.

Soviet progress was slower and required more interim steps bef
reaching the fully-fledged SSBN/SLCM combination with the Yankee/SS-N
Thereafter, progress was rapid and led to a large fleet of SSBNs, the bulk

ove: Typhoon, *by far the largest submarine ever built.*

which were of the Yankee- and Delta-classes, although the latter were lin
descendants of the Yankee design. The balance of the fleet was made up of
Typhoons, the largest submarines ever built.

The British Polaris force of four Resolution-class SSBNs was commission
between 1967 and 1969, with the Polaris missiles being bought direct from t
Unites States, although the re-entry vehicles and warheads were design
developed and produced entirely in the United Kingdom. This force was kep
service rather longer than had been planned, but was eventually replaced in t
1990s by the Vanguard-class.

France's nuclear deterrent was developed entirely within her o
resources, a remarkable achievement. The first SSBN, *Le Redoutable*, beca
operational in 1971 and was followed by further boats in 1973, 1974 and 19
respectively. However, unlike the British, the French then decided to buil
fifth ship, which became operational in 1980. A sixth, *L'Inflexible*, was built t
more advanced design, joining the fleet in 1985, but the next was a totally n
class, the Le Triomphant-class.

The end of the Cold War saw a sharp reduction in the number of operatio
SSBNs and a slowing down in the pace of development of new system

spite this the importance of the SSBN has grown as the emphasis on mbers and ICBMs has decreased. Thus, the position in 2002 was that the S. had a force of 14 Ohio-class boats, but with the possibility of either ucing to 12 or maintaining the figure at 14, but with single crews. Her former ponent, Russia, nominally operates seven Delta IVs and eight Delta-IIIs but st of these are of doubtful operational value; possibly no more than four lta-IVs and two Delta-IIIs are actually in a usable state.

The two European nuclear powers continue to operate their smaller SSBN ets, although it should be noted that the advent of MIRVs has given them a portionally greater capability than with their first generation systems. Thus, British have a force of four Vanguard-class SSBNs armed with 16 Trident II BMs, while the French have six ships, armed with French SLBMs, which will duce to four in 2004. In Asia, China has operated a single SSBN for some ars, but a new class is under development, while persistent rumours of the velopment of missiles and nuclear-propulsion in India may lead to an BN/SLBM in due course.

low: Ohio-class SSBN, USS Michigan (SSBN-727).

Daqingyu (Xia)-class (Project 092)

Total built: 1.
Completed: 1988.
Displacement: submerged 7,000 tons.
Dimensions: length 393ft 8in (120.0m); beam 32ft 9in (10.0m); draught 26ft (8.0m).
Propulsion: 1 x pressurised-water nuclear reactor, 58MW; 2 x steam turbin one shaft.
Performance: submerged – 22kt; maximum operating depth 985ft (300m).
Weapons: 6 x 21in (533mm) TT (bow); missiles – 12 x missile tubes.
Complement: ca 100.
Specifications for Xia (#406), as built.

History: The Chinese Daqingyu-class, pennant *#406,* is the first SSBN to designed and built in Asia, being constructed at Huladao, a major shipbuild centre some 120 miles (200km) north-east of Beijing. Laid down in 1978, submarine was launched in 1981, but then spent a lengthy period fitting out conducting tests with its 12 JL-1 (CSS-N-3) missiles. The system suffe several problems, not surprising in a first-generation system, and did become operational until 1987. It would appear that, just as the L lengthened the hull of a Skipjack-class SSN to produce the first Washingt class SSBNs, so the Chinese lengthened the hull of the Han-class SSN

Le Redoutable-class

Total built: 6.
Completed: 1971-85.
Displacement: surfaced 8,045 tons; submerged 8,940 tons.
Dimensions: length 422ft 0in (128.0m); beam 35ft 0in (10.6m); draught 33ft (10.0m).
Propulsion: 1 x pressurised-water nuclear reactor; 2 x steam turbines, turbo-alternators, 1 x electric motor, 15,000shp; 1 x auxiliary diesel, 2,670b one shaft.
Performance: surfaced – 20kt; submerged – 22kt; maximum operating de 656ft (200m).
Weapons: 4 x 21.7in (550mm) TT (bow) (18 torpedoes); missiles – 16 x mis tubes.
Complement: 135.
Specifications for Le Redoutable, as built.

History: In the early 1960s France embarked on the development of a *Force Dissuasion* (deterrent force) which was initially based on five SSBNs. overall design was similar to that of the U.S. Navy's Lafayette-class (qv) single hull design with a 16-missile SLBM compartment located directly al the sail, the machinery spaces aft and a single shaft. The propulsion syst was, however, different from contemporary U.S. and British designs in that single pressurised-water nuclear reactor did not drive geared steam turbir but drove two turbo-alternators instead, these, in turn, providing the power a single large electric motor. The fourth and fifth boats, *L'Indomptable* and *Tonnant,* had a metallic reactor core in place of the oxide cores in the ea

ght: Daqingyu, _China's first_
erational SSBN.

duce the Daqingyu. Only one boat is
own for certain to have been
nstructed. This entered service in
37. It then went into a long refit at
iadao in 1985, where the work,
ich was still in progress in early
)2, involved installing the new JL-2
S-NX-4) missile system, as well as
eral updating.

Western intelligence reports have
igested that a second Xia-class
3N may have been launched in 1981
I that one of the two was lost at sea
985. This has never been confirmed
I the only extant submarine became
erational in the late 1980s and
ved with the North Sea Fleet until
ng into refit. A new class of SSBN
)e 093) is now under construction.

In order to maintain one submarine on continuous patrol a navy requires
ninimum of four, preferably five, hulls. While the Daqingyu programme
s far short of this criterion, it does represent a major national
ievement and is a valuable first step for a country which traditionally
es a very long-term view.

ove: L'Inflexible, _sixth of the French Le Redoutable-class._

boats, while the sixth, *L'Inflexible*, was of an improved design and is sometim
regarded as a separate class.

The first two units, *Le Redoutable* and *Le Terrible*, initially carried the t
stage, single-warhead M1 missile with a range of 1,350nm, but this v
superceded in the third unit, *Le Foudroyant*, by the more capable M2 miss
The fourth and fifth units carried a mix of M2 and M20 missiles, the la
differing only in having a single 1mT thermonuclear warhead, with the
three later carrying the same mix. The sixth, *L'Inflexible*, carried the M4, a to
new missile, with greater range and a payload of six 150kT MRVs.

The first four ships were stricken between 1991 and 1999, leaving just
in service in 2002: *L'Indomptable* and *L'Inflexible*. These will strike in 2004
2007, respectively.

Right: **Le Tonnant***, one of the first five French
SSBNs which carried 16 M2/M20 ballistic
missiles. They also carried L5 and F17
torpedoes for self-defence.*

Le Triomphant-class

Total built: 4.
Completed: 1996-2008.
Displacement: surfaced 12,640 tons; submerged 14,335 tons.
Dimensions: length 452ft 8in (138.0m); beam 41ft 0in (12.5m); draught 34ft
(10.6m).
Propulsion: 1 x K15 pressurised-water nuclear reactor; 1 x electric mo
41,500shp; 2 x SEMT-Pielstick 8 PA-4 V200 stand-by diesels, 2 x 1,225bhp;
shaft (pump-jet).
Performance: submerged – 25+kt; maximum operational diving depth 1,6
(500m).
Weapons: 4 x 21in (533mm) (bow) (18 cruise missiles/torpedoes); missiles -
x missile tubes.
Complement: 121.

History: *L'Indomptable* was the last of the first series of French SSBNs
production then switched to a totally new second-generation design, with
first ship, *Le Triomphant*, being laid down in 1989, entering service in 1996
carrying out its first operational patrol in 1997. The French Navy origin
planned to build five, but it was announced in 1992 that only four would be b
Following a series of delays for budgetary reasons, the last will now e
service in 2008.

The Le Triomphant-class hull is constructed of NLES-100 steel and is
a better hydrodynamic shape than earlier designs, with a prop-jet propu

Right: **Le Triomphant***, first of the latest French SSBN class.*

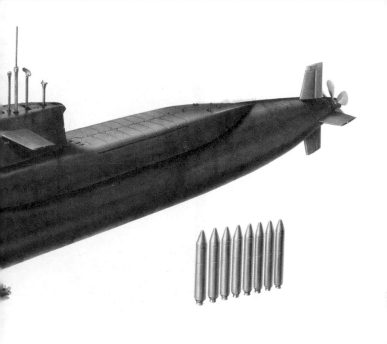

and end plates on the horizontal stabilisers. Internally, power is provided by the new K15 pressurised-water nuclear reactor, with all mechanical elements mounted on "rafts" to isolate them from the hull in order to reduce radiated noise. The final stage is a pump-jet propulsor, which provides both improved hydrodynamic efficiency and a greatly reduced acoustic signature.

The first three boats carry 16 of the new M45 SLBMs, but the fourth will have the M51 missile, which will then be retrofitted into the first three. The M51 will have a range of 3,240nm and carry 10-12 TN-75 MIRVs.

Right: Le Triomphant. The pump-jet propulsor is carefully screened from view.

Resolution-class

GREAT BRITA

Total built: 4.
Completed: 1966-80.
Displacement: surfaced 7,500 tons; submerged 8,400 tons.
Dimensions: length 425ft 0in (129.5m); beam 33ft 0in (10.1m); draught 30ft (9.1m).
Propulsion: 1 x Vickers/Rolls-Royce PWR.2 pressurised-water nuclear reac ca. 27,500shp; one pump-jet.
Performance: surface – 20kt; submerged – 25kt.
Weapons: 6 x 21in (533mm) TT (bow); missiles – 16 x missile tubes.
Complement: 143 (two crews).

History: In the late 1950s it was planned that the British Royal Air Force wc provide the British strategic nuclear deterrent into the 1960s and 1970s, us V-bombers armed with Skybolt air-to-surface nuclear missiles. But at Nassau conference in 1962, President John F. Kennedy told British Pr Minister Harold MacMillan that the USA was abandoning Skybolt, due apparently insuperable development problems. It was then agreed that United States would supply Britain with Polaris SLBMs, for which the Bri would build their own SSBNs, but that the missiles would have entirely Bri front-ends (ie, nuclear warhead and guidance package), thus giving the Bri government total control over the use and targeting of the weapons.

Four submarines were built of a planned total of five, the last boat be cancelled in the Labour Government's 1965 defence review. Much techn

Right: British Resolution-class SSBN approaches its base.

assistance was provided by the United States and the Resolution-class
generally similar to the American Lafayette-class, although the actual desig
based on that of the Valiant-class SSN, but with a missile compartm
between the control centre and the reactor room.

First-of-class *Resolution* was laid down in February 1964 and complete
October 1967, exactly on schedule. She then fired her first Polaris A-3 mis
off Cape Kennedy on 15 February 1968 and sailed on her first operational pa
on 15 June that year. Later, she was the third to receive the Chevaline upc
(1984) and created a record in 1991 when she conducted the longest-e
Polaris patrol, lasting 108 days. She paid off in October 1994 after 69 patro

Repulse underwent her Chevaline update in 1982 and completed the Bri
200th Polaris patrol in August 1990. One of her achievements was to take
in trials of the U.S. Navy's Deep Submergence Rescue Vehicle (DSRV), nar
Avalon, which was flown in from the United States and installed on *Repuls*
after casing. Once in deep water, *Avalon* disengaged, moved to HMS *O*
simulating a sunken submarine and took a number of *Odin*'s crew to *Repu*
in an entirely successful operation. *Repulse* completed the last Polaris pa
and her own 69th, on 5 May 1996 and paid off in August 1996.

Renown was the first of the four ships to be fitted with the Cheva
conversion and successfully tested the system in early 1982. She paid of
1995. *Revenge* launched her first Polaris missile in June 1970 and started
first operational patrol three months later. She was the last to receive
Chevaline update (1988) but became the first to be paid off in May 1992, ha
completed 56 deterrent patrols.

Right: The British operated four Resolution-class SSBNs.

Below: Resolution *was armed with 16 Polaris A3TK SLBMs.*

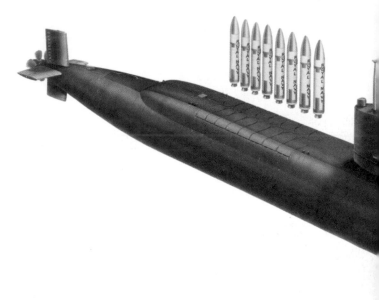

Vanguard-class

Total built: 4.
Completed: 1993-99.
Displacement: submerged 15,850 tons.
Dimensions: length 490ft 0in (149.3m); beam 42ft 0in (12.8m); draught 33ft (10.1m).
Propulsion: 1 x Vickers/Rolls-Royce PWR.2 pressurised-water nuclear reac ca. 27,500shp; one pump-jet.
Performance: submerged – 25kt.
Weapons: 4 x 21in (533mm) TT (bow) (Harpoon/Spearfish/Tigerfish torpedo missiles – 16 x missile tubes.
Complement: 135 (two crews).

History: After many years of discussion it was announced in 1980 that British government had selected the Trident missile as the replacement for Polaris A3TK missiles (Polaris A-3 with British Chevaline warhead). Initial pl were to buy the Trident I C-4, but this was later changed to Trident II D-8 ensure long-term compatibility with the U.S. Navy. This required a n submarine, considerably larger than the Resolution-class it replaced – in fact, far the largest submarine ever built in the UK – but still armed with 16 missi unlike the U.S. Navy's Ohio-class which has 24 missiles.

The arrangement for the missiles is unique and demonstrates extremely close relationship between the Royal and U.S. navies. Under this, UK did not purchase a specific number of Trident missiles which would th have been the sole property of the British government. Instead, the purchased a share of a common USN/RN pool which is held at King's E Georgia. Thus, when a British SSBN requires missiles it sails to King's I

Above: **Vanguard,** *first of the UK's second class of SSBNs.*

ove: British SSBNs are armed with 16 Trident II SLBMs.

where it is loaded with the next 16 available missiles, less their warheads, the
being no differentiation between British and American missiles. The ship th
returns to Coulport on the west coast of Scotland, where the missiles are fit
with British warheads. At the end of the commission the reverse process
followed, with the British warheads remaining in the UK and the missiles be
returned to the USA.

First-of-class HMS *Vanguard* was launched on 4 March 1992 and sailed
its first operational patrol in December 1994. The second, *Victorious*, ente
service in December 1995, followed by *Vigilant* in November 1996 a
Vengeance in November 1999. All four are based at Faslane in the Gareloch
the River Clyde in Scotland.

The class was just coming into service as the Cold War ended, and this
to a number of major changes in deployment. According to the Ministry
Defence, "...each submarine will deploy with no more than 96 warheads a
may carry significantly fewer." This was followed by an announcement that

nguard-class will have a "sub-strategic" mission..." which would involve the limited and highly selective use of nuclear weapons in a manner that fell monstrably short of a strategic strike, but with a sufficient level of violence convince an aggressor who had already miscalculated (British) resolve and acked us that he should halt his aggression and withdraw or face the ospect of a devastating strike." This involves fitting some Trident ssiles with a single warhead, which could be used to detonate the primary stem with a yield of less than 10kT and thus used as a demonstration of solve to "go all the way" unless the aggressor ceased his attack. This means at a proportion of the 16 missiles will carry an average of five warheads each, hile the remainder carry one warhead each; thus, one load-out might mprise 14 missiles with five warheads plus two single warheads, for a total 72 warheads.

elow: The escorting boats give the scale of this huge SSBN.

Zulu V-class (Project 611)

Total converted: 5.
Converted: 1954-58.
Displacement: surfaced 1,900 tons; submerged 2,350 tons.
Dimensions: length 324ft 1in (98.8m); beam 24ft 7in (7.5m); draught 17ft (5.2m).
Propulsion: 3 x diesel engines, each 2,000bhp; 3 x electric motors, 5,200sh three shafts.
Performance: surface – 18.0kt; submerged – 12,5kt, 20,000nm/8kt; maximu operating depth 656ft (200m).
Weapons: 10 x 21in (533mm) TT (bow – 6, stern – 4) (10 torpedoes); missi – 2 x missile tubes.
Complement: 83.

History: The first launch of a ballistic missile from a submarine took place 16 September 1955, one of many significant achievements by the Soviet Na during the Cold War period. It was launched from a modified Zulu IV pa submarine (qv), which was fitted with a single tube in the sail for a stand Soviet Army R-11 (Scud) tactical missile, which was mounted on an eleva

veloped fom a battlecruiser gun mounting. Once in position, with the
bmarine on the surface and only in relatively calm seas, the end-cap was
moved by an electric motor and the missile raised, held firmly in the grip of a
o-part cradle until the motor had fired.

Having achieved success in these trials with the Zulu IV, five Zulu-class boats
ere converted with two tubes in a lengthened sail, each carrying a navalised Scud,
signated R11FM. Generally known under their NATO reporting name of "Zulu V",
ese boats were slightly longer than the earlier Zulus, and no spare torpedoes
ere carried. The R11FM (also known as D-1) had a range of approximately 80nm
50km), carried a non-nuclear warhead and had an accuracy (circular error probable
CEP) of 4nm (8km). Only one missile could be raised and launched at a time,
hich meant that the submarine would have had to expose itself for some 10-15
nutes very close to the enemy shore while launching two relatively small and
ry inaccurate missiles. This missile was replaced by the R-13 (D-2) in 1967/68,
own to NATO as SS-N-4 (Sark). This had a range of some 350nm (650km) and
rried a 1mT nuclear warhead.

elow: Zulu V carried 2 x SS-N-4 in its enlarged sail.

Golf-class (Project 628)

Total built: 23 (plus 1 in PRC).
Completed: 1958-62.
Displacement: surfaced 2,350 tons; submerged 2,850 tons.
Dimensions: length 328ft 1in (99.0m); beam 27ft 11in (8.0m); draught 21ft 8
(6.6m).
Propulsion: 3 x diesel engines, each 2,000bhp; 3 x electric motors, 5,200sh
three shafts.
Performance: surface – 17kt, 9.500nm/5kt; submerged – 12kt; maximu
operating depth 656ft (200m).
Weapons: 10 x 21in (533mm) TT (bow – 6, stern – 4) (16 torpedoes); missi
– 3 x missile tubes.
Complement: 59.
Specifications for Golf I, as built.

History: The Golf I diesel-electric submarines were built using many Foxtr
class components, in parallel to the Hotel-class (qv) and as an insurance agair
the failure of the latter's nuclear propulsion system. The early Golf Is carri
three RF-11M (Scud) missiles in vertical tubes in the sail until the SS-N
became available. Even this new missile also had a short range and 13 boa
(known to NATO as Golf II) were converted to take three SS-N-5 (Serb) missile
The SS-N-5 Soviet D-4 (R-21) not only had much greater range but could also
launched when the submarine was submerged, limits being a depth of 20
(60m) and a forward speed of 4kt. Missile range was some 760nm (1,400kn

Some of the remaining hulls were used to test new msssile systems. G
III was lengthened by 33ft (10m) and carried three SS-N-8 (Sawfly), while G
IV was lengthened by 60ft (18.3m) to carry six SS-NX-13 and Golf V carried ju
one of the much larger SS-N-20. One curiosity about these three was that t
missiles in the Golf II and III were counted under U.S./USSR SALT-I agreeme

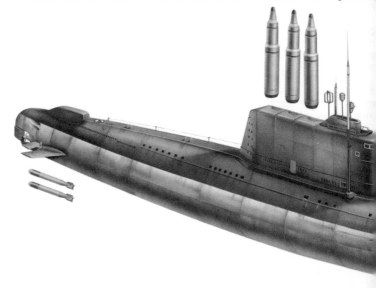

Above: Golf II carried 3 x SS-N-5 (Serb) SLBMs in its sail.

Above: Golf II on patrol; note huge sail and radio masts.

...t the hulls were not, while neither the Golf V nor its single missile were
...untable. Two of these boats were converted in the late 1970s by having their
...ssile and torpedo tubes removed and much communications equipment
...ded to be employed as communications relays – they were designated Golf
...Modified) or Golf SSQ by NATO. One Golf-class submarine is known to have
...en assembled in China as part of that country's SLBM programme and there
...ve been persistent rumours that a second was also built, and that one of the
...o exploded in the South China Sea in mid-1981.

One Soviet Golf II sank in the central Pacific in 1968. Part of it was later
...covered by the specially built *Glomar Explorer*, owned by Howard Hughes,
...t funded and controlled by the CIA. According to reports, this ship recovered
...e bow section, two nuclear-tipped torpedoes and a number of bodies, which
...ere given formal funerals.

In the 1970s, late in the Golf II's career, six were deployed to the Baltic as
...eatre assets to be used in direct support of any land battle in central Europe.
...e Golfs left service in the late 1980s, except for the three SSQs, which
...rvived into the 1990s.

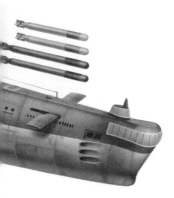

Hotel-class (Project 658)

Total built: 6.
Completed: 1960-64.
Displacement: surfaced 5,000 tons; submerged 6,000 tons.
Dimensions: length 377ft 4in (115.0m); beam 29ft 6in (9.0m); draught 23ft (
(7.0m).
Propulsion: 1 x HEN pressurised-water nuclear reactor; 2 x electric moto
30,000shp; two shafts.
Performance: surface – 20kt; submerged – 25kt.
Weapons: 6 x 21in (533mm) TT (bow) (16 torpedoes); 2 x 16in (406mm)
(stern); missiles – 3 x missile tubes.
Complement: 80.
Specifications for Hotel I, as built.

History: The first Soviet nuclear-powered ballistic missile submarines, t
Hotel I-class carried three SS-N-4 (Sark) SLBMs, with the tubes stretchi
from the keel to the top of the sail. The missiles were launched from t
surface, being raised clear of the sail by an elevator, as in the Zulu-V- a
Golf-class SSBs. Six were built, all at Severodvinsk, and all were power
by the same nuclear plant as used in the other two first-generation nucle
classes, leading to the NATO designation of HEN (Hotel-Echo-Novembe
The six boats were rebuilt in the mid-1960s: five were converted to ta
three SS-N-5 (Serb) missiles each and were redesignated by NATO as Ho
II. The sixth was converted to serve as trials boat for SS-N-8 (Sawfly), whi
subsequently was deployed aboard Yankee- and Delta-class SSBNs. Th
boat, which was lengthened to 426ft (130m), was designated Hotel III
NATO.
 The Hotel IIs were deployed off the western and eastern seaboards of t

Below: The nuclear-powered Hotel II carried 3 x SS-N-5.

bove: Hotel II in distress, one of many to suffer accidents.

ited States, posing a major threat to U.S. strategic bomber bases, since the ght times would have been some 6-10 minutes. First-of-class *K-19* had such appalling safety record that she was known as "*Hiroshima*" throughout the viet Navy. She suffered two very serious nuclear-related accidents with 10 rsonnel dying in one (July 1961) and 29 in another (February 1972), and also llided with USS *Gato* (SSN-615) in the White Sea (November 1969). In 1973 e unit was disabled off the coast of Newfoundland and towed back to rthern Russia. These boats were affected by the SALT agreements: two ere scrapped in 1982-83 and all surviving boats had their missile facilities moved by 1989. Two were re-roled as communications relays (SSQN) for a ort period.

Yankee-class (Project 667) RUSS

Total built: 34.
Completed: 19670-72.
Displacement: surfaced 8,000 tons; submerged 9,600 tons.
Dimensions: length 426ft 6in (30.0m); beam 39ft 4in (12.0m); draught 29ft 1
(8.8m).
Propulsion: 1 x VM-4 pressurised-water nuclear reactor, 90MW; 2 x elect
motors, 29,000shp; two shafts.
Performance: submerged – 27kt.
Weapons: 4 x 21in (533mm) TT (bow) (16 torpedoes); 2 x 16in (406mm)
(bow); missiles – 16 x missile tubes.
Complement: 120.
Specifications for Yankee I, as built.

History: The Soviet Navy lost its early lead over the U.S. Navy in SSBN/SLE
development when the first of the Polaris submarines went to sea in 1960, a
it was not until the Yankee-class became operational in 1967 that the Sovi
had their first submarines to mount SLBMs totally within the hull. The miss
tubes were arranged in two vertical rows abaft the fin, the first 20 ships be
armed with 16 SS-N-6 Mod I (Sawfly) SLBM, each of which had one 2r
warhead with a range of some 1,500nm and which, for the first time in a Sov
SLBM, were launched while submerged. The next 14 boats carried 16 of t
longer-ranged SS-N-6 Mod 3, with two MRV warheads.

Like all Soviet submarines, the Yankees were noisier than their Weste
counterparts and were correspondingly easier to detect. The relatively sh
range of the SS-N-6, even in its later versions, meant that the Yankees wo
have had to approach the American coasts in order to launch their missil
although they were less vulnerable than the earlier types which had to surfa
to launch their missiles. As the new Deltas entered service, the Yankees we
progressively withdrawn from the strategic role, starting in 1980, SSBNs
service being: 1980 – 34; 1991 – 12; 1992 – 6; 1993 – 0.

As they retired from strategic service, many of the Yankees were modifi
for different roles. One was armed with 12 SS-N-17 in a trial installation (Yank
II), while four were converted into carriers for SS-N-21 cruise missiles; t
NATO designation was Yankee Notch (qv). Another was converted to take
SS-NX-24 in vertical tubes in a new and much larger mid-body. Two othe
became Yankee Pod, designed to test new sonars, and Yankee Stretc
lengthened by 97ft 6in (29.7m), which was used as a support vessel for m
submarines. The five remaining boats were converted to SSNs by removing t
central missile section, shortening them by 95ft (28.9m), becoming Yankee

Yankees suffered a number of accidents in service, two of them in t
missile tubes (31 August 1973; 6 October 1986). One had a serious reac
problem which led to the boat being rebuilt, becoming the sole Yankee II.

*Right: A Yankee on fire off Bermuda in 1986. Note that the sail- mounte
hydroplanes are swung to the vertical, a capability necessary to
penetrate the ice when surfacing in the Arctic.*

Delta-class (Project 667B)

Class	Delta I	Delta II	Delta III	Delta IV
Project	667B	667BD	667BDR	667BDRM
Total built	18	4	14	7
Completed	1972-77	1975	1976-81	1985-92
Displacement surfaced submerged	9.000 tons 11,750 tons	10,000 tons 12,750 tons	10,500 tons 13,250 tons	11,740 tons 15.500 tons
Dimensions: length beam draught	459ft 4in (140.0m) 39ft 4in (12.0m) 28ft 7in (8.7m)	508ft 6in (155.0m) 39ft 4in (12.0m) 28ft 10in (8.8m)	508ft 6in (155.0m) 38ft 5in (11.7m) 28ft 7in (8.7m)	548ft 0in (167.0m) 39ft 4in (12.0m) 28ft 6in (8.7m)
Propulsion: reactor power shafts	2 x VM-4S 50,000shp 2	2 x VM-4S 50,000shp 2	2 x VM-4S 50,000shp 2	2 x VM-4SG 60,000shp 2
Performance submerged maximum operating depth	25kt	24kt	24kt	24kt
			1,250ft (380m)	
Endurance			80 days	
Weapons: 21in (533mm) TT torpedoes 406mm TT torpedoes missiles	4 12 2 6 12 x SS-N-8	4 12 2 6 16 x SS-N-8	4 12/SS-N-16 2 6 16 x SS-N-18	4 12/SS-N-16 – – 16 x SS-N-23
Complement:	120	126	130	135

History: The Soviet Navy's Delta-class has been one of the most successful all SSBNs, with 43 built over a 20-year period. It was the mainstay of t Soviet/Russian deterrent force throughout the 1980s and 1990s, exerting major influence on the strategic nuclear balance. By Soviet Navy standards t Yankee-class SSBN was a very satisfactory design, so when a new class SSBN was required to take the new SS-N-8 missile to sea it was decided avoid disruption in the shipyards by producing an evolutionary development the Yankee, thus avoiding the complications of a new missile *and* a ne submarine. As a result, the Delta had the same forward end (torpedo tube sonar, command centre and accommodation) and after end (nuclear reacto propulsion) as the Yankee, but with a totally new mid-section housing missiles. Because the SS-N-8 was longer than the SS-N-6, however, the miss section had to be higher and was covered by a raised casing, known in t West as a "turtleback".

ove: Delta III heads North on patrol under the Arctic ocean.

When the Delta I/SS-N-8 combination became operational in 1973, it
ded the superiority in both quality and performance which the U.S. Navy
d enjoyed since the appearance of the Washington/Polaris in 1960. The
rly Soviet SLBMs had short ranges which meant that the SSBNs had to
trol close off the U.S. coastline, where they were naturally more
Inerable. However, the SS-N-8 missile with its range of more than
300nm (7,720km) and a CEP of only 0.84nm (1.5km) enabled the Soviets
threaten the USA from "bastions" in the Sea of Okhotsk and the Barents
a, close to their own shores and thus much more easily protected by
eir own defensive measures.

Eighteen Delta Is were built, which were split equally between the
orthern and Pacific Fleets, the nine latter boats being the last SSBNs to be
nstructed at Komsomols'k in the Soviet Far East; once these had been
mpleted construction of all later SSBNs was concentrated at
verodvinsk. The Delta Is served from the mid-1970s to 1991 when nine
are retired, following by the remaining nine in 1992.

Next came four Delta IIs, an interim design which was lengthened to
able them to carry four more SS-N-8 missiles, thus matching Western
BNs. They were all built at Severodvinsk and all served in the Northern Fleet,
tering service in 1974-75 and retiring in 1993-94.

The Delta III introduced the SS-N-18 missile, which mounted either a large
gle or a number of MIRVed warheads (see table on page 430). The new
ssile was longer than the SS-N-8, requiring an even larger "turtleback". All 14
lta IIIs were built at Severodvinsk, being completed between 1976 and 1982,
t the force was split equally between the Northern and Far East Fleets. The
st to be stricken went in 1996, followed by another five until in 2002 only
ght remained nominally in service, although very few of these were actually
to go to sea.

Delta IVs were the last and largest of the Deltas. At least 10 were ordered,
which seven were completed between 1985 and 1992, while the
nstruction of another two was stopped on the stocks. All seven served in the
orthern Fleet and their planned use was to deploy under the Arctic ice and
en to surface to launch their missiles. In 2002 all seven were still nominally
erational.

In 1993 one Delta-class boat collided with the U.S. Navy's Sturgeon-class
ack submarine, USS *Grayling* (SSN-646). In 1998 one unit, *K-407*, was used
launch a Russian RSM-54 missile carrying a German telecommunications
tellite.

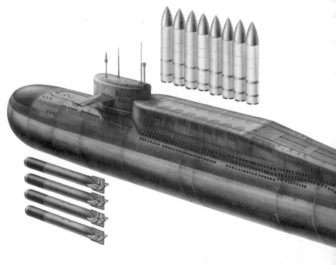

ove: First of a long line, Delta I armed with 12 x SS-N-8.

low: Delta III armed with 16 x SS-N-8 Stingray SLBMs.

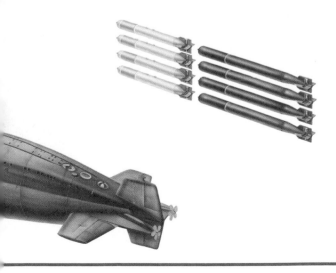

Missile	SS-N-8		SS-N-18			SS-N-2
	Sawfly		Stingray			Skiff
	Mod 1	Mod 2	Mod 1	Mod 2	Mod 3	Mod 1
SSBN	Delta I/II		Delta III			Delta I
Stages	2					
Propellant	Stored liquid					
Length	42ft 6in (13.0m)		46ft 3in (14.1m)			48ft 6 (14.8m
Diameter	5ft 11in (1.8m)		5ft 11in (1.8m)			6ft 2in (1.9m
Weight	73,413lb (33,300kg)		77,822lb (35,300kg)			88,845 (40,300k
IOC	1973	1977	1977	1979	1979	1986
Range	4,200nm (7,800km)	4,900nm (9,100km)	3,500nm (6,480km)	4,300nm (7,960km)	3,500nm (6,480km)	4,500n (8,300k
RVs	1 x RV	1 x RV	1 x RV	3 x MIRV	7 x MIRV	4 x MIF
Yield per RV	800kT	800kT	450kt	200kt	100kT	100kT
CEP (estimate)	5,250ft (1,600m)	5,250ft (1,600m)	2,950ft (900m)	2,950ft (900m)	2,950ft (900m)	500ft (152m)

ove: Delta IV carries 16 x SS-N-23 (Skiff) missiles.

ow: Delta II carried 16 SS-N-8 (Sawfly) missiles.

Typhoon-class
(Project 491)

Total built: 6.
Completed: 1981-89.
Displacement: surfaced 23,200 tons; submerged 33,800 tons.
Dimensions: length 566ft 11in (172.8m); beam 76ft 1in (23.2m); drau
37ft 8in (11.5m).
Propulsion: 2 x OK-650 pressurised-water nuclear reactor; 2 x ste
turbines, 100,000shp; two shafts (shrouded propellers).
Performance: surface – 12kt; submerged – 25kt; maximum operat
depth 1,300ft (400m).
Weapons: 2 x 21in (533mm), 4 x 24.8in (630mm) TT (bow) (22 weapor
missiles – 20 x missile tubes.
Complement: 179.

History: In the late 1970s there were persistent rumours in the West t
the Soviet Navy was constructing a new class of submarines of hu
proportions, but when the design was revealed in November 1980 it
came as a major surprise. Overall, the most astonishing factor was
enormous size – it was far bigger than any other submarine before or sin
and for many years there were arguments as to whether it had one or t

Below. Typhoon's size caused great alarm in the West.

ove: Typhoon is 76ft (23m) wide, 567ft (173m) long.

hulls inside the outer casing. Next, it was the first SSBN to have t
missiles located forward of the sail, and the number of missiles – 20 – w
greater than any of its contemporaries, until the advent of the U.S. Nav
Ohio-class.

The mysteries were gradually revealed, the main one being that the
were two identical and interconnected hulls, each 27ft 11in (8.5m)
diameter containing a full propulsion system, accommodation and oth
services. In addition, there were three pressure containers, housing t
torpedo tubes forward, sail and command centre amidships, and a smal
one aft for the steering and hydroplane control machinery. The missile tub
were located in two parallel rows of 10 between the two main pressu
hulls and forward of the massive sail.

The Typhoons were designed to operate under the Arctic ice-cap, usi
their enormous size to force their way to the surface in order to launch th
missiles. The missile was the SS-N-20 (Sturgeon), a three-stage, solid f
missile with a range of 4,470nm (8,300km) and a payload of 10 100kT MIRV

The main machinery comprised two quite separate power-trains, one
each hull, each unit comprising an OK-650 pressurised-water nucle
reactor (190mW) driving a steam turbine (50,000hp) and two 3,200k

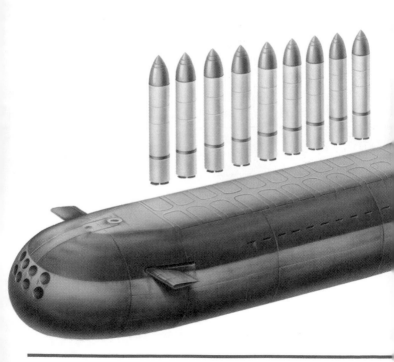

rbo-generators. Each unit also includes stand-by power from a single
0kW diesel generator coupled to the shaft line. Each power-train
lminates in a seven-bladed, fixed-pitch shrouded propeller. In order to
sist navigation at slow speeds, there were built-in bow and stern
rusters, each powered by a 750kW motor.

Six Typhoons were built at Severodvinsk on the White Sea near
changelsk, completion dates being: *TK-208* – 1981, *TK-202* – 1983, *TK-12*
1984, *TK-13* – 1985, *TK-17* – 1987 and *TK-20* – 1989. Work on a seventh
TK-210 – stopped in 1990 and it was then broken up. All were based with
e Russian Northern Fleet at Litsa Guba. First-of-class *TK-208* started a refit
1992, which included conversion to take SS-N-28 missiles, but work was
:er suspended and the combination of a shortage of funds and
ncellation of the SS-NX-28 mean that it will never be completed. *TK-12*
d *TK-13* were stricken in 1996, since funds were not available for a refit.
ork on scrapping most of these ships started in the late 1990s, the
ssian Navy being assisted by the United States under the Co-operative
ireat Reduction Programme, with U.S. funding being particularly
rmarked for the processing facilities to remove nuclear material and
nvert it into forms suitable for either re-use or long-term storage.

elow: In essence, Typhoon consists of two parallel hulls, each
ntaining its own missiles and nuclear power-train, with a third
mmand compartment on top and all encased, as always in Russian
bmarines, in a second, outer hull.

George Washington-class

Total built: 5.
Completed: 1959-61.
Displacement: surfaced 5,959 tons; submerged 6,709 tons.
Dimensions: length 381ft 8in (116.4m); beam 33ft 0in (10.1m); draught 26ft
(8.1m).
Propulsion: 1 x Westinghouse S5W pressurised-water nuclear reactor;
15,000shp; 1 x electric motor; one shaft.
Performance: submerged – 20kt.
Weapons: 6 x 21in (533mm) TT (bow); missiles – 16 x missile tubes.
Complement: 112 (two crews).

History: This historic design established a pattern which has been followed by the great majority of subsequent SSBNs, with 16 missiles mounted vertically in two rows of eight abaft the sail. Having decided in favour of the principle, the U.S. Navy was desperate to get SSBNs to sea as quickly as possible and the first-of-class was constructed by taking the hull of Skipjack-class USS *Scorpion* (SSN-589), which was already under construction, and adding a new 130ft (40m) missile section, while retaining the original powerplant and much of the SSN-type equipment. The result was an outstanding success and four more to the same design were completed between 1959 and 1961, each armed with 16 Polaris A-1 missiles. Such was the pace of progress, however, that by the mid-1960s the relatively short range of their first-generation SLBMs was making them vulnerable to Soviet countermeasures, so during their first re-coring they were fitted to launch the 2,855nm (4,595km) Polaris A-3. Their electronics and other systems were also upgraded.

These five boats were physically unsuitable for

nversion to take Poseidon missiles, so they were deactivated in 1980-81, and veral plans for their future were considered, including conversion to cruise-issile carriers. In the event, *Theodore Roosevelt* (SSBN-600) and *Abraham ncoln* (SSBN-602) were cut in two and have since been scrapped, while the her three had their missile tubes filled with concrete and were reclassified as Ns. They were then used as training boats for several years, but the last was commissioned in 1985.

elow: **George Washington** *SSBN receives a Polaris SLBM .*

Ethan Allen-class

Total built: 5.
Completed: 1961-63.
Displacement: surfaced 6,946 tons; submerged 7,884 tons.
Dimensions: length 410ft 5in (125.1m); beam 33ft 0in (10.1m); draught 24ft 7 (8.4m).
Propulsion: 1 × Westinghouse S5W pressurised-water nuclear reactor; 15,000shp; 1 × electric motor; one shaft.
Performance: submerged – 20kt.
Weapons: 4 × 21in (533mm) TT (bow); missiles – 16 × missile tubes.
Complement: 110 (two crews).

History: Whereas the George Washington-class was built to a modified SS design in order to get the Polaris missile into service as quickly as possible, t five Ethan Allen SSBNs were designed specifically as SSBNs. They we generally similar to the earlier class, but were some 28ft 9in (8.7m) longer, a when first commissioned were armed with the Polaris A-2 missile, which h a range of 1,725nm (2,776km). They had greatly improved crew quarters, important consideration in a boat intended to spend 60 days at a tir submerged. *Ethan Allen* (SSBN-08) was the first SSBN to launch a live SLBM May 1962) which detonated successfully on the Christmas Island test rang These boats were later converted to take the Polaris A-3 missile, but could r be further converted to take Poseidon.

In 1980-81 they were redesignated SSNs, but it was not until 1982 that th missile tubes were filled with concrete and their missile launch and fire cont equipment removed. Two never returned to service, but the other three served ur 1990-91 as SSNs, of which two – *Sam Houston* (SSBN-609) and *John Marsh* (SSBN-611) – were each capable of carrying 66 SEALs and could mount two C Deck Shelters on the upper casing. The last was decommissioned in 1992.

Below: Ethan Allen-class SSBNs carried 16 missiles.

Right: Ethan Allen-class carried Polaris A-1 or A-3 missiles.

Lafayette-class

Total built: 31.
Completed: 1963-67.
Displacement: surfaced 7,325 tons; submerged 8,251 tons.
Dimensions: length 425ft 0in (129.6m); beam 33ft 0in (10.1m); draught 2
10in (8.5m).
Propulsion: 1 x Westinghouse S5W pressurised-water nuclear reactor;
15,000shp; 1 x electric motor; one shaft.
Performance: submerged – 20kt.
Weapons: 4 x 21in (533mm) TT (bow); missiles – 16 x missile tubes.
Complement: 140 (two crews).

History: The 31 Lafayette-class SSBNs were the definitive U.S. SSBNs of t
1960s and 1970s. The first 19 to be built were slightly improved and enlarg
versions of the Ethan Allen design and were, at least outwardly, virtua
indistinguishable from the earlier class. The last 12 (ie, from SSBN-6
onwards) differed considerably, with improved, quieter machinery, many mir
improvements and 28 more crewmen, and are sometimes referred to as t

*Below: Earlier Lafayette-class SSBNs retained their original Poseidon C
missiles, but later boats, like* Daniel Boone *(SSBN-629) seen here, were
retrofitted to take Trident I C-4 .*

440

bove: Lafayette-class, George Washington Carver.

Benjamin Franklin-class, but are here treated as one.

The missiles were progressively improved. As built, the first eig[ht] Lafayettes (SSBN-616 – SSBN-625) carried Polaris A-2 SLBMs, while t[he] remaining 23 had the improved Polaris A-3, which had a range of 2,855[nm] (4,594km) and three 200kT MRV warheads. Then, between 1970 and 1978, [the] Lafayettes were converted to take the Poseidon C-3 missiles, which ha[d a] better range of about 3,230nm (5,200km) but, much more significantly, carri[ed] 10 50kT MIRVs, giving a very marked improvement in strategic capabili[ty.] Finally, 12 were refitted yet again (1978-1982), this time to take the larg[e] three-stage Trident C-4 with a range of 4,400nm (7,100km) and carried ei[ght] 100kT MIRVs. The first of these to be completed, *Francis Scott Key* (SSB[N-] 657), began the first Trident patrol on 20 October 1979. Another significa[nt] improvement was that, while the first five boats used compressed-air to eje[ct] the missiles from the tubes (as had been the case in the Washington- and Eth[an]

bove: **Benjamin Franklin,** *first of the modified Lafayettes.*

...len-classes), the remainder had the now-standard rocket-motor, which ...oduced a gas-steam mixture. Although these SSBNs did not have the same ...nderwater performance as an SSN they had a respectable self-defence ...pability against surface ships or other submarines, and were armed with ...onventional or wire-guided torpedoes and SubRoc. Normally, however, they ...ould attempt to evade detection or contact.

Daniel Webster (SSBN-626) of this class was fitted with diving planes on a ...sed and reinforced bow sonar dome, instead of on the fin. Although ...ccessful, this was not copied on other SSBNs.

SSBN-623, -635 and -636 were deactivated in the mid-1980s and the ...mainder in 1990-1994, the only exceptions being SSBN-642 and -645, which ...ere reclassified as SSNs, and converted to SEAL transports.

Ohio-class

Total built: 18.
Completed: 1981-97.
Displacement: surfaced 16,764 tons; submerged 18,750 tons.
Dimensions: length 560ft 0in (170.7m); beam 42.0in (12.8m); draught 3ft 0
(11.3m).
Propulsion: 1 x General Electric S8G natural-circulation, pressurised-wate
nuclear reactor; turbo-reduction drive, ca. 35,000shp; one shaft.
Performance: submerged – 25kt; maximum operational diving depth 984
(300m).
Weapons: 4 x 21in (533mm) TT (amidships); missiles – 24 x missile tubes.
Complement: 163 (two crews).

History: While the programme to upgrade the later Polaris SSBNs to car
Poseidon missiles was under way in the early 1970s, development of a
entirely new missile was started. This was to have a much greater range, whic
required a larger missile, and this in turn required a larger submarine to take fu
advantage of its capabilities. At first, Congress baulked at the immense cost o
the new missile, but its view was transformed into support when the Sovi
Navy introduced first the SS-N-8 (4,200nm/6,760km) followed short
afterwards by the SS-N-18 (4,846nm/7,800km). The U.S. Navy the
speeded up its programme and the first Ohio-colas ship was laid down o
10 April 1976. However, a variety of factors caused delays and first-of-clas
USS *Ohio* (SSBN-726) did not start trials until 17 June 1981; it fired its fir

Above: Fourth in the Ohio-class, USS Georgia (SSBN-729).

Below: Caps lift to expose the Ohios' awesome power.

445

Above: The dedication of USS West Virginia *(SSBN-736).*

successful missile on 17 January 1982 and sailed on its first operation deterrent patrol on 1 October 1982. This was considerably behind schedule and both submarine and missile were subjected to considerable criticism the time, but since then this has proved to be one of the most success naval weapons systems ever to enter service.

The Ohio-class boats are huge, being only marginally shorter than Ticonderoga-class cruiser – 560ft (170.7m) compared to 567ft (172.9m) – with a very much greater displacement – 16,747 compared to 9,466 tons. The immense destructive power, however, lies in their 24 Trident II D-5 missile each capable of carrying eight 475kT W-88 MIRVed warheads.

Eighteen were built, joining the fleet between 1981 and 1997, of which eight were armed with the Trident I C-4 missile and 10 with the Trident II D missile. In 2002, the plan was to retire the first four ships (SSBN-726 – SSB 729) and to rearm the second four (SSBN-730 – SSBN-733) with Trident II D missiles. This will leave the U.S. Navy's deterrent force comprising 14 ship with each of the 24 missiles carrying five warheads, for a grand total of 1,6 warheads. Of these warheads, some 400 are W-88s with a 300-475kT yie while the remainder are W-76s with a yield of some 100kT.

The Trident force is split equally between the east and west coasts of t United States, with nine based at Bangor, Washington, and nine at King's B Georgia. Of these, five are on station, five proceeding to or returning from pat (but still capable of launching their missiles) and the others are in port undergoing overhaul. Each boat has two crews, known as Blue and Gold.

In early 2002 the future of some elements of the Ohio-class was uncerta There have been periodic proposals to either reduce the active force to boats, or to reduce the crewing of all 14 to one crew each. This would produ a totally new deployment cycle and reduce the numbers available on station any one time; it would also drastically reduce both the manpower requireme and the annual operating costs.

Right: **Tennessee** *outward bound on deterrent patrol.*

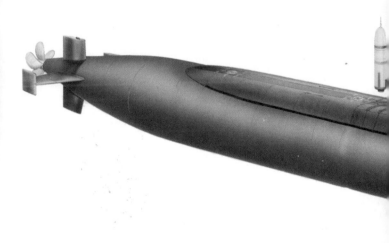

Above: Ohios carry 24 missiles, more than any other SSBN.

Special Role Submarines

Gun-armed Cruisers

In 1917 the German Navy started developing "U-cruisers" armed with lar[ge] calibre guns to attack enemy merchant shipping in remote areas. The Brit[ish] also developed the M-class (one 12in/305mm) followed by *X-1* (two tw[o] 5.2in/132mm), but neither proved satisfactory. The U.S. Navy considered ve[ry] large submarines mounting 8in (203mm) guns, but the only outcome was t[he] Narwhal-class with two 6in (152mm) guns. Largest of them all was the Frer[ch] *Surcouf* with two 8in (203mm) guns but, like the others, she was a failure.

Minelayers

The first specialised submarine minelayer was the Russian *Krab* laid down [in] 1908, followed by the German UC I-class in 1915, and small numbers [of] minelayers were subsequently built for most navies. The Russians used [a] horizontal conveyor belt atop the hull which moved the mines to the ste[rn] where they simply fell off, while the U.S. Navy, used a system in which min[es] were ejected along a tube. One German system used tubes on the boa[t's] centreline, but this required holes in the pressure hull, open at both ends. T[he] fourth was the simplest, using vertical tubes in the submarine's side tanks. T[he] specialised minelayer disappeared because small minefields could be laid mo[re] effectively by aircraft, and mines were developed which could be laid fro[m] torpedo tubes.

Aircraft-carrying Submarines

Aircraft-carrying submarines were conceived to extend the observation range of submarines, and both the British and Germans experimented with taking aircraft to sea aboard submarines during World War I. Nothing came of the idea until after the war, when several navies produced submarines carrying a small floatplane in a cylindrical hangar, with the submarine surfacing to launch and recover the aircraft. The U.S. Navy conducted experiments in the early 1920s with the submarine *S-1* (SS-105) and Martin MS-1 floatplane but did not pursue the idea. The British converted the monitor *M-2,* but after she was lost with all hands, they, too, abandoned the idea. In the mid-1930s the French built the *Surcouf* , which carried a small floatplane, but when war broke out the aircraft was removed. The Japanese built by far the most aircraft-carrying submarines which saw a great deal of action in World War II. A completely different approach was taken by the Germans in World War II who used a one-man, rotary-winged kite (Focke-Achgelis Bachstelze) which was assembled on deck and then towed aloft. The problem with all these schemes was that it took a relatively long time to assemble and launch the aircraft and to recover, dismantle and stow it after landing, during which the submarine was very vulnerable to attack..

Radar Pickets

Another special role for submarines was as radar

kets, a mission originated by the U.S. Navy which needed both to detect oming *kamikaze* attacks, and provide forward control for carrier aircraft erations. After heavy losses among surface warships, the role was passed to omarine radar pickets (SSR), operating radars while awash; they could omerge if threatened with air attack. Two boats (out of an intended 24) were nverted during the war and a few more conversions followed in the late 40s. In the 1950s three purpose-built radar pickets were commissioned, two nventionally powered (SSR) and one nuclear-powered (SSRN). The only other y to develop submarine radar pickets was the Soviet Navy, but this was to meet otally different operational requirement.

nsport, Cargo and Oiler Submarines
ally, throughout the 20th century submarines have had to transport people materiel, most often by misemploying operational boats. Some specialist nsports have been produced, eg, German World War I Deutschland-class and lian World War II Romolo-class, while the Germans also produced the Type F, a torpedo transport. The German Type XIV resupply submarines posed a rticular threat, but the Allied breaking of Enigma codes enabled these boats be sunk comparatively quickly. Another concept tried at various times by the rman, Japanese and U.S. navies was the use of submarines as floating uelling stations for seaplanes, but without great success.

low: USS Redfin *converted to radar picket (SSR).*

Surcouf-class

Total built: 1.
Commissioned: 1935.
Displacement: surfaced 3,252 tons; submerged 4,304 tons.
Dimensions: length 360ft 1in (110.0m); beam 29ft 6in (9.0m); draught 23ft
(7.25m).
Propulsion: 2 x Sulzer diesel engines, 7,600bhp; 2 x electric motors, 3,400sl
two shafts.
Performance: surface – 18.5kt, 10,000nm/10kt; submerged – 10kt, 75n
4.5kt; maximum depth 262ft (80m).
Weapons: 8 x 21.7in (550mm) TT (14 torpedoes); 4 x 15.7in (400mm) TT
torpedoes); 2 x 8in/50 (203mm) guns (600 rounds); 2 x 37mm guns (1,0
rounds); 4 (2 x 2) 13.2mm AAMG.
Aircraft: 1 x Besson MB 411 floatplane.
Complement: 118.

History: *Surcouf* was designed for world-wide commerce-raiding, mount
two 8in (203mm) guns in a twin turret forward and carrying a purpose-b
Besson floatplane, whose role was to obtain targets and to provide correctic
for gun engagements. She was the largest submarine of her time and w
superficially impressive, but suffered from a number of disadvantages. First
took some 2-3 minutes to get the guns into action following surfacing ar
second, the low height of the stereoscopic rangefinder limited effective fire
12,300yd (11,265m). Next, the aircraft was small and under-powered, and tc
all of 10 minutes to disassemble prior to submerging. The basic proble
however, was that it was never clear which nations' merchant shipping *Surc*

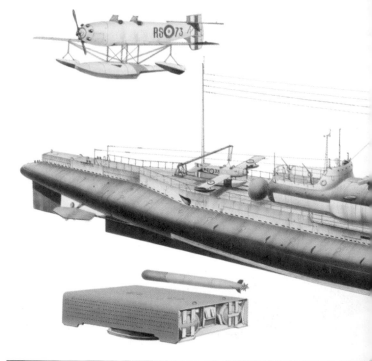

*ove: **Surcouf's main armament was two 8in (203mm) guns.***

ght be required to attack. If war was declared against the most likely enemy, rmany, that country's merchant fleet would be swept from the sea in a atter of weeks by surface warships, while no other potential enemy had a erchant fleet worth attacking.

Torpedo armament consisted of eight 21.7in (550mm) tubes, four in the w and four external aft, and four 15.7in (400mm) in a rotating mount on the er deck, the latter being intended for use against merchant ships. In World ar II *Surcouf* served as a convoy escort but on the French collapse went to mouth, England, where, after several weeks delay, she was forcibly taken er by the British. She served for some months in the Caribbean but was then dered to the Pacific and was en route to her new operating area when she appeared with all hands, the result of a collision with a U.S. freighter.

*low: **A spotter plane was built for Surcouf, but never used.***

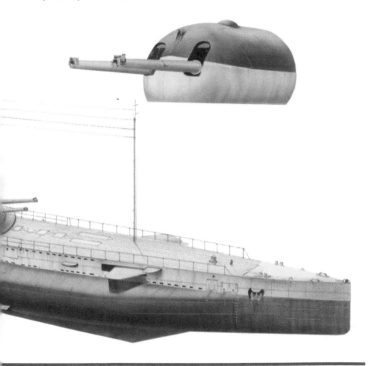

U-151-class

Total built: 7.
Commissioned: 1917.
Displacement: surfaced 1,512 tons; submerged 1,875 tons.
Dimensions: length 213ft 3in (65.0m); beam 29ft 2in (8.9m); draught 17ft (5.3m).
Propulsion: 2 x Germania 6-cylinder, 4-stroke diesel engines, 800bhp; electric motors, 800shp; two shafts.
Performance: surface – 12.4kt, 25,000nm/5.5kt; submerged – 5.2kt, 65nm/ maximum depth 164ft (50m).
Weapons: U-155 – 6 x 19.7in (500mm) TT, remainder – 2 x 19.7in (500mm) (18 torpedoes); 2 x 5.9in/45 (150mm) guns (2 x 1); 2 x 3.45in/45 (88mm) gu
Complement: 56 (plus 20 prize crew).

History: The Deutschland-class boats were originally designed as submar freighters, for which they were built to mercantile standards, managed b commercial company and manned by civilian crews. They mounted armament and could carry some 740 tons of cargo. First-of-class *Deutschl* made two successful return voyages to the United States in 1916, but second to be completed, *Bremen*, disappeared without trace on her f voyage. When the USA entered the war on the Allied side it was decidec convert the remaining boats into long-range, gun-armed U-cruise *Deutschland* was converted (becoming *U-151*) and the remainder w completed to the new design as *U-152 – U-157*, all seven becoming operatic in late 1917.

M-class

GREAT BRITA

Total built: 3.
Commissioned: 1917.
Displacement: surfaced 1,600 tons; submerged 1,950 tons.
Dimensions: length (M-1/2) 295ft 9in (90.1m), (M-3/4) 303ft 0in (92.4 beam 24ft 8in (7.5m); draught 15ft 1in (4.8m).
Propulsion: 2 x Vickers 12-cylinder diesel engines, 2,400bhp; 2 x elec motors, 1,600shp; 336 lead-acid cells; two shafts.
Performance: surface – 14kt, 3,800nm/10kt; submerged – 8kt, 80nm/2 maximum depth 200ft (61m).
Weapons: M-1/2 – 4 x 18in (457mm) TT (bow) (10 torpedoes), M-3/4 – 21in (533mm) TT (8 torpedoes); 1 x 12in/40 (305mm) gun (40 rounds); 3in (76mm) gun (72 rounds); 1 x 0.303in Lewis MG.
Complement: 68.

History: The original idea for the M-class was for a submarine armed v a single 12in (305mm) gun with 50 rounds, which could be used agai either sea or land targets. The hull was a new design, but the diesel a electric motors were taken from the L-class. Four boats were laid dowr 1916 and on trials with the first-of-class the gun proved to be success being capable of elevation between +12 and -5 degrees, and training o 15 degrees. The diving time was a surprisingly short 90 seconds.

Four were laid down in 1916, of which *M-1* was completed in 1917 a saw brief war service in late 1918 in the Mediterranean; it served on u 1925. *M-2* was to the same design as *M-1*, but *M-3* and *M-4* w lengthened by some 10ft (3m) to accommodate the new 21in (533m

All mounted two 5.9in (150mm) and two 88mm guns, but while *U-151* had
torpedo tubes (three per side) mounted under the upper deck and angled out
5 degrees, the remainder had two conventional bow-mounted, ahead-firing
es. There were two war losses, *U-154* being torpedoed by British submarine
5, while *U-156* was mined; the remaining five were ceded to the Allies (UK
, France – 2) and were sunk or broken up in the early 1920s.

*ow: **U-151**, formerly transport **Deutschland**, as a cruiser.*

*ove: British **M-1** armed with a single 12in (305mm) gun.*

pedo tubes. *M-2* and *M-3* were both too late to see war service and were
iverted in 1927-28, *M-2* to a seaplane carrier (qv), and *M-3* to a minelayer.
1 was rammed and sunk by a freighter in 1925 with the loss of all hands.
4 was cancelled while building and scrapped. Somewhat surprisingly, despite
s clear rejection of the concept by the British, the French built the *Surcouf* (qv)
ich was virtually identical in concept, and was, similarly, a failure.

X-1-class

Total built: 1.
Commissioned: 1925.
Displacement: surfaced 3,050 tons; submerged 3,600 tons.
Dimensions: length 360ft 6in (110.8m); beam 29ft 10in (9.1m); draught 15ft (4.8m).
Propulsion: 2 x Admiralty diesel engines, 6,000bhp; 2 x M.A.N. auxil diesels, 2,600bhp; 2 x G.E.C. electric motors, 2,400shp; two shafts.
Performance: surface – 20kt, 18,700nm/8kt; submerged – 9kt, 50nm/ maximum operating depth 350ft (107m).
Weapons: 6 x 21in (533mm) TT (bow) (12 torpedoes); 4 x 5.2in/42 (132m guns (2 x 2).
Complement: 109.

History: The German World War I concept of the lone submarine roaming world's sealanes had its attractions for the British who ordered *X-1* in 19 armed with four 5.2in (132mm) guns in two twin turrets, which were suppos

enable her to survive against destroyers and to attack enemy merchant hipping. She proved to have excellent handling characteristics both on the urface and when submerged, and provided a stable gun platform, while her nge-finder could be raised by 9ft (2.7m) to provide good gun control over dequate ranges. However, she suffered from severe mechanical problems: e main diesels and the electric motors proved to be unreliable, while the .A.N. battery charging diesels never produced their design output power. In ddition, the eternal fuel tanks leaked badly, leaving a tell-tale oil slick on the urface.

Once in service it became clear that her intended role against destroyers ould prove hazardous in the extreme, while it was unclear which nation's erchant ships she could be used against. As a result, she completed one four-ear commission in the Mediterranean, but was then placed in reserve, stricken 1935 and scrapped in 1936.

elow: British **X-1***, with 4 x 5.2in (132mm) guns.*

Pierre Chailley/
Saphir-classes

Total built: Pierre Chailley – 1; Saphir – 6.
Completed: Pierre Chailley – 1922 ; Saphir – 1928-35.
Displacement: surfaced 761 tons; submerged 925 tons.
Dimensions: length 216ft 2in (65.9m), beam 23ft 7in (7.2m); draught 14ft 1
(4.3m).
Propulsion: 2 x Normand-Vickers diesels, 1,300bhp; 2 x electric motor
1,000shp; two shafts.
Performance: surface – 12kt, 4,000nm/12kt; submerged – 9kt, 80nm/4
maximum depth 250ft (76m).
Weapons: 2 x 21.7in (550mm) TT (bow); 1 x 21.7in (550mm) TT ; 2 x 15.7
(400mm) TT (rotating mount aft); 1 x 3in (76mm) gun; mines– 32.
Complement: 42.
Specifications for Saphir-class, as built.

History: *Pierre Chailley*, ordered in 1917 and completed in 1921, was the fir
French purpose-built minelayer. It used the Normand-Fenaux system
externally mounted, vertical mine-tubes, which proved both safe and efficient
practice. There were 20 tubes, each containing two 441lb (200kg) mines. Th
Saphir-class was a modified version, with 16 mine-tubes, each containing tw
mines. *Pierre Chailley* was stricken in 1936, but the six Saphir-class boa
served on routine peacetime tasks until the outbreak of World War II, whe

UC-1-class (Project 35a)

Total built: 15.
Completed: 1915.
Displacement: surfaced 168 tons; submerged 183 tons.
Dimensions: length 111ft 6in (34.0m); beam 10ft 4in (3.2m); draught 10ft 0
(3.0m).
Propulsion: 1 x Daimler 6-cylinder 4-stroke diesel, 90bhp; 1 x electric motor
175shp; one shaft.
Performance: surface – 6.25kt, 780nm/5kt; submerged – 5.2kt, 50nm/4
maximum operating depth 164ft (50m).
Weapons: Mine tubes – 6 x 39.4in (100cm) sloped tubes (forward); 12
UC/120 mines.
Complement: 14.

History: The German land attack on France in the early months of World Wa
was most successful on its right wing. In early September it was proposed th
small minelaying U-boats should be built to take advantage of the new
captured naval bases on the Belgian coast. The first proposal was for an 80 to
boat driven by battery power alone, but was this was shelved and by Octob
the requirement was for a 150 ton boat based on the newly completed Type U
design. This would have a totally new forward section housing six tubes, ea
containing two mines. It was decided that the mines would be laid while th
boat was moving slowly forwards, so the tubes were angled aft at 26 degre
from the vertical, even though this caused some construction problems.
   Despite the novelty of the concept, the project proceeded with remarkab
speed: the requirement was stated on 14 October 1914; orders for 15 we

bove: Rubis *was the most successful minelayer in any navy.*

vo took up minelaying duties in the North Sea and four in the Mediterranean.

Following the French armistice in June 1940, two served with the Free ench Navy, of which *Perle* was sunk in error by the RAF in July 1944, while ubis became the most successful minelaying submarine in any navy, her ines accounting for 10 minor warships and 14 merchant ships. The other four erved in the Vichy Navy; one was scuttled in November 1942 and the other ree were captured in Bizerta in 1942. Two of these were then used as battery-narging hulks by the Italian Navy, but all three were scuttled in 1943. *Rubis* rvived the war, to be stricken in 1949. These were the only purpose-built inelayers built for the French Navy.

bove: German UC-1-class minelayer had sloping tubes.

aced on 23 November; the first to be completed left the yard on 26 April 915; and the last was completed in July. They were built by Vulkan (10) and Veser (5) and were broken down into sections and despatched by train, C-1 – UC- 11 to Flanders and *UC-12 – UC-15* to Pola on the Adriatic. Apart om the mines, the Type UC-1 boats were unarmed except for one of the landers boats, *UC-11*, which was fitted with a single external 17.7in 5cm) tube aft in 1916. *UC-2* sank off Yarmouth, England, on 2 July 1915 nd was detected and raised by the British, their first indication that ubmarines were being used to lay mines.

UC-III-class (Project 41a)

Total built: 29 (see notes).
Completed: 1918.
Displacement: surfaced 491 tons; submerged 571 tons.
Dimensions: length 214ft 10in (56.5m); beam 18ft 0in (5.5m); draught 12ft 6
(3.8m).
Propulsion: 2 x M.A.N. 6-cylinder 4-stroke diesels, 2 x 300hp; 2 x elect
motors, 2 x 385hp; 2 x 62-cell batteries; two shafts.
Performance: surface – 11.5kt, 9,850nm/7kt; submerged – 6.6kt, 40nm/4.5
maximum depth 246ft (75m).
Weapons: 3 x 19.7in (500mm) TT (see notes) (7 torpedoes); 1 x 4.1in/
(105mm) gun; mine tubes – 6 x 39.4in (100cm) (forward); 18 UC/200 mines.
Complement: 32.
Specifications for UC-90 group, as built.

History: Even the UC-II boats did not prove totally satisfactory and, in any cas
the German Navy needed more boats to replace the high loss rate amo
minelayers already in service. A requirement was therefore stated for ne
boats with a more powerful armament, greater surface speed and increas
submerged endurance. There was also feedback from the UC-II crews, w
criticised the diving time, adverse conditions for watchkeepers on the brid
during winter, and discomfort for the men below when the boats were travelli
on the surface. The result was a revised UC-II design, with a new hull shape
4.1in (105mm) gun on a raised mounting, and with the two forward torpe
tubes brought back to abreast the conning tower, where they were angl

U-117-class (Project 45)

Total built: 10.
Completed: 1917-18.
Displacement: surfaced 1,164 tons; submerged 1,512 tons.
Dimensions: length 267ft 4in (81.5m); beam 24ft 3in (7.4m); draught 24ft 3
(4.2m).
Propulsion: 2 x M.A.N. 6-cylinder diesels, 23 x 1,200bp; 2 x electric motors,
x 600hp; two shafts.
Performance: surface – 14.7kt, 9,400nm/8kt; submerged – 7kt, 35nm/4.5
maximum operating depth 246ft (75m).
Weapons: 4 x 19.7in (500mm) TT (bow) (12 torpedoes); 1 x 5.9in/45 (150mm
gun; mine tubes – 2 x 39.4in (100cm) horizontal tubes (stern); 42 mines (pl
30 mines in deck stowage).
Complement: 40.
Specifications for U-117 group, as completed.

History: A requirement for an improved and more reliable minelayer aro
in 1916, leading to Project 45, which began as essentially a marriage of t
main features of Project 43 (U-155-class) to the large mine storage spa
and twin, aft-mounted mine tubes of Project 38 (U-71-class). As wi
Project 38 there were two tubes, each of which carried three mines, pl
36 mines in the store room. One of the curious features of this desig
however, was that there were also storage bins in special troughs on t
upper deck abaft the conning tower, which could accommodate either
spare torpedoes or 30 additional mines. The latter were launched manua
over the stern of the surfaced submarine.

above: **UC-103***, a UC-III-class minelayer, after the war.*

atwards at some 10 degrees. The boats' flooding and ballast arrangements ere improved, but the mine tubes and other internal arrangements remained achanged.

A total of 39 boats were ordered (*UC-80 – UC-118*), but, in the event only *UC-)– UC-118*, all built by Blohm + Voss, were completed before the war's end, those Weser (3) and Danzig (9) being broken-up on the slips in 1919. None of the mpleted boats was lost in combat, although one was lost in an accident, and the mainder were allocated to the Allies, including two to the Japanese Navy, which ed them as the basis for their KRS-class minelayers.

The first five of these boats (*U-117 – U-121*) were built by Vulkan, Hamburg ad the second five (*U-122 – U-126*) by Blohm + Voss, the latter being 20in .5m) longer and having a slightly shorter range. All served in World War I and ere then allocated to the Allies: France – 3; Japan – 1; UK – 4; U.S. – 1.

At one point in the war the demand for U-cruisers became greater than that r minelayers and certain of these Project 45 boats were converted for such a le, with the mine storage space being used to accommodate the prize crews ad additional fuel.

elow: Ocean-going minelayer **U-122** *in the Kiel canal.*

Type XB-classes

Total built: 8.
Completed: 1941-43.
Displacement: surfaced 1,755 tons; submerged 2,143 tons.
Dimensions: length 294ft 7in (89.8m); beam 30ft 3in (9.2m); draught 15ft 5(4.7m).
Propulsion: 2 x Germania 9-cylinder, 4-stroke diesels, 2 x 2,100bhp; 2 x electr motors, 2 x 550shp; two shafts.
Performance: surface – 16.4kt, 14,450nm/12kt; submerged – 7.0l 188nm/2kt; maximum operating depth 394f t (120m).
Weapons: 2 x 21in (533mm) TT (stern) (15 torpedoes); 1 x 4.1in/45 (105mm gun; 1 x 20mm C30 cannon; mine tubes – 30 x 4ft 4in (1.33m) diameter tub (6 x 3-mine tubes forward; 12 x 2-mine tubes in each side tank); 66 x SN mines.
Complement: 52.

History: The largest submarine built in Germany, the Type X was design specifically to carry the SMA anchored mine. The original design (Type XA) w an update of the World War I Project 45 (qv) and was based on the need to s the SMA mechanism by hand immediately prior to launch, which necessitat the mines being held in a large storage chamber aft. When this need for man setting was overcome the entire design was recast, resulting in the Type X There were six vertical tubes forward, each containing three mines, whi protruded about 12in (305mm) from the foredeck and were open above a below. There were a further 24 tubes, 12 in each side tank, holding two min

---

Porpoise/
Grampus-classes

Total built: Porpoise – 1; Grampus – 5.
Completed: Porpoise – 1933; Grampus-class – 1936-39.
Displacement: surfaced 1,520 tons; submerged 2,157 tons.
Dimensions: length 293ft 0in (89.3m); beam 25ft 6in (7.8m); draught 17ft 3(5.3m).
Propulsion: 2 x Admiralty diesel engines; 2 x 3,300bhp; 2 x electric motors, x 1,630shp; battery 3 x 112 4,560AH cells; two shafts.
Performance: surface – 15.8kt, 5,880nm/9.3kt; submerged – 8.8kt, 64nm/4 maximum operating depth 300ft (91m).
Weapons: 6 x 21in (533mm) TT (bow) (12 torpedoes); 1 x 4in/40 (102mm) gu mine system – one horizontal conveyor-belt; 50 x Mk XVI mines.
Complement: 59.
Specifications for Grampus-class, as built.

History: *Porpoise* had a hull based on that of the Parthian-class (qv) combin with an improved version of the conveyor system tested aboard *M-3* (qv).The was only one conveyor carrying 50 mines and this ran down the centreline the boat, requiring the tower and periscopes to be offset to starboard wi balancing weights carried on the port side. The design was improved yet furth and the next five boats were longer, had a revised internal design and a straigl through casing, whereas *Porpoise* had a small step near the bow. *Porpoise* a the five Grampus-class boats had a very busy war, laying a total of 2,599 mine

ght: A Type XB minelayer iling into Portsmouth, NH, May 1945.

ch. The two torpedo tubes ere situated aft and the boats ginally mounted a 105mm gun, hough this was later removed.

The large size of the Type s made them suitable for her uses and they were often nployed as supply boats; deed, all six war losses were e to enemy action while rving in this role. The other two ats were converted for use as nsport boats on the Far East n, one of them, *U-219*, actually aching Malaya in 1944 and still ere at the time of the German rrender, when it was taken er by the Japanese as *I-505*. e last boat, *U-234*, left for the r East in April 1945 and was in mid-Atlantic when Germany capitulated. The otain surrendered to the United States and on arrival at Portsmouth, NH, his at was found to be carrying a large quantity of uranium, whose origin, ended use in Japan, and actual use in the USA all remain mysteries to this day.

ove: British minelayer, Rorqual, *is launched, 21 July 1936.*

t losses were heavy. Two were sunk by Italian surface units: *Cachalot* (30 ly 1941) and *Grampus* (16 June 1940). Two more fell victim to aircraft: the ftwaffe sank *Narwhal* (23 July 1940) and Japanese naval aircraft sank rpoise (19 January 1945). The fifth loss was *Seal*, which was sunk by a mine May 1940) but brought back to the surface, where it was unable to proceed d was captured by the Germans, who later employed it for a time as a ining boat. That left *Rorqual*, which was scrapped in December 1945.

Above: Rorqual's *conveyor-belt dropped mines over the stern.*

X-2-class

ITA

Total built: 2.
Completed: 1917-18.
Displacement: surfaced 403 tons; submerged 468 tons.
Dimensions: length 139ft 9in (42.6m); beam 18ft 1in (5.5m); draught 10ft 2 (3.1m).
Propulsion: 2 x Sulzer diesel engines, 2 x 650bhp; 2 x electric motors, 2 325shp; two shafts.
Performance: surface – 8.2kt; submerged – 6.3kt.
Weapons: 1 x 3in/30 (76mm) AA gun; mine system – 9 x sloping tubes; 18 x Italian AE1916/125t mines.
Complement: 25.

History: The German UC I-class minelayer, *UC-12*, was transported to the Adriatic where it operated under the Austro-Hungarian flag as *U-24*, but with its original German crew. While operating off Taranto on 16 March 1916, it hit one of its own mines and sank, but was subsequently raised by the Italians and completely rebuilt, joining the Italian Navy on 9 December 1916 as *X-1*. This led the Italian Navy to develop its own submarine-launched mines and to design a new class of boat to deliver them. The new boats, the

2-class, were somewhat larger than the German UC-1-class, enabling them
accommodate nine tubes (18 mines) as opposed to six tubes (12 mines) in
e German boat. Main armament was a 3in (76mm) AA gun mounted abaft the
wer. As built, no torpedo tubes were fitted, but in 1918 two 17.7in (450mm)
rpedoes were carried on the upper casing.

elow: Italian X-3 carried 18 mines in nine vertical tubes.

Bragadin-class

Total built: 2.
Completed: 1930-31.
Displacement: surfaced 965 tons; submerged 1,008 tons.
Dimensions: length 235ft 7in (71.5m); beam 20ft 2in (6.2m); draught 16ft
(5.0m).
Propulsion: 2 x Tosi diesel engines, 2 x 750bhp; 2 x Marelli
electric motors, 2 x 500shp; two shafts.
Performance: surface – 11.5kt, 4,800nm/6.5kt; submerged –
7.0kt, 86nm/2.2kt; maximum operating depth 288ft (90m).
Weapons: 4 x 21in (533mm) TT (6 torpedoes); 1 x 4in/35
(102mm) AA gun; 2 x 13.2mm MG; mine system – 2 x
horizontal tubes; 16-24 mines.
Complement: 55.

History: These were Italy's first post-World War I minelayers and
were designed by Bernardis, who had been responsible for the
rebuilding of the ex- German X-1 and the design and construction
of the X-2-class. Those earlier boats had used vertical tubes, but
the new boats used a horizontal system, with two tubes, ejecting
the mines at the stern. They were designed for short-range
operations in the Mediterranean, and were developed from the
Pisani-class, with a single hull and saddle-tanks. The design was
not satisfactory and after several years' service they underwent
major modification, with the stern being shortened by some 12ft

KiRai-Sen (KRS)-class

Total built: 4.
Completed: 1927-28.
Displacement: surfaced 1,142 tons; submerged 1,768 tons.
Dimensions: length 279ft 6in (85.2m), beam 24ft 8in (7.5m); draught 14ft
(4.4m).
Propulsion: 2 x M.A.N. 6-cylinder, 4-stroke diesel engines, 2 x 1,200bhp; 2
electric motors, 2 x 550shp; two shafts.
Performance: surface – 14.5kt, 10,500nm/8kt; submerged – 7kt, 40nm/4.5
maximum operating depth 250ft (76m).
Weapons: 4 x 21in (533mm) TT (bow) (12 torpedoes); 1 x 5.5in/40 (140m
gun; mine system – 2 x horizontal tubes; 42 x Type 88 mines.
Complement: 51-70.

History: One of the ex-German U-boats allocated to Japan in 1919 was U-12
a U-117-class minelayer (qv), which was renumbered O-6 and served un
1922. Experience with this boat prompted the IJN to build a class of its ow
designated KRS, which were slightly larger, but otherwise identical to t
original German design. They had two relatively short mine tubes aft, each
which carried three mines, with the balance of 36 mines in a large store roo
The Japanese boats were not particularly successful and in 1940 they we
given the additional task of refuelling reconnaissance seaplanes, for which th
were fitted with deck-mounted aviation fuel tanks. This task required them
rendezvous with seaplanes in remote islands and replenish them so that th
could carry out very long-range reconnaissance flights, but the submarin
retained their full minelaying capability.

m) and a watertight compartment installed in a raised bow to improve surface sea-
eping. They were not used as minelayers during the war, being employed instead
transport supplies to North Africa and the Aegean.

Below: Modified Bragadin-class, with raised bow, short stern.

All four boats took part in the offensive operations in December 1941, *I-21*
d *I-22* being part of the Malayan invasion, while *I-23* and *I-24* were with the
ilippines attack. All laid mines at strategic points and then became part of the
irveillance force. In January 1942 all four boats laid mines off the northern
ores of Australia, in the course of which *I-24* was attacked and sunk. Up to
is point the boats were numbered *I-21* to *I-24*, but in May 1942, in common
ith other Japanese submarines, they were renumbered, becoming *I-121* to *I-
24*, respectively. *I-123* was sunk off Guadalcanal on 29 August 1942. From
343 the two survivors were relegated to training, in which role *I-122* was
rpedoed by a U.S. submarine on 10 June 1945. The only surviving boat, *I-121*,
as broken up in 1946.

Below: Japanese KRS-class, the only minelayers built by the IJN,
though they were employed during World War II as transports.

O-19-class

Total built: 2.
Completed: 1939.
Displacement: surfaced 998 tons; submerged 1,536 tons.
Dimensions: length 265ft 9in (81.0m); beam 24ft 7in (7.5m); draught 163t 1 (4.0m).
Propulsion: 2 x Sulzer diesel engines, 2 x 2,600bhp; 2 x electric motors, 2 500shp; two shafts.
Performance: surface – 19.3kt; submerged – 9kt; maximum operating dep 320ft (100m).
Weapons: 8 x 21in (533mm) TT (bow – 4, stern – 2, amidships in rotating mou – 2) (14 torpedoes); 1 x 3.4in/45 (88mm) gun; 2 x 40mm Bofors AA; mi system – 20 x vertical tubes; 40 x mines.
Complement: 55.

History: These were the RNethN's first and only minelaying submarines, t overall design being based on that of the Orzel-class, then building for the Poli Navy, but with the addition of mine tubes. The 20 tubes were mounted with the saddle tanks, 10 on each side, with two mines in each tube. These boa were principally intended for use in the Far East and particularly powerful dies engines were installed to give a very high surface speed and a long range. T boats were also among the first to be fitted with air-breathing tubes – t prototypes of today's snorkels – which were intended to enable them to trav just submerged to avoid the heat of the tropical sun, but while continuing to u the diesel engines. Both boats spent the greater part of their service lives in t

Krab-class

Total built: 1.
Completed: 1915.
Displacement: surfaced 512 tons; submerged 740 tons.
Dimensions: length 173ft 3in (52.8m); beam 14ft 0in (4.3m); draught 12ft 9 (3.9m).
Propulsion: 4 x gasoline engines, 4 x 300bhp; 2 x electric motors, 2 x 200sh two shafts.
Performance: surface – 11.8kt, 1,700nm/7kt; submerged – 7.1kt, 82nm/4kt.
Weapons: 2 x 18in (457mm) TT (bow); 2 x Drzewiecki drop-collars torpedoes); 1 x 3in (75mm) gun; 2 x MG; mine system – 2 x horizontal tube 60 x mines.
Complement: 50.

History: *Krab*, the world's first submarine minelayer, was designed by railway engineer named Nalyetev, who not only conceived a very effectiv laying system, but also designed the submarine that carried it, which ha notably clean lines for its time. Work, however, proceeded at a very slo pace; the proposal was accepted in 1906, but construction did not begin the Admiralty Yard, Nikolayev, until 1908. She was launched in 1912 b was not completed until January 1915, by which time the German UC class (qv) was already in service. The Nalyetev system consisted of tv electrically driven conveyor belts mounted under the upper casing, whi propelled the mines aft until they fell over the stern, a system whi eventually proved more versatile than the vertical tubes, and was adopte by more navies.

bove: Dutch **O-19** *carried 40 mines in 20 vertical tubes.*

ar East. *O -20* had to be scuttled after a depth-charge attack by a Japanese estroyer on 20 December 1941, but *O-19* served until 8 July 1945 when it was vrecked in a storm in the South China Sea.

Krab proved somewhat unreliable in service but carried out several nining operations in the Black Sea in 1915-16, which sank several hostile essels. In the Revolution, she was captured first by the Ukrainians and hen by the Germans, who surrendered her to the British. The latter cuttled her in April 1918 but she was raised and scrapped by the Soviets n 1935.

elow: Russian minelayer **Krab** *carried 60 mines.*

Series II, XI, XIII, XIIIbis

Type	Series II	XI	XIII	XIIIbis
Completed	1931	1935-36	1937-38	194041
Total built	6	6	7	6
Displacement surfaced submerged	1,040 tons 1,335 tons	1,100 tons 1,400 tons	1,123 tons 1,414 tons	1,123 tons 1,414 tons
Dimensions length beam draught	265ft 8in ((81.0m) 22ft 7in (6.9m) 13ft 8in (4.2m)		273ft 3in (83.3m) 23ft 0in (7.0m) 13ft 5in (4.1m)	
Propulsion diesels electric motors shafts	2 x 1,100bhp 2 x 525shp 2	2 x 1,100bhp 2 x 725shp 2	2 x 2,100bhp 2 x 1200hp 2	
Performance surface submerged depth	14kt 9kt 246ft (75m)	14kt 9kt 246ft (75m)	18kt 10kt 246ft (75m)	18kt 10kt 246ft (75m)
Range: surface submerged	6,000nm/9kt 135nm/2kt		14,000nm/9kt 130nm/2kt	
Weapons: torpedo tubes torpedoes guns Mines	6 12 1 x 100mm 1 x 45mm 20	6 12 1 x 100mm 1 x 45mm 20	8 12 1 x 100mm 1 x 45mm 2 x 0.3 MG 20	8 12 1 x 100mm 1 x 45mm 2 x 0.3 MG 20
Complement	54	55	55	55

History: The Leninetz-class consisted of three groups – Series II, Series XI an Series XIII – together with a modified version of the last, Series XIIIbis. There ha been no submarine construction in the USSR following the Revolution until th Series I Dekabrist-class of 1926 (qv), which proved unsatisfactory. The Soviet Nav then raised the British submarine L-55 which had been sunk off Kronstadt in 191 and, having returned the bodies of the crew to Britain with complete correctness they returned the boat to service and closely examined its construction an operation. The lessons learnt were then used in the construction of the next class the Series II minelayers. These boats used a virtually unaltered version of th Nalyetev conveyor system, as used in *Krab* (qv), with two horizontal conveyor under the upper casing, dropping mines though holes in the stern.

The boats had hull numbers *L-1 – L- 25* and all were fabricated in yards in th western USSR. Six boats were built in Leningrad and allocated to the Baltic Flee

Above: Leninetz-class, one of many Soviet-built minelayers.

nd another six were built in Nikolayev and allocated to the Black Sea Fleet. The
emaining boats were prefabricated in Leningrad (10), Nikolayev (2) and Sevastopol
), and the parts were then sent by rail to the Dalzavod Yard in Vladivostok, where
hey were assembled and delivered to the Pacific Fleet, in what must have been a
major logistics undertaking. Nine were lost in the war and the survivors were
crapped in the 1950s.

Below: Series II; a conveyor belt laid mines over the stern.

Valen/Delfinen/ Neptun-classes

SWEDE

Class	Valen	Delfinen	Neptun
Total built	1	3	3
Completed	1925	1934-35	1942-43
Displacement: surfaced submerged	548 tons 730 tons	540 tons 720 tons	550 tons 730 tons
Dimensions length beam draught	187ft 4in (57.1m) 23ft 4in (7.1m) 10ft 2in (3.1m)	207ft 0in (63.1m) 21ft 0in (6.4m) 11ft 2in (3.4m)	205ft 5in (62.6m) 21ft 0in (6.4m) 11ft 2in (3.4m)
Propulsion diesels electric motors shafts	2 x 670bhp (Atlas) 2 x 350shp 2	2 x 600bhp (M.A.N.) 2 x 400shp 2	2 x 900bhp (M.A.N. 2 x 500shp 2
Performance surface submerged	14.8kt 7.4kt	15kt 9kt	15kt 10kt
Weapons torpedo tubes guns mines	4 x 17.7in (450mm) 1 x 75mm/42 1 x 25mm AA 20	4 x 21in (533mm) 1 x 57mm 1 x 25mm AA 20	5 x 21in (533mm) 1 x 40mm Bofors A 1 x 20mm AA 20
Complement	31	34	35

Below: Valen, *Sweden's first minelayer, designed by I.v.S.*

bove: Delfinen-class carried 20 mines in 10 tubes.

bove: The Neptun-class were Sweden's last minelayers.

istory: The first purpose-built minelayer for the RSwedN was the *Valen*, which vas laid down in 1923 and completed in 1925. The Swedes are known to have had ome dealings with the Netherlands-based German design office, I.V.S., in the early 920s and it is probable that German know-how was involved in the design. It was straightforward design, using the French Normand-Fenaux system of vertical ubes mounted in the side tanks, five each side, with two mines per tube, and four 7.7in (450mm) torpedo tubes, all in the bow.

This was followed by the three-strong Delfinen-class, a conventional design repared by I.V.S., but built in Sweden by Kockums to Swedish standards.Like *Valen*, ley had 10 mine tubes, but this time they were armed with four 21in (533mm) orpedo tubes (3 bow, 1 stern). Ordered in 1930, they were launched in 1934-35 and ompleted in 1936-37. The last of the minelayers was the Neptun-class, three of hich were laid down in 1942 and completed in 1943. The mission of these boats vas to lay mines in the Baltic if Sweden's neutrality was threatened, an event which ever arose. *Valen* was stricken in 1944, followed by the three Delfinen-class boats 1956-58, and the last of the line, the three Neptun-class boats, in 1966.

Argonaut-class (V-4)

UNITED STATE

Total built: 1.
Completed: 1928.
Displacement: surfaced 2,710 tons; submerged 4,164 tons.
Dimensions: length 381ft 0in (116.1m); beam 33ft 10in (10.3m); draught 15
4in (4.7m).
Propulsion: 2 x M.A.N. 6-cylinder, 4-stroke diesel engines; 2 x 1,400bhp; 2
Ridgeway electric motors, 2 x 1,100shp; 2 x 120-cell Elide ULS37; two shafts
Performance: surface – 15kt, 18,000nm/8kt; submerged – 8kt, 10nm/8k
maximum operational depth 300ft (91m).
Weapons: 4 x 21in (533mm) TT (bow) (12 torpedoes); 2 x 6in/53 (152mm) M
XII Mod 2 guns; 2 x 0.3in MG (see notes); mine system – 2 x horizontal 40
(102mm) tubes; 60 x Mk XI mines.
Complement: 88.

History: The U.S. Navy followed an international fashion in the 1920s when
constructed a large minelayer, USS *Argonaut* (SS-166). She was designed f
operations in the Pacific, which required long range and 90-day endurance, ar
the overall design was based on that of the Barracuda-class, but incorporatir
lessons learned from examination of surrendered German U-boats. Th
minelaying apparatus was of American design, in which mines were moved
a hydraulic system involving rotating cages and loaded, four at a time, into tw
40in (106mm) diameter tubes, from which they were ejected just under th
stern. There was also a complicated water compensation system to mainta
the boat's trim during the laying process. The submarine was theoretical

M-2-class

GREAT BRITAIN

Type: aircraft-carrying submarine.
Total converted: 1.
Converted: 1928.
Displacement: surfaced 1,788 tons;
submerged 1,950 tons.
Dimensions: length 295ft 9in (90.1m);
beam 24ft 6in (7.5m); draught 15ft 9in
(4.8m).
Propulsion: 2 x Vickers 12-cylinder
diesel engines, 2 x 1,200bhp; 2 x
electric motors, 2 x 1,300shp; 336
lead-acid cells; two shafts.
Performance: surface – 14kt,
3,700nm/10kt; submerged – 6.5kt, range
24nm/4kt; maximum depth 200ft (61m).
Weapons: 4 x 18in (457mm) TT (bow)
(10 torpedoes); 1 x 3in (76mm) gun (72
rounds), 2 x 0.303in Lewis MG.
Aircraft: 1 x Parnall Peto 2-seat
floatplane.
Complement: 55.

*Right: British M-2, converted to
aircraft-carrier, lost in 1932.*

bove: Built as a minelayer, Argonaut *was used as a transport.*

pable of laying eight mines in every 10 minutes, but the system was
mplicated and difficult to operate, although if well-maintained it was very
fective.

 Argonaut's engines were never sufficiently reliable or powerful for her to
tain her design speed and this, coupled with the complexity of the minelaying
ear, meant that she was never particularly successful as a minelayer. She was
ven a major refit in early 1942, which included installing four General Motors
esels in place of the unreliable M.A.N. machines, plus two new external
rpedo tubes aft. It was then decided to employ her as a transport and she
rried 120 Marines on the successful Makin Island raid. Next, she went to the
uth-West Pacific to continue serving as a transport and it was there that she
as sunk on 10 January 1943 with the loss of 120 lives, the U.S. Navy's worst
er submarine disaster.

History: The British carried out trials in 1916 in which two small aircraft we carried to sea aboard a submarine and then floated off, but there seemed lit future for the idea and it was shelved. The concept was, however, resurrect in the 1920s and the M-class monitor HMS *M-2* was converted; since it was a suitable size and it was no longer required in its original role (see M-1 entr It was reconstructed between April and November 1928, when the 12 (305mm) gun and the associated equipment were removed and replaced by watertight, cylindrical hangar, which was so large that the bridge had to raised to enable watchkeepers to see forward. A short launching rail was a fitted on the foredeck.

To launch the aircraft, the submarine was brought to the surface, whe the bottom-hinged hangar door was lowered, following which the aircraft its wheeled trolley was pushed forward onto the catapult. The submari then turned into wind and the aircraft was launched. This process to about five minutes. For recovery, the aircraft landed on its floats and taxi

J1M/J2-classes

Total built: J1M – 1; J2 – 1.
Completed: J1M – 1932; J2 – 1935.
Displacement: surfaced 2,080 tons; submerged 2,921 tons.
Dimensions: length 308ft 5in (94.0m); beam 29ft 9in (9.1m); draught 16ft 2 (4.9m).
Propulsion: 2 x M.A.N. 10-cylinder, 4-stroke diesel engines, 2 x 3,00bhp; 2 electric motors, 2 x 1,300shp; two shafts.
Performance: surface – 18kt, 24,00nm/10kt; submerged – 8kt, 60nm/3 maximum operational depth 260ft (80m).
Weapons: 6 x 21in (533mm) TT (bow) (10 torpedoes); 1 x 5.5in/40 (140mm gun.
Aircraft: 1 x 2-seat floatplane.
Complement: 93.
Specifications are for J1M, as built.

History: From the early 1920s onwards the IJN laid great emphasis on lon range scouting and one outcome was the development of aircraft-carryir submarines. The first was the J1Mboat, *I-5*, whose design was based on th J1 scouting submarine (qv), but with the after 5.5in (140mm) gun deleted ar replaced by facilities to carry a two-seat floatplane. There were two containe

the submarine where it was lifted onto its trolley and returned to the hangar. This recovery process was very dependent on the sea-state and could be protracted. The specially developed Parnall Peto aircraft was a two-seat, twin-float biplane, powered by a single 135hp engine; two prototypes and six production models were built. It was underpowered and had a poor performance, experiencing difficulty in taking-off and having a particularly low ceiling.

M-2 was on exercise on 26 January 1932 when it was lost with all hands. Subsequent investigation showed that the door of the hangar and the internal hatch into the pressure hull were both open, suggesting that the boat had been preparing to launch the aircraft and had been accidentally flooded. Attempts were made to recover the wreck but failed. The British never again experimented with aircraft-carrying submarines. Most of the major navies followed this path but only the Japanese made a success of it. The basic reason for this was that they had a very strong operational requirement; the others did not.

immediately abaft the sail, with the fuselage and twin floats in one and the wings and minor items in the other. The submarine surfaced, following which the aircraft had to be assembled on the open deck and then hoisted out by a crane, since there was no catapult. The aircraft then took off under its own power and on completion of its mission landed beside the submarine where the procedure was reversed. These arrangements were very awkward and time consuming, and no submarine commander likes to have to expose his boat on the surface in enemy waters. The aircraft facilities were removed in 1940, following which *I-5* served as a normal patrol submarine until it was sunk by USS *Wyman* (DE-38) on 19 July 1944.

The single J2-class submarine – *I-6* – was a development of the J1M design, marginally larger and with more powerful engines, which increased surface speed by 2kt but resulted in a decreased range of 4,000nm. Again, there was a single floatplane, but this time there was a long ramp and catapult on the after deck, a slightly more satisfactory arrangement than in *I-5*, except that take-off was over the stern, a most peculiar arrangement, since it deprived the pilot of the assistance of a head wind. *I-6* served through the Pacific campaign until it was sunk on 14 July 1944.

Below: I-5, before conversion to the IJN's first aircraft carrier.

AM-class

Total built: 2.
Completed: 1944-45.
Displacement: surfaced 2,620 tons; submerged 4,762 tons.
Dimensions: length 373ft 5in (113.7m); beam 38ft 5in (11.7m); draught 19ft
(5.9m).
Propulsion: 2 x Kampon 10-cylinder, 4-stroke diesel engines, 2 x 2,200bhp;
electric motors, 2 x 300shp; two shafts.
Performance: surface – 16.7kt, 21,000nm/16kt; submerged – 5.5kt, 60nm/
maximum operational depth 330ft (100m).
Weapons: 6 x 21in (533mm) TT (bow) (12 torpedoes); 1 x 5.5in/40 (140mm) g
7 x 25mm AAMG.
Aircraft: 2 x 2-seat floatplanes.
Complement: 114.

History: Originally planned to be a class of four, only two AM-class bo
were Completed: *I-13* and *I-14*. They were even larger than the A2-cla
and like them were intended to combine the roles of advanced scou
headquarters and aircraft-carrier. Once again, less powerful machinery w
fitted in order to enhance the surface range, although this was now sligh
less than in the A2-class. The hull was generally similar to that of the A
class, but was fitted with bulges to increase the reserve buoyancy and
give greater freeboard on the surface. A major innovation was
installation of a schnorkel, consisting of two tubes, one for air intake, c
for exhaust, but this early Japanese model was considerably le

B1/B2/B3-classes

Total built: B1 – 20; B2 – 6; B3 – 3.
Completed: B1 1940-43; B2 1943-44; B3 1944.
Displacement: surfaced 2,198 tons; submerged 3,654 tons.
Dimensions: length 356ft 7in (108.7m); beam 30ft 6in (9.3m); draught 16ft 1
(5.1m)
Propulsion: 2 x Kampon 10-cylinder, 4-stroke diesel engines, 2 x 6,200bhp;
electric motors, 2 x 1,000shp; two shafts.
Performance: surface – 24kt, 14,000nm/16kt; submerged – 8kt, 96nm/3
maximum operational depth 330ft (100m).
Weapons: 6 x 21in (533mm) TT (bow) (12 torpedoes); 1 x 5.5in/40 (140m
gun; 2 x 25mm AAMG.
Aircraft: 1 x 2-seat floatplane.
Complement: 101.
Specifications for B1-class, as built.

History: These were by far the most numerous classes of aircraft-carryi
submarines built by any navy. All three groups had identical hulls a
armament, but, compared to the B1-class, the B2s had marginally less power
engines (11,000bhp), while the B3s had engines of much less pov
(4,700bhp) in order to increase bunkerage and thus extend the surface range
21,000nm at 16kt.

The hangar was on the centreline with the bridge above it and to port, a
all boats were fitted with a schnorkel. In common with many other aircra
carrying submarines of the IJN, a number of these boats were converted
1941-42 to patrol submarines by deleting the hangar and adding a second 5.

phisticated than that developed by the Germans. The aircraft facilities
re, however, altered with a larger hangar accommodating two aircraft.
e hangar was offest slightly to starboard and faired into the forward part
the sail which was offset to port to compensate. *I-13* was sunk by U.S.
face forces on 16 July 1945, while *I-14* surrendered at sea on 27 August
45.

Below: **I-15; note hangar below bridge, ramp on the foredeck.**

Below: **I-37 dockside in 1939; refitted as a *kaiten* carrier in 1944.**

0mm) gun; later in the war some were converted into *kaiten* transports. A
mber were also converted into transports for resupplying isolated garrisons
the Pacific. One, *I-30*, undertook the voyage to France and returned
ccessfully to Singapore, only to hit a mine within hours of leaving that port on
e final leg back to Japan. The loss rate was very high and of the 29 boats
mpleted just one (*I-36*) survived the war, all the remainder being sunk by U.S.
ces, except for *I-27* and *I-34* which were sunk by the British.

STo-class

Total built: 3.
Completed: 1944-45.
Displacement: surfaced 5,233 tons; submerged 6,560 tons.
Dimensions: length 400ft 3in (122.0m); beam 39ft 4in (12.0m); draught 23ft (7.0m).
Propulsion: 4 x Kampon 10-cylinder, 4-stroke diesel engines, 4 x 1,920bhp; electric motors, 2 x 1,200shp; two shafts.
Performance: surface – 18.8kt, 37,500nm/14kt; submerged – 6.5kt, 60nm/3 maximum operational depth 330ft (100m).
Weapons: 8 x 21in (533mm) TT (bow) (20 torpedoes); 1 x 5.5in/40 (140mm) g 10 x 25mm AAMG.
Aircraft: 3 x 2-seat floatplanes.
Complement: 144.

History: These remain, by a wide margin, the largest diesel-electric submari ever built and were the outcome of a plan made by Admiral Yamamoto, the IJ commander-in-chief, to attack the locks on the Panama Canal, thus cutting shortest sea link between the USA's East and West coasts. The original desi started in 1942, would have carried two aircraft, but this was later enlarged to ta three, plus the parts for a fourth. These were housed in a 110ft (33.5m) long, 1 6in (3.5m) diameter cylindrical hangar, offset slightly to starboard, with the bric above and to port. The aircraft were warmed up in the hangar and then pul forward in turn onto the 85ft (25.9m) catapult track, where their wings were rota through 90 degrees and then extended, following which the pylons and floats w attached. Following training all three aircraft could be launched within 15 minutes surfacing.

The aircraft specifically designed for this class was the Aichi M6A1 Seiran single-engined, two-place monoplane, which was unquestionably the best aircr ever deployed aboard any submarine. The twin floats were detached for stora but were not, as some reports state, capable of being jettisoned in flight when a suicide mission. The Seiran had a top speed of nearly 300mph (483km/h) could carry one 800kg (1,288lb) or several smaller bombs.

I-400 and *I-401* took part in an attempted raid against the U.S. naval base Ulithi, but the Japanese sur-rendered while they were en route and they had choice but to surrender. A third boat – *I-402* – was completed as a fuel tanker.

Below: STo-class shows huge hangar and long launch ramp.